The French Defeat of 1940

THE FRENCH DEFEAT OF 1940

Reassessments

Edited by
Joel Blatt

Berghahn Books
New York • Oxford

First published in 1998 by
Berghahn Books
www.berghahnbooks.com

© 1998 Historical Reflections/Réflexions Historiques
Reprinted in 2006

All rights reserved. Except for the quotation of short passages for the purposes of criticism and review, no part of this book may be reproduced in any form or by any means, electronic or mechanical, including photocopying, recording, or any information storage and retrieval system now known or to be invented, without written permission of the publisher.

Library of Congress Cataloging-in-Publication Data

The French defeat of 1940 : reassessments / edited by Joel Blatt.
    p.   cm.
Includes bibliographic references.
ISBN 1-57181-109-5 (alk. paper) — ISBN 1-57181-226-1 (pbk: alk paper)
1. World War, 1939–1945—Campaigns—Western Front. 2. World War, 1939–1945—Campaigns—France. 3. France—History—1914–1940.
I. Blatt, Joel.
D762.F77   1997
940.54'214—dc21   96-53856
                                                                              CIP

British Library Cataloguing in Publication Data

A catalogue record for this book is available from the British Library.

Printed in the United States on acid-free paper.

Contents

Preface	*Joel Blatt*	vii
Introduction	*Joel Blatt*	1
I	Strategy and Scapegoatism: Reflections on the French National Catastrophe, 1940 *Nicole Jordan*	13
II	Marc Bloch and the *drôle de guerre*: Prelude to the "Strange Defeat" *Carole Fink*	39
III	Martyrs' Vengeance: Memory, Trauma, and Fear of War in France, 1918-1940 *Omer Bartov*	54
IV	Domestic Politics and the Fall of France in 1940 *William D. Irvine*	85
V	Edouard Daladier: The Conduct of the War and the Beginnings of Defeat *Elisabeth du Réau*	100
VI	The Missed Opportunity: French Refugee Policy in Wartime, 1939-1940 *Vicki Caron*	126
VII	Prelude to Defeat: Franco-Soviet Relations, 1919-1939 *Michael Jabara Carley*	171
VIII	France and the Illusion of American Support, 1919-1940 *William R. Keylor*	204
IX	In the Eye of the Beholder: The Cultural Representation of France and Germany by *The New York Times*, 1939-1940 *Robert J. Young*	245

X	Reflections on France, Britain and the Winter War Prodrome, 1939-1940 *John C. Cairns*	269
XI	"Fighting to the Last Frenchman"? Reflections on the BEF Deployment to France and the Strains in the Franco-British Alliance, 1939-1940 *Martin S. Alexander*	296
XII	French Defeat in 1940 and its reversal in 1944-1945: The Deuxième Division Blindée *Philip Farwell Bankwitz*	327
XIII	The Trauma of 1940: A Disaster and its Traces *Stanley Hoffmann*	354
Contributors		371

Preface

Joel Blatt

I thought that the time was right for a reconsideration of the catastrophe that befell France in 1940. Stuart Campbell, the Editor of *Historical Reflections/Réflexions Historiques*, encouraged me to become guest editor for an issue of his journal. Thus, with the essential participation of twelve authors, the core of this volume appeared as a special issue of *Historical Reflections/Réflexions Historiques* (Winter 1996, volume 22, number 1). Although a substantial audience had the opportunity to read the essays in the journal, their high quality prompted me to want to secure yet a wider readership for them. Dr. Marion Berghahn, Publisher of Berghahn Books, has now made that possible. For the American part of our audience, she encouraged the inclusion of an additional essay on relations between the United States and France; thus, William Keylor's contribution has been added to the original twelve. Gretchen Van Slyke has translated Elisabeth du Réau's article into English, and there are a number of other small changes.

I would like to thank all of the authors in this book for their labors. Marion Berghahn (and her staff) have given this book life with their skill, courtesy, and unfailing professionalism. Stuart Campbell, after participating in the inception of this project, nurtured it at every step. Yvonne Cassidy, Managing Editor of *Historical Reflections/Réflexions Historiques* in 1995-1996, helped bring the original version of this volume to fruition. My thanks to Gretchen van Slyke for her excellent translations of the articles by Stanley

Hoffmann and Elisabeth du Réau, and to Editions du Seuil for permission to publish once again Stanley Hoffmann's essay in translation. My wife, Felice Lesser, as always, offered invaluable support.

INTRODUCTION

The French Defeat of 1940: Reassessments

Joel Blatt

After months of waiting, on 10 May 1940, Hitler hurled the German armed forces against France and its ally, Great Britain. The French divided their defensive system essentially into three regions. The southeastern part of their defense system, the famous Maginot line, contained heavy fortifications that fulfilled their function. From the northwest, prime French troops and tanks rushed pell-mell northeastward toward Breda in Holland; from the western sector, too, other allied units moved north and east toward the Dyle River in Belgium. French strategy attempted to establish a northern defensive line outside France against the presumed main German thrust.[1] Assuming that rough terrain precluded an immediate German assault in the Ardennes, the French only defended the center of their line lightly. There, in the first days of battle, powerful German panzer units, supported by aircraft, broke through and streaked across northern France to the English Channel. Units that might have composed the missing French strategic reserve were far northeast of the primary German offensive. French counterattacks failed. During the last days of May and the first days of June, much of the British Army and part of the French escaped from Dunkirk. On 10 June, Mussolini "stabbed his neigh-

---

1. For the Breda aspect of the strategy, see Don W. Alexander, "Repercussions of the Breda Variant," *French Historical Studies* 8 (1974): 459-488.

bor in the back"; four days later, German troops entered Paris. Between 15 and 20 June, perhaps as many as six to eight million people were in flight on the roads of France. On 16 June, French Premier Paul Reynaud resigned, replaced by Marshal Philippe Pétain, who, the next day, broadcast an appeal to the nation for an end to the fighting. On 18 June, from a BBC studio in London, Charles de Gaulle affirmed enduring French "resistance." Four days later, in the same railroad car in the forest of Compiègne in which the Armistice of 1918 had been signed, the French capitulated, with the armistice going into effect three days later. During the first half of July political maneuvering by Pierre Laval and others shaped parliament's decision to replace the Third Republic with Marshal Pétain's authoritarian Vichy regime.

France had suffered a catastrophic, stunning, and total defeat. The French experienced heavy losses and huge numbers of prisoners of war, followed by occupation, collaboration with one of history's most brutal regimes (including participation in its most heinous crimes), and a civil war. Ever since the collapse, participants, observers, and historians have offered explanations. Most often, with the exception of Marc Bloch's classic account, early interpretations had the virtue (and faults) of apologetic simplicity. Allegedly, France had been overwhelmed by an enemy superior in terms of soldiers and machines, and its politicians and generals had failed to prepare for the maelstrom. Although victory usually has many parents while defeat is an orphan, in this instance defeat, too, had many parents. Every segment of the political spectrum shunted responsibility onto its enemies.

Over the decades, however, a far more dense and truthful web of understanding has been woven. In numbers of men and tanks, France and Great Britain roughly matched the Germans, although many more German planes were operational and France was deficient in antiaircraft weapons. Attention has shifted from sheer numbers to a host of concerns including France's utilization of men and machines, morale, domestic politics, culture, socio-economic considerations, and interallied relations. This volume of essays participates in that reconsideration.

In the first article Nicole Jordan, author of a recent study on the Popular Front's policy towards central and eastern Europe, focuses upon General Maurice Gamelin's military strategy: many of France's best troops and tanks dashed east and north to the Dyle River in Belgium and even up to Breda in Holland, leaving virtually no strategic reserves to contest the German breakthrough in the Ardennes sector. Jordan traces Gamelin's strategy to his deep-rooted pursuit of a "cut-price war on the peripheries" destined to avoid battles on French soil. Jordan also emphasizes how fear of revolution influenced the decision to seek a rapid armistice, and the scapegoating and myth making that followed in the wake of defeat.

Marc Bloch hovers over this volume more than fifty years after he died at the hands of the Gestapo and as a hero of the Resistance. Bloch's explanation of the defeat has retained its vitality and relevance. Carole Fink has written a biography of Marc Bloch as well as a book and articles about post-World War I French foreign policy and international relations. Here she reconstructs Bloch's thoughts during the "drôle de guerre" that contributed to his *Strange Defeat*. Bloch worried that France's *esprit* in 1939-1940 contrasted unfavorably with that of 1914, and he doubted the wisdom of an offensive into Belgium. While highlighting Bloch's emphasis upon the role of human choice in history, Fink also pays attention to the actions or inaction of France's potential allies as well as France's demographic and economic inferiority to Germany.

Omer Bartov places the memory of World War I at the epicenter of France's interwar crises and the defeat of 1940. He presents a searing assessment of the impact of World War I, the images and representations of that conflict and their influence on the war to come. He asserts that France and Germany ultimately remembered World War I differently, and this affected, even determined, the outcome of the Battle of France. During the 1930s complex images of war made it difficult for the French to comprehend the rationale for a second world war. Further competing images of the enemy – Germany and Bolshevism – sowed confusion between foreign and civil war. Bartov concludes that fear of war fueled domestic conflicts and ultimately paralyzed France's will in the face of Nazi Germany.

William Irvine, who has written on French conservatism during the 1930s and on Boulangism, considers the role of domestic politics. Questioning orthodoxy, he provides one of the volume's most revisionist pieces. He argues that historians must show, not merely assume, the linkage between social and political polarization during the 1930s and the collapse of 1940. If sharp divisions existed from 1935 through 1938, the Daladier-Reynaud tilt towards the Right in 1938-1939 brought renewed support for the government and its foreign policy by the elites. Furthermore, the Left grumbled, but not to the point of becoming intransigent. Meanwhile, workers produced the necessary war material, and although difficult to measure, pacifism on both the Left and Right waned. Irvine portrays a stiffening national will and a France "morally and materially ready" for war, thereby compelling a close reading of the events from 1938 to 1940.

Author of an extensive *thèse d'état* and a biography of Edouard Daladier, Elizabeth du Réau sketches Daladier's national defense policy. Daladier battled against a strong peace current in the Cabinet and legislatures and took France into war against Germany. Preparing for a long war, Daladier successfully crafted policies of economic and financial cooperation with Great Britain (far better than in 1914-1918) and with the United States ("cash and carry" brought much American-made material, particularly planes). He also fostered overall arms development through the appointment of Raoul Dautry as head of the Ministry of Armament. Although she recognizes important problems, du Réau characterizes Daladier's tenure as one of real accomplishments. She ascribes the defeat to the failure of military and civilian leaders to absorb the lessons of blitzkrieg and to "vulnerabilities" pointed out by Marc Bloch.

Vicki Caron's current research, based on exceptional digging in primary sources, investigates French responses to Jewish refugees during the 1930s. Here, she paints a mixed, but overall bleak, portrait of French refugee policies from the outbreak of war until the defeat. Committed ideological opponents of Nazism, many refugees wanted to join the French Army. Civilian authorities, however, often interned them, at times in horrendous, life threatening conditions. Caron assesses the sources of French refugee policy. She finds "countervailing forces," thereby distinguishing the late Third Republic from Vichy's overwhelming malevolence. Some refugees studied by Caron believed their plight provided a clue to France's defeat: it indicated a greater hatred of the Left than of Fascism, a lack of commitment to democracy, and an insufficient appreciation of the stakes posed by the struggle.

Author of a book on early French responses to the Russian Revolution, Michael Carley's recent writing has focused on Franco-Soviet relations between the two world wars. In this article, he illustrates long patterns of Franco-Soviet interactions; for example, the French bargained with the Soviets in order to keep them and Germany apart, but avoided clinching accords with them in the 1920s and the 1930s. Carley presents a complex picture with a small number of French governmental and military voices urging close Franco-Soviet cooperation, while opponents of this alliance prevailed. The latter predominated primarily because of the impact of ideology and domestic politics on foreign policy, but the longstanding French decision to follow the British lead also played a role. Carley empathizes with the realistic Maxim Litvinov, caught between a murderous Stalin and obdurate French and British governments. Working from French, British, and American archives as well as published Soviet sources, Carley concludes that anti-Communism distorted perceptions of French national interests, thereby contributing to the defeat.

With this second contribution in the section of essays on France's relations with allies or potential allies, William Keylor traces the French "mirage" of American assistance from the Paris Peace Conference of 1919 through 1940. Keylor, whose scholarship has explored a wide range of subjects including the history of twentieth century international relations, blames faulty French military strategy as the primary culprit in the defeat of 1940, but also emphasizes the absence of the United States at France's side. After President Wilson's stubborn opposition to compromise on the Versailles Treaty sank the Anglo-American Treaty of Guarantee of French security, France and the United States cultivated negative images of each other. Reparations and debt issues contributed to tensions, yet Keylor distinguishes between surface public perceptions and more complex subsurface actualities. French hopes in its distant potential "savior" never died, but the United States supported appeasement of Germany for a long time. One architect of American policy, Ambassador to France William Bullitt, feared the Soviet Union would dominate a postwar Europe, and also condemned the outcome of the Paris Peace Conference of 1919. Keylor studies the intensive French endeavors to utilize the United

States as an arsenal for airplanes. Premier Daladier's initiative was crowned by partial success, but "too late" for French survival if not for that of Great Britain.

Robert Young elaborates on a particular aspect of Franco-American relations in 1939-1940. Author of books and articles on French military planning and foreign policy during the 1930s and of a biography of Louis Barthou, Young explores with an innovative approach the realm of French cultural propaganda in the United States. He interprets the effectiveness of France's image-making in *The New York Times* as an indication of the late Third Republic's vitality. Although in the short run French cultural propaganda in the United States failed to sway the outcome of the Battle of France, in the longer term it may have influenced the American role in World War II.

John Cairns, whose previous labors have contributed substantially to our knowledge of the defeat of 1940, focuses on Franco-British discord in response to the Russo-Finnish winter war. Cairns sees the episode as an integral step towards May-June 1940, weakening the Anglo-French alliance and leading to the fall of Daladier, the French politician most capable of holding things together. In addition to noting the frayed condition of Anglo-French relations, Cairns' essay sketches the French domestic political scene of cliques, personal rivalries, and ideologies, and where politics revealed an enthusiasm for intervention against the Soviets not carried over to Nazi Germany.

Martin Alexander, author of a recent study of General Gamelin, here analyzes crucial dimensions of Franco-British interaction during the "phony war." Using a wide range of sources, Alexander probes issues such as the number of British troops and airplanes committed to France, and their subsequent impact on French morale and strategy. Sensitive about their relatively small contribution in men, British commanders followed the French lead in military strategy, thereby not questioning Gamelin's Dyle-Breda plan. Moreover, the smaller number of British mechanized forces in France than originally proposed contributed to Gamelin's lack of reserves at the crucial moment of mid-May 1940. Alexander's Gamelin anticipated a long war and failed to comprehend that his strategy was overly ambitious. Alexander also points to British "complacency" regarding the chance of a German offensive achieving a decisive victory over France.

The last two essays offer different kinds of overviews and closure for this volume. I asked Philip Bankwitz to analyze and reminisce, and to draw upon his extensive knowledge of the interwar French Army and his personal memories as a young American soldier assigned to General Philippe Leclerc's Second French Armored Division in 1944. He created a synthesis of the two experiences. In the first section of his essay Bankwitz elaborates upon and probes civil-military relations and military strategy in interwar France, subjects on which he has contributed pioneering work. He explains the genesis of a French military strategy that neglected the need for fall-back positions. In Bankwitz's passionate retelling, General Leclerc learned the lessons of defeat and four years later "reversed" the outcome of 1940. Bankwitz also remembers Paris on 25 and 26 August 1944, and he reminds us of profound Franco-American affections and connections too rarely expressed these days.

Stanley Hoffmann, whose work has shaped our understanding of twentieth-century France, analyzes the impact of the catastrophe.[2] He perceives the defeat as part of an historical unit stretching from 1934 through 1946. He alludes to a collective memory of "catastrophe" and "humiliation," and more particular Vichy, Communist, and Gaullist memories. He locates the defeat in part by sketching post-World War II "actions" in France impelled by a reaction against the debacle. Hoffmann also ponders unresolved issues posed by the defeat in such areas as national self-perception, the role of French intellectuals, France's relations with other countries, postwar political, social, and economic developments, and the future of the French nation state.

* * *

While presenting new findings and interpretations, the authors both agree and disagree. They agree, for example, on a negative

2. I asked Professor Hoffmann if he would consider such a piece for this volume; he responded that he had recently completed "Le trauma de 1940" for *La France des années noires*, directed by Jean-Pierre Azéma and François Bédarida. My thanks to Editions du Seuil, Michel Winock, and the editors of that collection for the opportunity to publish the essay, and my thanks to Gretchen van Slyke for her translation.

-7-

assessment of France's military strategy and concur that French leaders prepared for a long war. Memory, myth, scapegoating, ideology, personality, and other factors provide themes in their stories. Basic issues upon which they disagree include the weight to be attributed to different causal factors, the strength or weakness of the late Third Republic, the role of domestic politics, and to some extent the health of Franco-British relations.

My own explanation of the defeat is pluralistic. Material factors played long-term roles. Germany had over twenty million more people, more workers, a larger pool of soldiers, and greater industrial might. These disparities constantly strained France as she attempted to keep up and remain a major European power with the world's second largest colonial empire. Nevertheless, the collapse of 1940 was neither fated nor inevitable.

Confronting a stronger foe, France needed allies. In the central compromise among the victors at the Paris Peace Conference of 1919, the American President, Woodrow Wilson, and the British Prime Minister, David Lloyd George, promised Georges Clemenceau a guarantee of French security against another German attack. In return the French renounced ambitions to separate the Rhineland from Germany. When the American Senate refused to ratify the Versailles Treaty, the Treaty of Guarantee and the promises on which it was based evaporated.[3] Too often during the interwar years the United States and Great Britain wanted something from France in return for nothing or too little. Their absence (or limited presence) contributed substantially to European instability and ultimately to the defeat of France while endangering their own security.

Two profound memories haunted interwar France. First, World War I, with its horrendous 1,300,000 to 1,400,000 French dead and many more wounded, left war cemeteries, memorials, and widows. Understandably, most of the French regarded entry into a second charnel house with serious qualms; generals and politicians accordingly devised a defensive strategy and sought a war outside France that might somehow spare French lives.

---

3. See William R. Keylor, "The Rise and Demise of the Franco-American Guarantee Pact, 1919-21," *Proceedings of the Annual Meeting of the Western Society for French History* 15 (1988): 367-377.

A second decisive set of memories emerged from social, economic, and political divisions emanating from the past. The French Revolution, the Revolutions of 1830 and 1848, the June Days of 1848, and the Paris Commune of 1871, all left divisive residues of inspiration, nightmare, and anger. During the Third Republic the struggle between clerical and anticlerical, the Socialist demand for equality, and finally the divisive impact of the Bolshevik Revolution in Russia exacerbated earlier disagreements.

During the interwar years France experienced two moments of intense political polarization, 1924-1926 and 1934-1938. The second, marked by deep economic depression, gave rise to a malodorous stew of discontents. Further, the ideological attraction in France of Communist and Fascist regimes in major European countries placed pressure on the center of French politics. Whatever the role of a recalcitrant British ally, attempts to patch together an anti-Hitler alliance foundered in part on divisions within France.

The influence of domestic politics and ideology upon foreign policy undercut Franco-Soviet relations. Even though the Russian rush to combat probably saved France in 1914, the Soviet bullet became the hardest for French leaders to bite during the 1930s. French decision makers avoided a military alliance with the Soviet Union from 1935, well antedating Stalin's purge of the military in 1937, until at least 1939. Soviet documents may tell us more about Stalin's intentions, the terms for a possible accord, and whether it was feasible. Michael Carley's research, though, shows persistent approaches by Soviet representatives to their French counterparts, as do the Schweisguth papers, perhaps the best window into the minds of the French General Staff and other officials from 1935 to 1937.[4] Indeed, a military accord with the Soviet Union would have involved an alliance with one of history's most brutal tyrants,

---

4. My discussion draws on Michael Carley's essay in this volume and his articles: "End of the 'Low, Dishonest Decade': Failure of the Anglo-Franco-Soviet Alliance in 1939," *Europe-Asia Studies* 45 (1993): 303-341; Carley, "Five Kopecks for Five Kopecks: Franco-Soviet Trade Negotiations, 1928-1939," *Cahiers du monde russe et soviétique* 33 (1992): 23-58. My own research on Franco-Italian relations has drawn me to some of the same document collections as Carley, particularly the Schweisguth materials: the papers of General Victor-Henri Schweisguth, Vice-Chief of the General Staff from 1935-1937, including his reports and a kind of diary, Archives Nationales (351AP).

but a French war against Germany without Russian support held great danger.

Domestic French politics also influenced Franco-Italian relations, but probably not decisively. The French Right praised Mussolini's domestic policies while the French Left condemned them, but neither favored concessions to Italy involving French colonial territories.[5] The French General Staff rejoiced in 1935 when a substantive Franco-Italian military rapprochement followed the Laval-Mussolini accord of January. If the French military leadership had pursued the Soviet tie with the same zeal they sought an unlikely long-term accord with Fascist Italy, France's position might have been considerably stronger in 1940.

Fear of war, an unwillingness to pursue seriously a military alliance with the Soviet Union, and the ongoing courtship of Great Britain account for France's participation in the Munich Treaty of 1938. The General Staff claimed that only by transporting French troops across northern Italy could France aid central Europe, specifically Czechoslovakia, in the event of German aggression.[6] Where there was little will, no way would be found. Thus, the Czechoslovak crisis of 1938 reached a different resolution than the Serbian crisis of 1914, which it resembled. France's one major success became the alliance with Great Britain, but the French paid dearly for it.

One of the keys to defeat was the arrival of France at the railway station of 1940 pulling a train with few allies and few advantages. Hitler's remilitarization of the Rhineland in March 1936 cost France the Versailles Treaty and the German initiated Locarno Treaty, as well as Belgium and perhaps Fascist Italy. At Munich, the French betrayed Czechoslovakia with its highly-motivated army and population, democratic institutions, airfields minutes from Germany, and Skoda factories producing tanks.

5. For a suggestive exploration of Mussolini's price for an accord with Britain, see Alan Cassels, "Deux empires face à face: La chimère d'un rapprochement anglo-italien (1936-1940)," *Guerres mondiales* 161 (1991): 67-96.
6. For example, see General Victor-Henri Schweisguth, "Les données militaires actuelles d'une guerre de coalition européenne," Conférence faite par le Général Schweisguth au Collège des Hautes Etudes de Défense Nationale, 5 novembre 1936, Schweisguth Papers, Archives Nationales, 351AP 7, SC 4, Dossier 2, sous-dossier b; Schweisguth, "Réflexions sur la défaite française," possibly July 1940, Schweisguth Papers, Archives Nationales, 351AP 7, SC 4, Dossier 8.

Introduction

The story of the Battle of France includes, however, a partial French recovery of balance in 1938-1940. Edouard Daladier – Premier from April 1938 until March 1940, and Defense Minister from 1936 to 1940 – was a substantive figure (but not a statesman). Anticipating a long war, he cultivated better relations with Great Britain, opened the pipeline for materiel from the United States, and with considerable success continued rearmament. Politically, Daladier drew the French wagon train into a tight circle. The Daladier-Reynaud government broke with the Popular Front, orienting policies on a conservative axis with potential support stretching from moderate Radicals to the Center and well into the Right. The process resembled the "nationalist revival" before World War I. Daladier brought a measure of political stability and coalescence, but much of the Left lay outside his narrow circle. Unlike 1914, no *union sacrée* emerged.

Assessing French morale in 1939-1940 is an imprecise but worthy project. As William Irvine notes in this volume, when France entered World War II, citizens obeyed the call to the colors, but without the élan of 1914. Hitler wanted war, his opponents peace. The terrible losses in the Great War, the strain to maintain major-power status, perceptions of German strength, the paucity of allies, political divisions, and the lassitude of "the phony war" sapped energies. The Third Republic retained greater strength than her critics contended, but the sustained assaults on liberal-democratic values took their toll. Too many lacked a visceral commitment to the regime and its traditions. How many went to war feeling a conflict between their political passions and the Third Republic? These factors certainly influenced the Armistice, but how much did they inhibit the total effort necessary to blunt the blitzkrieg? Oddly, French leaders and the general population seem to have felt only episodically the sense of desperation appropriate to the magnitude of the crisis. From 1936 through 1940, why did French leaders not more often make tough minded choices and exhibit the political courage to explain them forthrightly to the public? Defense of the homeland ought to have been as strong a motivation for the French as revenge was for the Germans.

Perhaps France needed close to a "perfect war" in 1940, or, at a minimum, a war in which many of the key variables were resolved in her favor. This was the third armed conflict between the French and the Germans in seventy years. The Prussians had won in 1870-1871, and France had barely survived in 1914 by means of a successful strategic retreat, a timely counteroffensive, Russian aid in the east, and *esprit*. During the interwar years French decisions and uncontrollable developments had turned a number of the variables against France. General Gamelin's Dyle-Breda strategy became the last blow, one of the colossal blunders in the history of warfare.

Contrasting national strategies created the potential for French catastrophe. Hitler returned to the World War I obsession with the offensive, but this time with surprise, tanks, planes, daring, and his habitual use of terror. With hindsight, one can ask what might have happened if a French commander in May-June 1940 had resigned himself to the possibility of a battle on French soil similar to that of 1914, and had kept a large strategic reserve intact. France still would have missed its Russian, Italian, and American allies from the previous war. There still would have been a German breakthrough; the French still would have struggled with the pace of the battle, with their communications breakdown, and with German air superiority. But what if they had chosen well the moment for a counterattack? Necessity might have forced the grouping of French tanks recommended by Charles De Gaulle. If the French had weathered the initial German assault, perhaps they could have implemented their preparations for a long war.

Instead, time ran out. The French defeat and Hitler's resulting domination of Europe, given his transvaluation of the western Judeo-Christian-humanist moral tradition, posed the gravest crisis in the history of the West. The issue became survival of human dignity.

I

STRATEGY AND SCAPEGOATISM
Reflections on the French National Catastrophe, 1940

Nicole Jordan
(In memory of James Joll, 1918-1994)

The French military collapse in 1940 was one of the great military catastrophes in world history. A striking image of the defeat dates from 16-17 May: a sea of some ten thousand French prisoners, captured at a cost of one German officer and forty enlisted men, as Rommel's *Panzerkorps* drove deeply through the French lines.[1] Yet the French rout has been consigned to virtual oblivion by much of the recent literature, which presents Maurice Gamelin, the French Commander, as almost entirely disconnected from the events of May 1940. The defeat appears then as strangely diffuse, disembodied, the product of an absence.[2] Marc Bloch, a witness of these events, permitted no such evasion:

 1. B.H. Liddell Hart, ed., *The Rommel Papers* (New York, 1953), p. 26.
 2. For example, two monographs on the interwar French General Staff, Robert Young's *In Command of France* (Cambridge, MA, 1978) and Martin Alexander's *The Republic in Danger* (Cambridge, 1992), contain glowing assessments of its competence without in-depth consideration of the May-June 1940 campaign. Alexander has written on Gamelin in 1940, but like his subject, he gives more attention to military feuds with politicians in 1939-1940 than to military operations. Idem., "The Fall of France, 1940," *Journal of Strategic Studies* 13 (1990); "Maurice Gamelin and the Defeat of France" in Brian Bond's *Fallen Stars* (London, 1991), pp. 107-140.

Nous venons de subir une incroyable défaite. A qui la faute? Au régime parlementaire, à la cinquième colonne, répondent nos généraux. A tout le monde, en somme, sauf à eux. Que le père Joffre était donc plus sage! "Je ne sais pas, disait-il, si c'est moi qui ai gagné la bataille de la Marne. Mais il y a une chose que je sais bien: si elle avait été perdue, elle l'aurait été par moi." ... Au retour de la campagne, il n'était guère, dans mon entourage, d'officier qui en doutât; quoi que l'on pense des causes profondes du désastre, la cause directe – qui demandera elle-même à être expliquée – fut l'incapacité du commandement.[3]

In contradistinction to a recent historiography which attempts to rehabilitate the French Command, this essay will advance the following arguments. Strategy lay at the heart of the French military collapse and prepared the way for the armistice in 1940. Scapegoatism was Gamelin's response to the defeat, conceded by him on 16 May, before his dismissal on 19 May. In its most concentrated, contemporary form, this scapegoatism was directed against the Popular Front government of 1936-1937 and sheds crucial light on military acceptance of the armistice.

The Rhetoric of 1914 and the Doctrine of the Continuous Front

Those who wish to understand the strategic reasons for the French defeat might well begin by considering Gamelin's orders to the army

---

3. "We have just suffered such a defeat as no one would have believed possible. On whom or on what should the blame be laid? On the French system of parliamentary government, say our generals; on the rank and file of the fighting services, on the English, on the fifth column – in short, on any and everybody except themselves. Old Joffre was wiser. 'Whether I was responsible for the winning of the Battle of the Marne,' he said, 'I do not know. But of this I feel pretty certain, that, had it been lost, the failure would have been laid at my door.' ... When the Army was disbanded after the final campaign, it would have been hard to find a single officer among those with whom I was in daily contact who had the slightest doubt on the subject. Whatever the deep-seated causes of the disaster may have been, the immediate occasion (as I shall attempt to explain later) was the utter incompetence of the High Command. "Marc Bloch, *L' Etrange Défaite* (Paris, 1946), p. 45, and again, on pp. 90, 92 / *Strange Defeat*, trans. Gerard Hopkins (New York, 1968), p. 25. The present author can only second the moving tribute of J.-L. Crémieux-Brilhac to Bloch's superior qualities as analyst in *Les Français de l'an 40*, II (Paris, 1990), p. 369 and note.

before his dismissal. Rhetoric derived from the 1914-1918 war and strategic and tactical incoherence characterised these orders. At the German invasion on 10 May, Gamelin evoked Verdun:

> L'Allemagne engage contre nous une lutte à mort. Les mots d'ordre sont pour la France et ses Alliés: courage, énergie, confiance. Comme l'a dit il y a vingt-quatre ans le maréchal Pétain: "Nous les aurons."[4]

The dead hand of the past reappeared in Gamelin's last order to the army on 17 May, which again evoked the memory of Verdun:

> Toute troupe qui ne pourrait avancer doit se faire tuer sur place plutôt qu'abandonner la parcelle du sol national qui lui a été confiée. Comme toujours, aux heures graves de notre histoire, le mot d'ordre aujourd'hui est: VAINCRE OU MOURIR. IL FAUT VAINCRE.[5]

A text from the opposing side by General Franz Halder, a late but solid recruit to the Guderian-Manstein school, provides – in its iconoclasm and psychological grasp of the realities of combat – an almost cruel contrast to Gamelin's orders of 10 and 19 May. Halder wrote in anticipation of the German onslaught:

> The mission assigned to the German Army is a very difficult one. Given the terrain [the Ardennes] and the ratio of forces on both sides – especially with regard to artillery – *this mission cannot be fulfilled if we*

---

4. "Germany is engaged against us in a battle to the death. The watchwords for France and its allies are: courage, energy, confidence. As Marshal Pétain said twenty four years ago: 'We will beat the hell out of them.'"

5. "Every soldier who might not be able to advance must let himself be killed on the spot rather than abandon the portion of national soil which has been confided to him. As always, in the grave hours of our history, the order today is: CONQUER OR DIE. WE MUST CONQUER." Gamelin's Ordres du Jour, 10, 17 May 1940, cited in Pierre Le Goyet, *Le Mystère Gamelin* (Paris, 1976), pp. 302, 328. In these orders, Gamelin reverently evokes the *saignée* of Verdun and the name of the wooden colossus of French interwar defence doctrine, Philippe Pétain. In his postwar memoirs, allusions to the Marne crowded out Verdun and the discredited Pétain. M. Gamelin, *Servir* (Paris, 1946), III, pp. 418-419, 428-429. While Gamelin had written the orders for the Battle of the Marne in September 1914, his allegiance to the interwar doctrine of continuous fronts, discussed below, made impossible a 1940 repetition of the "Miracle at the Marne." Gamelin's strategy contained no serious provision for countering a consummated German breakthrough by falling back and redeploying with massive reserves.

employ those means which were relevant in the last war. We will have to use exceptional means and take the resulting risk. Whether the panzer divisions of the forward wave appear on the Meuse in full combat power is less important to me than the necessity of demonstrating resolute daring in pursuit of the retreating enemy and in making the initial crossing to the western Meuse bank decisive ... I am absolutely aware of the fact that these units, when dashing forward, will have hours of severe crisis on the western Meuse bank. The Luftwaffe will relieve them by fully bringing to bear its superior combat power. *Without taking this risk we might never be able to reach the left Meuse bank.* But I am convinced that in this operation, too, our panzer leaders will have an advantage, due to their energy and flexibility, combined with the effect of setting personal examples. *Against an enemy proceeding methodically and less trained in commanding panzers, they will be able to exploit the severe psychological burden imposed by the appearance of German panzers on a unit which lacks all battle testing.*[6]

On 13 May, learning of the German penetration in the Ardennes, an area he had dismissed as an invasion route despite parliamentary and staff concern over its poor defences, Gamelin issued the following order of the day:

Il faut maintenant tenir tête à la ruée des forces mécaniques et motorisées de l'ennemi. L' heure est venue de se battre à fond sur les positions fixées par le haut commandement. On n'a plus le droit de reculer. Si l'ennemi fait localement brèche, non seulement colmater mais contre-attaquer et reprendre.[7]

Gamelin was attempting to solve an immediate tactical problem. Yet the contradiction in his order leaps to the eye: how did one counter a furious and fast-moving armored enemy assault ("la ruée des forces mécaniques et motorisées de l'ennemi") if every breach

6. Halder, 12 March 1940, cited in John J. Mearsheimer, *Conventional Deterrence* (Ithaca, 1983), p. 128; my italics. On the inherent tension between Gamelin's and Halder's perspectives, see Michael Geyer's remarks on the "politics of restoration" versus those of "innovation" in "The Crisis of Military Leadership in the 1930s," *Journal of Strategic Studies* 14 (1991): 454-455.
7. "The onslaught of the mechanical and motorised forces of the enemy must now be faced. The time has come to fight to the bitter end on the positions fixed by the High Command. One no longer has the right to retreat. If the enemy locally breaches our line, it must not only be sealed off but counter-attacked and retaken." Gamelin, *Servir*, I, p. 337.

had to be counter-attacked, sealed off and retaken?[8] Gamelin's rhetoric of 1914-1918 and his strategically and tactically incoherent response to the rapidly breaking situation in the Ardennes drew on central elements of interwar French military thought: the doctrine of the continuous front and the related doctrine of integral defence of the frontiers.

The concept of the continuous front was devised to prevent a repetition of the German breakthrough to the outskirts of Paris in August-September 1914. Best understood as an uneven system of fortifications and military *ententes* gradually elaborated in the 1920s and 30s, it was designed to keep any future war away from French territory, a goal officially designated as integral defence of the frontiers. To achieve this end, the General Staff constructed the celebrated Maginot line along the Franco-Swiss border, and much lighter and often unfinished fortifications of the blockhouse sort along the Belgian frontier to the north. While Pétain, the "Victor of Verdun," played a leading role in elaborating these fortifications, he and his colleagues manifested an unshakable resolve that their principal line of resistance would be in Belgium. This proviso for the forward defence of France on Belgian soil was originally devised in the 1920s and remained a constant in French planning under Gamelin. A combined Franco-Belgian front, to which Gamelin added Holland in the mid-1930s, thus constituted the continuous front. The enemy was to bleed himself white in failed offensives outside of French territory without ever lastingly penetrating French soil – a repetition of the failed German tactic of Verdun, this time in Belgium.

8. Cf. Marc Bloch's critique of Gamelin's tactic of *colmatage*, the rapid sealing off of any breach by the enemy: "La surprise fut grande de devoir constater, à l'expérience, que l'échelon dit <<arrière>> se trouvait plus près de la vraie ligne de feu que l'échelon qualifié <<avant>>. Déjà, lorsque s'ouvrit la brèche de la Meuse, il avait fallu s'efforcer de modifier hâtivement, en cours de route, les points de débarquement d'une division, que, sous prétexte de colmater la poche, on s'apprêtait à jeter dans la gueule du loup." / "What was our surprise when it was borne in upon us that, in fact, the so-called 'rear' H.Q. was a great deal closer to the line than its advanced brother! When the Germans crashed through the Meuse defences, we were compelled to improvise at short notice alternative rail-heads for the division which we were preparing to rush into the lion's mouth in the hope of blocking egress from the pocket." *L' Etrange Défaite*, p. 64 / *Strange Defeat*, trans. Hopkins, p. 45.

French doctrine attempted to combine static and mobile elements. The invasion route of 1914, Lorraine, was to be protected by static fortifications, while much of the frontier with Belgium in the north remained essentially unfortified, open terrain. Complex technical and economic concerns accounted for this decision, but the single most important reason was the General Staff's strategy of advancing into Belgium, with or without Belgian cooperation, should Germany invade in the east or west.[9] Projected into Holland as well, forward defence was to provide the French Army an *espace de manoeuvre*. However, this was mitigated by the notion, also inspired by Philippe Pétain, of a prepared battlefield in the Low Countries. Virtually the sum of French operational doctrine in the interwar period, the concept stressed the careful and methodical delimitation of the battlefield under centralised command.[10] In a deteriorating international atmosphere and against an adversary bent on operational opportunism, French military plans carried enormous risk. Staking all on a prepared, distant battlefield made impossible timely defence in depth on French soil.

La Guerre Ailleurs and Allied Immolation

The doctrine of the continuous front based on forward defence and prepared battlefields in the Low Countries indicated that France was to be defended by a war which would take place elsewhere, *une guerre ailleurs*.[11] From 1933, in anticipation of an imminent reoccupation of the Rhineland which he believed would channel German force eastward, Gamelin counted upon the next war taking place in Central Europe. In that region, France had small (Czechoslovakia,

---

9. Service Historique de l'Armée de Terre [henceforth, SHAT], CSG, 28 May 1932.

10. The Belgians were not slow to understand the purposes to which the French General Staff intended to put the 1920 military entente. Dubious of the wisdom of arbitrarily prepared battlefields without confirmation of the enemy's intentions, and above all, not wishing to see their country preordained as the next killing ground, they reacted by turning to neutralism.

11. Nicole Jordan, "The Cut Price War on the Peripheries: The French General Staff, the Rhineland and Czechoslovakia," in Robert Boyce and E.M. Robertson, *Paths to War* (London, 1989), pp. 128-166.

Roumania and Yugoslavia) and medium-sized (Poland) treaty partners dating from the 1920s, as well as unstable arrangements with regional great powers, Italy and the Soviet Union. To grasp the French military's attachment to an eastern front for much of the 1930s, one has to return, as always in dealing with their root conceptions, to the 1914-1918 war. French officers were haunted by the tenacity of German artillery and the impossibility of breaking the German lines in 1914-1918. While continuous fronts were to protect France itself, the French General Staff sought a solution to the problem of stalemate on a northeastern frontier which they imagined as again rapidly saturated by Franco-German forces. A war fought primarily in the east, they believed, would make possible the strategic breakthrough which they sought as eagerly as their German adversaries. Thus, Gamelin in a meeting with the civilians in April 1936 stated that:

> ... en champ clos, sur un espace relativement étroit, les Armées française et allemande seraient en état, très rapidement, de saturer le terrain. Or l'expérience de la dernière guerre montre que, si les espaces vides ont permis initialement de manoeuvrer, la saturation des fronts a ensuite conduit rapidement à un équilibre de forces, qui n'a pu être rompu qu'après une usure péniblement acquise de la puissance allemande ... Puisque, sur terre, un conflit limité à la France et à l'Allemagne ne permet guère d'escompter des résultats décisifs, ceux-ci doivent être recherchés par l'extension des fronts de combat, c'est-à-dire *à l'aide d'alliances*.[12]

He spoke along similar lines the following year, insisting on the narrowness of the Franco-German frontier and the necessity of enlarging it in Belgium and southern Holland or in Central Europe "fut-ce par un détachement rapide et symbolique en attendant la possibilité d'une grande opération."[13]

12. "In a closed battlefield, a confined space, the French and German armies would very soon be able to saturate the terrain. Now the experience of the last war shows that if empty spaces initially allowed maneuver, the saturation of fronts rapidly led to a balance of forces, which could only be broken after painful attrition of German power ... Since, on land, a conflict limited to France and Germany would hardly allow decisive results, these should be obtained by an extension of fronts, that is, *with the aid of alliances*."

13. "if only by a rapid, symbolic detachment, while awaiting the possibility of a large scale operation." SHAT, 1N36, "Note résumant l'exposé fait par le général

Under Gamelin, the General Staff romanticised the eastern front as it had revealed itself in 1914-1918, fluid and fast-moving in contrast with the stalemated west. On this image, they superimposed Gamelin's interpretation of German developments in mechanised warfare. Gamelin's representative to the allied armies, General Schweisguth in April 1937 waxed enthusiastically about the singularities of the eastern front to an audience of high-ranking staff officers in the Collège des Hautes Etudes de la Défense Nationale:

> Ce terrain n'a pas de valeur en lui-même. Se battre ici ou là, qu'importe! On peut reculer de 50 kilometres sans découvrir ni une route importante, ni une ville, ni une usine, ni une voie ferrée. D'où des retraits rapides et profonds, nécessitant des avances de même ordre; il faut par conséquent des troupes susceptibles de rompre ou de prendre le contact: infanterie légère, cavalerie, chars.[14]

Preference for a war in the east was a constant in Gamelin's calculations from the time of Hitler's announcement of conscription in March 1935 until the eve of the war. As he explained to the Minister of War in April 1935:

> Il y aurait intérêt à ce que l'action commence en Europe centrale de façon que nous agissions en second contre une Allemagne déjà engagée de ce côté avec ses forces principales. Bien entendu, la condition d'une action efficace en Europe centrale est la collaboration de la Petite Entente et *comporte la possibilité d'user du territoire autrichien*.[15]

Gamelin à la réunion du 4 avril 1936," italics in the original; Papiers Schweisguth [henceforth, Schw.], Archives Nationales, 351 AP, 1SC2 Dr11, 24 Feb. 1937.

14. "This terrain has no value in itself. Fighting here or there makes absolutely no difference! One can retreat 50 kilometers without discovering an important road, a town, a factory or a railroad. So there can be rapid and deep withdrawals, necessitating advances of the same order; consequently, it is necessary to have troops able to break or resume contact with the enemy: light infantry, cavalry, tanks." Schw., SC4 Dr3, CHEDN lecture, 20 Apr. 1937.

15. "It is certain that the interest for us is in a conflict beginning in Central Europe, so that we could act as a secondary force against a Germany whose principal forces were already engaged in that region. Naturally, the condition of effective action in Central Europe is the collaboration of the Petite Entente and *entails the possibility of using Austrian territory*." *Documents Diplomatiques Français* (Paris, 1963 et seq.) [henceforth, *DDF*], I, 10, no. 155; italics in the original.

To his British colleague, Lord Gort, Gamelin spoke in July 1939 of a Franco-British interest in the war breaking out in the east, over Poland, and only gradually becoming a general conflict. France and Britain would thus gain necessary time to put all of their forces on a war footing. He concluded grandly that the sacrifice of the Poles would immobilise important German forces in the east.[16] This was the blood-of-others theme central to French strategy under Gamelin.

The theme of allied immolation extended from the war missed over Czechoslovakia in 1938 – when Gamelin had refused to move without an Italian alliance – through Franco-British inaction after the declaration of war in September 1939, to the tattered Belgian planning upon which Gamelin relied with Poland's defeat. His much vaunted planning for *une guerre de longue durée* concealed the mentality of the *drôle de guerre*, already evoked by the phrase *attente stratégique* in an Etat-Major de l'Armée (EMA) memorandum in late 1937.[17] He responded to the Czech crisis not with the idea of war, but negotiations to allow retention of Czechoslovakia as a strategic pawn in the French system. In a note written shortly before Munich, he argued that a Czechoslovakia shorn of the Sudetenland could play a part *à la Belgique* in a system to channel the German inundation away from France, a rather thankless task for the betrayed Czechs.[18]

As geography vanished with the Anschluss and Munich, Gamelin increasingly relied upon a strategy in time. Tutoring the British in the delicacies of grand strategy, in September 1938 he explained: "Il faut faire de la stratégie non seulement dans l'espace mais aussi dans le temps."[19] When chronic feelings of unpreparedness led him finally to adopt the sophism of *attente stratégique* over

16. SHAT, CSDN, "Conversations militaires franco-britanniques ... du 13 juillet 1939."
17. As the international tide turned against Czechoslovakia in November 1937, one of Gamelin's colleagues advocated *une attente stratégique*, that is, a plan for a war over Czechoslovakia exactly like that which occurred a year later over Poland: a Franco-British declaration of war followed by inaction, save for a small, local offensive in the Saar to mitigate the moral disadvantages of inaction. SHAT, 1N46, "Réflexions concernant la politique de guerre de la France," 20 November 1937.
18. DDF, II, no. 65.
19. "One must make strategy not only in space, but also in time." Cited in Le Goyet, p. 159.

Poland in 1939, his policy, as explained to Gort, was again allied immolation while France gained the mythic time necessary to launch an offensive.[20] At Poland's fall, when even the illusion of a two-front war collapsed, Gamelin blamed the Belgians for Poland's obliteration. Belgium, he thundered, would pay for its policy of neutrality in September 1939 by becoming the powers' battlefield.[21] The litany of allied immolation in the defence of France was monotonous, incessant and ruinous to any genuine allied effort.

Gamelin's allied diplomacy was central to his strategic failures, both in regard to a real two-front war in 1938-1939 and in regard to the defence in depth of France itself in 1940. Cynical miscalculation lay at the heart of his grand strategy, as it is sometimes tawdrily called. Gamelin consistently renounced a real two-front war – in which France would contribute to an allied effort by launching genuine offensives and fighting on its own soil – in favour of a cut-price war on the peripheries, in the east or in Belgium. As Hitler's conversations with his generals and Italian allies in 1939 demonstrate, only a genuine two-front war could have deterred him.[22]

The Breda Variant and the Fate of the French Strategic Reserve

The German inundation of France came in May 1940. Despite highly adverse political circumstances, and in the perennial hope of economising on French blood, Gamelin dispatched the cream of his army through northern Belgium to Breda in Holland, while the Germans broke through the Ardennes on to French soil in the south. Crucial reserves, including tank units designated to repulse

20. Mearsheimer remarks of the Franco-British relationship by 1939, "The British accepted the logic of [Gamelin's] policy, although they found its implications distasteful." By December 1939 the British concluded that, "... the French have no intention of carrying out an offensive for years, if at all." Mearsheimer, pp. 82-89. For a panoramic view of British perceptions in this period, P. M.H. Bell, *A Certain Eventuality: Britain and the Fall of France* (Farnborough, U.K., 1974).

21. Gamelin to Paul Reynaud, 9 October 1939, cited in M. Alexander, *The Republic in Danger*, p. 208.

22. D.C. Watt, *How War Came* (New York, 1989), pp. 317-318, 414-420, 426-429.

a German onslaught, were shifted northwards towards Breda even as German tank units appeared on the Meuse. The Breda Variant, meant to anchor the battle deep inside Belgian territory, has long been regarded by military historians as the most egregious command error of the campaign.[23]

This essay advances two new points. First, the Breda Variant was an extension of Gamelin's long-term strategy for a cut-price war on the peripheries. Second, Gamelin had long planned some form of the Breda Variant. He began transforming the French strategic reserve in 1936, and this proved critical in 1940. In the context of the evolution of Gamelin's mechanised doctrine, the Breda Variant was neither a strategic aberration nor a novelty.

After the Rhineland reoccupation of March 1936, Gamelin altered the traditional French conception of the strategic reserve. He redefined it as a highly specialised, mobile force to be committed to the Low Countries in the critical first days of conflict, rather than as an uncommitted force on French soil to be called to any front as needed.[24] By September 1936 Gamelin had transmuted a rearmament plan from earlier in the year for fortifications and manpower increases into a plan – with greater expenditures for tanks and mobile artillery – designed to carry war into the flat terrain of the Low Countries. His attention to the development of German mechanised forces had convinced him that Hitler would attack not against an organised position such as the Maginot line, but rapidly over free terrain in the east, against Poland, or against Belgium, where the French themselves might race to the encounter.[25] Gamelin's advocacy of mechanisation privileged tanks as the ideal means to regain lost ground and thus as a *defensive* weapon *par excellence*. This led him to transpose the defence of France far into the Belgian quadrant. EMA writers in 1936 spoke of holding the Albert Canal, which was on a line with Antwerp, in 1940 the embarkation point for the dispatch of the reserve to Breda.

The transformed strategic reserve was seen as offering maximum possibilities of maneuver, allowing Gamelin to transport the

---

23. Don Alexander, "Repercussions of the Breda Variant," *French Historical Studies* 8 (1974): 459-488.
24. SHAT, 7N3697, "Le problème militaire français," 1 June 1936.
25. SHAT, CSG, 29 Apr. 1936.

war outside French territory, his overriding priority. It was also thought to promise defensive security. While static defence by fortification troops on the Maginot line would ensure that the enemy did not break through onto French soil, the battle to defend France would be maintained entirely on Belgian soil by the so-called *Grandes Unités*, whose forces incorporated most of the mechanised reserve. France's security would be so increased by the specialised reserve that units in sectors regarded as static and relegated to the lowest priority by the Command, such as the Ardennes, could be reduced for the economies in manpower necessary to reorganise reserve units designated to fight in the Low Countries. A modernised strategic reserve, it was argued, could easily be accomplished by such a reorganisation of existing resources.[26] The implicit, further downgrading of the Ardennes sector was yet another aspect of the strategic reserve problem to be of great moment in 1940.

For many months after April 1936, when Gamelin undertook the task of redefining the strategic reserve, he believed that the next conflict would begin in Central Europe and spoke of a French offensive in Belgium to aid Czechoslovakia.[27] With the Nazi-Soviet pact and the fall of Poland, Gamelin's plans for a war in the east on the cheap had collapsed, or almost. There were schemes in 1939-40 for peripheral theatres: operations in Norway, Salonika, the Caucasus, the Ukraine and the Middle East. The recently published Doumenc papers present a General Staff still enticed in 1940 by a war of far-flung fronts. For some in the Army General Staff (EMA), the resulting dispersal of German force meant that Germany could not reasonably be expected to unleash a massive

---

26. The surface resemblance of Gamelin's plan for a mechanised strategic reserve to Charles de Gaulle's advocacy of a *force d'intervention* was not coincidental; cf. Elisabeth du Réau, *Edouard Daladier* (Paris, 1993), pp. 180-182. Gamelin customarily proceeded by incorporating elements from more innovative military thinkers in order to maintain his claim constantly to be modernising the army. The General Staff's emphasis was on reorganisation of existing resources rather than an in-depth reorganisation which would have departed from the doctrine of continuous fronts. Its plan also differed critically from de Gaulle's in that it posited a prepared battlefield in Belgium (how prepared this battlefield would be rested on Gamelin's covert diplomacy with the Belgian Command), as opposed to encountering the Germans wherever they attacked.

27. Schw., 1SC2 Dr8, 1 Apr., "Rapport," 4 Apr. 1936.

attack in the west. Gamelin, for example, restored normal leave in the army on 7 May 1940. For others, such peripheral plans, in place or to come, would pressure Germany to attack through Belgium in order to "briser le cercle de fer qui l'étreindra."[28] These speculations about dispersing German force were the last vestiges of military enthusiasm for a war in which an eastern counterweight would absorb the bulk of the German blow.

Germany's attack on 10 May narrowed French attention to the Low Countries. A supremely confident Gamelin believed that the enemy would play out the strategic scenario which he had written for it.[29] His attraction to the Belgian-Dutch theatre rested on the same search for open spaces, *terrain libre*, as had his earlier infatuation with the east:

> ... au cas où les Allemands envahiraient la Belgique (Hollande-Luxembourg) [les Alliés] pourraient avantageusement passer à la contreoffensive car l'ennemi s'offrirait à eux en terrain libre. Le champ de bataille Luxembourg-Belgique-Hollande du Sud permet seul l'usure et la décision hors des systèmes fortifiés et des parades d'obstacles.[30]

As Belgium's increasing neutralism had soured relations with France during the 1930s, Gamelin failed to reverse the doctrine of forward defence. Although he had pressed in the early years of the decade for light, supplementary fortifications just inside the French border as a fall-back position (albeit one precluding an improvised defence in depth), Gamelin lost interest in the project when it was later begun at Daladier's insistence, arguing that German motorisation required a rapid and firm commitment of the strategic

---

28. François Delpla, ed., *Les Papiers secrets du Général Doumenc* (Paris, 1992), pp. 145, 149, 163-164, 167; for Gamelin's view of operations in Salonika as dependent on Italian benevolence, *ibid.*, pp. 495-496.

29. Archives Nationales, Papiers Paul Reynaud, AN 74 AP/22, "Notes prises par le lt.-col. Villelume ... avril-mai 1940," 12 May 1940; see also General Doumenc's recollections in Delpla, pp. 206-207.

30. "In the case that the Germans invade Belgium(Holland-Luxembourg), [the Allies] could advantageously go onto the counter-offensive because the enemy would be exposed to them in unfortified territory. Only the battlefield of Luxemburg-Belgium-southern Holland permits attrition and breakthrough outside of fortified systems and a defensive line of obstacles." "Plan de Guerre pour 1940," 26 Feb. 1940, Gamelin to the Minister of War, *ibid.*, p. 497.

reserve to the Low Countries. As was his habit, he relied on a conflict to coalesce support for France, this time not in Central Europe but within a divided Belgium and a frightened Holland. Before 1940 he had relied on cultivating covertly the Belgian Chief of Staff, Van den Bergen (a disastrous pattern elsewhere discernible in his reliance on personal understandings with such foreign generals as Rydz-Smigly of Poland and Badoglio of Italy). Gamelin continued to plan for a war in the Lowlands after Van den Bergen's dismissal for excessive Francophilia in January 1940 and also after the Mechelen episode of the same month, when allied capture of German war plans forced an already eager Hitler to change his strategy from limited warfare to tactical breakthrough. By May 1940 so strong was Gamelin's *idée fixe* of a campaign in the Low Countries that he was prepared to meet the Germans in an encounter battle, as clear a violation of classic French doctrine as his redefinition of the strategic reserve.

The pivotal error in the Breda Variant concerned Gamelin's use of his strategic reserve which he deployed before ascertaining the main direction of the German attack. The original proximity of the reserves to the Ardennes is tantalising, but the area behind the Ardennes, located roughly at the centre of the French defensive system, served merely as a staging ground for the reserves which Gamelin had long intended to dispatch to the Low Countries.[31] The Belgians and Dutch had failed to coordinate their actions, yet Gamelin threw caution to the winds in his alacrity to join what would in effect have been a battle of encounter had the critical mass of the German Army moved into southern Holland.[32]

---

31. Gamelin did not commit his entire reserve to the Breda Variant, despite being taken in by the "matador's cloak," the action of German armies in Belgium and Holland to distract attention from the Ardennes. Once he sent the 7th Army to Breda, Gamelin maintained a large force behind the Maginot line to protect against an Italo-German eruption through Switzerland outflanking the line. When the significance of the Ardennes became inescapable, Goebbels threatened to invade Switzerland in order to persuade Gamelin that the attack at Sedan might not be the main attack after all, and so deter him from transferring troops from the Maginot line to stop the German advance. These various German attempts at disorientation proved successful.

32. The alternative to the Breda Variant, the Escaut Plan, would have situated the battle very close to the industrial centre of Lille with the system of strong points reaching back on French soil, the situation Gamelin was determined to avoid.

The Germans rapidly consummated their breakthrough in southern Belgium without serious opposition from the demoralised, grade B French troops guarding unfinished blockhouses in their path. Gamelin's Breda Variant fixed his vision northwards for the critical days of German action and fatally compromised his ability to respond. The primitive state of French military communications compounded this myopia.[33] Gamelin himself chose to be without radio contact with the front. In this sense, the defeat *was* the product of an absence. Furthermore, the irresponsible division of authority between himself and General Alphonse Georges led to a cumbersome liaison linking the two commands.[34] No wonder that for many hours into the German attack, Gamelin had almost no idea what was happening. French troops on the ground in Belgium and Holland went through the chaotic hell chronicled by Marc Bloch in *L' Etrange Défaite*. German progress proved so rapid that French Intelligence not only did not know the enemy's location, it often did not know where the remnants of the French Armies were. As for the Breda Variant, on 11 May, thirty-six hours into the battle, the advance guard of General Henri Giraud's mechanised divisions reached Breda only to find that the Dutch Army had fled. Gamelin's gamble with his mechanised reserve was a fiasco.

33. Army communications suffered from Gamelin's low estimation of their importance. Robert Doughty has argued that the low budgetary priority given to communications reflected French defence doctrine with its stress on prepared battlefields. R. Doughty, "The French Armed Forces, 1918-40," in Williamson Murray and Allan R. Millett, eds., *Military Effectiveness* (Boston, 1988), II, p. 58. Of the contrasting German case, Geyer writes: "The main task [of command] became coordination through communication rather than actual deployment and direct control of movement." "German Strategy in the Age of Mechanical Warfare" in P. Paret, ed., *Makers of Modern Strategy* (Princeton, 1986), p. 560.

34. Gamelin intended to assume a grandiose interallied command, and so gave Georges the putatively less significant command of the northeastern front. But Gamelin's dominant political concerns and the emerging fiasco of the allied armies, whose cooperation in battle proved chimerical, meant that he withdrew emotionally from any responsibility to take command of the battle. Responsibility for allied liaison devolved on to Georges, who passed it on to a manifestly unsuitable general, Gaston Billotte. General Doumenc, as head of the *Grand Quartier Général* assumed more and more responsibility, propping up a flagging Georges and ghostwriting Gamelin's last order for a north-south attack against over-extended German lines. Doumenc's account is in Delpla, pp. 211-215, 219 n. 35, 221 n. 38, 362.

When Gamelin finally grasped on 16 May the consequences of the German breakthrough in the Ardennes, he told Churchill that he could not counterattack given his lack of reserves.[35] Paul Reynaud had understood more rapidly than the ill-starred generalissimo the significance of the German rupture, realising on 14 May that " ... si notre front est crevé, *tout est perdu*. Il ne peut plus être question de bataille de la Marne. Nous avons opté pour le front continu."[36] The French strategic collapse stemmed not, as Gamelin later alleged, from a failure to implement the lofty conceptions of the Command, but from the doctrine of continuous fronts which vainly sought to retake every point of German breakthrough rather than regrouping for in-depth defence on French soil with an adequate strategic reserve.[37]

By the time of Gamelin's dismissal on 19 May, the French military accepted that the defeat had been consummated. In François Delpla's phrase, " ... désormais, toutes les décisions vont se prendre dans une atmosphère de pré-armistice."[38] Demanded not by Gamelin but by his successor – although as Marc Bloch wrote, there was no change in strategic response with Weygand's eleventh-hour reappearance[39] – the timing of the armistice served the two purposes for which Gamelin's strategy had been invented: it ensured that there would be no prolonged conflict on French soil and no repetition of the national bloodletting of 1914-1918. By attempting to fight the war elsewhere, Gamelin in effect made it impossible to fight at all.

 35. Winston Churchill, *Their Finest Hour* (Boston, 1949), pp. 45-49.
 36. "If our front has been broken, *everything is lost*. There can be no question of repeating the battle of the Marne. We have opted for the continuous front." Paul Reynaud, *Au Coeur de la mêlée* (Paris, 1951), p. 442; italics in the original. On hearing Gamelin's claim that between Laon and Paris there was not a single corps of soldiers at his disposal, Daladier concluded that the French Army would be destroyed. O. Bullitt, ed., *For the President: Personal and Secret* (Boston, 1972), p. 426.
 37. Once the Germans broke through in the Ardennes, the doctrine of continuous fronts decreed that counterattack be consistently sacrificed to the vain task of *colmatage*. By the same token, the doctrine of continuous fronts meant that French tanks were deployed in penny packets rather than massed in tactically independent units.
 38. " ... henceforth, all decisions were going to be taken in a pre-armistice atmosphere." Delpla, pp. 364-366.
 39. Bloch, *L' Etrange Défaite*, p. 61; Delpla, pp. 369-370, 372.

French weaknesses in 1940 were strategic and experiential. The French were not hopelessly outclassed in material terms.[40] Rather, the Breda Variant eloquently expressed the complete lack of will of the Command to resist on French soil, a problematic condition compounded by the French Army's lack of experience against a Wehrmacht embarked upon its fourth military excursion in three years.[41] The fall of France came about not from lack of weapons, nor until after Dunkirk from an insuperable lack of men, but from a virtual absence of planning for a German breakthrough on French soil. This fact resists explanation until placed in its strategic context, a war of continuous and extended fronts always to be fought outside of France's frontiers. More than any other single factor, strategy accounts for the armistice of June 1940.

Scapegoatism

Michael Geyer has remarked that the armistice spared France not only a repetition of the slaughter of 1914-1918, but also "the desperate and radicalizing struggles of 1870-1871 which are perhaps too easily overlooked in this context."[42] Certainly, social fears

---

40. On the material question, a central argument of M. Alexander's *The Republic in Danger* is that Gamelin's success in remedying a "re-equipment crisis" after the arms cuts and disarmament of the early 1930s still did not allow him to oppose Germany forcefully in the eastern crises of 1938-1939 or during the *drôle de guerre*. Alexander loses view of the essential point that in a situation of rough parity, the number of arms is less important than the use made of them. He also repeats Gamelin's own mistake of forgetting that the adversary too had his troubles and might deem himself unprepared. Michael Geyer goes to the root of the matter in arguing that European general staffs in this period almost uniformly considered themselves unprepared for war. The traditional strategic calculus no longer worked, which accounts for Hitler's growing attachment to "politically and militarily improvised warfare." M. Geyer, "German Strategy, 1914-45," pp. 570-572.

41. Beyond handwringing and transposing the war into Belgium and Holland, Gamelin and his colleagues had done little in real terms in the winter of 1939-40 to prepare the army for the Blitzkrieg. As an example, Alistair Horne relates that Gamelin's GQG issued some 19 pages of instructions during the *drôle de guerre* on the conduct of patrols, while making no provision for exercises simulating dive-bomber attacks. At Sedan, one of Gamelin's favourite young generals, Huntzinger, denied his terrified troops immediate air cover, saying that they should receive their baptism by fire. Horne, *To Lose A Battle* (Boston, 1969), pp. 191, 288.

42. Geyer, "The Crisis of Military Leadership," p. 449.

played a prominent role in the scapegoatism that characterised the reaction of Gamelin and his colleagues to the German breakthrough. On 16 May, Gamelin informed Georges Mandel, the strongly *résistant* Minister of Colonies, that the Army, permeated with Communism, had not held. Such an interpretation of the tragedy at the Meuse lent itself to the false rumours that flooded the capital, to the effect that fugitives from the broken, Communist-infiltrated divisions on the Meuse were marching on Paris to make revolution.[43] The brilliant Manstein-Guderian strategy for an attack at the centre of the French continuous front had left unclear in what direction the Germans would next move: to Paris, or to the south to take the Maginot line from behind, or to the north to cut off the Franco-British forces in Belgium. Gamelin believed for some days that their target would be Paris, and he spread the alarm, which carried with it the message to ward off popular disorder in the capital.

On the eve of his dismissal Gamelin composed a lengthy explanation for the defeat. Its most prominent themes were self-justification and scapegoatism. He censured the troops for indiscipline and failure of morale, and included a scarcely veiled censure of the social reforms associated with the Popular Front government of Léon Blum:

> Porté à critiquer sans cesse tous ceux qui détiennent une parcelle d'autorité, *incité, sous prétexte de civilisation à jouir d'une vie quotidienne facile*, le mobilisé d'aujourd'hui n'avait pas reçu durant les années d'entre-deux-guerres l'éducation morale et patriotique qui l'aurait préparé au drame dans lequel allaient se jouer les destinées du pays.[44]

43. Horne, pp. 385-386, 391.

44. "Apt ceaselessly to criticize all those who hold an iota of authority, *encouraged to take life easy as a mark of civilisation*, today's mobilised soldier did not receive during the interwar years the moral and patriotic education which would have prepared him for the drama in which would be played out the destinies of the country". Archives Nationales, Papiers Paul Reynaud, Gamelin to Minister of National Defence, 18 May 1940, my italics; see also Gamelin's comments to an unnamed confidante in June 1940, cited in Le Goyet, pp. 350-1. Philip Bankwitz has written of Gamelin's 18 May censure of his troops: "It is perhaps Gamelin's misunderstanding of heroism and his debasement of the French people that shocks the most after over 50 years: his letter to Reynaud of 18 May 1940 is unworthy of a demoralised subaltern." "Comment," *Journal of Strategic Studies* 14 (1991): 444; for the reflections of J.-L. Crémieux-Brilhac on the same topic, *Les Français de l'an 40*, II, pp. 363-364, 507-517, 710-711.

The indictment of the values which infused the French educational system after the Dreyfus Affair struck a distinctly *pétainiste* note. The popular linkage between Gamelin and the Republic was seriously frayed well before the German attack. During the Blum government in 1936-1937, Gamelin's comportment was marked by private disquiet and professional mutism.[45] By 1939, he freely castigated republican politicians, including his civilian protector, Daladier. Long dismissive of the rigours of operational planning, he complained as Poland fell that military operations were as nothing compared to the tribulations of dealing with the government, the politicians and their cliques.[46] From March 1940, he was increasingly distracted by political concerns as he fought for his job amid rumours of Reynaud's intention to dismiss him. With the onset of the German attack he refused to move into a modern command centre at Montry, preferring to remain in the medieval gloom of the Château de Vincennes: "Je ne me sens pas assuré sur mes arrières ... je n'ose pas m'absenter une minute d'auprès du gouvernement."[47] Several months after the Battle of France, the Vichy Government, composed of his erstwhile colleagues, imprisoned Gamelin with political figures also blamed for the defeat; he was later placed on trial at Riom in a dock with Blum and Daladier.

Gamelin's loathing of the Popular Front emerged fully only at the Riom trial in 1942. While declining the opportunity to defend himself by taking the stand (apparently from apprehension at washing military dirty linen in public, as well as from a long-standing reluctance to speak his mind), Gamelin submitted to the court

45. Schw., 1SC2 Dr9, "Rapport," 9 June 1936. Gamelin later acknowledged: "La crise de mai-juin 1936, terrorisa une grande partie de la bourgeoisie française. Pour beaucoup d'entre nous elle fit perdre de vue les dangers de l'hitlérisme et du fascisme voisins ... "/"The crisis of May-June 1936 [which marked the advent of Blum's Popular Front] terrorized a large section of the French bourgeoisie. It made many of us lose sight of the dangers of Hitlerism and Fascism ... because behind the Popular Front one saw the spectre of Bolshevism." *Servir*, II, p. 219.

46. Martin Alexander, "Maurice Gamelin and the Defeat of France," in Brian Bond, ed., *Fallen Stars*, p. 117.

47. "I don't feel secure on the home front ... I dare not absent myself one minute from the seat of government." Author's note: the literal translation of Gamelin's statement, 'I don't feel that my back is covered ...,' conveys a strong fear of being stabbed in the back. Gamelin, cited in Doumenc's journal entry for 12 May 1940, in Delpla, p. 215.

a lengthy appraisal of French interwar policy.[48] In this memorandum he vented his spleen against the Popular Front in ideological terms which at times made him hardly distinguishable from his Vichyite judges. He blasted "la criminelle démagogie du front populaire et le vain orgueil de ceux qui nous ont entraînés jusqu'au fond de l'abîme" projecting on to the Popular Front the image of the nation's irrevocable descent into defeat.[49] By the time of Riom, Gamelin had come to reject the republican regime which he felt had ruined him.[50]

After the defeat, the Popular Front supplied the litmus test for republicanism in France. Marc Bloch wrote candidly that he had no wish to undertake an apology for Blum's government, which had been surpassed by events, but he deplored the annihilation of collective, patriotic memory in class and ideological division which he had witnessed among the bourgeoisie and many of the officers with whom he served. In passages which contrast strongly with the dismissal of social reform in Gamelin's note of 18 May 1940, Bloch argued that the Popular Front had ended working-class subservience for the good of the nation. Of its place in French history, he wrote in a justly famous passage:

> Surtout, quelles qu'aient pu être les fautes des chefs [du Front populaire], il y avait, dans cet élan des masses vers l'espoir d'un monde plus juste, une honnêteté touchante, à laquelle on s'étonne qu'aucun coeur bien placé ait pu rester insensible ... .Il est deux catégories de Français qui ne comprendront jamais l'histoire de la France: ceux qui refusent

---

48. Gamelin as "silent" victim at Riom, the vignette which opens Martin Alexander's *The Republic in Danger* (pp. 4-5, 7), thus needs modification. Alexander, himself, cites Gamelin's Riom memorandum elsewhere (*ibid*., p. 352). Also problematic are the intertwined leitmotifs of Gamelin as apotheosis of the republic and as victim which are central to Alexander's study. This double martyrdom of Gamelin omits consideration of his increasing estrangement from the régime and of his incompetence.

49. "The criminal demagoguery of the Popular Front and the empty arrogance of those who dragged us to the edge of the abyss ..." Gamelin's defence of Daladier's September 1936 rearmament programme led into renewed ideological attacks on the Popular Front. Fondation National des Sciences Politiques, Papiers Léon Blum, Maurice Gamelin, "La Politique Etrangère de la France 1930-39 au point de vue militaire," n.d.

50. After the war, Gamelin had some success in resuscitating his reputation as a republican warrior in his burnished, highly tendentious memoirs. *Servir* replaced the worn scapegoat of the Popular Front with that of Pétain, Gamelin's freshly dishonoured comrade-in-arms.

de vibrer au souvenir du sacre de Reims; ceux qui lisent sans émotion le récit de la fête de la Fédération. Leur imperméabilité aux plus beaux jaillissements de l'enthouisasme collectif suffit à les condamner. Dans le Front populaire – le vrai, celui des foules, non des politiciens – il revivait quelque chose de l'atmosphère du Champ de Mars, au grand soleil du 14 juillet 1790.[51]

Bloch observed that this élan of the masses towards a more just world left the bourgeoisie and the officer class cold. The social fears resurrected by the Popular Front destroyed the happiness and security of these groups and estranged them as surely from the sources of national feeling as those Frenchmen who could not thrill at once to the memory of the coronation at Reims and to an account of *la fête de la Fédération*.

A student of false rumours in the First World War,[52] Marc Bloch in the course of the Second World War was struck by a more perverse phenomenon, the concatenation of scapegoatisms and false claims to represent *la vraie France* by which traditional military aspirations to embody the nation were being revived. The *mentalités* which produced the Riom trial, already palpable to Bloch in the summer of 1940, had a part, like the armistice to which Gamelin's strategy had been pivotal, in Bloch's determination to write his much cited, little understood classic. At Riom the Vichy regime sought to perpetrate its own stab-in-the-back legend. The underlying thesis of Riom, with which Gamelin concurred, was

51. "But whatever the faults of which the [Popular Front] movement may have been guilty, there was in that striving of the masses to make a juster world a touching eagerness and sincerity which ought not to have been without effect on any man animated by ordinary human feelings ... There are two categories of Frenchmen who will never really grasp the significance of French history: those who refuse to thrill to the Consecration of our Kings at Rheims, and those who can read unmoved the account of the Festival of Federation. I do not care what may be the colour of their politics today: such a lack of response to the noblest uprushes of national enthusiasm is enough to condemn them. In the Popular Front – the *real* Popular Front of the masses, not the one exploited by the politicians – something lived again of the spirit that had moved men's hearts on the Champs-de-Mars under the hot sun of 14 July 1790." Bloch, *L' Etrange Défaite*, pp. 182-183/*Strange Defeat*, trans. Hopkins, pp. 166-167.

52. Bloch's observations on false rumours in the 1914-1918 war were published in "Réflexions d'un historien sur les fausses nouvelles de la guerre," *Revue de synthèse historique* 33 (1921): 41-57; see also Carole Fink's excellent introduction to Marc Bloch, *Memoirs of War 1914-15* (Cambridge, 1988), especially pp. 28, 43-44, 47, 66-67.

that a decadent Popular Front had brought about the defeat by sapping French national energies from within. To this scapegoatism were added forms of national atonement and contrition through which the serried ranks of Vichy for a time won wider acceptance of the *pronunciamiento* which followed the armistice.[53]

Bloch's willingness to pass from an indictment of the military in the opening parts of *L' Etrange Défaite* to a magisterial analysis of the parochialism of French society and politics has supplied a popular source of quotation in writings on 1940. The underlying theme of the final part of Bloch's book, however, has been grossly neglected: it is that the military and the bourgeoisie, separated from the profound sources of popular feeling represented by the Popular Front, went on to capitulate completely to the invader. This recurrent theme of estrangement from the nation, which in the military's case Bloch dated from the Dreyfus affair, links the different parts of his book in a culminating argument:

> Mal instruits des ressources infinies d'un peuple resté beaucoup plus sain que des leçons empoisonnées ne les avaient inclinés à le croire, incapables, par dédain comme par routine, d'en appeler à temps à ses réserves profondes, nos chefs [militaires] ne se sont pas seulement laissé battre. Ils ont estimé très tôt naturel d'être battus. En déposant, avant l'heure, les armes, ils ont assuré le succès d'une faction. Quelques-uns, certes, cherchèrent, avant tout, dans le coup d'Etat, le moyen de masquer leur faute. D'autres cependant, dans le haut commandement, presque tous dans les rangs de l'armée étaient loin de poursuivre consciemment d'aussi égoïstes desseins. Ils n'ont accepté le désastre que la rage au coeur. Ils l'ont accepté, cependant, trop tôt, parce qu'ils lui trouvaient ces atroces consolations: écraser, sous les

---

53. "Le troupier, conscient de ses propres sacrifices, refuse de se tenir pour responsable pour leur inutilité. Ses chefs, qui redoutent son jugement, l'encouragent à chercher les coupables partout ailleurs que dans l'armée. Ainsi naît la fatale légende du coup de poignard dans le dos, propice aux redressements à rebours et aux pronunciamientos."/ "The soldier is only too conscious of the sacrifices he has been called upon to make. If they turn out to have been useless, that, he feels, is not *his* responsibility. His leaders, ever fearful of his criticism, encourage him to find scapegoats anywhere rather than in the Army. Thus is born the fatal legend of the 'stab in the back' which reactionary movements and military *coups d'état* always find so useful. "*L' Etrange Défaite*, p. 146/*Strange Defeat*, trans. Hopkins , p. 127. Bloch identified both the paradox by which military régimes posed as the saviors of their defeated societies, and the origin of stab-in-the-back legends in military scapegoatism. Ibid., pp. 45, 46, 187.

ruines de la France, un regime honni: plier les genoux devant le châtiment que le destin avait envoyé à une nation coupable.[54]

The perception of national decadence projected on to the Popular Front preceded and made possible both the military acceptance of the armistice and the claim to legitimacy of the Vichy regime. This, then, was the strangeness of France's defeat. Or as Bloch wrote elsewhere, "Les faits historiques sont, par essence, des faits psychologiques."[55]

Concluding Myths

Let us in conclusion return to the image with which this essay began, Rommel's capture of 10,000 French prisoners in mid-May

54. "Ill informed about the infinite resources of a people that has remained far healthier than they, as the result of poisonous teaching, have been inclined to believe; rendered incapable by inherited contempt and by the limited routine of their training to call in time upon its inexhaustible reserves of strength, our leaders not only let themselves be beaten, but too soon decided that it was perfectly natural that they should be beaten. By laying down their arms before there was any real necessity for them to do so, they have assured the triumph of a faction. Some of them, to be sure, strove hard, by backing the coup d'état, to disguise their fault. But others there were, in the High Command and in almost every rank of the Army, who were very far from pursuing any such selfish design. They accepted the disaster, but with rage in their hearts. However that may be, they did accept it, and long before they need have done. They were ready to find consolation in the thought that beneath the ruins of France a shameful regime might be crushed to death, and that if they yielded it was to a punishment meted out by Destiny to a guilty nation." *Ibid.*, pp. 186-187; cf. pp. 144, 184 / *Ibid.*, trans. Hopkins, p. 170.

Bloch throughout his text rejected the notion of national decadence so popular among military figures at Riom and Vichy. "Au fond de leur coeur, ils [nos chefs militaires] étaient prêts, d'avance, à désespérer du pays même qu'ils avaient à défendre et du peuple qui leur fournissait leurs soldats. Ici, nous quittons le domaine militaire. C'est plus loin et plus profond qu'il faut chercher les racines d'une malentendu trop grave pour ne pas devoir compter parmi les principales raisons du désastre." (p. 144)/ "In their hearts, they were only too ready to despair of the country they had been called upon to defend, and of the people who furnished the soldiers they commanded. At this point I leave the purely military field. The roots of misunderstanding so grave that we cannot but rank it among the main causes of our disaster, must be sought elsewhere and at a much deeper level." (P.125) It was this inquiry that prompted his cross-sectioning of French society.

55. "Historical facts are in essence psychological facts." M. Bloch, *Apologie pour l'histoire ou Métier d'historien* (Paris, 1974), p. 145.

1940 during his lightning advance. Such episodes and the ensuing imprisonment of huge numbers of French soldiers in Germany – believed to total one-half of young Frenchmen of arms-bearing age in 1939 – gave immediate and pulverising reality to the defeat.[56] From this catastrophic situation arose two structurally-related myths.

First came the seductive Vichyite myth of honourable French military resistance in 1940 to the Germans. After all, it was not the strategic conceptions of the Command, but the decadent politicians and broader society who were to blame for the defeat. "Military honour is safe," sighed Weygand after the signature of the armistice which provided for surrendering to the Reich all political refugees on French soil, a provision soon to be more widely defined among the Jewish population of France. In the face of a revolutionary German strategy for victory which brought ideological, and ultimately genocidal, warfare, the French Command in 1940 was unable to resolve the strategic problems of the conflict by traditional means, in the absence of an eastern front. The strategy of Gamelin and Weygand, which led to acceptance of the armistice, failed to meet the needs of the time, whatever the armistice did for military honour.[57]

---

56. A French observer of another such scene in May 1940 reported to Gamelin: "Débandade intégrale. Sur 70,000 hommes et de nombreux officiers, aucune unité commandée, si petite soit-elle ... 10% à peine d'hommes ont conservé leurs fusils ... Il ne m'a pas été possible, sur les milliers qui ont été triés, de former une compagnie pour la défence du pont de Compiègne [où l'armistice a été signé plus tard]. Cependant, les pertes subies ne paraissent pas avoir été élevées. Aucun blessé parmi ces milliers de fuyards ... Ils ne comprennent pas ce qui leur est arrivé. La vue d'un avion leur inspire de la terreur."/"Complete disintegration. Out of 70,000 men and numerous officers, no single unit is commanded, however small ... 10 percent at most of men have kept their rifles ... Out of the thousands we sifted, it was not possible for me to form one company for the defence of the bridge at Compiègne [where the armistice was later signed].However, the losses suffered do not seem to have been high. There were no wounded among the thousands of fugitives ... they do not understand what has happened to them. The sight of an airplane inspires terror in them." Cited in J. Minart, P.C. Vincennes Secteur 4, II, pp. 221-222. Contemporary figures on prisoners of war were compiled by the Commissariat au reclassement des prisonniers de guerre rapatriés, SHAT, 2P68, cited in Pierre Péan, Une Jeunesse française (Paris, 1994), p. 205.

57. For Weygand's quest from 21 May for an anachronistic concept of military honour rather than victory, Delpla, pp. 371, 404, 422. This quest in no way diminishes the human valour of individual French soldiers chronicled by Marc Bloch, as well as such legendary episodes of group resistance as that of some 2000 officer cadets of the

The Germans shrewdly saw political interest in salving the wounded honour of a demoralised French officer corps by the wording of the preamble to the armistice: "After an heroic resistance, France, in a unique series of bloody battles, has been vanquished and has collapsed. Thus, Germany does not propose to give to ... the negotiations for the armistice the character of an affront to such a brave adversary."[58] Such language was also meant to dampen any spirit of resistance by conveying to a bewildered populace the message that the time had come to lay down arms with honour.

A second seductive myth arose from the ashes of 1940, the Gaullist postwar vision "positing an identity between a mythical Resistance (with a capital R) and the French people as a whole."[59] In reality, the widespread popularity of *la Résistance* inside France had to await the Vichy government's imposition in February 1943 of *le Service du Travail Obligatoire*, compulsory labour in Germany or German-controlled factories in France for French youth, who were to be exchanged for French prisoners of war. It was the S.T.O. which transformed the *Maquis*, the guerilla arm of the Resistance, into a veritable army. Estimates of numbers fleeing the S.T.O. into active resistance reach 100,000.[60]

The defeat of 1940 continues to exert a profound influence on French collective memory, an influence perhaps the deeper for

---

cavalry school of Saumur on the Loire from 18 to 20 June that occurred despite Pétain's appeal of 16-17 June for an end to hostilities; see Crémieux-Brilhac's *Les Français de l'an 40*, II, pp. 695-699.

58. Cited in Annie Brassié, *Robert Brasillach ou encore un instant de bonheur* (Paris, 1987), p. 216.

59. Michael Marrus, review of Henry Rousso's *Le Syndrome de Vichy* in the *Times Literary Supplement*, 24 Apr. 1992, p. 23; for a meditation on the complexity of Resistance loyalties, Pierre Vidal-Naquet, *Le Trait empoisonné: Réflexions sur l'affaire Jean Moulin* (Paris, 1993).

60. Mireille Johnston, Appendix to the British script of Marcel Ophuls, *The Sorrow and the Pity* (St. Albans, 1975), p. 183; H. Rousso, *Les Années noires: vivre sous l'Occupation* (Paris, 1992), pp. 106-108.

having run so long in subterranean channels. The myths to which the armistice and defeat gave rise, so many means to disguise the keen national sense of degradation, are only now painfully and slowly being confronted and disentangled from their various claims to military honour.[61]

---

[61]. To speak thus of military honour is not to enter into the debate over "legitimacy" and the "true nation" between Vichy and France Libre. One might take as symbolic of the confused claims of military honour in 1940-1944 the case of Miron Zlatin, director of the orphanage at Izieu, deported with his charges in an April 1944 *rafle*, but classified by the post-war republic as an *ancien combattant*. While a *résistant*, he had not been deported for facts of armed resistance; nor had he fought in 1939-40. S. Zlatin, *Mémoires de la Dame d'Izieu* (Paris, 1992), pp. 52, 93, 101. On the difficulty of distinguishing between war crimes and crimes against humanity in the full-blown period of Gaullist myth, see Alain Finkielkraut's luminous essay on the Barbie trial, *La Mémoire vaine* (Paris, 1989), pp. 37-38; for a transgenerational perspective on the French search for military honour if not grandeur, Robert Gildea, *The Past in French History* (Oxford, 1994), pp. 112-165.

II

MARC BLOCH AND THE DRÔLE DE GUERRE

Prelude to the "Strange Defeat"

Carole Fink

Shortly after the Pétain government signed the armistice with Nazi Germany in the forest of Rethondes near Compiègne, an outraged demobilized officer surreptitiously took up his pen and bore witness to "the most terrible collapse" in France's history.[1] *Strange Defeat*, the title given to the historian Marc Bloch's unfinished book published after his heroic death as a resistance leader, has remained a compelling work for over a half century. It is the outpouring of a brilliant, anguished patriot who analyzed a calamity that exceeded Waterloo, Sedan, and even Dien Bien Phu, in its consequences for France, Europe, and the world.[2]

1. Marc Bloch, *L' Etrange Défaite* (Paris, 1957) (hereafter *ED*), p. 21: "(Le) plus atroce effondrement de notre histoire."
2. "... The fall of France opened an abyss of uncertainty for the whole continent and shook the imagination as perhaps nothing had shaken it since the victory of the Turks at Mohács in 1526." Peter Calvocoressi and Guy Wint, *Total War: Causes and Courses of the Second World War* (Harmondsworth, 1979), p. 131. For the momentous local and global consequences, see Gerhard Weinberg, *A World at Arms: A Global History of World War II* (Cambridge, 1994), Chap. 3: "A World Turned Upside Down," pp. 122-186.

During the eight and a half months preceding the battle of France, the fifty-three-year-old reserve captain – a distinguished professor of economic history at the Sorbonne, the co-editor of the journal *Annales*, and the father of six children aged nine to nineteen – occupied the personal and national antechamber known as the *drôle de guerre*, the "phony war." In the autumn of 1939 Marc Bloch had just completed his long-awaited *magnum opus*, *La Société féodale*. As the war clouds grew, he and his wife were preparing to attend the International Congress of Historical Sciences in Bucharest, and he ruefully anticipated another sojourn in Aix-les-Bains to treat the arthritis he had contracted in the trenches in World War I.[3]

Instead, on 24 August 1939, Marc Bloch and thousands of other reservists were mobilized for the third time in less than a year. Torn from normal behavior and from normal expectations, suspended from history and from common-sense responses, members of a huge French army became separated for an indefinite period from their work and their loved ones. Sixty-seven divisions, lacking strong leadership, public support, and solid allies, waited almost three-quarters of a year to be attacked by a ruthless, stronger foe.[4]

Like many of his generation, Marc Bloch went off to a second world war without the resolute high spirits of 1914.[5] A quarter of a century earlier, the twenty-eight year-old Bloch had fully shared with his fellow *poilus* the Marne victory, the Argonne privations, the Somme bloodletting, and the repulse of the Germans before Paris in 1918 as well as the sweetness of the liberation of Alsace.[6]

3. Marc Bloch to Henri Berr, Fougères, 13 Aug. 1939, in Marc Bloch, *Ecrire "La Société féodale": Lettres à Henri Berr, 1924-1943* (Paris, 1992), p. 106; Marc Bloch to Etienne Bloch, 12, 17 Aug. 1939, Etienne Bloch Collection (hereafter EBC).
4. Cf. Weinberg, *World at Arms*, p. 68: There was no question of saving Poland; French leaders intended to wait patiently for the British army and focus their concern on defending the soil against a German offensive, "whenever it came."
5. Marc Bloch to Lucien Febvre, 17 Sept. 1939, Bloch-Febvre correspondence, Archives Nationales (hereafter AN) Microfilm (hereafter MI) 318 1: "J'ai au fond de moi même sincèrement bon espoir. Mais tout cela n'empêche pas que je n'ai plus 20 ans ni comme en 1914 28, et que c'est la deuxième fois!" Cf. Marc Bloch, *Souvenirs de guerre 1914-1915* (Paris, 1969), pp. 10-11.
6. See Introduction by Carole Fink to translation of Marc Bloch, *Memoirs of War, 1914-1915* (Cambridge, 1988).

By 1939-1940 much had changed. In the two decades after World War I, Marc Bloch's professional career and personal life had succeeded brilliantly; but between the armistice and Munich the power and influence of his beloved *patrie* had markedly declined.[7] Nonetheless, Bloch's ties to France were long and deep, from his great-grandfather's service in 1793, to his father's defense of Strasbourg in 1870, to his own four citations in World War I. As a patriotic, and thoroughly assimilated French Jew, Bloch had been reassured and gratified by the outcome of the Dreyfus Affair and was secure and proud of his French identity. By the 1930s, however, Bloch was jolted by the recrudescence of French anti-Semitism, which touched him personally, and by the menace of the Third Reich which the Third Republic appeared too feeble to combat.[8]

Thus, when he arrived at the front, Marc Bloch had begun to distance himself intellectually and emotionally from his comrades and leaders.[9] If France's best prospect was a long war, Bloch considered the *patrie* unprepared, poorly organized, and insufferably complacent; the worst possibility, even more appalling, was a Polish-style *Blitzkrieg*, which would mutilate France and place Jews like the Blochs under direct Nazi control.[10] In early August Bloch had viewed Goya's graphic depiction of the May 1808 executions, which reinforced his foreboding of the impending conflict.[11] During the entire *drôle de guerre*, an isolated Bloch both feared and hoped that he would not be the only Frenchman to stand up to Hitler.

* * *

7. The image of the weak mother (France) and the disappointed, berating suitor (Bloch) is strongly expressed in ED, pp. 167, 197.
8. Carole Fink, *Marc Bloch: A Life in History* (Cambridge, 1989), pp. 79-204.
9. This article is based on Marc Bloch's private, unpublished correspondence with his family, colleagues, students and friends during the *drôle de guerre* of 1939-1940. Twenty-seven of Bloch's letters to his son, Etienne (some with important deletions) have recently been published: *Marc Bloch à Etienne Bloch: Lettres de la "drôle de guerre,"* François Bédarida and Denis Peschanski, eds., *Cahiers de l'Institut d'Histoire du Temps Présent* 19 (1991).
10. Already in 1935 Bloch had speculated whether within the next three years he might find himself in a concrete bunker or in a concentration camp: cf. Bloch to Febvre, 20 Dec. 1935, AN MI 318 1.
11. Marc Bloch to Etienne Bloch, 12 Aug. 1939, EBC.

Bloch's earliest correspondence during the *drôle de guerre* reveals an anxious, burdened spirit. His primary concern was his family, whom he had installed in an apartment in Guéret near their country-home in the tiny village of Fougères. Recalling the bombardments of 1914, many Parisians decided to move their children to places safely distant from air-raid threats and from any imaginable battle zone; but Bloch was one of the few middle-aged academics to take up arms.[12]

During this first long separation from his beloved wife, Simonne, Bloch was apprehensive over her health and regretted leaving her with the care of six children and his aged mother in an isolated, provincial town far from her family and friends.[13] However great his chagrin at "abandoning" his flock, Bloch's ingrained sense of duty prevented him from seeking a discharge on the basis of family obligations.[14]

The absent parent remained the concerned and overbearing *paterfamilias*. Bloch lectured his oldest child, Alice, about fulfilling her family duties, her selection of reading material, and her spelling mistakes.[15] He chided his son, Daniel, on his poor penmanship and frequent bouts of boredom.[16] He was hardest on his oldest son, Etienne, in regard to his studies and personal habits. Caustically critical of the eighteen-year-old, Bloch sprayed reproaches in many of his letters concerning Etienne's bad manners, willfulness, and laziness as well as the "evil demons" which occasionally possessed him.[17]

   12. Bloch to Febvre, 17 Sept., 4 Oct. 1939, AN MI 318 1; Bloch to Mollat, 4 Dec. 1939, courtesy of Prof. Michel Mollat.
   13. Bloch to Alice Bloch, 31 Aug., 11 Sept. 1939 and to Etienne Bloch, 11 Sept. 1939, EBC.
   14. "J'ai grand désir de servir n'importe où même," Bloch to Febvre, 5 Sept. 1939, AN MI 318 1; Bloch to Ferdinand Lot, 3 Oct. 1939, Archive of the Institut de France. Cf. Etienne Bloch, "Marc Bloch. Souvenirs et réflexions d'un fils sur son père," in *Marc Bloch aujourd'hui: Histoire comparée & sciences sociales*, eds. Hartmut Atsma and André Burguière (Paris, 1990), p. 26: "Un trait de caractère a commandé toute sa vie: un sens exacerbé du devoir."
   15. Bloch to Alice Bloch, 14 Sept., 9,17 Oct.1939, 15 Feb. 1940, EBC.
   16. Bloch to Daniel Bloch, 18 Jan. 1940, EBC.
   17. Etienne Bloch, "Marc Bloch. Souvenirs," pp. 23-24, characterized his father with one word: "sévérité." See e.g., Bloch to Etienne Bloch, 24 Aug., 11 Sept. 1939, 18, 21, 25 Jan., 14, 17 Feb. 1940, EBC. In a letter on 25 Apr. 1940, Bloch accused

The war made Bloch see his children as more than tiresome, immature dependents; they were *his* future as well. With his "vieux Tiennot," he discussed military and political affairs along with family matters, school subjects, music, and literature.[18] All too soon, despite his protectiveness and sacrifices, his young ones would be shouldering burdens, taking risks, and incurring dangers against which he might not always be able to shelter them. Marc Bloch clung to an austere personal creed that was admittedly "old-fashioned." His sexual advice to his adolescent son was based on the "principle of a sound body and spirit" (the avoidance of contact with "contaminated females") and on reconciling "the problem of the physical and the sentimental."[19] Admitting that he too had once been quite "timid" with the "fair sex," Bloch revealed that his scruples had not prevented him from finding happiness with his wife, from giving her pleasure, and from living with her in a sense of complete fulfillment.[20] Bloch urged his headstrong son to follow a disciplined path: to be natural and agreeable, and to avoid the youthful temptations of excessive introspection, mockery, and vulgarity. He appealed for Etienne's trust, "not because I am your father, but because I abhor falsehood."[21]

* * *

The oldest reserve officer in the French army, Marc Bloch was first posted to Strasbourg, where his duties involved evacuating civilians behind the shelter of the Maginot Line, and then to Molsheim, where he arranged provisions and transit facilities for the Sixth Army. Bloch's spirits soared with stimulation and responsibility and fell with menial details and boring routine.[22] After a brief stay in

---

Etienne of behaving like a *Feldwebel* (sergeant) when he spoke rudely to the maid, and, on 5 May of exhibiting the mentality of the "SS" when he acted arrogantly towards his mother and grandmother.
  18. See, e.g., Bloch to Etienne Bloch, 24 Aug., 14, 28 Sept., 5, 16, 22, 27 Oct., 13 Dec. 1939, EBC.
  19. Bloch to Etienne Bloch, 3 Nov. 1939, EBC.
  20. Bloch to Etienne Bloch, 11 Nov. 1939, EBC.
  21. Bloch to Etienne Bloch, 11 Nov. 1939, EBC: "J'ai horreur du mensonge."
  22. Marc Bloch to Alice Bloch, 31 Aug., 14 Sept. 1939, EBC; Bloch to Febvre, 5 Sept. 1939, AN MI 318 1. In Molsheim, Bloch's party consisted of five persons, a brigadier general, a lieutenant colonel, two captains and a lieutenant who spent their time sitting in their schoolroom office "longing for a runner to arrive unexpectedly

Saverne, performing "equally dreary tasks," Bloch on 15 October 1939 was reassigned to First Army headquarters in Picardy.[23]

Following weeks of entreaties to well-placed friends, Bloch traveled north to First-Army headquarters where the Maginot line had not been extended. Across the border neutral Belgium lay open to a German attack and to an Anglo-French incursion. The French High Command believed that the war would begin, and hopefully stay, outside France.[24] Bloch was skeptical. A historian devoted to the science of change, he was convinced that French leaders had read the past incorrectly and failed to keep up with current realities. "The massacres of 1915" laid bare the "obsession with offensive in 1914." In his opinion a prudent, alert defensive line would hold, even against tanks.[25] Bloch doubted that air power would play a decisive role in the impending campaign.[26] He recognized that a strategy involving a massive Allied thrust into Belgium required extraordinary preparation, coordination, and provisions, incurring all the risks of an offensive on foreign soil while relinquishing the moral and material advantages of defending one's own homeland. Bloch was convinced – accurately so – that the Allies were incapable of countering a German *Blitzkrieg* in the low countries.[27]

Bloch's first posting in the north was to the Intelligence Branch as liaison with the British.[28] He had studied English medieval history and knew the language fluently; he had traveled in England, lectured at London and Cambridge and had several close friends in

---

with some official form that would provide us with an excuse for filling up still further forms." *ED*, pp. 27, 92-93.

23. Bloch to Alice Bloch, 9 Oct. 1939, EBC; Bloch to Febvre, 5, 17 Sept., 8 Oct. 1939, AN MI 318 1; *ED*, p. 28.

24. "La mission en Belgique," Opérations de la 1ère Armée, Service Historique de l'Armée de Terre, Château de Vincennes. Cf. *ED*, pp. 65-66; Barry R. Posen, *The Sources of Military Doctrine: France, Britain, and Germany Between the World Wars* (Ithaca, NY, 1984), pp. 105-140.

25. Bloch to Etienne Bloch, 28 Sept. 1939, EBC.

26. Bloch to Etienne Bloch, 14 Sept. 1939, EBC. "Je continue à penser que l'aviation ne décide rien, à elle seule. Elle est un élément de combat puissant. Rien qu'un élément."

27. Bloch to Etienne Bloch, 27 Oct.1939, EBC.

28. Bloch to Etienne Bloch, 16 Oct. 1939, to Alice Bloch, 22 Oct.1939, EBC.

British academic life, which he considered in many ways more comfortable and open than in France.[29] Among his acquaintances, two eminent Jewish historians, Richard Koebner and Roberto Lopez, had been given refuge from Fascism in Britain.[30] Bloch's anglophilism was sorely tried by his experience in Picardy. If the British seemed more diligent than their French counterparts, they also offended ordinary Frenchmen with the soldiers' looting and lechery and their officers' detachment and snobbery. The *drôle de guerre*, with its prolonged inactivity and limited contact between Allied soldiers and commands, resumed the cold partnership of 1914-1918, bitterly experienced by Robert Graves. Bloch was keenly aware of the embedded British francophobia, of strong Nazi sympathies in British intellectual circles, and of the widespread pacifism within the British public.[31] Above all, he feared that another *mésentente* would come out of the war, especially if France again practiced "Poincarism" against a defeated Germany. When Bloch decided to end his unproductive visits to Lord Gort's headquarters, he apparently removed the British factor from his concerns until it reemerged in combat.

A new challenge presented itself. Bloch was placed in charge of petrol supplies, assuming responsibility for moving the most heavily motorized army on the whole French front when battle began. His predecessor, an eminent financier employed by the Lazard bank, had ostensibly "juggled the figures," providing Bloch with a labyrinthine assignment. He plunged into the details of fuel supplies, learning to "count petrol tins and ration every drop." Lacking sufficient knowledge of Belgian fuel supplies, he made a successful, if unauthorized inquiry into petrol dumps on neutral territory.[32] Bloch's hasty apprenticeship coincided with Hitler's original timetable for an

29. Bloch to Febvre, 27 Jan., 15 Feb. 1934, AN MI 318 1. Bloch's article, "La grande pitié des lecteurs," *Annales d'histoire économique et sociale* 10 (1938): 54-55, contained a scathing critique of the Bibliothèque Nationale in comparison with the British Museum.
30. Bloch to Koebner, 25 Jan. 1934, courtesy of Prof. Yehoshua Arieli, Jerusalem; Bloch to Lopez, nd, (1938) courtesy Mme. Claude-Anne Lopez.
31. Bloch to Etienne Bloch, 22, 27 Oct. 1939, EBC; see especially his comments on the anti-war letter of G.B. Shaw in *The Times* on 20 Sept. 1939, which Bloch found "paradoxical and dangerous."
32. Bloch to Etienne Bloch, 11 Nov. 1939, EBC, to Febvre,12 Nov. 1939, AN MI 318 1, to Le Bras, 15 Nov. 1939, EBC. Cf. *ED*, pp. 29-31, 114-116, 133-138.

attack on the West; but when harsh weather and disagreements among the Führer's generals delayed the assault for another half year, Bloch and his comrades dug in for a strange and unnerving experience; alternating periods of frenetic activity with bouts of idleness, they stood before a peaceful frontier worrying constantly when it would ignite.[33] The initiative belonged to Adolf Hitler.

In his periods of enforced idleness, Bloch reflected on national and international politics. He approved the cabinet reshuffle of 13 September, which essentially removed the appeaser Bonnet from power but fell short of a Union Sacrée – which, after all, had "rarely produced good results."[34] He nevertheless was as disdainful of Daladier ("ce mauvais professor de lycée") as of the other *munichois*, Neville Chamberlain ("ce boutiquier de Birmingham"), both of whom, along with three or four other diplomats, had been schooled in "ersatz Sorel or Bourgeois."[35] He faulted the Daladier government for its partisan repression of the French Communists, for its failure to deal with the equally subversive radical right,[36] and for its essentially "spiteful" policies.[37]

During the excruciating period of Allied inactivity while Poland was being crushed, Bloch perched uneasily between resignation and reproach. Fearing an imprudent war fever in the civilian population, he opposed "mobilizing" the home front. The "great duty" of good French people, he counseled his children, was "to accept": to be as patient, stoic, and good humored as he was in whatever modest tasks

33. "Quelle étrange guerre! Reserve faite de quelques rares coups de DCA et de quelques exercises de tir, je n'ai pas entendu une fois le canon." Bloch to Mollat, 4 Dec. 1939, courtesy of Prof. Michel Mollat; cf. Bloch to Ferdinand Lot, 3 Oct. 1939, Archive of the Institut de France. The twenty-nine postponements undoubtedly benefited the Germans, who made good their losses in Poland and studied the lessons of the Polish campaign. Weinberg, *World at Arms*, p. 122.
34. Bloch to Etienne Bloch, 14 Sept. 1939, EBC.
35. Bloch to Lucien Febvre, 17 Sept. 1939, AN MI 318 1.
36. Bloch to Etienne Bloch, 14 Sept. 1939, EBC. Despite his detestation of Stalin ("La vérité est que Staline a justifié le trotskisme."), the Nazi-Soviet Pact, and the Soviet assault on Poland as well as the tergiversations of French communism, Bloch disapproved of the closing of the two dailies, *L'Humanité* and *Ce Soir*, on 26 August in retaliation for the Nazi Soviet Pact and of the dissolution of the PCF one month later (after the French Communists endorsed the partition of Poland, denounced the "imperialist" war, and urged an end of hostilities).
37. Bloch to Etienne Bloch, 3 Nov. 1939, EBC.

they were assigned.[38] Yet Bloch was not entirely comfortable with those in power. The man who abhorred falsehood was infuriated by the clumsy censors of the mail and the press who were obsessed with suppressing all predictions of a "long war" but allowed rumors to circulate of the adulteration of the wine by the medical corps (which caused a deplorable reaction among the soldiers). He detested the style of official propaganda, which "recalled the worse days of 1914."[39] Nevertheless, the aged *poilu* clung to the quixotic hope that France would fully prepare for a German attack but demand a less prodigious squandering of human blood than in 1914.[40]

Bloch was strikingly unsympathetic toward France's ally, Poland. Its foreign minister in 1939, Colonel Beck, was the man who had signed a treaty with Hitler in January 1934 which had overturned French policy in Eastern Europe.[41] Bloch admired the bravery of the Polish people but called their leaders "stupid." He was ironically prescient in his harsh criticism of the Rydz-Smigly strategy: by placing the bulk of the Polish army on the frontiers, Poland's leaders had ensured that a German breakthrough would produce total defeat within ten days.[42] As the Soviet army advanced, Bloch commented that the "too large Poland of Versailles," the "historic Poland" reborn "of conquest" was an "artificial creation"; he prophesied that the Ukraine would never again fall under Poland's rule.[43]

From the first moments of the *drôle de guerre*, Bloch was hyperconscious of his situation, his surroundings, and the momentous events before him. From his school-room office in Alsace, on 8 October, he poured out his chagrin to his colleague and collaborator, Lucien Febvre, over his "bad conscience":

> I have a bad conscience; we all have one. This is not a new idea for me. In 1919-1920 and afterwards, we allowed quite terrible things to

38. Bloch to Alice Bloch, 14 Sept., 17 Oct. 1939, EBC.
39. Bloch to Etienne Bloch, 27 Oct., 3 Nov. 1939, EBC. "La censure, extrêmement partiale, est une honte. Il y aura à faire après la guerre."
40. Bloch to Etienne Bloch, 5 Oct.1939, EBC.
41. Bloch to Etienne Bloch, 14 Sept.1939, EBC.
42. Bloch to Etienne Bloch, 28 Sept. 1939, EBC.
43. Bloch to Etienne Bloch, 28 Sept. 1939, EBC; Bloch later wondered if it would be possible to restore pre-Munich Czechoslovakia, Bloch to Etienne Bloch, 27 Apr. 1940, *ibid*.

happen without protesting, or protesting too little. We turned ourselves over to a poor lot. We sold our souls for a little respite, intellectual work, and personal freedom ... to live fully after four years of horror. We were wrong.[44]

When this war was over, Bloch insisted, the aged would have to guide the young in another direction. Indeed, he already heard the menacing sounds of a renewed nationalist truculence. "Mourir pour Danzig" had been a deceptive right-wing taunt in 1939. When the Allies two decades earlier "yielded the Ukraine to the Polish '*pans*,'" they had made "the arrival of Premier Stalin and the burning of the châteaux" inevitable.[45] This time France and its problematic ally must learn limits.

Bloch the historian, fascinated by the "human spectacle" around him, was especially interested in the kinds of people with whom he had not been in contact since the Great War.[46] It was a world far distant from the Sorbonne and the *Annales*![47] His young fellow staff officers, although well-trained and well-intentioned, were "quite stupid" when it came to politics; they had an "incredible ignorance" of social problems, of the political and social contours of Europe, and of the nature of non-traditional parties. Bloch reported little "overt" anti-Semitism in his small circle.[48]

In the first days of the war, he decided to use his idleness and "exorcise the demons of the present" by writing a history of France. Emulating his beloved deceased *maître*, Henri Pirenne, "who, at the time his country was fighting beside mine for justice and civilization, wrote in captivity a history of Europe," Bloch hoped to write a history of the French people; without excluding politics, wars, or great individuals, he would concentrate primarily on the "profound realities" of his nation's history within the broad context of European civilization. He purchased a notebook and, according to his usual practice, began to compose a discourse on method.

---

44. Bloch to Febvre, 8 Oct. 1939, AN MI 318 1. Cf. *ED*, pp. 215-216: "J'appartiens à une génération qui a mauvaise conscience ... Puissent nos cadets nous pardonner le sang qui est sur nos mains!"
45. Bloch to Febvre, 8 Oct. 1939, AN MI 318 1.
46. Bloch to Alice Bloch, 31 Aug. 1939, EBC. Cf. Bloch, *Souvenirs de guerre, passim*.
47. Bloch to Febvre, 12 Nov. 1939, AN MI 318 1.
48. Bloch to Etienne Bloch, 22 Oct. 1939, EBC.

The book on France was never completed; but the discourse was the germ of his final, posthumous work, *The Historian's Craft*.[49] By December he had completed only a few pages on historical method. In his cold, poorly-lit rooms, Bloch spent his free time reading, worrying about his family, and suffering a "cold and prolonged lassitude."[50]

The onset of an idle, icy winter reduced the morale of the French army and increased Bloch's dismay. No one had yet answered the question, "Why are we fighting?"[51] Bloch considered, and again rejected, the idea of requesting a release from service. He fretted over his "monotonous existence" and over "a nation at arms that does not fight."[52] Bloch's scolding of his children grew more strident: he berated Etienne for shirking his duty while his father sacrificed himself for them all.[53] He found some comfort in his English mysteries, read Montaigne, and savored classical music performances over the radio from London and Berlin.[54]

Bloch was keenly disappointed when an expected invitation to give a series of lectures across the border in Liège on "Belgian Neutrality" did not materialize. He deplored the equivocations of his timid colleague, and of timid Belgium, whose aloofness and secretiveness undermined the Allies' military strategy and "gave the ini-

---

49. The surviving manuscript from this period, "Histoire de la société française dans le cadre de la civilisation européenne," Molsheim, 22 Sept. 1939, EBC, contains a nine-page discussion of criticism of sources. Cf. Bloch to Etienne Bloch, 5 Oct. 1939, EBC, to Alice Bloch, 9 Oct., EBC, to Lucien Febvre, 8 Oct. 1939, AN MI 318 1. Lucien Febvre, "Comment se présentaient les manuscrits de 'Métier d'historien,'" in Marc Bloch, *Apologie pour l'histoire* 7th ed. (Paris, 1974), pp. 161-162, describes the original publication. The newest edition, Marc Bloch, *Apologie pour l'histoire ou métier d'historien. Edition critique préparée par Etienne Bloch* (Paris, 1993), combines Bloch's several manuscripts.
50. Bloch to Febvre, 23 Dec. 1939, AN MI 318 1.
51. Bloch wanted a frank discussion of war aims, although "chez nous la chose soit quasiment impossible." Bloch to Etienne Bloch, 27 Oct. 1939, EBC.
52. Bloch to Alice Bloch, 6, 22, 28 Jan. 1940, EBC, to Lucien Febvre, 31 Jan., AN MI 318 1, and to Philippe Wolff, 4 Jan. 1940, courtesy of Prof. Wolff.
53. Bloch to Etienne Bloch, 18 Jan. 1940: "Ai-je tort ou raison de me laisser mobiliser? De préférer en somme ce que j'ai estimé mon devoir envers mon pays à mon clair devoir envers les miens? Je m'interroge là-dessus avec angoisse. Une chose est sûre: je croyais que mes enfants me faciliteraient mon sacrifice. Je suis triste de m'être trompé."
54. Bloch to Alice Bloch, 11, 22, 27 Jan. 1940, EBC.

tiative to the enemy."⁵⁵ When a German plane carrying invasion plans was forced to land in Belgium on 10 January the Belgian government refused to involve the French army.

The alert provoked by this incident was a reminder of Bloch's heavy responsibilities.⁵⁶ Consequently, he turned down an opportunity to escape his "sclerosis" by serving as an attaché to the French Military Mission to Oslo. Bloch was tempted. His knowledge of the language and the country made him an ideal candidate for a post where he could at last be "useful." But "this French family animal" shrank from putting so much distance between himself and his children.⁵⁷ In February 1940 he made two trips to Paris – which displayed signs of "fatigue" – where he saw his wife, visited relatives and friends, and savored the joys of civilian life: a sandwich in a café, a concert, and several good films.⁵⁸

Bloch was saddened by the Soviet defeat of Finland, which he attributed to the West's abandonment of another small country.⁵⁹ In mid-March he was hospitalized in a military clinic in Paris with a severe bronchitis; he recuperated in his apartment in Paris and later in the Creuse. The Allied expedition to Narvik began and would lead to a fiasco. Bloch, who might have been there, took the setback with equanimity ("A war is not won by a continuous line of victories"). He was skeptical over the political fallout. He raged over the "stupid and disturbing" official efforts to represent the failed initiative as a success.⁶⁰ Since the Dreyfus Affair, Bloch had been fascinated and repelled by distortions of reality, by half-truths and manufactured "facts" – a phenomenon which had become embedded in his historical analysis.⁶¹

55. Bloch to Etienne Bloch, 2 Jan., 14 Feb. 1940, to Alice Bloch, 3 Jan. 1940, EBC, Bloch to Lucien Febvre, 31 Jan. 1940, AN MI 318 1.
56. Bloch to Alice Bloch, 20 Jan. 1940, EBC.
57. Something he believed an Englishman would not have hesitated to do: Bloch to Alice Bloch, 1 Feb. 1940, EBC.
58. Simonne and Marc Bloch to Alice Bloch, 3 Feb. 1940, Simonne Bloch to Alice Bloch, 14 Feb., Marc Bloch to Alice Bloch, 6, 12, 14 Feb., EBC.
59. Bloch to Etienne Bloch, 14 Feb. 1940, EBC.
60. Bloch to Etienne Bloch, 5 May 1940, EBC.
61. Marc Bloch, "Réflexions d'un historien sur les fausses nouvelles de la guerre," *Revue de synthèse historique* 33 (1921): 13-35; cf. Bloch to Febvre, 17 Sept. 1939, AN MI 318 1, in which Bloch expressed his "horror of propaganda" and insisted that "historians maintain clean hands."

Bloch returned to the front in a grim mood over the long war of nerves. Despite the replacement of the wavering Daladier by the more resolute Reynaud, little had changed. Bloch complained about the officers' "garrison mentality," which eroded the troops' morale; over a spring "which could not decide to give us our legitimate portion of sunshine and greenery"; and over the "waiting" for something undefined and perhaps quite terrible, which at least gave a purpose to their "absurd existence." Bloch searched vainly in France's leadership for the presence of new, large, and enlightened spirits. He regretted the accumulation of past "errors" that weighed heavily now – the alienation of neutrals, the abandonment of a "defendable" Czechoslovakia, the alliance with an "undefendable" Poland, the blunders in Norway – mistakes that were irreparable only because they were repeated and not understood. Furious at feeling idle and ill-used, Bloch contemplated a return to the Sorbonne, on special assignment, in the fall.[62]

In the final days of the *drôle de guerre* Bloch meditated on France and on history. He tried to understand the identity of the "France" he was about to defend: bourgeois France, peasant France, and workers' France. He recognized that the June days of the Popular Front – "one of the great moments in French history" – had offered a chance for cohesion, and that the denouement produced a hardening of all the class and regional divisions.[63] Bloch sought the idealized France he had known as a young apprentice scholar in 1914, his intense comradeship with the miner from the Pas de Calais and the waiter from the Bastille quarter. He felt isolated in the milieu he now occupied, deploring the narrowness and ignorance of the ruling classes, their attitudes "si peu humaines."[64] For eight months he had sought to comprehend the forces that had placed him in Picardy; his life as a scholar had prepared him for this meeting with destiny.

In September, he had written Etienne about his absorption in the entire human spectacle. He had used all his faculties to over-

62. Bloch to Febvre, 6 Apr. 1940, AN MI 318 1; cf. Bloch to Etienne Bloch, 28 Mar., to Alice Bloch, 31 Mar. 1940, EBC. Bloch to Daniel Bloch, 16, 26 Apr. review his daily routines, EBC.
63. Bloch to Febvre, 3 May 1940, AN MI 318 1. Cf. *ED*, pp. 205-10.
64. Bloch to Febvre, 3 May 1940, AN MI 318 1.

come his passivity, to be useful and to serve, and above all to affirm his existence through *understanding*.⁶⁵ At the edge of the precipice Bloch linked the present, the past, and the future in his dedication to history:

> The profession of the historian ... is a beautiful, but difficult profession ... To be well achieved, it requires much work, diverse forms of knowledge, and a real intellectual force: curiosity, imagination, an orderly spirit, and the faculty of explaining human thoughts and feelings clearly and accurately .... A great scholar requires force of character as much as intellect.⁶⁶

On 10 May 1940 at 4:30 A.M. Guderian led the 1st Panzer Division across the Luxemburg border followed by Rommel and his 7th Panzers across the Belgian frontier. Bloch, who had been at General Headquarters in Meaux, hastened back to his post and jotted his first letter in action: "Je vais bien. J'ai beaucoup de travail. Je t'embrasse."⁶⁷

* * *

Just two months later, after the debacle, Bloch wrote to Febvre: "It is useless to comment on the events. They surpass in horror and in humiliation all we could dream in our worst nightmares."⁶⁸ Despite his shock over the devastating German attack and France's collapse, Bloch recovered to write a scathing personal and national indictment in his hidden manuscript of *Strange Defeat*.⁶⁹

Throughout the *drôle de guerre*, Bloch had tried to read the future by drawing deeply on his own and on France's past. With his unique mixture of idealism and reason, patriotism and critical

---

65. Bloch to Etienne Bloch, ca. 17 Sept. 1939, EBC. "Un mot, pour tout dire, domine et illumine nos études: 'comprendre.' Ne disons pas que le bon historien est étranger aux passions; il a du moins celle-là. Mot, ne nous le dissimulons pas, lourd de difficultés; mais aussi d'espoirs." Bloch, *Apologie pour l'histoire*, p. 121.
66. Bloch to Etienne Bloch, 25 Apr. 1940, EBC.
67. Bloch to Daniel Bloch, 13 May 1940, Simonne Bloch to Alice Bloch, 13 May 1940, EBC.
68. Bloch to Febvre, 8 July 1940, AN MI 318 1.
69. Bloch to Febvre, 8 July 1940, AN MI 318 1: "Tâche bien platonique. Il faudra verser ce texte, s'il est jamais écrit, dans mes archives." Cf. Simonne Bloch to Alice Bloch, 16 July 1940, EBC.

objectivity, hope and skepticism, he was a sensitive antenna in the *drôle de guerre* antechamber, more conscious, more engaged, more enraged, and more vulnerable than those around him. This experience, even more than the actual events of May-June 1940, left an indelible trace on his written testimony.

Bloch attempted to explain how the "strange war" of 1939-1940 turned into the Strange Defeat. He blamed the ruling class, the military and the politicians, the press and the teachers, for a flawed national policy and a weak defense against the Nazi menace, for betraying the real France and abandoning its children. Germany had won because its leaders had better understood the methods and psychology of modern combat.

In *Strange Defeat* Marc Bloch ignored the roles of Soviet Russia and Italy and the United States, and he minimized the role of the British. He left out the economic and demographic forces that had placed France at a disadvantage against its richer, larger neighbor. Like Polybius, Marc Bloch singled out the human causes of his own and his people's catastrophe, seeking behind the great abstractions "the only concrete realities: human beings."[70] Good historian that he was, he unflinchingly analyzed the tragedy neither he nor France could prevent.

---

70. *ED*, p. 51.

III

MARTYRS' VENGEANCE

Memory, Trauma, and Fear of War in France, 1918-1940

Omer Bartov

On 13 December 1927 at 10:15 AM, Mme Marie-Pauline Murati, a war widow, attempted to kill the mayor of Toulon, M. Emile Claude, in the course of an interview in his office at the town hall. According to the account given by M. Berry, the head clerk (*commis principal*) at the mayor's office, Mme Murati was the last of three ladies to have been shown into M. Claude's office that morning. The widow Delort, 35 years old, resident of 9, rue Hippolyte-Duprat, entered the office leaving the door ajar. M. Berry, however, who was still on the landing, pushed the door shut for reasons of discretion.

As he did so, he heard the sound of quick steps, followed by calls for help from M. Claude. M. Berry pushed the door open, entered the room, and was confronted by an unexpected and tragic spectacle: the widow Delort, clutching a long knife in her hand, was furiously striking M. Claude on his face, neck, and chest. The mayor, covered with blood, tried to escape the attacker, but she chased him around his desk, arm raised in the air. At this point M. Berry leaped at the would-be assassin, immobilized her and, following a fierce struggle, managed to disarm her. "Unfortunate woman! What are you doing?" he reportedly said to her. Beside herself, her hands red with blood, the widow Delort cried at him, "Let me go! Let me go!" M. Claude, blinded by the blood streaming from one of his wounds, now approached the woman and asked her: "What have I done to you?" to which she responded furiously: "I've been martyred for too long, it's become a scandal. That's what it is!" "Better say that it's an assassination!" M. Berry said to her, at which point the woman suddenly turned pale and fell unconscious on the carpet.

M. Claude, who was stabbed four times, swiftly recovered from his injuries, though he was unable to take part in the congress of mayors due to take place in Paris that week. The war widow Delort, it was reported, had acted under the spell of a mental crisis, or temporary insanity, to which she had frequently succumbed since the death of her husband, a lieutenant in the colonial infantry, from wounds sustained in battle. While the widow Delort was held in detention and undergoing mental examination by the specialist forensic pathologist (*médecin légiste spécialiste*) Doctor Ernest Rapuc, a search of her domicile uncovered letters written by her to a public prosecutor (*Procureur de la République*), and several journalists, in which she wrote: "I pass my days crying; I have looked for the reason in vain. I finally know that it is because strange things are happening in Toulon, and it is necessary to punish the abusers and defend the truth."[1]

1927 was the year in which the film *Napoléon vu par Abel Gance* was first screened. But the images which haunted the widow Delort were most probably not those of Gance's celebrated triptych, which in a fit of (artistic) rage he had once tried to destroy. Napoleon's melancholy and tragic greatness as seen by this proponent of artistic suffering do not seem to have been of central concern to the French of the interwar period. Rather, it was images of meaningless, horrible death, boundless, inexplicable suffering, inarticulate rage, madness, and violence which surfaced in innumerable forms during an era of recovery from one massacre and

---

1. This account is taken from reports in *Journal*, 14 Dec. 1927, *Avenir*, 15 Dec. 1927, and *Volonté*, 15 Dec. 1927, all to be found in the Archives Nationales (henceforth AN), F7 13021. In some of the reports the name is given as Veuve Delord, rather than Delort. The same reports refer to Veuve Delort also as Mme. Murati, probably because one of these is her maiden name.

growing anxiety with the approach of another. This was not a good time for Napoleon, not even when projected on three screens simultaneously. It was a time of guilt, accusation and fear. Gance's *J'accuse* (1919), with its terrifying image of dead soldiers rising from their graves, and Raymond Bernard's *Les Croix de bois* (1931), based on the novel by Dorgelès, in which a soldier becomes mad at the moment of attack, reflected much better the atmosphere of the period and people's attitudes to war.[2]

These were not merely artistic hallucinations and creative phantasies. The war had produced a reality which few minds of the *Belle Époque* could have conjured up. Both the nature and the scale of the killing stretched the boundary between sanity and madness, perception and perversion to the limit. The widow Delort's fit of rage and madness, whatever its specific causes, must be viewed within the context of postwar (and interwar) France. Strange things were happening in Toulon; perhaps the strangest of all was the attempt to go back to normality, to forget the events and erase the images which had scarred the consciousness of so many Europeans in the slaughterhouse of the front. Was a war widow's plea for attention to her suffering madder than society's indifference? Was her violence less legitimate than that which had taken so many lives only a few years before?[3]

In speaking about France of the *entre-deux-guerres*, it is therefore impossible to understand any of the major political, cultural, military or popular trends and attitudes without realizing that visions of war, memories of past massacres and fears of their recurrence

---

2. Alan Williams, *Republic of Images: A History of French Filmmaking* (Cambridge, MA, 1992), pp. 86-88. For a still picture from the film "Napoleon," see Douglas and Madeleine Johnson, *The Age of Illusion: Art and Politics in France 1918-40* (New York, 1987), p. 71; for scenes from *J'accuse* and *Les Croix de bois*, see Antoine Prost, *Les Anciens Combattants 1914-40* (Paris, 1977), between pp. 96-97.

3. For some photographic representations of the horrors of the "Great War," see, e.g., the following: dead soldiers hanging from a treetop (censured by the military during the war), soldiers recovering from the first shock of battle, and the effects of a delayed-action shell which exploded in the liaison bunker of the 23rd Infantry Regiment on 18 November 1918, all in Prost, *Anciens Combattants*, between pp. 96-97; delegation of French *Mutilés de Guerre* to the Congress of the Versailles Treaty, 28 June 1919, in Kenneth E. Silver, *Esprit de Corps: The Art of the Parisian Avant-Garde and the First World War, 1914-25* (Princeton, 1989), p. 188.

dominated the minds of the French. Moreover, familiar distinctions were increasingly blurred due to the impact of the war and the growing sense that it had, after all, not been the *der de der*, the war to end all wars. Some soldiers may well have been brutalized by the fighting, turning to the extreme right and to paramilitary organizations and leagues, while others became ardent pacifists. But the distinction between these two reactions should not be overdrawn, since extreme right-wing street fighters came to oppose another war in the 1930s, while pacifists used an increasingly violent and aggressive tone in their speeches and proclamations. Similarly, violence was not only a product of direct experience at the trenches, but also of the suffering, anger, and frustration caused by the death of those who had been there, and the urge of the state's officials to bracket this suffering by means of organized and controlled commemoration, marking out geographical and chronological spaces for mourning surrounded by a sea of normality and indifference in which the victims (or the victims' victims) had nevertheless to lead their own daily lives.[4]

Was this effort successful? After all, most war widows did not try to assassinate their local mayor, and most Frenchmen did indeed go about their business. Paris was a great cultural centre in the 1920s,[5] and, despite growing political and economic turmoil in the 1930s, the Third Republic did not succumb to fascism.[6] It was only

4. On commemoration in interwar France, see, Annette Becker, "From Death to Memory: The National Ossuaries in France after the Great War," *History and Memory* 5 (1993): 32-49; idem., *La Guerre et la foi: De la mort à la mémoire, 1914-30* (Paris, 1994); Daniel Sherman, "Art, Commerce, and the Production of Memory in France after World War I," in *Commemorations: The Politics of National Identity*, John R. Gillis, ed. (Princeton, 1994), pp. 186-211; idem., "Monuments, Mourning, and Masculinity in France after World War I," (unpublished paper, presented at the Rutgers Center for Historical Analysis, 1994). For the wider European scene, see George L. Mosse, *Fallen Soldiers: Reshaping the Memory of the World Wars* (New York, 1990); and for a series of even more wide-ranging discussions, see the above cited Gillis, *Commemorations*.

5. See, e.g., William Wiser, *The Crazy Years: Paris in the Twenties* (New York, 1990 [1983]); Jerrold Seigel, *Bohemian Paris: Culture, Politics, and the Boundaries of Bourgeois Life, 1830-1930* (New York, 1987 [1986]), part III.

6. See. e.g., Jean-Louis Loubet del Bayle, *Les Non-conformistes des années 30: Une tentative de la renouvellement de la pensée politique française* (Paris, 1969); Serge Berstein, *La France des années 30* (Paris, 1988). On the last months of the Third Republic, see Jean-Louis Crémieux-Brilhac, *Les Français de l'an 40*, 2 vols. (Paris, 1990); Jean-Pierre

in the wake of military defeat that France came under the rule of a quasi-fascist, autocratic regime.[7] Yet this view of interwar France, itself an image created by scholars of various interests and political inclinations, fails to grasp some of the most crucial aspects of a society torn between competing images of war, and whose ultimate inability to reach a consensus on the meaning and implications of domestic and foreign conflict was at the root of its collapse under the impact of German attack in May-June 1940.

The links between the war of 1914-1918 and the debacle of 1940 are both obvious and open to abuse. There was, after all, a degree of agreement among fascists (both French and German), Communists, and not a few liberals, that France was about to collapse (or in retrospect, that France had collapsed), due to its cultural and political degeneration. Excluding the Communist expectation of social revolution (or of orders from Moscow), the implicit argument here was either that French *"civilisation"* had reached the end of the road, and would now be overtaken by German *"Kultur,"* or that only by accepting a fascist order would France be rejuvenated and able to stand up to its foes. Consequently, the opponents of these two social-darwinian versions of fascist perceptions were left with only one option, namely, the argument that France's collapse in 1940 was merely caused by military inferiority, misjudgment and incompetence, which had little bearing on the previous twenty years. Moreover, it was assumed that the ills exposed by the debacle could be healed with relative ease by means of firm leadership, professional military command, and patriotic education, as well as a thorough purge of those who had betrayed the *patrie*. It took the debacle in Indochina and the war in Algeria to demonstrate that such superficial interpretations and makeshift solutions could not treat the root of the problem. But by then these very same crises had had the effect of diminishing the interest in 1940 and its interwar origins, as it receded into

---

Azéma, *1940, l'année terrible* (Paris, 1990); Philippe Richer, *La Drôle de guerre des Français: 2 septembre 1939 – 10 mai 1940* (Paris, 1990); René Rémond and Janine Bourdin eds., *La France et les français 1938-39* (Paris, 1978).

7. See especially Robert O. Paxton, *Vichy France: Old Guard and New Order 1940-44* (New York, 1975 [1972]); and Philippe Burrin, *La Dérive fasciste: Doriot, Déat, Bergery 1933-45* (Paris, 1986).

a distant pre-Vichy memory of far lesser public concern than the era of Pétain and his assistants.[8] Only recently have historians of France shown a renewed interest in the interwar period and begun to note the impact of memories, visions and premonitions of war on that generation of Frenchmen. Even now, however, most of this work tends to focus on specific political groups, ideological trends and extra-parliamentary organizations. In this manner an impression is created that each of these groups had formed a more or less coherent image of war which consequently guided its perception of events and its political (or cultural) activity.[9] In fact, however, existing images of war in France, though immensely influential, crossed political, ideological, and social barriers. The confusion over a predominant image was in itself the reflection of, as well as the cause for, the general climate of uncertainty and bewilderment. In an era dominated by fresh cemeteries on the one hand and by growing armament production on the other, the fluidity of war imagery was a crucial factor in destabilizing and undermining French society as a whole.

The first, and quite probably the most insightful, survey of the debacle and its causes was written shortly after the event, by a man who had seen it and who combined the perceptive eye of a great historian with the experience of soldiering.[10] But by and large, the challenge posed by Bloch's outline for a kind of total history of interwar France as a means to understand the debacle was not taken up by those who, unlike him, had survived the occupation unscathed. Whether the new emphasis on the *longue durée*, taken up with great energy by the new leadership of the *Annales*,

---

8. See Henry Rousso, *The Vichy Syndrome: History and Memory in France Since 1944*, trans. Arthur Goldhammer (Cambridge, MA, 1991).
9. See, e.g., Prost, *Anciens Combattants*; Robert Soucy, *French Fascism: The First Wave, 1924-33* (New Haven and London, 1986); Zeev Sternhell, *Ni droite, ni gauche: L'idéologie fasciste en France* (Brussels, 1987 [1983]); Norman Ingram, *The Politics of Dissent: Pacifism in France 1919-39* (Oxford, 1991).
10. Marc Bloch, *Strange Defeat: A Statement of Evidence Written in 1940*, trans. Gerard Hopkins (New York, 1968 [1948]). See now also Carole Fink, "Marc Bloch and the *drôle de guerre*: Prelude to the 'Strange Defeat'," in this volume; and idem., *Marc Bloch: A Life in History* (New York, 1989). I wish to thank Professor Fink for allowing me to consult her paper and for many illuminating discussions on this issue during her tenure at the Rutgers Center for Historical Analysis.

served the purpose of avoiding the need to come to terms with recent events, just as the *Sonderweg* theory implied a convenient *Stunde Null* after which normality was restored, is a moot point.[11] Historians' unwillingness to undertake an analysis of interwar France with an eye to the deep roots of the collapse was, and still is, probably mainly due to the discomfort of discovering in a post-1945 world that fear of war could lead to collaboration in atrocity, that antimilitarism can bring about fascism, and that lack of a certain ruthlessness in policy-making can easily allow for much greater abuse by others. Some of the pitfalls awaiting any examination of this period through the perspective of attitudes toward war are indicated by the debate over the nature of (French) fascism, and especially over the extent to which it had originated in the left or the right.[12] A rigorous examination of the roots of the debacle, taking into account the bewildering blur of distinctions and the confusion of moral imperatives which characterized the interwar period, will doubtlessly raise some disturbing moral and political questions for scholars and their audience. Indeed, the expectation of such troubling findings seems to have had an inhibiting effect on research into the long-term causes of France's collapse.

In speaking about the impact of war (past and future) on France of the *entre-deux-guerres*, it should be noted that although other nations were just as traumatized by the events of 1914-1918, in the long run they reacted very differently to this trauma. Here a glance at the case of Germany is especially illuminating. German soldiers returning from the front in 1918 were probably just as brutalized by four years in the trenches as their French counterparts. Some of them turned to pacifism, some to militant right-wing activity, some to Communism. In Germany of the 1920s there were as many different images of war as in France. Some glorified the conflict as a grand experience of fraternity and sacrifice, while others abhorred it as a mechanical slaughterhouse; some were willing to practice

---

11. See esp. Fernand Braudel, *On History*, trans. S. Matthews (Chicago, 1980 [1969]); and David Blackbourn and Geoff Eley, *The Peculiarities of German History: Bourgeois Society and Politics in Nineteenth-Century Germany* (Oxford, 1984).

12. See works by Sternhell, Soucy, Berstein, and Burrin cited above. See also René Rémond, *The Right Wing in France: From 1815 to de Gaulle*, trans. J. M. Laux, 2d ed. (Philadelphia, 1971 [1966]); and Robert Aron, *Histoire de Vichy 1940-44* (Paris, 1954).

violence in order to eliminate the possibility of *any* future war (or at least a capitalist war or a revolutionary war), while others were adamant never to use violence again, even against the violent. But the differences between France and Germany are just as evident as the similarities. By the time of the great 1929-1933 economic and political crisis, the wide-range of attitudes toward war and violence in Germany rapidly coalesced into a powerful stream leading to the breakup of the Weimar Republic and the subsequent establishment of the Nazi dictatorship. German positions on war, or at least on the only war that mattered, had become increasingly uniform over the years preceding Hitler's "seizure of power." The war, it was said, would and should have been won but for the "stab in the back" (*Dolchstoss*) by a treasonous minority in the rear, and the resulting Versailles treaty was presented as a travesty demanding correction before Germany forgave the world for the suffering and humiliation to which it had been subjected.[13] Conversely, in France the constant flux in attitudes toward war and violence led to a gradual disintegration of the Republic without the emergence of any alternative political system. In other words, the increasingly pessimistic view of the triumph of 1918 as a Pyrrhic victory introduced a growing sense of confusion and unclarity as to the nature, necessity and potential profit of war: if the cost of winning was so great, would it not have been better to have lost the war? Defeatism, at least in the case of France, can thus be said to have had its roots in victory, not defeat. Hence we can say that while in Germany attitudes toward war, whether pacifist or militarist, Communist or fascist, by and large leaned more toward the use and organization of violence, in France precisely the opposite development can be seen, whereby even the militarists tended to reject the option of war, while those sincerely opposed to it were unwilling to act forcefully enough to prevent it (or were much more willing to

---

13. The widespread acceptance of this view in other European counties, and especially in England, is subtly depicted in Kazuo Ishiguro's finely crafted novel, *The Remains of the Day* (New York, 1989), and only slightly less subtly in the recent film based on the novel. To be sure, while some well-meaning, aloof, and politically naive English aristocrats felt that the winners had been unfair, many realistic and profit-oriented businessmen wanted to tear up the Versailles treaty in order to stabilize Germany's economy and thereby to go back to business as usual.

be forceful on the domestic, rather than on the international front). To put the matter differently, in Germany the trauma of war caused a resurgence of destructive energy; in France it resulted in increasing paralysis.

In most post-1918 Western countries, such as Britain, France, Germany, and Italy, one can easily recognize two views of war. The first focused on war as a great national and personal experience, and in its more fascist version wished to do away with the distinction between war and peace, the military and the civilian spheres, the professions of soldier and worker. It idealized the community of battle and hoped to recreate the same imagined solidarity of soldiers among all sectors of society. The second was ostensibly the opposite, based on the disillusionment experienced by those who had confronted the realities of modern war. It depicted war as a meaningless, hopeless, monstrous event, where primitive conditions and base instincts combined with modern industrial techniques and organization to create an endless cycle of guns and victims, production and destruction. Curiously, however, the convenient distinctions between these two powerful images of war, drawn along commonly accepted political and moral lines, do not faithfully reflect the complexity of contemporary representations of 1914-1918. Rather, the imagery of war was characterized much more by baffling paradoxes, painful ironies, confusing overlaps, and jarring contradictions, at least some of which remain as part of our own present understanding of war and violence. It is this more complex view of armed conflict that must be grasped if we wish to comprehend the anxieties, motivations and actions (or inactions) of our historical protagonists, if not, indeed, of our own contemporaries. To illustrate this point, let us briefly examine the manner in which these conflicting attitudes toward war were reflected in the writings of a few French and German authors.

* * *

This war, in fact, made no sense at all. It couldn't go on. Had something weird got into these people? Something I didn't feel at all? I suppose I hadn't noticed it ...

"In a mess like this," I said to myself, "there's nothing to be done, all you can do is clear out ..."

I never felt so useless as I did amid all those bullets in the sunlight. A vast and universal mockery ... Could I, I thought, be the last coward on earth? How terrifying! ... All alone with two million stark raving heroic madmen, armed to the eyeballs? With and without helmets, without horses, on motorcycles, bellowing, in cars, screeching, shooting, plotting, flying, kneeling, digging, taking cover, bounding over trails, root-toot-tooting, shut up on earth as if it were a loony bin, ready to demolish everything on it, Germany, France, whole continents, everything that breathes, destroy destroy, madder than mad dogs, worshipping their madness (which dogs don't), a hundred, a thousand times madder than a thousand dogs, and a lot more vicious! A pretty mess we were in! No doubt about it, this crusade I'd let myself in for was the apocalypse!

You can be a virgin in horror the same as in sex. How, when I left the Place Clichy, could I have imagined such horror? Who could have suspected, before getting into the war, all the ingredients that go to make up the rotten, heroic, good-for-nothing soul of man? And there was I, caught up in a mass flight into collective murder, into the fiery furnace ... Something had come up from the depths, and this is what happened.[14]

This is a passage from the first novel of the French writer, Louis-Ferdinand Céline. Born in 1894 and a doctor by profession, Céline published several anti-Semitic and pro-fascist essays in the late 1930s, called for an alliance between France and Nazi Germany, and was tried for treason after the war. His hatred of war and eventual contempt for humanity originated in his war experience. Nothing in his depiction of war makes one wish to be there; it is gruesome, ugly, murderous, repulsive and, as he tirelessly reminds us, totally insane. Erich Maria Remarque, four years younger than Céline, published his novel *Im Westen Nichts Neues* in 1928. Probably the most widely read war novel of all time, it is generally considered to be an antiwar, if not pacifist, work. Significantly, some of its passages greatly resemble those of Céline (as well as many other novels of that genre):

> The front is a cage in which we must await fearfully whatever may happen. We lie under the network of arching shells and live in a suspense of uncertainty. Over us, Chance hovers. If a shot comes, we

---

14. Louis-Ferdinand Céline, *Journey to the End of the Night*, trans. R. Manheim (New York, 1983 [1932]), pp. 7-9.

can duck, that is all; we neither know nor can determine where it will fall.[15]

And further:

> We have become beasts. We do not fight, we defend ourselves against annihilation. It is not against men that we fling our bombs, what do we know of men in this moment when Death is hunting us down – now, for the first time in three days we can see his face, now for the first time in three days we can oppose him; we feel a mad anger. No longer do we lie helpless, waiting on the scaffold, we can destroy and kill, to save ourselves, to save and to be revenged.
>
> We crouch behind every corner, behind every barrier of barbed wire, and hurl heaps of explosives at the feet of the advancing enemy before we run ... crouching like cats we run on, overwhelmed by this wave that bears us along, that fills us with ferocity, turns us into thugs, into murderers, into God only knows what devils; this wave that multiplies our strength with fear and madness and greed of life, seeking and fighting for nothing but for our deliverance. If your own father came over with them you would not hesitate to fling a bomb at him.[16]

Remarque is just as appalled by the war as Céline, just as filled with its senseless killing and brutality. Yet there is something in his account which is missing from Céline's more sophisticated text. Consciously or (most probably) not, Remarque provides us with more than he is directly willing to admit, indeed, with more than many of his critics seem to have noticed. To be sure, Remarque laments the human and material destruction of war, but nevertheless, antimilitarist though he may be, he is also fascinated by it, by the tremendous energy and passion of battle, by the expansion of the self in a situation of great urgency, by the drive to kill and the will to survive that surpass any previous knowledge and make for a new, frightening, yet immensely liberating and empowering perception of human capacities. Total, industrial war may annihilate the individual, but it also liberates him from moral and social constraints and takes him beyond familiar frontiers of physical and mental experience into new territories never imagined. Elements

---

15. Erich Maria Remarque, *All Quiet on the Western Front*, trans. A. W. Wheen (New York, 1991 [1928]), p. 102.
16. Ibid., pp. 113-114.

of this subtext were well sensed, if not understood, by Lewis Milestone, the American director of the Hollywood film version of the book, whose work retained the same protean quality of being both an antiwar production (and seen as such by the Reichswehr authorities and the Nazis who successfully fought to have it banned), and a presentation of war as an adventure, perilous and frightening to be sure, but immensely appealing in its ruthless nihilism.[17]

What is more, Remarque also expresses that same sentimental longing for comradeship at the front extolled by veterans of a very different political persuasion. This idealized representation of frontline existence, encapsulated in the German term *Frontgemeinschaft* (later recoined *Kampfgemeinschaft* by the Nazis), maintained that true friendship could be found only among comrades in battle, to the extent that even soldiers on leave quickly became disenchanted with the corruption and hypocrisy of the rear and hurried back to their new "family," a battle community forged by fire and sacrifice.[18] Memories of that pristine, simple world, where barbed wire clearly marked the dividing line between friend and foe, and battle was confined to a narrow strip of no-man's-land, were not infrequently mixed with the trauma of taking part in an unprecedented enterprise of industrial killing. Hence, the desire to prevent war from

17. See John Whiteclay Chambers II, "All Quiet on the Western Front (1930): The Antiwar Film and Image of the First World War," *Historical Journal of Film, Radio and Television* 14 (1994): 377-411. A report by the central censorship office in Berlin, dated December 11, 1930, noted that the Reichswehr was particularly incensed by the fact that such "foreign film strips ... caricature, disparage, and scorn the war and the German Wehrmacht." Oberprüfstelle, Nr. 1254: Deutsche Zentralarchiv / Reichsministerium des Innern / Band 1: Okt. 1930 - Febr. 1933, 26080. I wish to thank professor Chambers for allowing me to see this document. See also Modris Eksteins, "War, Memory, and Politics: The Fate of the Film *All Quiet on the Western Front*," *Central European History* 13 (1980): 60-82.

18. On Siegfried Sassoon's (and many other of his poet-officer peers') devotion to the men at the front, and their criticism of and contempt for the rear (along with the aristocratic officers, the generals and their staffs), see, e.g., Robert Wohl, *The Generation of 1914* (Cambridge, MA, 1979), pp. 85-121; much of Robert Graves' remarkable *Good-Bye to All That* deals with similar themes. On the same reactions among French soldiers returning from leave, see the chapter "The Anger of Volpatte," in Henri Barbusse, *Under Fire: The Story of a Squad (Le Feu)*, trans. F. Wray (New York, 1917 [1916]), pp. 107-32. Here I refer, of course, to Chapter Seven in Remarque's *All Quiet*, in which Paul returns home on a brief leave from the front. The chapter ends with the line: "I ought never to have come on leave." *Ibid.*, p. 185.

happening again was accompanied by the feeling that the only way to rekindle the true and honest friendship of the trenches was to bring back war itself, either as domestic strife or as international conflict. It is precisely because there *was* no clear dividing line between these two reactions to the war experience that this aspect of the *Freikorps*, SA, SS, and *Arditi* mentality was not wholly absent also from the memoirs of other soldiers, such as Robert Graves and Siegfried Sasoon, or from the poetry of Wilfred Owen and Charles Péguy.[19] Remarque, for his part, puts it in the following manner:

> It is a great brotherhood, which adds something of the good-fellowship of the folk-song, of the feeling of solidarity of convicts, and of the desperate loyalty to one another of men condemned to death, to a condition of life arising out of the midst of danger, out of the tension and forlornness of death – seeking in a wholly unpathetic way a fleeting enjoyment of the hours as they come. If one wants to appraise it, it is at once heroic and banal – but who wants to do that?[20]

Finally, of course, upon the death of his best friend and soldier-mentor, Remarque's protagonist Paul Bäumer loses all desire to go on living; war had created friendship and smashed it too, but it was only thanks to war that Paul could have known such comradeship.

Ernst Jünger, whose renewed popularity in Europe and the United States in this so-called postmodern age still needs to be explained,[21] can hardly be presented as an opponent of war. Neither in his early writings on the First World War, nor in later editions of these works, did he try to conceal his eagerness for war, his excitement and pleasure (even if mixed with pain, fear and sorrow) while participating in battle, and his contentment at having been awarded medals for bravery after the event. Yet Jünger is interesting not only as a forerunner of fascism who refused to join

---

19. See, e.g., Wohl, *The Generation of 1914*; Paul Fussell, *The Great War and Modern Memory* (Oxford, 1975); Samuel Hynes, *A War Imagined: The First World War and English Culture* (New York, 1991); Modris Eksteins, *Rites of Spring: The Great War and the Birth of the Modern Age* (New York, 1989).
20. Remarque, *All Quiet*, p. 272
21. The remarkable surge in scholarly and intellectual interest in Jünger was quite noticeable, to cite just one example, in the recent conference, "War, Violence and the Structure of Modernity," sponsored by the Department of Germanic Languages and Literatures at New York University in October 1993.

the Nazis, but also because of his nihilistic, pessimistic view of war. There is little in his writing that smacks of fighting for a cause; not even fighting for one's comrades. Jünger fights for his own pleasure, is motivated by a fascination with the phenomenon of war. Yet he sees no gain in war. From his perspective, between 1914 and 1918 war had become the natural state of things, and he therefore enjoyed participating in it. In 1930, in his essay on total mobilization, Jünger recognizes that the world is once more preparing for war, and he suggests that one had accordingly best be armed. In his 1980 postscript to this essay he acknowledges that this universal condition of conflict has not fundamentally changed. Hence war, for Jünger, much as he may personally enjoy it, exists beyond personal desires, and can be viewed almost as a natural phenomenon. Making war is not unlike hunting: the big game is there whether you set out to enjoy a day of slaughter or not; it has no need of ideological justification.[22]

Jünger notes in his essay *Total Mobilization* that "Germany lost the war by making a greater investment in the West, by winning over to itself civilization, freedom and peace in the sense of Barbusse." Not untypically, Jünger does not state clearly whether he approves of this perceived choice made by Germany, though his ambiguity is especially interesting considering that within three years of his writing this essay Germany chose a wholly different path. Nevertheless, Jünger seems to imply that Germany might have done better to "conduct war outside of that 'wall, which ties Europe together'," as indeed it would do within a few years, whether what he meant was geographic expansion beyond Europe's frontiers or, more metaphorically, release from European norms and customs.[23] In any case, Jünger's evocation of Henri Barbusse is revealing, since it was Barbusse who first published a realistic novel,

22. Ernst Jünger, "In Stahlgewittern" (1920) and "Kriegsausbruch 1914" (1934), both now in *Sämtliche Werke* I, Tagebücher I (Stuttgart, 1980), pp. 9-300, 539-545; and "Die Totale Mobilmachung" (1978), *ibid.*, VII, *Essays I* (Stuttgart, 1980), pp. 119-142.
23. Jünger, VII, p. 139. "Deutschland verlor den Krieg, indem es stärkeren Anteil am westlichen Raum, indem es die Zivilisation, die Freiheit und den Frieden im Sinne der Barbusse gewann. Aber wie konnte man ein anderes Ergebnis erwarten, da man doch selbst beteuert hatte, an diesen Werten Anteil zu nehmen, und um keinen Preis gewagt hätte, den Kampf zu führen außerhalb jener 'Mauer, die Europa umschnürt'. Das hätte eine tiefere Erschließung der eigenen Werte, andere Ideen und andere

by and large autobiographic, on the First World War, and did so almost two years to the day before the war ended. Barbusse, along with Romain Rolland, was the pacifist *par excellence* of France, if not of the whole of Europe, in the 1920s. And yet, his war is a far more meaningful event than Jünger's. To be sure, *Le Feu* is not a novel about the writer's pleasure at taking part in battle; it is an optimistic book filled with the sense that the war will not only be the *der de der*, but, even more ambitiously, that it will bring social justice and an end to misery and proletarian slavery:

> One of the pale-faced clairvoyants lifts himself on his elbow, reckons and numbers the fighters present and to come − thirty millions of soldiers. Another stammers, his eyes full of slaughter, "Two armies at death-grips − that is one great army committing suicide."
> "It should not have been," says the deep and hollow voice of the first in the line. But another says, "It is the French Revolution beginning again." "Let thrones beware!" says another's undertone.
> The third adds, "Perhaps it is the last war of all." A silence follows, then some heads are shaken in dissent whose faces have been blanched anew by the stale tragedy of sleepless night − "Stop war? Stop war? Impossible! There is no cure for the world's disease."...
> ... But the thirty million slaves, hurled upon one another in the mud of war by guilt and error, uplift their human faces and reveal at last a burgeoning Will. The future is in the hands of these slaves, and it is clearly certain that the alliance to be cemented one day by those whose number and whose misery alike are infinite will transform the old world.[24]

It is here that we find the extent to which both pacifism and militarism were Janus faced, especially in the interwar period, and most confusingly, if not perniciously, in France. Yet let us not forget that while French bewilderment and ambiguity, contradiction and frustration, ultimately resulted in a whole nation turning against war, in Germany − despite similar fears, anxieties and forebodings − those who wanted another war won over those who hoped to prevent or at least avoid it.[25]

Verbündete vorausgesetzt. Die Anschürfung der Substantz hätte mit und durch den Fortschrittsoptimismus geschehen können, wie es in Rußland sich andeutet."
    24. Barbusse, *Under Fire*, pp. 3-4.
    25. On reactions to the outbreak of war in Germany, see Wolfram Wette, "Ideologien, Propaganda und Innenpolitik als Voraussetzungen der Kriegspolitik des Dritten

Jean Renoir's masterpiece "The Grand Illusion" (1937) may serve as a useful link between the images of war discussed above, and prevalent especially in the 1920s, and two images which gathered momentum, particularly in France, during the 1930s. Renoir's film is overtly a powerful antiwar statement, which provides hope for the victory of the working class, embodied by Jean Gabin, over the old and corrupt bourgeoisie and aristocracy. In this sense, Renoir created a cinematic version of Barbusse's vision. Yet "*La Grande Illusion*," and the less explicit but even more critical "The Rules of the Game" (*La Règle du jeu*, 1939) contain a much darker and more pessimistic subtext, one which may have not suited the purposes of the Popular Front's *cinéma engagé*, but which reflected Renoir's own sensibilities. For here we find a statement not only on the corruption of the postwar world, but also on the codes of conduct and honor, which were destroyed by that apocalypse. Renoir may be politically on the side of Maréchal (Gabin), but he laments the loss of such men as the French aristocrat Boeldieu (Fresnay) and the physical and mental distortion of his German counterpart, Rauffenstein (von Stroheim). Gabin wins, but his victory is not that of a class, but of his type, the tough survivors, the fittest. Neither courage nor justice had been victorious, but raw instincts, physical strength and will power. These, combined with the now corrupt and degenerate remnants of the old society, are what makes for the world of "The Rules of the Game," a world so clearly on the brink of an abyss.[26]

There is little doubt that Renoir's films reflected the increasing bewilderment in 1930s France over the nature of the anticipated next war. Here was a perplexing image of war with neither clear-

---

Reiches," in *Das Deutsche Reich und der Zweite Weltkrieg*, ed. Wilhelm Deist, Vol. I (Stuttgart, 1979), pp. 25-173, esp. 137-142. See also F. L. Carsten, *War Against War: British and German Radical Movements in the First World War* (Berkeley, 1982); Sandi E. Cooper, *Patriotic Pacifism: Waging War on War in Europe, 1815-1914* (New York, 1991); Richard Evans, *Comrades and Sisters: Feminism, Socialism and Pacifism in Europe, 1870-1945* (New York, 1987).

26. See, esp., Leo Braudy, *Jean Renoir: The World of His Films* (New York, 1972); Célia Bertin, *Jean Renoir: A Life in Pictures*, trans. M. Muellner & L. Muellner (Baltimore, 1991 [1986]); Alexander Sesonske, *Jean Renoir, The French Films, 1924-39* (Cambridge, MA, 1980); Jonathan Buchsbaum, *Cinema Engagé: Film in the Popular Front* (Urbana, 1988).

cut frontiers nor easily identifiable protagonists, where domestic strife was constantly confused with international conflict, and the identity of friend and foe alike became progressively uncertain. Hence France became torn over the expected form of future confrontation, fighting a debilitating battle over the nature and implications of war. Along with this image of the elusive enemy came another image of war as apocalypse, as the end not only of all future wars, but of civilization itself, perhaps even of humanity as hitherto known. Could the anticipated destruction of war have the benefit of wiping out the old and preparing a clean slate for the construction of a "brave new world," a "workers' paradise", or a "racial utopia"? Or was the danger of universal apocalypse so great that it must be prevented at any cost, even if that meant submitting to the forces of evil?

* * *

Curiously, in the context of the political realities of 1930s France, these apparently contradictory images, constantly clashing on the street and in the media, ended up by promoting similar attitudes to war and almost identical actions (or inactions) once armed conflict began in earnest. The proponents of war, those who hoped to build a new world on the ruins of the old, found their loyalties stretched between patriotism, on the one hand, and their foreign models and supporters, on the other. The fascist fascination with war therefore attracted them to France's prospective enemies, and especially to Nazi Germany; hence, instead of supporting war, which would have inevitably involved them in confronting their own model, they increasingly leaned toward compromise and collaboration. Conversely, the Communists, finding themselves torn between their animosity against the right (and the military establishment) in France and their obedience to the conflicting orders of the Kremlin, failed to pursue a coherent policy (domestic or foreign) as late as the German invasion of the Soviet Union in June 1941.[27]

27. On fascism in France, see, e.g., J. Plumyène and R. Lasierra, *Les Fascismes français 1923-63* (Paris, 1963); Pierre Milza, *Fascisme français: passé et présent* (Paris, 1987); Pierre-Marie Dioudonnat, *Je suis partout 1930-44: Les maurassiens devant la tentation fasciste* (Paris, 1973). On communists and socialists, see, e.g., Annie Kriegel, *The French Communist Party: Profile of a People*, trans. Elaine P. Halperin (Chicago, 1972

The opponents of war, too, were not free of contradictions. French pacifism evolved from what has been called the *ancien style* to the *nouveau style*, i.e., from a belief in the ability to reach peace through international organizations and support of just causes (even through war), to an assertion of absolute opposition to war, distrust of the state or any international body, and a willingness to compromise at any price (even capitulation). Hence while the Old Pacifism was quite willing to support war against aggressors, the New Pacifism was willing to cut a deal with aggressors so as to prevent war. Moreover, while the former was composed of liberal patriots with strong nationalist inclinations, the latter developed a tendency toward strongly violent language against the existing social order, as well as against those who were more interested in changing the social order than in preventing war per se, namely the Communists.[28]

These ambivalent attitudes, this bizarre overlap between the images propagated by conflicting political camps, indeed, this bewildering plethora of contradictory and complementary representations of war, can be documented from a variety of sources. A few examples will suffice.

The town of Domme erected a monument to commemorate its "heroic soldiers who died for France" during the Great War (see illustration 1). This assertive statement contrasts with the more ambivalent plaque put up for "the victims of the war 1939-1944," who are in turn listed under three categories: "deportees," "killed in combat," and "executed." From the perspective of the debacle, the occupation, and the resistance, the "Great" War forms a more coherent framework: chronologically it ends in the same year as the war of France's allies and enemies; contextually, all Frenchmen who died in it died for an indisputable cause, France; and essentially, all those deaths were, by definition, heroic. Not so among the "victims" of that other conflict, whose numbers were smaller, whose loyalties and affinities were often in conflict, and whose

---

[1968]); Tony Judt, *Marxism and the French Left: Studies on Labour and Politics in France 1830-1981* (Oxford, 1989 [1986]), chapter 3; Nathanael Greene, *Crisis and Decline: The French Socialist Party in the Popular Front Era* (Ithaca, NY, 1969). Also see David Caute, *Communism and the French Intellectuals, 1914-60* (London, 1964).

28. The best book on this now is Ingram, *Politics of Dissent*.

Illustration 1

deaths frequently occurred far from the battlefield. And yet, when we raise our gaze above the names, we find the heroic soldier of 1914-1918, though holding the flag, being struck by a bullet (see illustration 2).[29] For seventy years since the end of the war this soldier has been dying in the central square of this little town. Other striking representations of war in memorials to the fallen of 1914-1918 can be found throughout France. Such are, for instance, the sprawled, dead stone soldiers of Lilas, or the soldier of Levallois breaking his sword on his knee, while his dying comrades look toward heaven, searching for mercy, meaning or hope. The sculpture *"Vive la guerre"* by Pouvreau-Baldy, a war veteran himself, depicts a grimacing skeleton still wearing its uniform and medals, its arms tied with barbed wire. Although the Prefect of Police prevented the work from being shown in 1926, the inhabitants of Paris, who had watched the march of the wounded – which preceded the victory parade of 1919 at the demand of the soldiers – knew very well the cost of the war.[30]

The commemoration of fallen soldiers and war, victory and its price, necessarily delivered mixed messages. To be sure, many other monuments celebrated victory more than they mourned the dead. But even in those cases, what mattered most were the endless lists of names inscribed on hundreds of memorials in the towns and villages of France. The government might have erected vast cemeteries not far from the actual battlefields; but those lists of familiar names at the central (and often only) square of the town, or in the local cemetery, were indeed a constant reminder of the price a particular community had paid. Nor were the dead left out of the political and economic conflicts of the postwar years, but were occasionally dragged from their graves in protest against the disappointments of peace. Thus, for instance, while France's former allies fumed at its insistence on reparations from Germany, the French asked whether the human sacrifice they had made to win the victory was not sufficient to excuse them from paying back their own war debts (see illustration 3).[31]

29. Both photographs were taken by the author.
30. All pictures referred to in the text, including the march of the wounded, can be found in Prost, *Anciens Combattants*, between pp. 96-97.
31. Photograph taken by the author of a pamphlet in AN, F7 series.

Illustration 2

Illustration 3
Discours de M. Louis MARTIN, député
SUR LES DETTES INTERALLIEES

Soon memories of the previous war were mobilized to assist in the political conflicts of the present. On the eve of the 1928 election a right-wing poster warned that electing the left would bring about an evacuation of the left bank of the Rhine, the annexation of Austria by Germany, and swiftly thereafter invasion and war (see illustration 4). The right played on the public fear of war without, however, assuring the electorate that in case of an invasion it would be able to deal firmly with the enemy. This curious tactic followed by the right throughout the interwar period had a devastating effect on public morale; while arguing that the left would bring about war, the right never promised that its own rule could either prevent or win it. Similarly, the extreme right-wing league, Jeunesses Patriotes, presented itself as a bulwark against domestic strife and civil war, on the one hand, and Bolshevik conquest, on the other; however, its own solution of "social peace" was somewhat difficult to take at face value considering that this league was heavily supported by big capital (see illustration 5). Thus, as early as the mid-1920s the discourse on war involved two enemies (Germany and Bolshevism), and two types of war (international and civil); and while the threats were menacing enough, none of the proposed solutions seemed sufficiently convincing.[32]

The rhetoric of conflict intensified during the 1930s, when the danger of a new war increased and domestic strife became ever more dangerous. Following the attempted *coup d'état* of 6 February 1934, the Socialist Party's daily, *Le Populaire*, promised that fascism would not pass, evoking the famous war cry of the French *poilus* of 1914-1918 (see illustration 6). Fascism, therefore, was identified with Germany, the domestic opponent with the foreign threat. But while the left reacted to the threat by organizing the Front Commun, which in turn eventually led to the establishment of the Popular Front, the right saw this move as *casus belli*. Consequently, the argument was made that a left-wing government would inevitably lead to war, and such a war was now inevitably depicted in the form of German bombers attacking Paris (see illustrations 7 and 8). The conclusion to be drawn was that the Popular Front would

---

32. Photographs of illustrations 4 and 5 taken by the author of posters in AN, F7 series.

Illustration 4

Illustration 5

Le Fascisme ne passera pas!

PARIS OUVRIER A REPONDU HIER AUX PROVOCATEURS DU ROY ET AUX "CROIX DE FEU"

A l'appel du Parti Socialiste auquel se sont associés le Parti Communiste et toutes les organisations d'avant-garde, plus de 150.000 travailleurs ont clamé, Cours de Vincennes et place de la Nation, leur haine du fascisme et affirmé leur volonté de défendre les libertés politiques et syndicales

Illustration 6

Illustration 7

Illustration 8

bring the Germans, whereas the right would keep them out. Yet no suggestion was made as to why the latter would be better equipped to defend French cities from German bombers than the former. Rather, it was implied that the right would prevent a conflict that France could not conceivably win. In these posters we see the emergence of a right-wing defeatism under the guise of antileftist sentiments. This was a major shift from the position taken by the veteran association of the Jeunesses Patriotes only a few years earlier, when it warned that in the East nothing had changed (an instructive pun on the French title of Remarque's novel), that German pacifism was always a guise for war, and that the duty of French patriots was to be ready for war while working toward a Franco-German economic rapprochement (see illustration 9).[33]

Finally, there came that strange consensus between the left and right, the militarists and pacifists, whose links to the strange defeat of 1940 cannot be ignored. "Die for the Soviets! Die for the Negus! Die for Red Spain! Die for China! Die for the Czechs! Die for the Jews!" "Thank you," says the morose *poilu* in a 1938 poster, "I'd rather: 'live for France!'" We might conclude that the soldier is speaking on behalf of the New Pacifists, but in fact the poster was issued by none other than the right-wing *Je suis partout*.[34] Jean-Paul Sartre, whose novel *The Reprieve* takes place during the war scare of 1938, puts similar sentiments in the mouths of many of his protagonists, and whatever we might think about his position at the time, there is little doubt that these feelings were shared by a large majority of the French population, left, right and center. As a trade union poster issued in 1939 put it, the workers of Europe were united behind the slogan "Enough!" with war and arms production.[35] This same slogan united French, German and Italian pacifist veterans who gathered at Douaumont, by Verdun, in 1936 to make sure that the previous war would also remain the last.[36]

* * *

33. Photographs and copies of illustrations 6-9 taken by the author of posters and newspaper clipping in AN, F7 series.
34. A copy of this poster can be found in Johnson, *Age of Illusion*, p. 147.
35. Ibid.
36. See photograph in Prost, *Anciens Combattants*, between pp. 96-97.

Illustration 9

In March 1936 one of the leaders of French pacifism, Félicien Challaye, in a response to Romain Rolland, stressed that the ultimate evil was war, not Nazism. Hence he concluded that war had to be avoided at all cost. Furthermore, Challaye insisted on the distinction between external and internal antifascism:

> The struggle against internal Fascism is the civil battle which we accept ... This is the national front which we must occupy in the international struggle against Fascism. But the struggle against external Fascism takes on necessarily the aspect of war. We want nothing to do with war, even that which is baptized antifascist and revolutionary. We are convinced, moreover, that one does not bring freedom on the tip of a sword, nor democracy in foreign troop carriers.[37]

This was an admirably steadfast position, and one that eventually led Challaye to claim that Pétain had "saved the country in imposing the armistice" and to insist on the "duty to collaborate with Germany ..."[38] On the other extreme of the political map, the Jeunesses Patriotes proclaimed in its leaflets: "*Le Communisme, voilà l'Ennemi!*" while the new fascist league La Solidarité Française warned that the Red Fascism of social-communist Judeo-freemasons posed a deadly threat to freedom, the family and the nation, and threatened to bring revolutionary tyranny to France as it had to central Europe and Russia.[39]

War had thus become mainly a struggle between competing forces within France, all of which, for one reason or another, feared or rejected the idea of war against a foreign enemy, and vented their rage by combating each other. It is not that France became a pacifist society. Quite the contrary, even the most extreme pacifists were willing to fight those who, in their opinion, were French proponents of war. Blood, sacrifice, and destruction, these were terms on everyone's lips. War became a general obsession, perhaps even greater than in Germany of the late 1930s; and yet, it was civil war about which everyone spoke, whether to prevent another catastrophe such as that of 1914-1918, or to ward off a Franco-Bolshevik uprising. There is little doubt that the ample evidence of the

---

37. Ingram, *Politics of Dissent*, pp. 192-193.
38. *Ibid.*, pp. 318-319.
39. See leaflets in AN, F7 13233, 13235, 13239.

price of war did its share in diminishing the public's desire to take part in another massacre. The fact that fear of war, and obsessive preoccupation with that fear, brought not domestic reconciliation but increased political tensions and a new brutality to political and intellectual discourse, indicated the immense impact of 1914-1918 upon France. That the abhorrence of foreign war reached such proportions is admittedly quite laudable; that it ultimately led not only to military defeat but also to willing collaboration with the Nazis is a trauma that France is still trying to overcome.[40]

40. For a photograph of the march of the *"grands mutilés"* past the Arc de Triomphe, yet one more reminder of the atrocity of war, see *Le Matin*, 12 July 1926, in AN F7 13242. See further in Pierre Laborie, *L'Opinion française sous Vichy* (Paris, 1990); Henri Michel, *Pétain, Laval, Darlan, trois politiques?* (Paris, 1972); Pascal Ory, *Les Collaborateurs 1940-45* (Paris, 1976); Jean-Pierre Rioux, *La Vie culturelle sous Vichy* (Brussels, 1990); Robert Aron, *Histoire de l'épuration: De l'indulgence aux massacres, novembre 1942 – septembre 1944* (Paris, 1967); Peter Novick, *The Resistance Versus Vichy: The Purge of Collaborators in Liberated France* (London, 1968).

IV

DOMESTIC POLITICS AND THE FALL OF FRANCE IN 1940

William D. Irvine

Ever since Marc Bloch's *Strange Defeat* historians have believed that the military defeat of France in May-June 1940 can only be understood in terms of the social and political crises of the last years of the Third Republic. Serge Berstein's recent textbook on the 1930s is typical in this respect. He concludes:

> The long crisis which marked the 1930s – a crisis both economic but also moral, social and political – therefore led to what appeared to be a total collapse. If, in the short run, one can invoke the strategic errors of the general staff rather than that inferiority in material which the generals stressed in order to hide their responsibilities ... the explanation for the collapse is to be found elsewhere .... One must ... take into account the doubts about the validity of the regime ..., the sclerosis of ideologies and the fear of risk of a morally exhausted people. [All of which] seemed *a posteriori* to lead the country ineluctably towards the tragedy of 1940.[1]

---

1. Serge Berstein, *La France des années 30* (Paris, 1993), pp. 170-171. Berstein is hardly unique in this respect. Jean-Louis Crémieux-Brilhac, in his otherwise superb study, *Les Français de l'An 40* (Paris, 1990), V.II, p. 369 speaks of *"L' Etrange Défaite* de Marc Bloch dont pas une page, après cinquante ans, n'appelle une réserve." Jean Doise and Maurice Vaisse, *Diplomatie et outil militaire, 1871-1969* (Paris, 1987), p. 334, while insisting that "the defeat of 1940 was above all military," nonetheless assert that "Marc

At first blush the proposition advanced by Berstein seems self evident. Marc Bloch, after all, was but the most distinguished of many contemporary observers who saw a direct connection between the crisis of the 1930s and the collapse of June 1940.[2] Especially when viewed retrospectively, it is hard to deny that the late 1930s provided a host of ingredients for an eventual military collapse. The political polarization brought on by the fascist challenge and the counter-attack by the Popular Front in particular created an atmosphere of civil war. Certainly Frenchmen of all political persuasions could believe in the aftermath of June 1940 that the roots of defeat went back to the crisis of the previous decade. At Riom the Vichy authorities attempted, albeit unsuccessfully, to indict a Socialist government for failure to adequately rearm France; Léon Blum countered that the origins of the collapse could be traced to the right-wing enemies of the Republic.[3] Indeed, not least of the reasons for the enduring belief that June 1940 began in the mid-1930s was the delightfully bipartisan quality of the argument. Conservatives could, with varying degrees of plausibility, blame Socialist economic mis-management, pacifist machinations and the general bad faith of the Communists. Left-wing historians could attack a French Right seduced by the charms of fascism, increasingly sympathetic to Nazi Germany or Fascist Italy and, if they never actually uttered the words, prepared to behave as if they preferred Hitler to Blum. Taken together these

---

Bloch has written the definitive pages on that subject." In the last twenty years a number of historians have expressed skepticism about what might be called the "decadence" school of the French defeat although they rarely deal directly either with Bloch or domestic politics. Among the most stimulating are: John C. Cairns, "Some Recent Historians and the 'Strange Defeat' of 1940," *Journal of Modern History* 46 (1974): 60-85; Don W. Alexander, "Repercussions of the Breda Variant," *French Historical Studies* 8 (1974): 459-488; Robert J. Young, *In Command of France. French Foreign Policy and Military Planning, 1933-39* (Cambridge, MA, 1978); Jeffery A. Gunsburg, *Divided and Conquered: The French High Command and the Defeat of the West, 1940* (Westport, CT, 1979); and Martin S. Alexander, *The Republic in Danger: General Maurice Gamelin and the Politics of French Defense, 1933-40* (Cambridge, 1993).

2. See, for example Georges Friedmann, *Journal de la guerre 1939-40* (Paris, 1987).

3. For the best discussion of the Riom trials and an effective analysis of the early debate on responsibility for the military collapse of 1940 see Henri Michel, *Le Procès de Riom* (Paris, 1979).

undeniable aspects in crisis would appear to have doomed France to defeat in 1940.

Yet at some levels the argument risks being a *post hoc ergo propter hoc* one. Social and political crises have not, after all, always accompanied spectacular military defeats. A prosperous economy and political stability did not prevent France from suffering a defeat in September 1870 which was as sudden as that of 1940. By contrast, the total political chaos of September 1792 did not prevent France from winning the battle of Valmy. The First Battle of the Marne was – as Wellington would have had it – a "near run thing." Had Germany won in September 1914, it would not have been difficult to find the roots of that defeat in the acute social, political and religious tensions of the previous fifteen years in France.[4] Significantly, Marc Bloch's indictment of prewar France seems not to have antedated her defeat. Certainly his letters to his son, written in the months prior to May 1940, reveal neither a preoccupation with French domestic politics nor any pessimism about the prospect of a French victory.[5] The same can be said for Georges Friedmann's wartime memoirs.[6]

It is not enough, then, merely to establish that in the years before 1940 France experienced social and political upheaval. What, exactly, was it about those crisis years that rendered France vulnerable to the German military machine? Marc Bloch – so often evoked – is actually disappointing on this point since much of his analysis deals primarily with the perceived incompetence of the military rather than the socio-political preconditions for defeat. Still, in the few pages devoted to the prewar, he evokes one theme that has been systematically explored by a later generation of historians. "In the France of 1939," he wrote, "the members of the upper middle classes were never sick of declaring that they had lost all power."[7] Bloch was careful to qualify these sentiments as an "exaggeration,"

---

4. Douglas Porch, "Arms and Alliances: French Grand Strategy and Policy in 1914 and 1940," in Paul Kennedy, ed. *Grand Strategies in War and Peace* (New Haven, CT, 1991), pp. 125-144, makes an effective argument on this point.

5. François Bedarida and Denis Peschanski, eds. "Marc Bloch à Etienne Bloch: Lettres de la 'Drôle de guerre'," *Cahiers de l'Institut d'Histoire du Temps Present* 19 (1991). See especially, pp. 13-16.

6. Friedmann, *Journal*, see esp. p. 239 (dated 29 May 1940).

7. Marc Bloch, *Strange Defeat* (New York, 1968), p. 134.

but there can be no doubt that in the mid-1930s significant elements of France's ruling elite shared similar views. Serious historical scholarship has depicted the reactions of a beleaguered French ruling class to the supposed political instability of the regime, the rise of the Communists, the triumph of the Popular Front and, above all, the great victories of the working class in the summer of 1936. This apparent shift in political power severely shook the self-confidence of a previously republican bourgeoisie. Significant elements of the middle classes embraced movements and ideologies overtly contemptuous of French political democracy and in many cases openly admiring of foreign fascist models. Moreover, the latent menace of the Popular Front moved most French conservatives to abandon two generations of Germano-phobic nationalism and to embrace appeasement. In a seminal study done shortly after the fall of France, an American scholar, Charles Micaud, demonstrated why so many erstwhile conservative nationalists abandoned their anti-German resolve in the era of the Popular Front.[8] The great majority of the French Right believed that diplomatic firmness with respect to Germany might lead to war, and war – given the French domestic situation – enhanced the danger of revolution. The war/revolution nexus, implausible though it sounds in retrospect, dominated conservative thinking from 1935 until 1938 and manifested itself most clearly during the Munich crisis. In short, there was, on the part of the French Right, both a willingness to embrace domestic fascism and an equal complacence with respect to the aggressive designs of foreign fascism. In theory, these attitudes, taken together, ought to have conditioned France, or a substantial part of it, to accept defeat in June 1940.

While there can be no dispute about how widespread these views were, the impact of such values in 1940 is not self-evident. The *grande peur des bienpensants* was, after all, characteristic of the period 1935-1938. By 1939 things were very different. The Daladier-Reynaud ministry, the decree laws modifying the forty-hour work week and above all the failure of the general strike of 30

---

8. Charles A. Micaud, *The French Right and Nazi Germany, 1933-39* (New York, 1964 [1943]). A similar argument can be found in William D. Irvine, *French Conservatism in Crisis* (Baton Rouge, 1979), pp. 159-203.

November 1938 protesting these measures dealt the organized working class a decisive blow. Both government and private businessmen took severe measures against the strikers of November; in the weeks that followed large numbers of CGT militants were fired. By the spring of 1939 the "patrons" were firmly back in the saddle as the ranks of the CGT dwindled. The "deliberate, systematic and unpitying repression" meant that by the summer of 1939 "for the government as for the *patronat* there was henceforth no social problem."[9]

For most of the Right, 30 November 1938 represented *un grand tournant* almost as dramatic as June 1936. Certainly the press controlled by *le grand patronat*, *Le Temps*, *Le Journal des débats* and *Le Capital* abandoned its unconditional hostility to the government.[10] François de Wendel, head of the Comité des Forges and symbol of die-hard capitalism, certainly gave the Daladier-Reynaud ministry his qualified support; whatever hesitations he retained about the Radical leader, he was wholeheartedly behind him when war broke out.[11] The political formations of the Right ceased their systematic opposition and, significantly, altered dramatically their attitudes towards foreign policy. If much of the French Right had heretofore been, in the words of Charles Micaud, "conditional nationalists," the condition had been the end of the Popular Front. By 1939 that condition had been met and resulted in a dramatic *revirement* in the position of the French Right – a shift every bit as radical as that of 1935. The classical Right, typified by Louis Marin's Republican Federation quickly forgot its obsession with war and revolution and returned to its favorite role as the pre-eminent advocates of Germanophobic nationalism. Philippe Henriot, one of the party's vice-presidents, had been among the most violent critics of the Popular Front and one of the most outspoken opponents of war in 1938. By September 1939 there was no more intransigent opponent of

9. Antoine Prost, "Le climat social," in René Rémond and Janine Bourdin, *Edouard Daladier, chef du gouvernement* (Paris, 1977), p. 110.
10. Jean-Louis Crémieux-Brilhac, "L'opinion publique française, L'Angleterre et la guerre (septembre 1939-juin 1940)" in *Français et Britanniques dans la drôle de guerre* (Paris, 1975), p. 7.
11. Jean-Noël Jeanneney, *François de Wendel en République: L'Argent et le pouvoir, 1914-40* (Paris, 1976), pp. 588, 591-592.

Hitler. His celebrated article, "Peace, yes, war on the installment plan, no," (published in, of all places, *Gringoire*) was utterly Jacobin in its call for resistance against the German dictator and its willingness to contemplate peace only if Hitler abjectly abandoned his foreign policy ambitions.[12] Colonel de la Rocque's PSF, every bit as Munichois as the Federation in 1938, followed suit in its shift to diplomatic intransigence in 1939. The center-right Democratic Alliance, traditionally less hostile to Germany than the Federation, had been, if possible even more Munichois than its right-wing cousins. The president of the Alliance, Pierre-Etienne Flandin had, after all, sent a letter of congratulations to Hitler in the wake of the Munich accord. By the end of 1938 Flandin had become an obvious embarrassment to many leaders of the party who took some pains to distance themselves publicly from his Munich stance. On domestic policy the Alliance now supported the Daladier-Reynaud ministry – a natural enough role for a party that traditionally wooed the right wing of the Radical party.[13] On foreign policy, even Flandin was now declaring, "We must firmly declare to the dictators: You will obtain nothing more by threats and violence." These sentiments only became firmer in the course of the prewar summer. As the historian of the Alliance has noted: "It is ... beyond dispute that by the time the Third Republic went to war in 1939, it did so with the emphatic support of Pierre-Etienne Flandin and the Alliance Républicaine Démocratique."[14]

In fact, what is striking about so much of the French Right in 1939 is the degree of *discontinuity* with their position a year earlier – or a year later. Neither Flandin's role in Vichy, nor – still more – that of Henriot, should blind us to the stand they took on the eve of war. Moreover the willingness to resist Hitler was not limited to

12. Elisabeth du Réau, *Edouard Daladier, 1884-1970* (Paris, 1993), p. 366.
13. On the evolution of the Alliance Démocratique, the best source is the important but as yet unpublished work by Donald G. Wileman, "L' Alliance Républicaine Démocratique: The Dead Centre of French Politics, 1901-47," Ph.D. Dissertation, York University, 1988; see his "P.-E. Flandin and the Alliance Démocratique, 1929-39," *French History* 4 (1990): 139-173; see also Rosemonde Sanson, "L' Alliance Démocratique" in René Rémond and Janine Bourdin, eds, *La France et les Français en 1938-39* (Paris, 1978), pp. 327-340.
14. Cited in Wileman, "L'Alliance Républicaine Démocratique," p. 313. Ibid., p. 315.

those on the Right – like Marin and Flandin – who remained content to work within the democratic system. The contagion of diplomatic firmness hit even those who were clearly bitter opponents of the democratic Republic. Perhaps nothing has more graphically symbolized a degenerating republicanism than the political evolution of André Tardieu. Premier in the early thirties, Tardieu was once the incarnation of the reformist center-right politicians who had given the Third Republic its tenacity. By the mid-1930s, however, a failed and embittered Tardieu had given up on the democratic regime and had drifted into the camp of its most outspoken enemies. The spectacle of a former editor of *Le Temps* writing for an ugly right-wing *torchon* like *Gringoire* has so struck historians that they have rather overlooked the fact that, at least with respect to Germany, Tardieu remained a committed partisan of a strong French foreign policy. As his biographer notes with some justifiable frustration, posterity's abhorrence for Tardieu's later political associates is such that scholars have ignored the fact that on the issue of Munich nothing whatsoever separated him from better known right-wing antiappeasers: Reynaud, Kérillis, Buré and Mandel. Not only was he an outspoken opponent of the Munich accords, but by the summer of 1939, shortly before his disabling stroke, he was a particularly able advocate of a policy of national firmness.[15]

What the case of Tardieu so strikingly illustrates is that a rejection of the democratic republic and even a distinct preference for more authoritarian political systems – even fascist ones – did not necessarily entail an enthusiasm for the foreign policy goals of the Third Reich or an unwillingness to resist Hitler. Jacques Doriot's PPF was by all accounts an authentically native French fascism, and its leader enthusiastically welcomed the Munich accords. Yet many leaders of the PPF were profoundly troubled by this stance. Whatever it was that led Bertrand de Jouvenel to associate himself with Doriot, it was not the Nazi destruction of the regime headed by his personal friend, Edouard Beneš. In fact, Doriot's outspoken defense of the Munich settlement was one major (albeit not the

---

15. François Monnet, *Refaire la République; André Tardieu, une dérive réactionnaire (1876-1945)*, (Paris, 1993), pp. 495-502, 505-513.

only) reason for profound disagreements within and resignations from the PPF in late 1938 and early 1939. After March 1939 the PPF advocated a policy of diplomatic firmness with respect to Nazi Germany, and its newspaper, *L' Emancipation nationale*, "became one of the most chauvinistic newspapers in the country."[16] Even the overtly pro-fascist *Je suis partout* was affected by the altered climate of 1939. By the summer both traditional royalists like Pierre Gaxotte and more modern "fascists" like Robert Brasillach were taking a firm line on the demands of both Italy and Germany. The newspaper pointedly reminded pacifists like the neo-socialist Marcel Déat that whereas Czechoslovakia, whose destruction they had so gleefully welcomed the previous year, was not a real nation, Poland, by contrast, most certainly was.[17]

What of the political Left? In 1940 Marc Bloch suggested that at least *one* of the reasons why France "was not turning out enough aeroplanes, engines or tanks" was because too many workers "thought first and foremost about selling their labour at the highest price, about doing as little as possible, for the shortest time possible, in return for as much money as possible."[18] The notion that the social legislation of the Popular Front was responsible for the nation's defeat is, of course, an oft debunked myth. As early as the 1942 Riom trial, the speciousness of the argument was evident: postwar scholarship, most notably the momentous work of Robert Frankenstein,[19] has demonstrated both that France, for the most part, *was* producing enough war material and that this was largely due to the Popular Front and its successors. By 1939 Socialists and Communists had reverted to the opposition but they objected to the domestic policy of the Daladier government, not its foreign policy. The Socialists, to be sure, had a refractory pacifist wing to deal with, but by the Congress of Nantes of May 1939 the policy of diplomatic firmness advocated by Léon Blum appeared to have prevailed.[20] The

16. Jean-Paul Brunet, *Jacques Doriot* (Paris, 1986), p. 301
17. Pierre-Marie Dioudonnat, *Je suis partout, 1930-44* (Paris, 1973), pp. 296-311.
18. Bloch, *Strange Defeat*, p. 135.
19. Robert Frankenstein, *Le Prix du réarmament français 1935-39* (Paris, 1982).
20. Georges Lefranc, *Le Mouvement socialiste sous la Troisième République* (Paris, 1963), p. 372. To be sure, the Blum position appeared to prevail largely because Faure wanted to avoid a total rupture in the party.

Communists, for all their denunciations of Daladier's reactionary social policies, remained firmly committed to national defense up to – and probably for a good while after – 26 August 1939. Still, November 1938 did represent something of a defeat for the French working class. Did the triumphant reassertion of nationalism in 1939 on the part of the bourgeoisie have, as its logical corollary, the bitter disillusionment of the working class? There is little doubt that the working-class élan of 1936 was largely gone by the end of 1938.[21] Few workers mobilized for the 1939 May Day celebrations, leading prefects, somewhat predictably, to congratulate workers for "a magnificent example of their patriotic spirit."[22] Social historians of the period are more inclined to explain the lack of working-class militancy in 1939 in terms of disillusionment with a government that had destroyed the highly symbolic benefits of the forty hour week and the "week of two Sundays." It is equally possible, of course, that working-class quiescence owed something to the fact that longer hours, combined with the recently implemented family allowances yielded higher nominal weekly earnings and, as a result of decreased inflation, at least stable real incomes. Rather more important, however, is the working-class contribution to national defense. Here, recent research is unambiguous. Herrick Chapman's recent expert analysis of the workers in the aviation industry discusses in some detail the demoralizing effect of Daladier's decree laws. Yet, and despite ritualistic obeisance to Marc Bloch, he also demonstrates that between the summer of 1939 and June 1940 the rate of aircraft production in France increased more rapidly than in either Great Britain or Germany.[23] Similarly, Jean-Louis Crémieux-Brilhac demonstrates that despite working upwards of 60 hours a week, seven days a week, and despite having most of their extra earning clawed back through taxation, French workers in war industries matched or exceeded their Ger-

21. The single best discussion of this topic is Guy Bourdé, *La Défaite du Front Populaire* (Paris, 1977).
22. Marcel Gillet, "La situation sociale en Province: Le Nord," p. 155, and Pierre Guillen, "La situation sociale en province: l'Isère," p. 167, in René Rémond et al., *Edouard Daladier*.
23. Herrick Chapman, *State Capitalism and Working-Class Radicalism in the French Aircraft Industry* (Berkeley, 1991), p. 223.

man counter-parts in the months preceding the collapse of 1940.[24] Whatever else explains the "strange defeat" of 1940, it cannot have been – as Marc Bloch would have had it – the unpatriotic egotism of the working class, or – as more modern historians might suggest – their disaffection with a regime run by Daladier and Reynaud. Disaffected they might have been – although here all the evidence is ambiguous – but this disaffection never took the one form that meant anything: unwillingness to rearm France.

One of the more powerful currents in prewar France – but also in prewar Great Britain – was doctrinaire pacifism. Influential segments of French society abhorred war as an instrument of national policy. But there is a critical distinction to be made between the more traditional pacifists who believed that war should be avoided if possible and those, the so-called integral pacifists, who believed that war should be avoided at all costs. As Norman Ingram has recently demonstrated, by 1938 at the latest, most of the former had come to recognize that Hitler might have to be stopped by force. The integral pacifists clung to their doctrine more tenaciously but by the spring of 1939 ruefully admitted that their support was collapsing.[25] Moreover, although pacifism of some kind was prevalent in certain milieus – notably school teachers and intellectuals in general – evidence as to its impact on the popular classes is more ambiguous. At least one analyst of the defeat in 1940, for example, has emphasized the inherent pacifism of the peasantry convinced that "tout le monde s'embusque, excepté moi."[26] Yet, as he admits, his claim is not grounded on any actual study of the peasants themselves as opposed to what city-dwellers said about them. Significantly, Isabel Boussard's more recent study, based on the peasant press, concludes that a latent aversion to war on the part of the French peasantry "in no way excluded a real patriotism and a willingness to defend the nation should it be in danger." In September 1939 "there was no peasant pacifism."[27]

---

24. Jean-Louis Crémieux-Brilhac, *Les Français de l'an 40*, v. II, *Ouvriers et soldats* (Paris, 1990), esp. pp. 348-355.
25. Norman Ingram, *The Politics of Dissent* (Oxford, 1991), pp. 112-118; 235-243.
26. Ladislas Mysyrowicz, *Autopsie d'une défaite* (Paris, 1973), p. 331.
27. Isabel Boussard, "Le pacifisme paysan," in *La France et Les Français*, pp. 74-75.

Assessing the depth of pacifist sentiment is uncommonly difficult. Which had greater influence on the average Frenchman? Jean Giraudoux's successful Parisian production of the pacifist play, "La guerre de troie n'aura pas lieu"?, or Edith Piaf's first great hit, the powerfully patriotic "Mon Légionnaire"?

Although knowing exactly how the "average" Frenchman felt in 1939 is difficult, there is reason to believe that neither the views expressed in the press nor those of the political elite entirely captured the mood of "la France profonde." The year before the war saw the first manifestations of French public opinion polls. Although crude by today's standards, they are suggestive of a public mood that differed somewhat from "la France officielle." The Munich accords, for example, were welcomed, albeit with varying degrees of enthusiasm, by the quasi-totality of the non-Communist political elite and the great majority of the French press. Yet the first "sondages" taken immediately afterward indicated that only 57% of Frenchmen interviewed approved of the accords. Fully 37% – several times, as scholars have noted, the presumed constituency of the Communist party – disapproved. All of the polls taken in 1939 indicate a hardening of public opinion with respect to Germany. When asked in July 1939 if France ought to resort to force to prevent Germany from seizing Danzig, five Frenchmen out of six responded in the affirmative.[28] The 17% of Frenchmen who were unwilling to die for Danzig in July of 1939 should be compared to the 17% of the citizens of Great Britain who, when interviewed in the last week of September (!) 1939, indicated that they were in favor of peace negotiations with Germany.[29]

All the evidence, therefore, suggests that in the summer of 1939 France was morally and materially ready to confront Nazi Germany. As Jean-Louis Crémieux-Brilhac has noted, "The shift in French public opinion between October 1938 and September 1939 is an extraordinary psychological phenomenon, probably greater in scale – even if it seems less dramatic – than the stiffening of British public opinion after the occupation of Bohemia in

---

28. Christel Peyrefitte, "Les premiers sondages d'opinion," in René Rémond et al., *Edouard Daladier*, pp. 265-278.
29. P. M.H. Bell, "L' évolution de l'opinion publique anglaise à propos de la guerre et de l'alliance avec la France," *Français et Britanniques*, p. 58.

March 1939."[30] France had just completed the most extensive series of domestic reforms in the history of the Third Republic. The Daladier-Reynaud ministry had modified but not destroyed the social reforms of its Popular Front predecessors. If, by 1939 it had sacrificed the highly symbolic forty-hour week legislation to the exigencies of military preparation, it also succeeded in ensuring a degree of economic growth that had eluded its predecessors. The Daladier government was arguably the most popular that France had seen for a decade; it enjoyed an unprecedented degree of support from the Radicals to the traditional Right. Although both the Communists and Socialists opposed the government's domestic policy, all of the former – at least until 26 August – and a majority of the latter supported its foreign policy. The ideological cleavages of 1936-38 had largely – if not entirely – disappeared on the eve of war. And for the past four years governments of whatever stripe had undertaken an extensive and increasingly successful campaign of rearmament.

When war came in September, France mobilized without a hitch. The percentage of "insoumis" – draft dodgers – was low (1.5%) and no higher than in 1914.[31] True, almost all contemporary observers noted that the enthusiasm of 1914 was missing in September 1939; resignation more accurately typified the national mood.[32] This ought not be very surprising since the same could be said of Germany and Great Britain. Everywhere memories of the carnage of the Great War dampened the enthusiasm of prospective combatants. Moreover, this time France was fighting not to recover lost provinces but to preserve the freedom of Danzig. But there were few manifestations of pacifism. The outbreak of war found Marceau Pivert, the articulate Socialist advocate of "revolutionary defeatism," in the United States. Significantly he chose not to return to France. Romain Rolland, one of the most effective pacifist spokesmen of the 1930s, sent a message of support to Daladier.[33]

There were, of course, pacifist elements in parliament: Georges Bonnet, Anatole de Monzie, Pierre-Etienne Flandin, Pierre Laval,

30. Crémieux-Brilhac, "L'opinion publique," p. 6
31. Pierre Laborie, L' Opinion française sous Vichy (Paris, 1990), p. 202.
32. Guy Rossi-Landi, La Drôle de guerre (Paris, 1971), p. 168.
33. Cremieux-Brilhac, "L'opinion publique," p. 8.

Jean Montigny. Both Right (Jean-Louis Tixier-Vignancour, Georges Scapini, René Dommange) and Left (Gaston Bergery, René Chateau, René Brunet) were represented. They formed a semiformal parliamentary group which met at most six times. In September 1939 they attempted, without success, to argue that a vote for war credits was not necessarily a vote for war. At the end of March 1940 they attempted, again fruitlessly, to orchestrate a cabinet shuffle to put the pacifist Pierre Laval in the Quai d'Orsay. Many of the most outspoken prewar pacifists were, to say the least, passive during the phony war. Paul Faure, secretary general of the Socialist party and leader of the party's prewar pacifist wing, manifested his feelings by *not* writing in the Socialist newspaper, *Le Populaire*, for the first five months of the war.[34] Georges Bonnet lapsed into silence after September 1939.[35] Many of the leading pacifists either refused to sign or retroactively withdrew their signature from the one significant pacifist manifesto of the phony war.[36]

Certainly all of the information received by Daladier stressed the excellent morale of Frenchmen, both at the front and at the rear.[37] Even those among the military who were most pessimistic, such as the highly placed and frankly defeatist Paul de Villelume, had few reservations about the fighting spirit of the French army. The entries in his wartime diary abound with skepticism about the strategic wisdom of the commander in chief, General Gamelin, but as late as 13 May 1940 he believed the morale in the army to be excellent.[38]

Given the dramatic political polarization of the prewar years, there ought to have been soldiers who believed themselves to be fighting for a regime they despised. This would almost certainly have been the case of Sergeant Jacques Doriot. Yet Doriot's private political views did not prevent him from fighting courageously and

---

34. Rossi-Landi, *La Drôle de guerre*, p. 121.
35. Guy Rossi-Landi, "Le pacifisme en France," in *Français et Britanniques*, p. 142.
36. *Ibid.*, p. 135.
37. By far the most thorough discussion of French military morale is in Crémieux-Brilhac, *Les Français de l'an 40*, v. II, especially pp. 518-531. See also Patrice Buffotot, "Le moral dans l'armée de l'air française de Septembre 1939 à juin 1940," in *Français et Britanniques*, p. 186.
38. Paul de Villelume, *Journal d'une défaite* (Paris, 1976), p. 335.

with distinction in June of 1940, actions which earned him the Croix de Guerre.[39] Indeed, all of the evidence suggests that in the crucial hours of May-June 1940 even the most savage opponents of the democratic republic nonetheless believed France worth fighting for. On 24 May 1940, when the French army was in an advanced state of disarray, the overtly fascist, anti-semitic and pacifist newspaper, *Je suis partout*, chose to write an editorial in praise of the recently appointed Minister of the Interior, Georges Mandel. A Jew and longtime partisan of resistance to Nazi Germany, Mandel had been a favorite target of the extreme Right and of *Je suis partout* in particular. But at the end of May 1940 the newspaper chose to forget its prewar vendetta against Mandel, to remember only his association with Georges Clemenceau and to celebrate him as the man France now needed most.[40] It would be a mistake to make too much of this eleventh-hour conversion on the part of the fascist Right. Mandel, for example, seems not to have been unduly impressed, because he promptly arrested several of the newspaper's editors! Nonetheless, this extreme example does suggest that in the spring of 1940 something of the spirit of the Union Sacrée was alive in France.

Of course France was defeated and the Vichy regime promptly succeeded the democratic republic. The ease with which embittered and disillusioned politicians of both the Left and Right rallied to a regime that was both authoritarian and pro-German helps sustain the view that French defeat in 1940 resulted from domestic politics. Vichy did not arise from nowhere, and, so the reasoning goes, the same domestic political forces that prepared France for Vichy caused the collapse of 1940.

Such an argument seriously confuses cause and effect. The immediate cause of Vichy was the crushing defeat of 1940. Similarly, it was the decisive defeat at Sedan on 2 September 1870 that caused Imperial France to become a republic two days later. But few historians would argue that prewar republican forces, a distinct minority of Frenchmen, had somehow caused the defeat of the Imperial armies. All the available evidence suggests that until

39. Brunet, *Doriot*, p. 306.
40. Pierre-Marie Dioudonnat, *Je suis partout 1930-44* (Paris, 1973), p. 323.

France collapsed in 1940, most Frenchmen, including the most intransigent opponents of the regime, actively sought a French military victory. Only in the wake of a crushing defeat did they avail themselves of the newfound opportunities to remodel France. As Guy Rossi-Landi has observed, between September 1939 and May 1940 "one finds no trace ... of a plot against the Republic. The enemies of the regime were not responsible for its fall; they exploited the situation rather than provoking it."[41]

In a 1975 colloquium on the fall of France a British historian, R.A.C. Parker, remarked that had Germany lost the war, scholars would be remembering how Germans complained in 1939 that their soldiers lacked the zeal of their counter-parts in 1914, that their morale was low and that their equipment, notably tanks, were inadequate.[42] By the same logic historians of modern France would be explaining the "victory of 1940" in terms of the amazing resilience of a democratic regime which in four years managed to parry the forces of domestic fascism, integrate the working class into the nation, rally the bulk of an obdurate Right, all the while rearming the nation. Events turned out differently, which permits historians of the stature of Jean-Baptiste Duroselle to qualify the 1930s as a period of "decadence." But it was not decadence that led to 1940; it is 1940 that has led us to view the late Third Republic as decadent.

---

41. Rossi-Landi, "Le pacifisme en France," p. 137.
42. See the intervention of R.A.C. Parker in *Français et Britanniques*, p. 218.

V

EDOUARD DALADIER

The Conduct of the War and the Beginnings of Defeat

Elisabeth du Réau

In April 1938 Edouard Daladier, the Popular Front's National Defense Minister since June 1936, became the President of the Council. In September 1938 he signed the Munich Pact, reckoning on a reprieve that would allow France to speed up its rearmament program. Yet France, one year later, was at war with the Third Reich.

On 22 October 1939, while France and its citizens were settling into the "phoney war," Colonel de Gaulle wrote these words to Paul Reynaud: "In my humble opinion, there is nothing more urgent nor more necessary than galvanizing the French people, instead of cradling them with absurd illusions of defensive security." He clarified his thoughts further on, hoping to make himself understood: "We must, just as soon as possible, be ready to make an active war by getting ourselves all the necessary equipment: planes, ultra-powerful tanks organized in huge armored divisions."[1]

Addressing himself to Daladier's Finance Minister who had cast a favorable eye on his theses since 1935, Colonel de Gaulle was drawing attention here to the very tasks incumbent upon the nation's government. According to the provisions of the law adopted

---

1. Charles de Gaulle, Lettres, *notes et carnets – juin 1919 – juin 1940* (Paris, 1980), pp.485-487.

in July 1938 concerning "the organization of the Nation in time of war," the government was responsible for the overall conduct of war.

* * *

What were the specific missions entrusted to the nation's government in time of war? Its charge was to determine the overall goals to be achieved by force of arms. It was called upon to equip the High Command with the necessary means to ensure the execution of those measures designed to satisfy the needs of the armed forces and the Nation.

At a meeting of the National Defense High Council (le Conseil Supérieur de la Défense Nationale) under the authority of the President of the Republic, the government received advice from both the Head of the National Defense Joint Chiefs of Staff and the Commanders in Chief. These figures, however, played only a consulting role. In this matter the civilian authority was pre-eminent. The National Defense High Council should have met in September 1939. Yet this unwieldly structure had not assembled since 1935; nor did it meet in either 1939 or 1940. This is one of the first dysfunctions which deserves underlining.

Within the government a specific role had been allotted to the National Defense Minister. Since the creation of that ministry in June 1936, the Minister was in charge of coordinating the activity of three departments: the Army, the Navy, and the Air Force. In particular, the Minister was to see to coordinating the employment of the armed forces along with the establishment and execution of armament programs. Using the General Secretariat of the National Defense High Council as his instrument, the Minister in peacetime presided over the National Defense Permanent Committee (Comité Permanent de la Défense nationale), which was in charge of the nation's preparation for war.

Edouard Daladier had taken on that heavy task in the Popular Front's first government. He was still in that capacity in September 1939 and would continue until 19 May 1940 in Paul Reynaud's Cabinet. Therefore, a study of the overall conduct of the war from September 1939 up until the French campaign calls first of all for a critical analysis of the government's activity in its own specific domain. This means carefully examining the government's deliberations concerning the goals of the war as well as reviewing the measures the government took in order to provide France with the means necessary to defend itself and to pursue the goals which it initially determined. Such a study must also take into account an essential fact, i.e. that France belonged to a coalition, an alliance system that provided for close consultation between the French and the British governments. Concerned with understanding the reasons behind the "strange defeat" of 1940 and assessing the specific responsibilities of the civilian authorities, historians must not hide certain facts – they must endeavor to render the whole reality. Thus, any presentation of the phoney war in France must take a high view of things.

Such a presentation cannot boil down to an overly "hexagonal" view of the conflict. The formula "immobile war" which has been used to evoke the period before the French campaign takes account of the land-forces on the borders of France, but it is too reductive. Indeed, it neglects the naval dimension of the conflict and the first peripheral operations in northern Europe. It also lends credit to a very static vision of the first months of the war.

This period is marked by important initiatives. The two Allies, convinced that Germany would make a western strike only late in the game, indeed hoped to have time to mobilize their potential for economic war against Germany, which was vulnerable because of its dependence on other countries for supplies. In the event of a long and total war that had already assumed a global dimension on the naval level, economic weapons would be necessarily privileged. Organizing this "economic war" preoccupied London and Paris when they envisaged peripheral operations.

The implementation of this economic war, the remarkable spurt in arms-production in France and Great Britain and the coordination brought about by Jean Monnet will receive only brief mention here; yet they must be taken into account before any attempt to evaluate the government's policy during the phoney war.

Defining the Stakes: the Military Leadership of the War During the Daladier Government

Given its responsibility for the overall conduct of the war, the government, as early as the tense period of August 1939, should have called a meeting of the National Defense High Council. A meeting on a smaller scale, however, was called on 23 August by the Foreign Affairs Minister Georges Bonnet. Participating members were the National Defense Permanent Committee, i.e. those ministers concerned with defense matters and the Chiefs of Staffs (with voting rights), along with the Minister of Foreign Affairs and a few key military figures.

Although the Council of Ministers, presided over by the President of the Republic Albert Lebrun, met the day before, the meeting on 23 August was decisive. It will allow us to study what decisions were to be made regarding the new German challenge in central Europe.

The President of the Council put the question: "Can France just stand by and watch Poland and Roumania disappear from the map of Europe?" Next he queried about the means that France had at its disposal in order to oppose the German move.

In his explanation of the diplomatic situation George Bonnet presented the most pessimistic scenario, i.e. western Europe would be attacked soon after Poland fell. In point of fact, he expected a negative response from the military figures. Would they, a year after Munich, weigh the pros and cons once again in order to seek a reprieve?

That was not the case, as the debates demonstrated. Indeed, General Gamelin expressed himself unambiguously: "The thing to do is to fulfill our commitments to Poland."[2] He thought he could put up worthy resistance and asked for the opinion of the Air Force. Here, the attitude of Guy La Chambre, the Air Force Minister, created an element of surprise. Favorably disposed toward compromise with Germany back in September 1938, now he did not want a repetition of Munich. Thanks to the progress in France and its cooperation with Britain, the nation ought to be able to keep its promises and accept the risk of a conflict. Yet it must be noted that General Vuillemin, the Air Force Chief of Staff, said nothing. In his view, France's strength still did not compare at all well with Germany's since British help would not come immediately. Guy La Chambre, however, set the tone: "Our air-power sit-

---

2. Fonds des Services historiques français – Service historique de l'Armée de Terre, henceforth referred to as SHAT, 5 N 579 – dossier 1 – Service historique de l'Armée de l'Air (SHAA) – Fonds Guy La Chambre, Z.12.1948.

uation must not weigh upon the government's decisions as it did in 1938." A bit later General Gamelin and Admiral Darlan declared: "the Army and the Navy are ready."

So France would fulfill her commitments, Daladier concluded, announcing the measures to be taken if in fact the Danzig crisis deteriorated and war broke out. A few hours later there was confirmation that the German-Soviet Pact had been signed, a diplomatic event bearing heavy consequences. It meant a crashing failure for Franco-British diplomacy which had started negotiations with the USSR that spring in order to avoid this collusion, a dreadful prospect since the 1920s and the Treaty of Rapallo.

From 24 August through 3 September several efforts were deployed in order to deflect the decisions made on 23 August. Those in favor of a pacifist solution did their best to see that compromise prevailed. There was set up a vast public opinion campaign, a veritable "remake" of the one organized in September 1938 in order to keep France in the peace-camp.

Aided from within the government by Georges Bonnet, Camille Chautemps and Anatole de Monzie, the pacifist current of the parliamentary Right, led by Pierre Laval and Joseph Caillaux in the Senate along with Jean Mistler and Pierre-Etienne Flandin in the Chamber, endeavored to win the day. The news about the German-Soviet Pact was considered proof that France's foreign policy had failed: the "Soviet betrayal" steered toward the choice of realistic solutions. Germany, fortified by its eastern neighbor's neutrality, had become a more formidable enemy. It was too dangerous to enter war in these conditions; therefore, it was necessary to battle for peace and, for the time being, to gain the help of another power considered as pacifist: Italy. At that point Pierre Laval reportedly made contact with the Italian ambassador to France (Guariglia) and Marshall Pétain (then in Spain), who could play the strong-man in a later scheme. Well informed about all these intrigues, the President of the Council, advised by Alexis Léger, the General Secretary of the Quai d'Orsay, and the Cabinet "hawks," Paul Reynaud and Georges Mandel, tried hard to foil Laval's plans. Yet his room for maneuver was limited.[3]

---

3. For more details about the attitude of the President of the Council, refer to my book *Edouard Daladier* (Paris,1993).

From late August until 2 September France played a certain "waiting game," before entirely committing itself to a steadfast course of action and declaring war on Germany. On 2 September Daladier's speech left little hope for the parliamentarians in favor of appeasement and the "doves" who, from within the government, were still invoking the possibility of Mussolini's mediation. The Munich way, brushed aside in Great Britain, was definitively excluded in France after the latest temporizing maneuvers to which General Gamelin lent his hand. "France and England," declared Edouard Daladier, "cannot stand by and watch a friendly nation destroyed, a forewarning of new undertakings directed against themselves." Thus, the government put France "in condition to act in accord with her vital interest and her honor."[4] On 3 September, at five o'clock in the afternoon, a few hours later than Great-Britain, France declared war on Germany.

After studying the initial stakes defined on 23 August and restated by Daladier on 2 September, one ought to ponder the evolution of the war-objectives of France and her British ally during the conflict's first months, marked by the crushing of Poland and Hitler's peace proposals.

The High Command's wait-and-see attitude and the inter-Allied decisions made at Abbeville by the Inter-Allied Supreme Council on 12 September are well known. A few unpublished documents, drawn from private French sources, reveal a great deal about the state of mind of French officials and military figures.[5]

Immediately after the German victories in Poland and the first manifestations of the Blitzkrieg on the eastern front, Gamelin realized that he needed to revise totally his initial assessments regarding Poland's ability to resist.

A fact of capital importance should be added here. It is clear that at the beginning of September Gamelin had received information about the Soviets' intentions, if not the exact terms of the secret protocol of 23 August. A note written to the President on 7 September 1939, the eve of the meeting of the War Committee,

---

    4. Declaration of Edouard Daladier to the Chamber of Deputies, 2 September 1939.
    5. Daladier collection in deposit at the Fondation Nationale des Sciences Politiques (FNSP) – 3 DA 1, dr 1, recently located in the Archives Nationales. See also SHAT, 5 N 581, dr 1.

clarifies: "One must bear in mind that Germany could not have got the Soviet-German pact free-of-charge. The advantages that were secretly granted to Russia came about only at the expense of Poland and the Baltic states."

On that date the text concluded on the need to give Poland emergency assistance. Yet the document specifies: "help compatible with the availability of French personnel and equipment."

These problems were brought up within the War Committee, an agency set up by the statutes regarding the organization of the nation in time of war. This agency, which was in charge of the military conduct of the war, was composed of the National Defense Permanent Committee. Under the authority of the President of the Republic, this joint structure drew together the main civilian and military authorities concerned with defense problems.

Edouard Daladier thought it preferable to debate the matter before the restricted audience of this War Committee, which was in principle responsible only for the military conduct of the war. At this decision-making level, the mission entrusted to the War Committee was to study the overall directives for the conduct and coordination of operations as well as the general distribution of resources.

The divisions within the Cabinet, hidden from the eyes of public opinion, had not grown fainter once war was declared. "At bottom," noted the President of the Senate Jeanneney, "the Cabinet reverts to its weak stance of 1939. Too many of its members are or will be hostile to war, no matter what happens."[6] Consequently, the head of the government, who had to wait a week before reshuffling his Cabinet, deliberately abstained from calling a meeting of his entire ministerial team in order to dodge the latest maneuvers of Georges Bonnet, who still held the portfolio of the Quai d'Orsay. Yet he knew that the Minister of Foreign Affairs had, in the person of General Gamelin, a fervent defender of the wait-and-see thesis. Now, the head of the National Defense Chiefs of Staff would play the determining role in deciding what assistance would be given to Poland. Indeed, on 7 September, in a select committee, Gamelin crudely stated to President Daladier and his colleagues: "Let's not hide from the facts and brain-wash ourselves about Poland. The

---

6. Jules Jeanneney, *Journal politique, septembre 1939 – juillet 1942*, Paris, 1972, p.8.

country's 'screwed'." The next day he specified: "The very fact that we find it impossible to extend our battle-lines rapidly limits our means of attracting the majority of the German forces and keeping them in front of us."[7]

Such were the orientations that led to the Franco-British summit on 12 September. Its conclusions were in fact the following: "No rush to begin massive land operations before we've maximized our means." As for Poland: "We cannot do much for her; the war will be won on the western front." These off-the-record remarks are a good translation of a conviction expressed by Neville Chamberlain, the British Prime Minister: "Time is on the side of the allied coalition." So why commit military resources prematurely, asked certain members of the High Command in Paris and in London?[8] Thus, national interests were given first priority, and for France there prevailed a very hexagonal conception of security. On 17 September news about the Soviet aggression in Poland confirmed Gamelin's prognostication. Poland was living its final days. While the ally "was sinking into the dark" after being struck by that bolt of lightning, a massive diplomatic offensive got under way. Set in motion by Germany, it was relayed in Europe by the Third International. News about the second German-Soviet pact on 28 September only confirmed the solid association between the Third Reich and the USSR. Would the two States intensify their cooperation? The government, which remained very vigilant and was doing its best to analyze how the conflict might evolve after the collapse of Poland, took this threat very seriously.

During the first days of October, the two parliamentary commissions for Foreign Affairs, one in the Senate and the other in the Chamber of Deputies, demanded a meeting with the President of the Council who, after the reshuffling that took place on 13 September, was in charge of the Ministry of Foreign Affairs. Once again it was necessary to study the evolution of the goals of the war. That coincided with the start of the peace campaign very cleverly organized by Chancellor Hitler, under Goebbels' advice.

7. SHAT, 5 N 581, dr. 1.
8. British papers, available for consultation at the Public Record Office (PRO) – CAB, 65, 3 WM 1939. See also François Bédarida, *La Stratégie secrète de la drôle de guerre* (Paris, 1979), pp.94-95.

German Peace Proposals, the Rebirth of Pacifism and the Government's Responses (October 1939)

Daladier's Cabinet had been reorganized on 13 September, and this eagerly awaited change had disappointed public opinion in France and abroad. While Bonnet's dismissal from the Quai d'Orsay was welcome news, all those who had hoped for the departure of the most notorious proponents of the Munich Pact objected to the fact that he remained on the ministerial team. The President, who was now handling the onerous tasks of National Defense and Foreign Affairs simultaneously, was therefore the main target of the parliamentarians' questions. Thus, Pierre-Etienne Flandin asked him on 29 September: "Is the government determined to pursue hostilities, despite any offers or proposals of mediation, truce or negotiation? If the answer is yes, what are France's war-objectives? Is the government determined to have these objectives debated and ratified by the parliamentary Assemblies?"[9] Here, of course, the point was to protest the lack of formal consultation of Parliament when war was declared and to test the government's intentions.

The replies given at that time were rather firm, even though they failed to elucidate all the questions that came up. On 6 October the head of the government made his clearest statement before the Senate in reply to a question regarding the objectives of the war after the fall of Poland. "In order to ensure France's indisputable security all the while avoiding unnecessary bloodshed for the nation, we must fight alongside others so that we do not one day find ourselves alone facing Hitler's Germany. England and France agree on the objectives of this war. Elbow to elbow, the two countries are struggling to survive." Yet one must note that the ideological aspect of the struggle is no longer stressed. "The goal is not to overthrow this regime or that, since each nation is free to choose how it will be governed. The goal is to put an end to a system of international relations founded on brute force."[10] Daladier manifested the same spirit on 10 October in an important radio address in response to Hitler's peace-proposals.

9. FNSP, 3 DA, dr 5 – Commissions parlementaires.
10. *Ibidem, idem.*

During this new phase of the war, the belligerents made ample use of psychological warfare. The Reich undertook a huge offensive whose purpose was to persuade France and Great Britain to put down their arms. That public opinion campaign relied particularly on the radio, and it can be said that there was a veritable "war of the air-waves." The German Chancellor and the head of the French government launched their appeals to public opinion from in front of microphones. Recorded on the air and widely broadcast, these speeches played a significant role in mobilizing opinion. The same can be said for Chamberlain's radio address in England.

On 6 October Hitler voiced Germany's desire for peace. Speaking at the Reichstag, he was in fact addressing international opinion and, in particular, London and Paris. After having justified Germany's annexations, he explained that there was no longer any reason for war because Germany's demands had been satisfied. Yet he also launched a challenge to the western Allies by proposing a great summit of the principal European powers, with controlled arms-reduction, the transfer of colonies to Germany and the solution of the Jewish problem on the agenda. He concluded with these words: "Let those who consider war a solution refuse this outstretched hand."[11]

While pacifist propaganda was being redeployed in France, the President's advisors, in particular the European associate-director Henri Hoppenot, transmitted to Edouard Daladier a very suggestive note that would inspire his radio address on 10 October. This unpublished note clearly stated France's war-objectives, formulated in relation to the situation: "The government," he wrote, "urgently needs to overturn this psychological climate in order to give Germany, the neutral countries, and the United States, the most powerful of these, the impression that we are as determined as the British." France's war-objectives had to be reaffirmed. Under what conditions could France one day put down arms? These conditions were the following: the reconstitution of an independent

11. Regarding these peace proposals, one may consult Charles Bloch, *Le IIIe Reich et la guerre* (Paris, 1986), pp.350-1. The author demonstrates well the pressure exercised by the High Command (in particular the OKH) in order to persuade Hitler to put off attacking on the western front. From this perspective, a diplomatic offensive toward the West was welcome: a new variant of psychological warfare was at work.

Poland with territorial guarantees; the revision, by a plebiscite conducted under international control, of the territorial modifications effected by force or the threat of force since 1938 in the political status of central Europe and the granting of an international guarantee for that revised status; the elimination of Nazism in Germany; finally, the convocation of an international conference for the purposes of establishing a basis for general cooperation "in order to facilitate the transformation of war-economies to peacetime economies and to prepare the groundwork for an equitable redistribution of raw materials."[12] This was the rough sketch of a program that could serve as a foundation for the elaboration of a future peace, at a time when Europe would be liberated from the threat of aggression.

It was in this frame of mind that, despite the pressure being exerted on him, the President of the Council made a speech on 10 October in reply to Hitler's proposals. "We will not put down our weapons," he affirmed, "without first having received sure guarantees of security. Our security must not be thrown into doubt every six months. Our victory must create a Europe freed from all forms of servitude."[13] While the speech contained a few statements of a more conciliatory nature, it was a blunt refusal of Hitler's proposals. This meant failure for the intrigues of the peace-clan and disappointment for Laval who had been hoping to play a diplomatic role in Rome and dreaming of a compromise brought about by Italy's mediation. The rather favorable reception that French opinion accorded Daladier's speech did not permit him to implement the political move he had been preparing: changing his team and setting up another government in which Philippe Pétain would be a player, or even, failing that, a transitional ministry in the hands of a resolutely conservative new majority. Still it must be noted that up until then a firm course had been maintained, and the notion of a "sham peace" (*paix blanche*) seemed pushed aside for a long time to come.

---

12. Private papers of the Ministère des Affaires Etrangères, MAE, France.
13. FNSP, Fonds Daladier, 3 DA 1, dr 2, sdra – Speech of 10 October. See also the press of 11 October that hailed the firmness of the speech, with only a few exceptions.

The Daladier Government and the Conduct of the War: Convergences and Divergences in the First Months of the Phoney War

The Direction of the War and Franco-British relations:

From October 1939 to May 1940 the two allies enjoyed a reprieve of seven months before the German attack on the western front, which began on 10 May after having been deferred several times. In the event of a long war, the two partners had to take advantage of the delays that resulted from the evolution of the conflict in order to conjugate their efforts and organize their cooperation in various areas. This was initially the task of the governments in charge of the overall conduct of the war and brought into association by the Supreme Inter-Allied Council.

Contrary to the conventional notion, this cooperation began in an altogether cordial climate, which is demonstrated by the correspondence between Neville Chamberlain and Edouard Daladier. The cooperation between England and France also implied consultation regarding war-objectives and the overall conduct of the war. Here divergences began to show up very early on. There was consensus by mid-September on the matter of aid to Poland; yet very soon the first differences of opinion set the government teams at cross-purposes. The main problem was their stance regarding neutral countries.

At the end of September the two heads of government brought up the "Balkan" questions and considered setting up a south-eastern defensive front which would rely on an allied Turkey. Yet Great Britain had a major worry: that of handling Italy with kid gloves. France, on the other hand, was hoping to take some risks and envisaged operations around the Dardanelles.[14] On this terrain, though, the military had the floor.

Indeed, from the beginning of the phoney war, different notions regarding the military conduct of the war began cropping up. An attentive reading of the Inter-Allied discussions shows

---

14. William Manchester, *Churchill*, v. 2: *L'Epreuve de la solitude* (Paris, 1990), and my essay in *Balkan Studies* 29 (1988), "Les Balkans dans la stratégie méditerranéenne de la France, avril 1939 – mai 1940," pp.71-88.

the growing influence of military leaders. While their designated role in these councils was to provide advice, they in fact came to exert very strong pressure and endeavored to win the day. On the British side, the presence of Churchill, Lord of the Admiralty and an influential member of the War Cabinet, was decisive. Thus, Winston Churchill, who first gained experience of the "hornets' nest of the Dardandelles" in the First World War, opposed premature engagements in the eastern Mediterranean and moderated the French fervor.

Later, there would be another conflict between General Gamelin who, with the agreement of Edouard Daladier, hoped to lend a hand to Finland and the British High Command, which was much more reserved. Facing the Soviet Union, the British, who were also defending their interests in the Far-East, remained wary. On this matter the British made their views clear during the Inter-Allied meeting on 5 February 1940. "The British Admiralty does not wish to have Russia as a declared enemy because of the two hundred submarines that this country could mobilize in the Far-East and in distant seas, and finally because of the threat that would weigh on the borders of India."[15]

While the French and the British were more and more clearly set against each other regarding the conduct of the war, internal divergences were becoming pronounced in France. In point of fact, the politico-military crisis was developing on several levels. In the High Command there reigned a serious malaise that initially seemed to be on a functional and technical level. It concerned the matter of the organization of the High Command and the distribution of tasks and functions. Yet behind the major conflict between General Gamelin and General Georges there emerged a political background.

General Gamelin should have retired in the fall of 1940. He had planned to leave the army by the end of 1939 in order to allow his successor, General Georges, to pick up the reins in the new year. Now, he modified his plans and endeavored more and more to deprive his colleague, General Georges, of any real means of action by fractioning to the extreme the organization of the general head-

---

15. Francois Bédarida, *La Stratégie Secrète de la drôle de guerre*, op. cit., p. 256.

quarters. The personal archives of the two men are very revealing regarding the political undertones of the matter, and these also appear in the private papers of the President of the Council. At the end of 1939 the prospect of another "succession" took shape, meaning a change in the government team.

The latent conflict between Edouard Daladier and Paul Reynaud burst out into the open over the Finnish question. Yet the matter really concerned older disagreements. Regarding the conduct of the war, the two men faced off against each other, though with buttoned foils at first. Paul Reynaud enjoyed solid support within the army: close to General Georges, he was also in relations with Weygand, Commander in Chief for the eastern Mediterranean front. He had also been very close to Colonel de Gaulle since 1935.

What was Marshall Pétain's role at this time? A confidential letter, written to General Georges in January 1940, is worth quoting here: "I spent three days in Paris incognito. I saw common friends and military men who filled me in on the poor organization of the Armed Forces' Command ... I earnestly request that you not leave your post for any reason, even if you have to swallow a few snakes. Nobody's in the right place; responsibilities are all tangled up; it's anarchy. Hang on and trust in the future."[16] This letter of 28 January sheds interesting light on the politico-military crisis of the winter of 1940. A few weeks later the political crisis was resolved by Edouard Daladier's resignation.

Harassed by the Parliament since November, the President of the Council had become personally involved in the debate over assistance to Finland, the victim of Soviet aggression. Looking favorably on diversion operations which, to his mind, would give the Allies a new reprieve, Edouard Daladier thought that public opinion would support him. A few weeks later criticism began raining down, and within Parliament the conservative Right allied with Paul Reynaud's friends in order to deal the head of the government the final blow once the fall of Finland was announced on 13 March. Yet the change did not occur in good circumstances. After Edouard Daladier's resignation on 20 March, Paul Reynaud

16. SHAT, Private papers of General Georges.

did not succeed in setting up a real War Cabinet, comparable to the one that Churchill was able to set up a bit later. The composition of the new team, which included several notorious pacifists like Frossard and Lamoureux, was worrisome. Bearing in mind the disagreements that opposed Daladier and Reynaud, one may wonder about the role of those who heavily contributed to the deterioration of the political climate in France over the course of the winter. The parliamentarians, whose role we have noted in September-October 1938, the men favorable to a "sham peace" ("*paix blanche*") were bound and determined to destroy the initial understanding between Daladier and Reynaud. They also inspired a decision made after Sedan: making Pétain part of Paul Reynaud's reshuffled Cabinet, vice-president of the Council.

Historians have not yet totally clarified this "hidden face" of the phoney war. Recent publications, however, ought to facilitate a better understanding of Pierre Laval's role during this first phase of the conflict.[17]

Edouard Daladier and the Economic War: A Poorly Known Aspect of the Phoney War

One also ought to ponder another dimension of the struggle against Germany, the use of economic warfare. The economic war began to get organized in September 1939. The creation of an Arms Ministry was the most eagerly awaited innovation at the time of the cabinet reshuffling on 13 September 1939. As we have noted, the Daladier Cabinet was to be recast on that date. Both in France and abroad, noteworthy upheavals were expected. One hoped for, as Jean Zay remarked, "a Cabinet of energetic war" that would include men of diverse opinions, plus a few experts; in short, something new![18] In fact, the Sacred Union (*l'Union Sacrée*) was in the background of the first combinations. Edouard Daladier, who already back in 1938 had dreamed of bringing SFIO representatives into the ministerial team he was forming in April, hoped to

---

17. A biography by Jean-Paul Cointet, *Laval*, published by Fayard in 1993.
18. Jean Zay, *Carnets secrets* (Paris, 1942), p.87.

gain their cooperation right after the declaration of war. Sounding like Viviani, he had tried to persuade Léon Blum to repeat the experience of which he himself had been a part alongside Marcel Sembat in August 1914. The SFIO's refusal was a serious failure. With the participation of the socialists, Edouard Daladier would have been better able to gain the cooperation of those who represented "these vital forces of the nation" that the President of the Council hoped to mobilize in his grand project of revitalizing the rearmament program.[19]

Implementing the measures concerning the nation's economic mobilization implied constraints that the defenders of liberalism could find worrisome. Such arguments had been stressed by the parliamentary pacifists. Choosing the Arms Minister was therefore a delicate operation. The President of the Council, who had become the Minister of Foreign Affairs, had to be able to delegate important responsibilities to the person holding that post. He had to choose a competent, well-known figure who was above political intrigue. In short, Edouard Daladier was looking for a man whom he could trust. He chose Raoul Dautry and assigned him a heavy mission: that of giving fresh impetus to the French rearmament program.

While public opinion was disappointed by the mere patch-up job for the cabinet as a whole, the choice of the Arms Minister was very broadly endorsed. Lucien Lamoureux wrote on 15 September: "The new Cabinet really rankles the press and almost all the parties ... It wasn't worth the trouble to labor six days in order to give birth to such a mousy thing."[20] Still he noted that public opinion welcomed the arrival of Raoul Dautry, an expert from the world of industry.

Raoul Dautry's itinerary is completely different from that of Edouard Daladier's other colleagues. Starting out in 1903 as simple overseer in the North rail-network at Saint-Denis, this technician moved quickly up the ranks. In 1928 he became the director of the West network. In 1937 he played an essential role when the networks were fused, and he actively participated in the creation of

19. See the Dautry collection at the Archives Nationales, AN, 307 AP 104.
20. Lucien Lamoureux, Unpublished memoirs, available for consultation at the BDIC, Paris.

the SNCF, of which he became the director. In January 1938 he became a member of the Commission of Industrial and Economic Organization, which first endeavored to chart the economic situation, then recommended measures necessary for the renovation of France's industrial fabric. In contact with the world of research, he was known for his independent mind and concern with helping people coming from different worlds work together. It was hoped that Dautry, who was appreciated for his fine management skills and scientific rigor, would be a minister who would know how to enter into dialogue with labor-union representatives and various individuals involved with industrial mobilization.

Installed at the Majestic Hotel, he surrounded himself with a dynamic team headed up by the Polytechnician Jules Antonini, his former colleague at the SNCF. Politicians labeled this move "the invasion of the technicians." It was also the arrival of a young generation of official representatives.[21]

Henceforth, the constant preoccupation of the new Minister was to keep on doing field-work and to escape bureaucratic sluggishness. He thought it necessary to adopt a method right from the start, which he presented in the following terms: "select precise goals and set up the order of their priority, galvanize energy, always keep the departments on tenterhooks, get them organized, shield them from interference, from wherever it may come."[22]

It is interesting to note that Dautry's tone here brings to mind remarks made by Colonel de Gaulle. After a few weeks Raoul Dautry realized the massive scale of the task awaiting him. Indeed, France in the fall of 1939 was handicapped by long-standing structural deficiencies. Despite a few good recent performances and a notable rise in the indicator of industrial production after January, severe failings in the industries producing capital equipment still held back the development of the arms sector. Anxious to boost productivity, Raoul Dautry had at great length explained to Edouard Daladier just what had to be done.

---

21. Bichelonne and Jean Jardin were among Dautry's colleagues. See the Dautry papers in the collections deposited at the Archives Nationales, AN 304 AP 104, also Pierre Assouline, *Jean Jardin, 1904-76: Une éminence grise* (Paris, 1986).

22. Dautry Papers, idem., ibidem.

There were three goals to pursue: accelerating the mobilization of industrial means, facilitating financial mobilization, reinforcing the mobilization of labor. Achieving these three goals presupposed the implementation of economic and social policies that would "blow up" certain obstacles. It was a matter of going far beyond the measures already undertaken by Paul Reynaud since November 1938. Furthermore, the acceleration of the armaments program presupposed close cooperation with Great Britain, especially with regard to organizing the purchasing missions undertaken by the two Allies abroad.

Since the spring of 1938, during which there were exchanges with London at the end of April, Edouard Daladier and his close colleagues had set up the foundation of economic cooperation between the two partners in order to avoid, in the event of a conflict, the errors that had been committed at the beginning of the First World War. In the case of a long and total war, the organization of a Franco-British coalition hostile to Germany would plan the concerted mobilization of the two nations' economic resources. It would examine the matter of supplies and freight in war-time, plan the organization of financial cooperation and study the distribution of war-expenditures between the Allies. As soon as the new government was formed on 13 September, Edouard Daladier, Paul Reynaud, Dautry, Gentin, the Commerce Minister and Pernot, the Blockade Minister constituted a think-tank concentrating on the problems posed by Franco-British cooperation. Advised by Daniel Serruys, the High Commissioner of the National Economy, the President of the Council was well aware of all the stakes, and he was convinced that it was urgent to set up structures of coordination.

In Great Britain there was also a new team directing the war-effort. Here the entry of Winston Churchill, one of the fiercest opponents of "appeasement," into Neville Chamberlain's War Cabinet was the most outstanding feature.[23] Very much in favor of this cooperation, Churchill acted as the "goad" in the War Cabinet. Aware of the need to reinforce naval cooperation, he played a

---

23. The most important English sources may be consulted at the Public Record Office. This collection contains a very important exchange of letters between Edouard Daladier and Neville Chamberlain under the call-number PREM 1-4-10.

very important role in the Inter-Allied discussions that took place within the framework of the structures set up by the statutes instituting Inter-Allied cooperation.[24]

On 20 September, two days after the meeting of the Supreme Inter-Allied Council at Brighton, Edouard Daladier wrote to Neville Chamberlain in order to propose the creation of a Franco-British Economic Coordinating Committee[25] and to suggest the name of a person suited to lead it. He was already thinking about Jean Monnet, hoping to gain London's support.[26]

Jean Monnet's role in setting up structures of coordination during the First World War is well-known. Afterwards, he had also carried out the first purchasing mission in the United States. The choice of Monnet was accepted by London on 27 September, and his mission was studied at an Inter-Allied meeting devoted to economic coordination in London on 30 September.[27] The organization was set up during October and November. It relied on permanent executive committees specialized in various domains: supplies, armaments and raw materials, oil, aeronautics, production and purchases, maritime transport. The first agreements were made on 17 November regarding the essential matter of maritime transport, given France's insufficiency, especially regarding oil transport. The organization of purchasing missions was also made a priority. That began taking shape in December, when the first joint mission for purchasing aeronautic equipment was to take place in the United States. On the other hand, technical cooperation in the area of armament production took longer to set up. Tank construction only became effective in March, and semi-product production in April.[28]

One may note that, despite the limited nature of this collaboration, by the end of the winter the Allies had achieved a degree of

24. Concerning Churchill's role, see William Manchester, *Churchill*, vol. 2: *L'Epreuve de la solitude, op.cit.*
25. PRO, PREM, 1.4.10 – Daladier-Chamberlain correspondence about Franco-British economic cooperation.
26. Collection available for consultation in Washington, NACA, R9 59, 711 and the book by John McVickar Haight, *American Aid to France 1938-40* (New York, 1970).
27. Public Record Office (PRO), PRO CAB 21, 748.
28. See Dautry papers, AN, 307 AP, 104.

cooperation that had not been approached four years after the start of the First World War.

This coordination presupposed financial agreements that were signed on 13 December 1939. Paul Reynaud and the Chancellor Sir John Simon had managed, after numerous meetings since the end of September, to lay the foundation for real financial cooperation. This accord planned monetary solidarity, the division of war-expenditures and economic solidarity. France was able to negotiate as a partner because Paul Reynaud, the previous autumn, had been able to bring about the return of a great part of exiled capital, which means that one can talk about the reconstitution of a "real war treasury." The two countries undertook to make a fair share of the expenditures in dollars or in gold borne by each and necessitated by the conduct of the war. They were to cooperate on price-policy in order to avoid any detrimental disparity and attempt to take out joint-loans.[29] Their purchasing missions in the United States are a good illustration of the positive aspects of this cooperation.

The Paris-London-Washington Axis, The First Stages of Transatlantic Cooperation During the Phoney War

The efforts deployed since the fall of 1938 for the purposes of laying a foundation for Atlantic cooperation and associating the United States with the Franco-British war effort represent one of the essential axes of Paris's foreign policy.

It often escapes attention that one of Edouard Daladier's first initiatives just after Munich was to organize an impromptu lunch with the American ambassador to Paris, William Bullitt, Jean Monnet, Guy La Chambre and the French President in order to set up an initial purchasing mission for aeronautic material.

Given the clear insufficiency of French aeronautical production that was revealed shortly before Munich, the French government

---

29. In addition to the collections already cited, Robert Frank's work on financing rearmament must be consulted, especially *Le Prix du réarmement français* (Paris, 1982). See also the Fonds Paul Reynaud at the Archives Nationales, AN 74 AP 17.

thought it indispensable to obtain help from the most powerful nation in the world, the former partner of London and Paris in 1917 and 1918. Many obstacles had to be overcome in order to convince Congress and the Roosevelt administration to modify the Neutrality Act's rules of application. The situation, already litigious in peace-time, worsened after the declaration of war. Indeed, the arms embargo was officially declared on 5 September 1939.

Yet on 8 September Daladier received William Bullitt, who had become a friend of his, and urged him to approach Roosevelt in order to obtain a revision of the Neutrality Act. There began a real race against the clock. Indeed, these modifications had to come about very quickly since big orders had already been placed with the Glenn Martin and Curtiss firms; other contracts were being negotiated. Would they have to cancel the arrangements already made and reconsider the contracts?

While public opinion was evolving in the United States and various pressures were at work inside Congress, Jean Monnet worked to bring about tripartite negotiations. Washington hoped to negotiate with joint Franco-British missions.[30] In favor of boosting American aeronautical production in the event of a world conflict, several of Roosevelt's colleagues had succeeded in interesting industrialists in a construction program that presupposed significant investments. The prospect of the demand offered by the French and British markets would allow for faster profits on the initial investments. Theodore R. Wright, who was the director of the Curtiss Wright Corporation and an expert advisor to the Defense Council, played an essential role. The assurance, which was soon forthcoming from experts of the French and British governments, of speedy financial settlements made it possible to propose a solution that gained the approval of Congress. After lengthy debate, Congress passed a new law of "neutrality" that modified the previous clauses. On 4 November 1939 the text voted by Congress eliminated the embargo. Arms and munitions, like all other commodities, would henceforth ben-

---

30. The most important papers on this subject may be consulted at Washington's National Archives (NACA). See NACA R9 59.711 and Record Group 18, Army Air Force Files, File 452-1. French books on this matter are rare – please refer to my contribution in the collective work: *L'Economie de guerre* (Montpellier, 1989).

efit from the cash-and-carry clause. This was an important personal triumph for Roosevelt as well as a victory for Franco-British diplomacy. It was also an important turning-point in the history of the cooperation among the three democracies. Indeed, the new clauses made it possible to regularize pending contracts and to increase future orders. Yet it must be noted that France played the driving role in getting these negotiations going; Daladier hoped to hasten the conclusion of new contracts while Chamberlain was temporizing. The technical and financial problems that were cropping up worried the French President of the Council. According to the testimony of Bullitt, who was asked to lunch on 20 November with the Air-Force Minister, Guy La Chambre, the head of the French government expressed his concerns in these terms: "If it is truly impossible to get the planes that we are requesting from the United States, I had better step down as President of the Council. I won't be the one to make peace in conformity with Germany's wishes."[31]

For a few weeks, as we have seen, parliamentary commissions had been harassing the President of the Council. Inside the Senate the clan of the Italophiles had roused themselves in order to recommend examining Hitler's peace-proposals. Why couldn't one contemplate resorting to the good offices of Italy and calmly consider examining these peace-proposals on an honorable basis! The arguments made by these pacifist parliamentarians were mainly founded on an acknowledgment of the relative strength of the parties. France and Great Britain had entered the rearmament race too late. Especially in the aeronautical domain, they could not make up for their late start since the rhythm of production was faster in Germany than in France and Great Britain.

It was in order to respond to these arguments, which were not devoid of realism, that Edouard Daladier attached so much importance to the success of the purchasing mission of aeronautical material. The last obstacles were overcome at the end of November. According to the terms of the Franco-British accord of 25 November, the Allies' United States Purchasing Committee was

---

31. William Bullitt, *For the President, Personal and Secret*, O. Bullitt (ed.) (London, 1973). See also Daladier papers, FNSP, 3 DA 3, dr 4, s drb.

set up with Purvis as its London president and Bloch-Lainé as its Paris president. Under the Committee's authority, two missions, French and British, acting in concert, would negotiate with the American administration and the firms through a Liaison Committee placed under the responsibility of Morgenthau, the American Secretary of the Treasury. The French orders were for various kinds of planes, diving fighter-bombers, cargo bombers, air-plane motors, projectors (*projecteurs*) ....

While most of the orders were placed from January through April 1940 with delivery-dates spread out from the fall of 1940 through the fall of 1941, older contracts drawn up in 1939 planned deliveries for the spring of 1940. In fact, before the armistice, 1,000 planes made in the United States had been delivered and 469 had been taken into account by the Air-Force. Yet the highest performance machines had not been delivered by this time. Moreover, certain deliveries made in North Africa took place in miserable conditions; some, which occurred at the start of the French campaign, were improvised jobs from start to finish.[32]

Must one conclude that the French mission to the United States was a failure? Cooperation among England, France and the United States had not produced all the anticipated results; yet it marked a decisive turning-point in the relations between the Allies and the United States. The Franco-British financial contribution facilitated a significant spurt in investments which helped modernize the American production-apparatus. While France had not been able to benefit from a noteworthy part of the orders, Great Britain would take over a significant number of units that were initially meant for France. Finally, in the United States, despite whatever reservations remained in certain military and civilian circles, the principle of economic cooperation was no longer in doubt. The contacts that had been established would later facilitate the development of a collaboration of a totally different scope. Yet the foundations of transatlantic cooperation had been laid down in 1938-1940.

---

32. Archives SHAA, Fonds Guy La Chambre and personal testimony from General Gallois, September 1985. See also John McVickar Haight, *American Aid to France 1938-40, op.cit.*

An Assessment of the Rearmament Effort on the Eve of the French Campaign

Soon after the defeat there began a debate about the value of French equipment and the opponent's relative strength at the time of Germany's attack to the West. We all know that at the end of summer the Vichy regime inculpated the designated culprits, Edouard Daladier and Robert Jacomet, the National Defense Minister and the General Inspector of Arms. The Riom trial aimed to prove the lack of war-preparation and the civilian authorities' incompetence. Now, this trial came to a sudden end when the defense began its arguments. Based on important documents drawn from official sources, the defendants, Daladier in particular, did their best to underscore the positive aspects of the rearmament work started in 1936 without denying the indisputable insufficiency of the French military apparatus and the limits of the work accomplished by the spring of 1940. We recall that France did not begin massive rearmament until after the adoption of a four-year plan for the Army and the Navy that had been established in September 1936. Most of the materials ordered starting in the winter of 1937 were to be delivered in 1941. In the aeronautical domain the delays were still longer since the modernization plan for the Air Force did not materialize until April 1938.[33]

The implementation of social legislation, especially the application of the 40 hour work-week law, as well as various situational and structural factors led to a slow-down of the impetus given to rearmament starting in 1936. The situation was critical during the summer of 1938, since the productivity-index fell off significantly for the entire industrial sector and bottlenecks blocked upstream the development of branches working for rearmament. At this point Paul Reynaud, who arrived at the rue de Rivoli in November 1938, managed to have orders in council approved that introduced "liberal surgery" and unblocked the situation. The return of capital facilitated the resumption of investment, and production took off again in 1939.[34]

33. Charles Christienne et Pierre Lissarague, *Histoire de l'aviation militaire – L'armée de l'Air, 1928-81* (Paris, 1981), p.310, Archives du SHAA, Fonds Guy La Chambre.
34. Emmanuel Chadeau, *L'Industrie aéronautique en France, 1900-50 – de Blériot à Dassaul*, (Paris, 1987).

Yet significant results did not appear until the beginning of 1940 when there occurred a spurt in production capacity which allowed massive increases in the deliveries made to the armed forces. However, the man-in-charge of the rearmament effort, Raoul Dautry, bitterly noted that he had inherited a heavy liability. Citing important labor-documents which showed a conflict between two conceptions of "man-power mobilization," he also denounced errors that could be attributed to the poor relations between civilian and military authorities. Numerous dysfunctions continued to affect the organization of industrial mobilization and risked compromising the fragile results that had been obtained. Still the right picture of the situation is not as grim as the one drawn by the Vichy authorities, who were trying to stigmatize the work of the last governments of the Third Republic. The right picture is in half-tones.

* * *

The last governments of the Third Republic had inherited a difficult situation. Incumbent upon them was the onerous task of straightening out the French economy, which was still in crisis in the spring of 1938. All the while pursuing this goal, they had to prepare the nation for a showdown with Germany, which the general staff had foreseen very early on.

The civilian authorities, endorsing the views of the official strategists, had counted on a long war which would allow the Franco-British coalition to get organized and to boost the war-industries. In the event of a "world and total" war, the French decision-makers and certain experts like Jean Monnet counted on the intervention of the United States, which was already providing aeronautical material and backing loans.

While the later evolution of the conflict, long and world-wide, confirmed these views, the French strategists had still made certain weighty analytical errors. They had not taken into account a certain scenario, even though it was foreseeable, and one enacted by the German High-Command: the Blitzkrieg which, after having struck to the East, would strike in the West in the spring of 1940. Underestimating information about this method, General Gamelin also refused to draw a lesson from the war in Poland.

Thus, in the first phase of the war, neither the military nor the civilian authorities took advantage of the reprieve granted them in order to try and adapt the military apparatus and the civilian structures to the adversary's strategy. While certain voices spoke up in various circles in order to denounce this lack of foresight, they did not manage to make themselves heard.

After long months of firm reliance on the status quo while discord was developing on the highest levels, the French did not have the clear sense that "the nation was in danger." The brutality of the German offensive and the enemy's swift thrust would bring about a dramatic "moral surprise" for French public opinion. The tragic events that tossed millions of French men and women on the roads "in a state of shock" would create lasting traumatism. The war revealed weaknesses in the French military system. It also illuminated the vulnerability of the political regime and the fragile nature of the entire social body, as Marc Bloch pointed out so well in his book *L'Etrange Défaite*.

Translated by Gretchen van Slyke

VI

THE MISSED OPPORTUNITY

French Refugee Policy in Wartime, 1939-1940[1]

*Vicki Caron**

"Contemporary history has created a new kind of human being – the kind that are put in concentration camps by their foes and internment camps by their friends."

Hannah Arendt[2]

Throughout the 1930s, France's treatment of Central and East European refugees fluctuated between a hard-line policy that sought to get rid of them and a more liberal one that allowed at least some to remain in order to strengthen the country economically and militarily. When war was declared on 3 September 1939, the tension between these alternatives did not disappear, but instead became sharper. Already in the spring of 1939, despite the harsh anti-immigrant decree laws of the previous year,[3] the gov-

---

1. The translations of passages included in the text are generally mine. Many of the documents located in the American Joint Distribution Committee (henceforth JDC) Archives, New York, however, were already translated.
2. Cited in Michael R. Marrus, Introduction, *Refugees in the Age of Total War*, Anna C. Bramwell, ed. (London, 1988), p. 6.
3. According to the decree law of 2 May 1938, the police had the right to impose stiff fines and even prison sentences on illegal refugees. The decree law of 12 November 1938 created a special border police to keep out illegal immigrants and mandated the creation of internment camps for those unable to depart. For the texts

ernment passed a series of measures that indicated a willingness to use the country's 3,000,000 immigrants to prepare for the war effort. On 12 April, in response to pressure from the General Staff and public opinion, the government announced a new decree law that facilitated the enlistment of foreigners into the regular army. Henceforth, all male foreigners who had been in the country more than two months were required to serve during peacetime either in the regular army or the Foreign Legion, while during wartime they were required to serve either in the *prestataire* service – noncombatant auxiliary labor service – or in the regular army if they were beneficiaries of the right of asylum.[4] On 21 April another decree law attempted to facilitate the settlement of foreign industrialists on French soil, especially those whose activities might prove useful in the event of war.[5] When war became a reality, however, these plans fell by the wayside. In response to fifth column fears the government completely banned foreigners from serving in the regular army, while it resorted to a policy of mass internment for Central European males, who were now declared "enemy aliens."

Nevertheless, until the German invasion of the Low Countries in May 1940, pressures militating in favor of a more liberal refugee policy continued to operate. In response to public pressure at

---

of these decree laws see *Journal officiel: lois et décrets* (henceforth, *JOLD*), 12-13 November 1938, pp. 12920-12924; *Le Temps*, 5 May 1938, p. 4; "Surveillance et contrôle des étrangers," *Le Temps*, 14 November 1938, p. 2; "La surveillance et le contrôle des étrangers," *Le Matin*, 13 November 1938, p. 6. See also Hanna Schramm and Barbara Vormeier, *Vivre à Gurs: Un camp de concentration français, 1940-41*, trans. Irène Petit (Paris, 1979), pp. 206-207, 223-224.

4. On the decree law of 12 April 1939 see *JOLD*, 16 April 1939, pp. 4910-4911; "Conférence interministérielle relative au régime des étrangers," *Le Matin*, 14 April 1939, p. 2; "Le statut des étrangers résidant en France," *Le Matin*, 16 April 1939, p. 1; "Le statut des étrangers," *Le Temps*, 18 April 1939, p. 1; "Les décrets-lois sur les étrangers," *Le Populaire*, 17 April 1939, p. 5; Arieh Tartakower and Kurt R. Grossmann, *The Jewish Refugee* (New York, 1944), pp. 142-144; Schramm and Vormeier, pp. 239-240. Beneficiaries of the right to asylum included Nansen and Saar refugees and German beneficiaries of the League of Nations' "Provisional Arrangement Concerning the Status of Refugees Coming from Germany," signed in Geneva on 4 July 1936. As a result of this accord, approximately 6,500 German refugees were officially granted asylum in France during the Popular Front.

5. On the decree law of 21 April 1939, see *JOLD*, 22 April 1939, p. 5,237, mimeograph extract in Archives of the Préfecture de Police, Paris (APP) DA 783 (Règlements).

home and abroad, the government created *criblage* or *sifting commissions* to review the dossiers of all internees to determine who were Nazi sympathizers and who were loyal to the Allied cause. Moreover, despite considerable delays, efforts were eventually made to utilize the refugees militarily. Certain groups of refugees – the Poles and Czechs – were allowed to join their respective national legions. Others, depending upon their age and fitness, were given the option of joining the Foreign Legion or enlisting for prestataire service.

This progress was brought to an abrupt halt by the German invasion. In response to a second wave of fifth column hysteria, the government resorted again to wholesale internments of Central European refugees. These were far more comprehensive than those of September, and for the first time included women. It was only at this moment, when France most needed additional manpower, that the effort to utilize refugees was abandoned. Whether a more determined and efficient use of the refugees would have made any difference to the outcome of the battle for France is impossible to know. What is clear, however, is that the government lost a significant opportunity to draw upon an important and highly spirited source of anti-Nazi fighting power. Military exigencies gave way to suspicion of fifth columns, procrastination, bureaucratic ineptitude, and even overt xenophobia and antisemitism, suggesting that the administration never understood the urgency of mobilizing every available resource. From the vantage point of the refugees, this missed opportunity became emblematic of the political ineptitude and lack of determination that led to the debacle of June 1940.

Although the internment of "enemy aliens" was certainly a possibility with the outbreak of war,[6] it was by no means predestined. Until 1 September, there were numerous indications that France intended to treat German, Austrian, Czech and Saar refugees with considerable leniency and to use them, together with the large mass of stateless refugees, including East European Jews, to serve

---

6. As early as 29 December 1937, Rudolf Breitscheid expressed the fear that "tous les réfugiés allemands seront, en cas de conflit, envoyés dans des camps de concentration." Cited in Rita Thalmann, "L'émigration allemande et l'opinion française de 1936 à 1939," in *Deutschland u. Frankreich, 1936-39* (Munich, 1981), p. 57.

in some capacity in the armed forces. According to a police report of February 1939, only White Russian émigrés were suspected of harboring pro-Nazi sympathies. Germans, however, were regarded as politically reliable. Despite their strong sense of German identity, these refugees, this report maintained, felt they had been "cast out of the 'German national body,'" and regarded a "European conflagration ... [as] a generalized form of civil war."[7]

Moreover, the government did nothing to deter those Central European refugees, who, together with thousands of other foreigners, turned out *en masse* to sign up for military service. Already in the spring, just after the proclamation of the 12 April decree law, both the police and press reported thousands of foreigners volunteering,[8] and in September this trend reached a crescendo. Only days after the outbreak of war, French military authorities admitted they were unable to cope with this deluge, and they turned the registration process over to private associations, such as the Amis de la République and the Ligue Internationale contre l'Antisémitisme (LICA).[9] According to the newspaper *L' Epoque*, the Amis de la République registered over 1,000 foreigners per day in September, while the Jewish War Veterans registered over 9,000 Jewish immigrants for regular army service as of 8 October, and another 9,000 for duty in the Polish and Czech Legions.[10] This registration drive

7. Police Report, "L' émigration en face de la perspective d'une guerre européenne," February 1939, APP BA Provisoire 407, dos. 13. pp. 112-4.
8. Police Report, 20 April 1939, APP BA 1812, 79.501-882-C; "Autour des enrôlements d'étrangers," *Le Petit Parisien*, 19 April 1939, p. 5. See also "Les étrangers et la France: Une délégation des Amis de la République française chez M. Albert Sarraut," *Le Petit Parisien*, 11 May 1939, p. 2; Paul Delon, "Si la démocratie française était en danger, les immigrés répondraient à son appel," *L' Humanité*, 16 April 1939; Tartakower and Grossmann, pp. 144-145.
9. "Pour les étrangers amis de la France," *L' Oeuvre*, 6 September 1939, p. 4.
10. "L' enrôlement des volontaires étrangers est entré dans sa phase de réalisation," *L' Epoque*, 11 September 1939, p. 4; "Des étrangers appartenant à 55 nationalités offrent leurs services à la France," *L' Epoque*, 17 September 1939, p. 3; "Pour les étrangers amis de la France," *L' Oeuvre*, 6 September 1939, p. 4; "L' enrôlement des étrangers," *L' Oeuvre*, 11 September 1939, p. 5; "Les étrangers résidant en France se mettent au service du pays," *Le Populaire*, 2 September 1939, p. 2; "30,000 Aliens Aid France: Foreigners from 55 Nations ask for War Duties," *New York Times* (henceforth, *NYT*), 5 March 1940, p. 5; Ruth Fabian and Corinna Coulmas, *Die Deutsche Emigration in Frankreich nach 1933* (Munich, 1978), p. 67; Zosa Szajkowski, *Jews and the*

was enthusiastically endorsed by the various émigré associations. German refugees, the Fédération des Émigrés d'Allemagne en France declared, "will fulfill their duty with the same devotion, the same spirit and the same courage as other Frenchmen."[11] As the émigré writer and journalist, Leo Lania, explained, for these refugees "who had lost ... everything ... faith in France was the only barrier between themselves and bottomless despair."[12]

Despite this outpouring of pro-French loyalties, the government ultimately chose to ignore the provisions of the 12 April decree law and instead fell back on a policy treating foreigners in general and Central Europeans in particular as potential "enemy aliens." On 8 September Prime Minister Edouard Daladier declared that "foreigners are authorized to enlist for the duration of the war in the Foreign Legion and the Foreign Legion only."[13] This order came as a bitter pill for most foreigners since they wanted above all to serve in the regular army, and service in the Legion, even if "only" for the duration of the war rather than the regular five-year stint, was not an attractive option given its harsh disciplinary regime and reputation as a haven for hardened criminals. An even more severe fate lay in store for German, Austrian, Czech and Saar refugees. On 4 September a decree was announced ordering all males from "Greater Germany" and between the ages of 17 and 50 to report to

---

French Foreign Legion (New York, 1975), p. 60; Leo Lania, *The Darkest Hour: Adventures and Escapes* (Boston, 1941), p. 10; Pierre Lazareff, *Deadline: The Behind-the-Scenes Story of the Last Decade in France* (New York, 1942), p. 249.

11. "Appel des étrangers vivant sur le sol français," *Le Populaire*, 30 August 1939, p. 4. For statements of other émigré organizations, see "Un vibrant appel des organisations des étrangers vivant en France," *L' Epoque*, 30 August 1939, pp. 1, 5; "Le loyalisme des émigrés," *L' Oeuvre*, 30 August 1939, p. 5; "Les étrangers et les événements actuels," *Le Peuple*, 1 September 1939, pp. 1-2. For statements of Jewish immigrant organizations, see "France: Les Juifs immigrés au service de la France," *L' Univers israélite*, 5 May 1939, p. 595, clipped in Archives of the Alliance Israélite Universelle, Paris (AIU) Ms. 650, Boîte 13 (46); "Les immigrés aux côtés de la France," *Le Populaire*, 29 August 1939, p. 3; "Le loyalisme des immigrés," *L' Oeuvre*, 29 August 1939, p. 7; J. Biélinky, "L'Immigration juive en France," *La Juste Parole*, No. 63, 1 December 1939, pp. 7-9.

12. Lania, p. 9.

13. President of the Council, Ministry of National Defense and War, Circular No. 464, 8 September 1939, Archives, Service Historique de l'Armée de Terre (SHAT) 7N 2475 (dos. 3).

designated assembly centers; ten days later this age limit was extended to 65. Those summoned were told to bring a two-day supply of food, as well as blankets, underwear and eating utensils. All other subjects of "Greater Germany" – men and women – were ordered to report to police headquarters or city halls to apply for new identity papers and were henceforth forbidden to leave their neighborhoods without police authorization.[14] Most seriously, the government froze the bank accounts of the detainees, inflicting severe economic hardship on their families.[15]

Although the refugees had been told to prepare for a 48-hour stay, most were detained for at least ten days and sometimes up to a few weeks.[16] At the Colombes Stadium outside Paris it took several days to register the 10,000 refugees who reported. Living conditions were abysmal. A single water pump served the entire camp

14. This decree was issued on 1 September 1939 and appeared in the Journal Officiel on 4 September. See JOLD, 1939, pp. 11091 ff; "Appendix No. 20," 3 September 1939, JDC, No. 617; Schramm and Vormeier, pp. 244-247; Vormeier, "La situation des émigrés allemands en France pendant la guerre," in Emigrés français en Allemagne; Emigrés allemands en France, 1685-1945 (Paris, 1983), pp. 155, 159; Vormeier, "La situation des réfugiés en provenance d'Allemagne, septembre 1939-juillet 1942," in Jacques Grandjonc, ed., Les Camps en Provence: Exil, internement, déportation, 1933-44 (Aix-en-Provence, 1984), pp. 88-89; "Le premier camp de concentration pour les ressortissants allemands est créé," L' Oeuvre, 7 September 1939, p. 6; "L'internement des sujets allemands," L' Oeuvre, 18 September 1939, p. 4; Hans Escher, "Avec les réfugiés ex-autrichiens dans les camps: Du Stade de Colombes à Meslay-du-Maine (Septembre 1939-mai 1940)," Archives juives, No. 1, 1982, pp. 9-18; Hans-Albert Walter, "Internierung in Frankreich zur Situation der exilierten deutschen Schriftsteller Politiker und Publizisten nach Beginn des Zweiten Weltkriegs," Jahresrins, 1970, p. 285; Walter F. Peterson, The Berlin Liberal Press in Exile (Tübingen, 1987), p. 241; Michael Schapiro, "German Refugees in France," Contemporary Jewish Record, vol. III, 1940, p. 137; Robert M.W. Kempner, "The Enemy Alien Problem in the Present War," The American Journal of International Law 34 (1940): 449-450; Fabian and Coulmas, p. 67; Kristina Pfoser-Schewig, "L' exil autrichien-France (1934-40)," Institut d'Histoire du Temps Présent (CNRS), Mimeographed Proceedings, "Colloque: Réfugiés et immigrés d'Europe Central dans le mouvement anti-fasciste et la résistance en France (1933-45)" (Paris, 17-18 octobre, 1986), vol. III, pp. 5-6; Dieter Schiller, et al., Exil in Frankreich: Kunst u. Literatur im anti-faschistischen Exil 1933-45 (Frankfurt a/M, 1981), p. 382.

15. Cable, Morris Troper (Amsterdam), to JDC, NY, 9 October 1939, JDC 617; Lania, pp. 93-96, 99; Schapiro, p. 137; Lion Feuchtwanger, The Devil in France, trans. Elisabeth Abbott (New York, 1941), p. 77

16. Edith Peters, "German Exiles Interned," NYT, 3 December 1939, sec. IV, p. 9.

population, and water was strictly rationed. Food consisted of dry bread and pork liver paté; kosher food was unavailable. Large pails set up in the corners of the stadium served as toilets, and the refugees had to sleep in the open air. Chaos reigned outside the camp as well. Government officials refused to release any information to desperate wives and relatives who congregated outside the camp daily, and journalists were strictly banned.[17]

Within days, the scope of the internments was widened considerably. On 9 September, the Minister of the Interior, Albert Sarraut, issued another decree law that allowed even naturalized foreigners to be stripped of their citizenship on the mere suspicion of involvement in activities injurious to national security.[18] Another decree law of 17 September, 1939 authorized police to arrest all politically suspect foreigners and either expel them or send them to an internment camp.[19] Armed with these decrees, the police initiated a fierce crackdown against hundreds of foreigners in France, most of whom were stateless communists or left-wing dissidents who, as a result of the Nazi-Soviet non-aggression pact of 23 August, had been transformed overnight into enemies of the state.[20] Males were initially brought to the Roland Garros tennis stadium, while the women were sent to the Petite Roquette prison in Paris.

17. On conditions at the Colombes stadium, see Magdeleine Paz, "Aux portes du camp de rassemblement des sujets allemands et autrichiens," Le Populaire, 12 September 1939, pp. 1, 3; Schramm and Vormeier, pp. 248-249; Jean-Michel Palmier, Weimar en exil: Le Destin de l'émigration intellectuelle allemande antinazie en Europe et aux Etats-Unis, vol. II (Paris, 1988), pp. 119-120; Françoise Joly, et al., "Les camps d'internement en France de septembre 1939 à mai 1940," in Gilbert Badia, et al., eds., Les Barbelés de l'exil (Grenoble, 1979), pp. 175-178; Heinz Pol, Suicide of a Democracy (New York, 1940), pp. 24-25; Lania, pp. 36-45; Hans Escher, "Avec les réfugiés ex-autrichiens," pp. 10-14.

18. Schramm and Vormeier, pp. 7, 246-247; Vormeier, "La situation des réfugiés," pp. 88-89.

19. Minister of the Interior, "Circulaire ayant pour objet de déterminer la situation en temps de guerre des étrangers suspects ou dangereux," 17 September 1939, APP DA 783 Règlements. See also Schramm and Vormeier, pp. 248-249; Vormeier, "Législation répressive et émigration (1938-39)," in Badia, et al., eds., Les Barbelés de l'exil, p. 165; Badia, "Réfugiés et immigrés d'Europe Centrale dans le mouvement antifasciste et la résistance en France (1933-45)," in Institut d'Histoire du Temps Présent (CNRS), Colloque: Réfugiés et immigrés, vol. I, p. 2.

20. For Arthur Koestler's account of his arrest during these roundups, see Koestler, Scum of the Earth (New York, 1941), pp. 57-69.

By mid-September it became clear that the vast majority of detained refugees were not about to be released soon. Instead, they were offered the choice of enlisting in the Foreign Legion or of being interned. Although the Ministry of Defense stipulated that the Germans were to be allowed to sign up only for the regular five-year term of service, Austrians were supposed to be allowed to serve solely for the duration of the war.[21] In practice, however, it appears that everyone was offered only the five-year term of service.[22] As one refugee complained bitterly to Emile Buré's conservative but pro-refugee paper, *L'Ordre*, the choice of internment or the Legion was "cruel" and "undeserved," since nearly all male refugees of military age had already volunteered for regular army service.[23] Fearing that enlistment in the Legion would foreclose this possibility, most refugees opted for internment.[24]

At the end of September, therefore, the military began to redistribute the approximately 18,000 detainees, of whom about 5,000 were Austrians and the rest Germans, to one of the 80 or so internment camps throughout the country.[25] Some of these camps, like

21. General Louis Colson, Chief of Staff for the Army of the Interior, to the Military Governor General of Paris and the Commanding Generals of the Paris regions, 17 September 1939, No. 1270, 1/EMA, SHAT 7 N 2475, dos. 1₂.
22. Morris Troper, "War Relief Activities of the JDC," pamphlet, spring 1940, JDC No. 165, pp. 10-11; "Jewish Life in Paris Today: The Situation of the French Jews and the Situation of the Refugees – What is being done for them?" Special correspondence to the "Day" by Clipper B. Smollar, *The Day*, 3 October 1939, JDC, No. 617.
23. "Nos lecteurs nous écrivent: Les réfugiés allemands," *L'Ordre*, 10 September 1939, p. 4. See also Pol, pp. 229-232.
24. According to Schramm and Vormeier, by the end of September, only 532 internees who had served in the International Brigades in Spain had enlisted in the Foreign Legion. According to *Le Populaire*, however, significant numbers of Austrian Jews did enlist in September. Schramm and Vormeier, p. 263; "Des Israélites autrichiens s'engagent dans la Légion étrangère," *Le Populaire*, 8 September 1939, clipped in AIU Ms. 650, Boîte 11 (41).
25. Although government sources claimed that 15,000 "enemy aliens" had been interned in September and October, private organizations, such as the JDC, generally set the figure at around 18,000. Many sources set the number of camps in the fall at 60, while the JDC claimed there were 80, and Françoise Joly, Jean-Baptiste Joly, and Jean-Philippe Mathieu have recently estimated that there were over 100 camps. Two problems in establishing these numbers are that many smaller camps were actually annexes of larger ones, and throughout the fall some camps were consolidated and others eliminated altogether. For the JDC estimate see Troper, "JDC activities during

St. Cyprien, Argelès, Barcarès and Gurs, had been erected in March of 1939 to absorb the half-million Spanish refugees who had flooded across the border.[26] Others, such as Rieucros in the Lozère, which held politically suspect women, served as detention centers for foreigners considered dangerous to national security but who could not be expelled.[27] Still other camps, particularly in the north, had been hastily improvised in September for the sole purpose of absorbing Central European refugees.[28] The worst camp was almost certainly Le Vernet in the Ariège, which housed politically suspect foreign males; of the approximately 900 refugees interned as of mid-October, the majority were either Spanish or Central and Eastern Europeans, including many who had fought in the International Brigades. By December, after most of the Spaniards had been inducted into the Foreign Legion, one relief committee estimated that 80 to 90 per cent of the remaining inmates were Jews.[29] According to Arthur Koestler and others,

---

early months of the war," 14 March 1940, JDC No. 165. For sources setting the number at 60, see "French Speed Aid for Enemy Aliens," *NYT*, 17 December 1939, p. 37; Edith Peters, "German Exiles Interned," *NYT*, 3 December 1939, sec. IV, p. 9; Pfoser-Schewig, pp. 5-6; Schapiro, p. 138; Kempner, p. 450; *American Jewish Year Book 5701*, 3 October 1940 to 21 September 1941, vol. XLII, p. 449. For Joly's estimate, see Françoise Joly, et al., pp. 180-181.

26. Louis Stein, *Beyond Death and Exile: The Spanish Republicans in France, 1939-55* (Cambridge, MA, 1979), pp. 27-28, 93; Anne Grynberg, *Les Camps de la honte: Les internés juifs des camps français, 1939-44* (Paris, 1991), pp. 40-63; Michael R. Marrus and Robert O. Paxton, *Vichy France and the Jews* (New York, 1980), pp. 63-64; Marrus, "Vichy before Vichy: Antisemitic Currents in France during the 1930s," *Wiener Library Bulletin* 33 (1980): 19; Marrus, "Vichy avant Vichy," *H-Histoire* 3 (November 1979), p. 91.

27. On the creation of Rieucros on 21 January 1939, see "Un premier camp de concentration vient d'être installé dans la Lozère près de Mende," *Le Matin*, 17 February 1939, pp. 1-2; "Les réfugiés et les indésirables qui ont inauguré le premier camp de concentration ...," *Le Matin*, 18 February 1939, pp. 1-2; *Le Temps*, 22 February 1939; *L' Oeuvre*, 18 February 1939; *Journal des débats*, 22 February 1939, all cited in Report on the decree laws, n. auth., n. title, n.d, AIU Ms. 650, Boîte 14 (1939); Schramm and Vormeier, pp. 237-239; Vormeier, "Législation répressive," p. 163; Grynberg, pp. 19-20; *Esprit*, 7e année, No. 82, 1 July 1939, p. 504; JDC, European Executive Committee (Euroexco), February report, 1939, "Excerpts from the Press, February 1939," JDC No. 189, p. 143.

28. Morris Troper, "War Relief Activities of the JDC," pamphlet, spring 1940, JDC No. 165, pp. 10-11. For a map of the camp locations, see Grynberg.

29. "Rapport sur la visite de MM. Davis et Guillon, secrétaires des UCJG (Comité Universel des Unions Chrétiens de Jeunes Gens) aux Centres de Rassemble-

those sent to Le Vernet were treated worse than German POWs. The camp was cordoned off by barbed wire, the guards carried whips, and the inmates' heads were shaven. Despite the rigorous work discipline, proper clothes were not provided, and the inmates were sent out in rags. Military in character, the camp held four roll calls a day, and visits from friends and relatives were strictly forbidden. The barracks were overcrowded, unlit and poorly insulated, and the sole furnishings consisted of bare wooden planks that served as beds. Except for the food, which was meager, French authorities provided nothing: blankets, eating utensils, soap, clothing, even furniture, had to be provided by private relief agencies. "[A]s regards food, accommodation and hygiene," Koestler commented, "Vernet was even below the level of Nazi concentration camps." And although the inmates were not deliberately tortured, the sum total of suffering experienced here was, according to Koestler, not significantly different.[30]

Although this harsh disciplinary regime was unique to Le Vernet, living conditions at other camps were not perceptibly better. At Meslay-du-Maine in the Mayenne west of Paris, neither barracks nor tents had been set up when the first detainees arrived. According to Lania, only the long ditch that served as the latrine had been prepared. It was three weeks before a hot meal was served, and fresh water was even scarcer than at Colombes.[31] Although Meslay may have been more primitive than other camps, it was by no means exceptional. Furniture, heat and lighting were everywhere lacking. Many camps had no beds, and refugees had to sleep on straw. As one former German statesman testified, "No means to wash oneself; no

---

ment d'Etrangers de France," 15-22 December 1939, Archives, Ministère des Affaires Etrangères, Paris (MAE) Z (Europe, 1930-40) 791 (Régime des sujets allemands en France), pp. 2-8.

30. Koestler, *Scum of the Earth*, pp. 98, 94, 123-124; Hicem (Jewish Emigration Society) report on Marmagne camp, 17 November 1939, sent from E. Oungre, Hicem, to JDC Paris, 29 November 1939, JDC, No. 617. On Le Vernet see also Stein, pp. 73-74; Palmier, vol. II, pp. 121-123; Schiller, et al., pp. 444-453; Badia, "Camps répressifs ou camps de concentration?" in Badia, et al., *Les Barbelés de l'exil*, pp. 310-332; Grynberg, pp. 69-70; Magazine excerpt, "Germans in France: The War against Hitler finds thousands of anti-Nazi fighters in French Concentration Camps," in *Friday*, vol. I, No. 10, 17 May 1940, clipped in JDC No. 617.

31. For Lania's description of conditions at Meslay-du-Maine, see pp. 46-83. See also, Hans Escher, "Avec les réfugiés ex-autrichiens," pp. 11-18.

canteen was ready, and I am no longer a youngster to lie on straw and hard stone floors."[32] By early November the American Joint Distribution Committee (JDC) reported that refugees were dying due to the lack of heat and winter clothing. Family visits and mail were extremely limited, and overcrowded conditions and lack of solitude drove many to the breaking point.[33] By contrast, the camp food was considered even by inmates to be "very good – both as to quality and quantity," and relief committees also noted that guards generally treated the internees with respect as opposed to those at Le Vernet.[34]

Beyond these material deprivations, however, the greatest torment for many refugees was the conviction that France had betrayed them. As Lion Feuchtwanger explained, the only reason he had remained in France since emigrating there in 1933 was his hope to participate in the impending battle against Hitler. Now, he commented bitterly, "The French not only refused any cooperation from us German anti-Fascists, they locked us up."[35] Compounding

32. Cited in Kempner, p. 450; Tartakower and Grossmann, p. 147. See also Feuchtwanger, pp. 27-28; Lania, pp. 94-95; W. Bein, "Digest of Letter dated 24 October 1939 from a lady in Paris who visited a concentration camp for German aliens in France," 27 November 1939, JDC No. 617.

33. W. Bein, "Digest of Letter dated 24 October 1939 from a lady in Paris who visited a concentration camp for German aliens in France," 27 November 1939, JDC No. 617; "Record of Telephone Conversation with Mr. Troper in Geneva on 6 November 1939, 3:30 PM," JDC No. 175; Feuchtwanger, pp. 34, 52, 55.

34. "Le Vrai visage du Camp de Gurs," La Flèche, 11 August 1939, AIU Ms. 650, Boîte 12 (43); L. Oungre, Hicem, to JDC, Paris, 7 November 1939, JDC 617; Jewish Telegraphic Agency report on camps of Orléans and Montargis, 22 November 1939, JDC No. 617. For other Hicem reports on the camps, see Report on Marmagne Camp, 17 November 1939, sent from E. Oungre, Hicem, to JDC Paris, 29 November 1939, JDC, No. 617; "Minutes of plenary meeting of Commission des Centres de Rassemblement de l'Intercomité des Oeuvres Françaises," 1 December 1939, JDC No. 617; Dossier of Félix Chevrier at the Centre de Documentation Juive Contemporaine, (CDJC), cited in Françoise Joly, et al., pp. 173-174 and Grynberg, pp. 74-75; "Rapport sur la visite de MM. Davis et Guillon, secrétaires des UCJG (Comité Universel des Unions Chrétiens de Jeunes Gens) aux Centres de Rassemblement d'Etrangers de France," 15-22 December 1939, MAE Z 791, pp. 2-8; Tartakower and Grossmann, p. 147. Grynberg claims that the reports of Chévrier and the Commission des Centres de Rassemblements tended to whitewash camp conditions so as not to alienate government authorities (p. 75), but these reports were often quite critical.

35. Feuchtwanger, p. 15, and also p. 21. For similar comments, see Heinz Soffner, "The internment of refugees in France during the War: Legal situation, facts, conclusions," JDC No. 618; Dr. Hans Rott, President, 1939-1940, document of Ligue

this disappointment, internees were not allowed to participate in noncombatant defense work. Instead, they were either left idle or given what seemed senseless work unrelated to the war effort. The French government, Koestler lamented, "did not want us, even as canon fodder."[36] Moreover, while most refugees recognized the government's need to sift out the fifth columnists among them, the inordinately long delays in implementing this process eventually provoked anguished protests. In his famous plea on behalf of the refugees, *L'Allemagne exilée en France*, the émigré writer Ernst Erich Noth warned in the fall of 1939 that if the process were not completed quickly, France would lose a vast reservoir of fighting power. At the same time, he pointed out, the internments were providing grist for the Nazi propaganda mill, which delighted in showing that the West despised the refugees no less than the Germans.[37]

Given that the vast majority of Central and Eastern European refugees were known to be antifascist, why did France decide in favor of wholesale internments? This question cannot be settled definitively even today since the government has not yet released all pertinent archival records. Nevertheless, it is striking that France alone of the major western powers resorted to such a policy during the period of the "phony war." Belgium and the Netherlands, although they, too, had camps for illegal refugees, did not indiscriminately intern all German and Austrian males in September 1939. Similarly, Great Britain did not resort to mass internments until May 1940 after the German invasion of the Netherlands. Instead, to guard against possible fifth column threats during the "phony war," the British set up a network of tri-

---

Autrichienne, Archives Nationales, Paris (AN) F7 14717; Memorandum, Ligue Autrichienne, 1939, n.d., AN F7 14717; Pol, pp. 229-237; Palmier, vol. II, p. 119; Lania, pp. 73-84.

36. Koestler, *Scum of the Earth*, p. 187; see also Miss Rott, American Friends, "Memorandum on Conditions in the "Camps de Rassemblement" of the Loire and Cher departments in France," 1 November 1939, attached to JDC, Paris, to JDC, NY, 11 November 1939, JDC No. 617; Feuchtwanger, pp. 3-4; Ernst Erich Noth, "15 jours dans un centre de rassemblement," *Nouvelles Littéraires*, 7 October 1939, clipped in AIU Ms. 650, Boîte 13 (dos. 1939-40).

37. Ernst Erich Noth, *L'Allemagne exilée en France: Témoignage d'un allemand proscrit* (Paris, [1940]), p. 27 ff. See also Maurice Carité, "Ernst Erich Noth nous parle ...," *L'Aube*, 18 December 1939, p. 1.

bunals to review on a case-by-case basis the dossiers of German and Austrian refugees, who, meanwhile remained free.[38] Why then did France act so swiftly in this matter? First, there can be no question that fifth column fears, while hugely overblown,[39] were not entirely fanciful. The police reported in October that at least some refugees still crossing the border illegally from Italy were "suspect individuals and probably ... in the pay of Germany [and] who hide their true designs under false identities ...."[40] In December, the Minister of the Interior alerted the border police that he had received word that Nazi spies were infiltrating enemy countries disguised as Jewish refugees and bearing passports marked with a "J."[41] Some historians have dismissed these claims as utter nonsense, or, more seriously, as a smoke screen behind which Daladier's already "fascisticized" government could lock up its foreign enemies on the left.[42] Yet, even many pro-refugee spokesmen as well as the majority

38. On the British reaction in the fall, see Kempner, pp. 444-449; Maximilian Koessler, "Enemy Alien Internment: With Special Reference to Great Britain and France," *Political Science Quarterly* 57 (1942): 98-127; *American Jewish Year Book 5701*, 3 October 1940 to 21 September 1941, vol. XLII, pp. 450-452; Bernard Wasserstein, *Britain and the Jews of Europe, 1939-45* (London, 1979), pp. 82-86; David Cesarani, "An Alien Concept? The Continuity of Anti-Alienism in British Society before 1940," *Immigrants and Minorities* 11 (1992), p. 44; Françoise Joly, et al., in Badia, et al., *Les Barbelés de l'exil*, p. 171; Sir Herbert Emerson, League of Nations, "Assistance Internationale aux Réfugiés," A.18(a) 1939, XII, Rapport supplémentaire, 23 September 1939, in MAE, Société des Nations (SDN) I M (Questions sociales, Réfugiés en France) 1814, p. 387; Bernhard Kahn, to Paul Baerwald, Memorandum, 13 October 1939, JDC, No. 255; "Telephone Conversation with Mr. Troper in Amsterdam today at 2 PM," 9 October 1939, JDC No. 175; "Meeting of the Officers of the IGC [Intergovernmental Committee] on Political Refugees, Department of State, Washington, DC," 17 October 1939, in Myron Taylor Papers, Box 7, Franklin Delano Roosevelt (FDR) Library (Hyde Park, New York).
39. For several examples of how fifth column hysteria seized the population, see Feuchtwanger, pp. 44, 47; Procureur Général de Nancy, to M. le Garde de Sceaux, 24 September 1939, and 14 October 1939, in AN F7 14882 (propos défaitistes); Alma Mahler-Werfel, *Ma Vie*, trans. Gilberte Marchegay Juillard (Paris, 1961), p. 314.
40. French consul, Ventimiglia, Italy, to the General Inspector (Criminal Police), Sûreté Nationale, 20 October 1939, AN F7 14776 (divers).
41. A. Castaing, Contrôleur Général, Ministry of the Interior, Circular, No. S. O./G. 400, to the Commissaires spéciaux des portes et frontières, des ports aériens, les Commissaires de la surveillance du Territoire, 23 December 1939, AN F7 14662; Grynberg, pp. 67-68.
42. Fabian and Coulmas, p. 69.

of refugees themselves, admitted the existence of some German spies among the émigrés. Moreover, as Michael Miller has pointed out, the proliferation of false passport and visa schemes made refugees a propitious target for fifth column suspicions.[43]

Some analysts have also argued that September's mass internments were triggered in part by the military's long preparation for such an exigency, and that the General Staff was unable to differentiate the situation in 1939 from that of the First World War, when Germans had also been interned.[44] As one contemporary observer put it, in the eyes of the French military, "'A boche is always a boche.'"[45] Moreover, the existence of an already extensive camp network made mass internments more probable.

Yet none of the above explanations fully accounts for the government's decision to intern Germans and Austrians in September. While some evidence suggests that internments were a conditioned reflex to the outbreak of war, other factors indicate that this policy had not been planned far in advance. The police report of February 1939, which described German émigrés as generally trustworthy, as well as the military registration of Germans and Austrians up until September, suggest that this policy was motivated by more immediate concerns. The fact that no preparations had been made for mass internments prior to the outbreak of war also suggests the improvised nature of this policy. Except for Rieucros and those camps already in place for Spaniards, most internment centers were erected at the last moment in great haste.[46] Furthermore,

43. Louise Weiss, *Mémoires d'une Européenne*, vol. III (Paris, 1970), p. 238; Lazareff, p. 109; Michael B. Miller, *Shanghai on the Métro: Spies, Intrigue, and the French between the Wars* (Berkeley, 1994), pp. 144-172; "Situation of the Refugees in France during the Year 1939," n.d., in JDC No. 604.
44. Koessler, p. 115; Miller, pp. 152-153.
45. Grynberg, pp. 66-67. See also Lisa Fittko, *Escape through the Pyrennees*, trans. David Koblick (Evanston, IL, 1991), p. 11; Henry Pachter, *Weimar Etudes* (New York, 1982), p. 314, cited in Peterson, p. 76.
46. This lack of preparation was noted in the report of the subcommittee of the parliamentary Commission on Civil and Criminal Legislation headed by Marius Moutet. For the text of this report, which had been compiled with the cooperation of the Foreign Affairs Commission of the Chamber, see "Rapport présenté par MM. Marius Moutet, André Le Troquer et Gaston Moreau devant la délégation permanente de la Commission de la Législation Civile et Criminelle, et adopté le 16 novembre 1939," in AN F60 391.

although the British began to implement their criblage or sifting process almost immediately, it was months before the French began to review the internees' dossiers systematically.[47] It therefore seems that some specific event occurred on the eve of the war that tipped the scales in favor of mass internments, and there can be little doubt that this incident was the Nazi-Soviet nonaggression pact. While the government may previously have felt confident in recognizing friends and foes, the signing of the nonaggression pact on 23 August cast a cloud of suspicion over all foreigners in France as well as Communist Party members, citizens and foreigners alike. Already on 22 August, as news of the pact became known, the Minister of the Interior issued a circular instructing prefects to inscribe in the Carnet B, the list of politically suspect foreigners, all foreigners who had ever received expulsion or deportation orders for national security reasons. On 28 August this list was expanded to include "all naturalized foreigners whose loss of citizenship has been envisaged," and on 9 September the government issued a decree law that enabled it to strip suspect individuals, French or foreign-born, of their citizenship.[48] Furthermore, the government unleashed a fierce crackdown against the Communist Party: on 26 September the party was legally dissolved and its publications banned, and the following January, Communist Party deputies, despite having voted for military credits, were forced to forfeit their seats in parliament.[49] To be sure, many Communists, especially among the émigrés, denounced the pact and proclaimed their loyalty to France,[50] but their appeals fell on deaf ears. Whether

47. Kempner, pp. 443-458. On the British response, see also note 38 above.
48. Schramm and Vormeier, p. 245, esp. note 4, p. 247, n. 11. On the decree law of 9 September 1939, see *JOLD*, 14 September 1939, p. 11400; Ministry of the Interior, Circular of 21 September 1939 (au sujet du décret-loi du 9 septembre 1939), AN F7 14662.
49. Alfred Cobban, *A History of Modern France*, vol. III (Middlesex, G.B., 1965), p. 174. See also Elisabeth du Réau, *Edouard Daladier, 1884-1970* (Paris, 1993), pp. 374-377.
50. "Une déclaration des socialistes allemands," *Le Populaire*, 31 August 1939, p. 6; "Les étrangers résidant en France se mettent au service du Pays," *Le Populaire*, 2 September 1939, p. 2; "Les protestations de l'opposition allemande contre le pacte Hitler-Staline se multiplient," *Le Populaire*, 2 September 1939, p. 2; "Une protestation des allemands de l'émigration," *Journal de débats*, 29 August 1939, clipped in AIU Ms. 650, Boîte 14 (48); Lania, pp. 9-10; Palmier, vol. II, p. 117; Rita Thalmann, "L' émigration allemande et l'opinion française de 1936 à 1939," p. 68.

the government was indulging in a witchhunt, as many émigrés and contemporary historians have claimed,[51] or whether it truly believed that Communists constituted a serious security threat, remains unclear. The fact is, however, that the Comintern did instruct its followers to sabotage the war effort and spread defeatist propaganda.[52] Seeing the internments largely as a response to the non-aggression pact also helps explain why the government felt compelled to resort to mass roundups, despite the fact that the dossiers of several thousands of refugees had been scrutinized. While these individuals may have been screened for pro-Nazi leanings, possible pro-Communist sympathies may not have received close attention.[53]

Aside from interning German and Austrian refugees, the government, in conjunction with British authorities, proceeded to force all German and Austrian male nationals of military age to disembark from neutral ships, even though most of these were Jewish refugees carrying visas for either the United States or some Latin American country. According to international law, belligerents had the right to remove enemy aliens from neutral ships if those aliens were thought to be possible members of the enemy's armed forces; as the JDC explained, "The French authorities, naturally, were anxious to eliminate every possibility for agents of the German government to go overseas, and the Jewish refugees unfortunately were caught up in the[ir] nets ...."[54] Men removed from the ships were subsequently directed to internment camps; the women and children were allowed to proceed.[55]

---

51. Arthur Koestler, *The Invisible Writing* (New York, 1954), p. 419; Badia, et al., eds., *Les Barbelés de l'exil*, pp. 92-93.
52. Kempner, p. 449. On the defeatist propaganda of the Communist Party, see du Réau, pp. 374-377. She claims the extent of this sabotage was extremely limited.
53. Curt Reiss, "Refugees in France: Their Treatment Unfortunate but Forced by Circumstances," NYT, 10 December 1939, sec. IV, p. 9; Schapiro, p. 140; Kempner, p. 451. Under the Popular Front a Consultative Commission had been set up to screen German refugees eligible for asylum according to the terms of the League of Nations' "Provisional Arrangement Concerning the Status of Refugees Coming from Germany," signed in Geneva on 4 July 1936.
54. "JDC Activities during early months of the war," 14 March 1940, JDC No. 165. On the legal basis for these seizures, see Kempner, p. 453.
55. Bernhard Kahn, to Paul Baerwald, Memorandum 13 October 1939, JDC No. 255; Paul Baerwald, teleg., to George L. Warren, President's Advisory Committee on

In light of these internments as well as seizures at sea, the situation for German and Austrian refugees did not look bright in the fall of 1939. Nevertheless, several pressure groups continued to lobby the government to ameliorate camp conditions and to utilize the refugees in the war effort, and their efforts eventually yielded some success. Jewish relief agencies, for example, demanded access to the camps in order to bring desperately needed aid. They further pressed the government to stop those activities – such as blocking internees' bank accounts and seizing refugees from neutral ships – that were costing them huge sums of money by making the families of the victims entirely dependent on charity.[56]

France's internment policy came under fierce attack abroad. Already in October the French Foreign Ministry instructed its embassies and consulates to stress that camp conditions were not as terrible as depicted in the foreign press, and that a criblage or sifting process had been implemented to screen the internees so that those judged friendly to the Allied cause could be released.[57] As long as internments continued, however, efforts at damage control had only limited success. In January The *New Republic* carried

---

Refugees (PAC), 25 October 1939, JDC No. 658; Dr. Feldmann and Dr. Speigel, from the Camp des Passagers du Pacific Line, Montguyon (Charente Inférieure), to the JDC, NY, 15 September 1939, JDC 617; Robert Pilpel, Secretary, Subcommittee on Refugee Aid in Central and South America, to Erna Zweig, Santiago, Chile, 16 October 1939, JDC No. 617; August Rothschild, Santiago, Chile, to Ike G. Cadden family, 18 November 1939, JDC No. 617; Jeanette Robbins, Personal Inquiry Dept. of the JDC, to Mr. Paul Herzog, 22 December 1939, JDC No. 617; JDC, NY, to Morris Troper, Amsterdam, 5 October 1939, JDC No. 617; Chargé d'Affaires de France, to M. le Ministre du Blocus, 15 December 1939, MAE Z 790 (Régime des sujets allemands en France), pp. 21-23; Hertha Kraus, American Friends Service Committee, to Clarence Pickett, 19 November 1939, in Jack Sutters, ed., *American Friends Service Committee, Philadelphia*, part 1 (1932-39), Doc. No. 204, p. 594, vol. II of *Archives of the Holocaust*, eds., Henry Friedlander and Sybil Milton (New York, 1990); André Fontaine, "L' internement au Camps des Milles et dans ses annexes, septembre 1939-mars 1943," in Grandjonc, ed., p. 119. For an excellent summary of this issue, see Kempner, pp. 453-454.

56. On JDC protests against seizures of refugees from neutral ships, see "JDC Activities during early months of the war," 14 March 1940, JDC No. 165; "Budgetary Forecast of the Hicem for 1940," JDC No. 675; Cable, JDC, NY, to Troper, Amsterdam, 29 September 1939, JDC No. 658; J.C. Hyman, Memorandum, to JDC Officers, 8 February 1940, JDC No. 617; Françoise Joly, et al., p. 191.

57. Foreign Ministry, to the French ambassador in Madrid, teleg., No. 514, 22 October 1939, MAE Z 790, p. 8.

a vitriolic piece entitled "France Copies Hitler." "France," it declared, "is supposed to be fighting this war for democracy. Some people in America would be more willing to accept this point of view if it were not for the shocking treatment the French are now giving to foreign Jews."[58]

There was also a ground swell of criticism at home. In the Chamber of Deputies, two of the most outspoken refugee advocates, the Socialists Marius Moutet and Salomon Grumbach, used their positions on the influential Commissions on Civil and Criminal Legislation and Foreign Affairs to attack the government's policy. As Moutet proclaimed in November, the internments, while perhaps justifiable in September, were no longer so today, and he called on the government to speed up the criblage process and follow the British example of allowing non-suspect refugees to remain at liberty, but under police surveillance. If the administration hoped to avoid further tarnishing France's image abroad and to maintain the loyalties of those refugees eager to fight for France, it would have to end the "bureaucratic delays, xenophobic prejudices, [and] obtuseness," that until now had impeded all progress on this issue.[59]

The domestic debate also focused on the practical problem of how France might better utilize the huge population of foreigners in general, including the internees. After the declaration of war, popular pressure to recruit foreigners into the military became vociferous. In late September, Senator André Honnorat, a long-time refugee advocate, appealed to the administration to allow the internees to serve in the army, or at least in the Foreign Legion for the war's duration. Otherwise, he claimed, the combative spirit of

58. "France Copies Hitler," *The New Republic*, 15 January 1940, clipped in JDC No. 617. See also Edith Peters, "German Exiles Interned," *NYT*, 3 December 1939, sec. IV, p. 9.
59. Moutet, "Quel sort réserver aux réfugiés politiques?" *La Lumière*, 17 November 1939, pp. 1-2; "La Chambre veut une prompte solution du problème des réfugiés politiques," *La Lumière*, 15 December 1939, pp. 1-2. These criticisms were echoed in the report of the subcommittee of the Parliamentary Commission on Civil and Criminal Legislation, headed by Moutet. See "Rapport présenté par MM. Marius Moutet, André le Troquer et Gaston Moreau devant la délégation permanente de la Commission de la Législation Civile et Criminelle, et adopté le 16 novembre 1939," AN F60 391.

the refugees would be lost forever. Honnorat further contested the government's ban on foreigners serving in regular French regiments. At the very least, he argued, foreigners who had resided in France many years deserved to be exempted.[60] The conservative daily, *L'Ordre*, concurred, and lambasted the authorities for allowing the huge reservoir of foreign manpower to go to waste. If the army refused to enlist non-naturalized foreigners, every effort should be made to speed up naturalization procedures, particularly for long-time foreign residents, many of whom had already requested naturalization.[61] Most significantly, this view was endorsed by the Ministry of Defense, which pressed relentlessly to speed up the naturalization process, so that at least some of the 64,000 foreigners who had volunteered for military service might be incorporated into the regular army. At the same time, the Ministry also called for swifter recruitment of the internees into the Foreign Legion.[62]

These pressures came to a head on 8 December when Moutet and Grumbach brought the refugee question to the floor of the Chamber. Speaking on behalf of the Commission on Civil and Criminal Legislation, Moutet asked the administration to clarify a number of issues: what was the situation of the wives and families of the internees?; were the internees who had signed up for the Foreign Legion being granted military allowances and pensions, and would they eventually be naturalized?; were those still in the camps "interned" or merely "detained"?; and what would happen to those previously guaranteed asylum? Alluding to the recent spate of criticism from abroad, Moutet concluded his speech with a ringing denunciation of the internments: "We must not allow public opinion abroad to perceive France as more cruel toward the victims of Hitler than Hitler himself. We cannot permit those who

60. Honnorat to the President of the Council, n. date, but forwarded to the Ministry of Defense on 28 September 1939, SHAT 7N 2475 dos. 1₂.
61. Jean-L. Prim, "Paris en guerre, toujours les étrangers," *L'Ordre*, 14 October 1939, p. 1. See also "Jewish Life in Paris Today: The Situation of the French Jews and the Situation of the Refugees – What is Being Done for Them?" Special correspondence to the "Day," by Clipper B. Smollar, *The Day*, 3 October 1939, JDC, No. 617; Jean-Louis Crémieux-Brilhac, *Les Français de l'an 40*, vol. I (Paris, 1990), p. 480.
62. Army Chief of Staff, 1er Bureau, No. 8312, "Note pour le Cabinet Militaire du Ministre," 13 November 1939, SHAT 7N 2475 (dos. 1).

have escaped Hitlerian concentration camps to remain interned in French camps[.] That would be too unjust and too cruel!"[63]

Sarraut, who spoke on behalf of the administration during the debate, prefaced his remarks by attacking foreign governments that had criticized France's refugee policies. Given their own restrictionist policies, Sarraut declared, they had no right to lecture France. He then proceeded to explain that the internments had initially been necessary since the administration had no means of identifying genuine suspects. Nevertheless, Sarraut admitted that the arbitrary nature of the internments "may have created painful situations," and he announced that the government was now prepared to remedy this situation. Criblage commissions had been set up, and Sarraut noted that 7,000 of the original 15,000 internees had already been released. And while conceding that these commissions did not always operate as efficiently and fairly as possible, he promised to correct this situation in the near future. In the end, the Minister's message was clear: the administration shared the goals of the reformers, and it was prepared to liquidate nearly all the camps and recruit as many internees as possible into the Foreign Legion.[64]

Although Sarraut's figures were inflated, since Jewish organizations estimated the number of refugees remaining in the camps as of mid-December at about 10,500,[65] there is little doubt that the administration intended to accomplish the goals announced by the minister. In an attempt to meet the demands of Jewish relief organizations, the military authorities in charge of the camps encouraged the formation of a new refugee committee in mid-November, the *Commission des Centres de Rassemblement*, funded primarily by

---

63. *Journal officiel, Débats, Chambre des Députés* (henceforth JODCD), 8 December 1939, pp. 2109-2110, 2120-2123. See also Schramm and Vormeier, pp. 254-255; J. Biélinky, "L'immigration juive en France," *La Juste Parole*, No. 63, 1 December 1939, p. 7; Koessler, p. 118; Kempner, pp. 450-451; Tartakower and Grossmann, p. 150. For the Commission's earlier report on which Moutet's remarks were based, see "Rapport présenté par MM. Marius Moutet, André Le Troquer et Gaston Moreau devant la délégation permanent de la Commission de la Législation Civile et Criminelle, et adopté le 16 novembre 1939," AN F60 391.

64. JODCD, 8 December 1939, p. 2121. See also Schramm and Vormeier, pp. 255-256.

65. "French Speed Aid for Enemy Aliens," *NYT*, 17 December 1939, p. 37; JDC, *Aid to Jews Overseas: Report for 1939*, pp. 33-34, JDC No. 156.

the JDC, but also by the Groupement de Coordination, a coalition of French refugee organizations created in the fall of 1938.[66] Albert Lévy, director of the Jewish relief committee, the *Comité d'Assistance aux Réfugiés* (CAR), served as president, while Robert de Rothschild served as Honorary Chairman. Most significantly, the new Commission was brought under the aegis of the Minister of Public Health, and an official of that ministry, Félix Chevrier, was appointed general secretary.[67] The humanitarian impact of the Commission's work was felt almost immediately. By the end of November, the Commission had spent over 600,000 francs on blankets, shoes, clothing, medicines, and even heating and furniture.[68] Moreover, during the coming months, Chevrier and his associates visited every camp to assess the material conditions as well as the state of morale among the internees. So improved were camp conditions by the end of the year, that the *New York Times*, the League of Nations High Commissioner for Refugees, and the Red Cross all commended the government on these efforts.[69]

66. On the Groupement and the reorganization of the Jewish refugee relief effort in late 1938, see Robert de Rothschild, "Le consistoire de Paris et la coordination des oeuvres," *L' Univers israélite*, 2 June 1939, pp. 661-664; Franz Gravereau, "Le problème des étrangers," *Le Petit Parisien*, 4 March 1939, clipped in AIU, Ms. 650, Boîte 14 (48); Vicki Caron, "The Politics of Frustration: French Jewry and the Refugee Crisis in the 1930s," *Journal of Modern History* 65 (1993): 333-335.

67. On the creation of the Commission, see "Minutes of plenary meeting of Commission des Centres de Rassemblements de l'Intercomité des Oeuvres Françaises," 1 December 1939, JDC No. 617; "Group Formed to Aid Refugees in France," *NYT*, 15 November 1939, p. 2; "Memorandum on Camps of German Refugees in France," n.d [Nov. 1939], JDC No. 617; JDC, *Aid to Jews Overseas: Report for 1939*, pp. 33-34, JDC No. 156; J.C. Hyman, Memorandum to JDC Officers, 8 February 1940, JDC No. 617; "Situation of the Refugees in France during the Year 1939," n.d., JDC No. 604; Grynberg, pp. 72-76; Françoise Joly, et al., pp. 216-217; Schapiro, p. 139.

68. "Situation of the Refugees in France during the Year 1939," n.d., JDC No. 604. On the Commission's impact, see "Minutes of Plenary Meeting of Commission des Centres de Rassemblement de l'Intercomité des Oeuvres Françaises," 1 December 1939, JDC No. 617. For reports on camp conditions, see note 34 above.

69. "French Speed Aid for Enemy Aliens," *NYT*, 17 December 1939, p. 37; Emerson, to George L. Warren, 19 March 1940, AN AJ 43 12 (18/56:3); Various reports of Dr. Junod and Minister F. Barbey and other Red Cross delegates on the occasion of their visits to internment camps for civil internees and POW's, 19 February 1940-24 February 1940," SHAT 7N 2480 dos. 5; President of the Council, Foreign Ministry, to Ministry of National Defense and War, EMA, 1er Bureau, 19 March 1940, SHAT 7N 2480 dos. 5.

By late 1939 many of the problems Jewish organizations had experienced were on their way to being resolved. In late October the Groupement and the Jewish emigration organization, Hicem, were granted permission to enter the camps to facilitate the emigration of internees. Camp officials cooperated fully in this effort, and the government even created two special camps for internees awaiting departure. By the end of the year some 250 internees had emigrated with their families, and Hicem expected many more to leave in the near future.[70] Furthermore, the question of military allowances was finally settled in November, with the announcement that all foreigners serving in the army, including those in the Legion, were henceforth to receive payments equivalent to those of French soldiers.[71] Finally, by early 1940 the government bowed to pressure from the U.S. State Department, as well as personal interventions by Robert de Rothschild and the League of Nations High Commissioner for Refugees, to stop the seizures of refugees from ships at sea. Although French naval officials continued to check the identities of German nationals on board these vessels, once it was certified that they were bonafide refugees, they were allowed to continue their journeys.[72]

70. Françoise Joly, et al., p. 191; Schramm and Vormeier, p. 249; Schapiro, p. 139; *American Jewish Year Book 5701*, 3 October 1940 to 21 September 1941, vol. XLII, p. 450; Amédée Bussière, Director, Sûreté Nationale, Ministry of the Interior, Circular No. 413, 27 October 1939, AN F7 14662; E. Ricard, Secretary, President of the Council, Ministry of National Defense and War, 1/EMA, to the Military Governor General of Paris and the Commanding Generals of the Paris regions, teleg. No. 5.343, 26 October 1939, SHAT 7N 2462 dos. 3; Ricard, to the Military Governor General of Paris and the Commanding Generals of the Paris regions, 1/EMA, Circular No. 7458, 9 November 1939, SHAT 7N 2475 dos. 1; JDC Paris, Cable to JDC, NY, 30 October 1939, JDC No. 617; "Memorandum on Camps of German Refugees in France," n.d [Nov. 1939], JDC, No. 617; L. Oungre, Hicem, to JDC, Paris, "Expedition of Refugees interned in camps," 7 November 1939, JDC No. 617; Jewish Telegraphic Agency, report on camps of Orléans and Montargis, 22 November 1939, JDC No. 617; "Budgetary Forecast of the Hicem for 1940," JDC No. 675; "Report on the Activity of the Hicem," 3 January 1940, JDC, No. 675; J.C. Hyman, Memorandum, to JDC Officers, 8 February 1940, JDC No. 617; Joseph J. Schwartz, JDC, NY, to Frances G. Marshall, 7 March 1940, JDC No. 617.

71. "Les allocations militaires seront accordées aux familles des étrangers combattants en France," *Le Populaire*, 2 November 1939, p. 3.

72. "Report on the Activity of the Hicem," 3 January 1940, JDC No. 675; "JDC Activities during early months of the war," 14 March 1940, JDC No. 165; Sir Herbert

Paralleling these reforms, Sarraut also revamped the criblage process in an effort to make it more fair and efficient. Already in September the Ministries of the Interior and Defense had set up regional criblage commissions to begin reviewing the internees' dossiers and determining which individuals were loyal.[73] Yet, by all accounts these tribunals worked at an inordinately slow pace. Although certain categories of refugees had been designated as early as mid-September as likely to be released – refugees with French wives or children, refugees who had enlisted in the Foreign Legion, and refugees personally recommended by the Minister of the Interior – it was weeks before further action was taken on their behalf.[74]

After the chaos of these initial weeks, it was clear that measures would have to be taken to speed up the criblage process. In October, Sarraut ordered the prefects to stop the wave of arbitrary arrests that had resulted in too many innocents being sent to Le Vernet and Rieucros.[75] At the same time, in an effort to coordinate the process, the administration established a Central Interministerial Criblage Commission in Paris, which included representatives from the General Staff, the Foreign Ministry, and the Ministry of the Interior.[76] Even then, the rate of release was "discouragingly

---

Emerson (Intergovernmental Committee on Refugees), to George Warren, 30 November 1939, p. 4, AN AJ 43 12 (18/56:2). On the relative satisfaction of Jewish organizations with the direction of French policy, see also "Memorandum on Camps of German Refugees in France," n.d [Nov. 1939], JDC No. 617.

73. Colson, Army Chief of Staff for the Interior, Ministry of National Defense and War, President of the Council, Circulaire No. 5.008 1/E.M.A., (Secret and Very Urgent), 23 October 1939, SHAT 7N 2462, dos. 3. See also Vormeier, "La situation des réfugiés," pp. 89-90.

74. Colson, Army Chief of Staff for the Interior, Ministry of National Defense and War, President of the Council, to the Commanders and Generals, No. 1270, 1/EMA, 17 September 1939, SHAT 7N 2475, dos. 1$_2$.

75. J. Berthoin, Secretary General, Ministry of the Interior, Sûreté Nationale, Circular, 29 October 1939, AN F7 14662. On this decree and subsequent orders by the Ministry of the Interior to cut down on arbitrary arrests, see also A. Bussière, Director General, Sûreté Nationale, Ministry of the Interior, 7ème Bureau, to the Prefects, 23 March 1940, APP DA 784 Règlements; Badia, "Camps répressifs ou camps de concentration?" p. 295; Badia, "Réfugiés et immigrés d'Europe Centrale dans le mouvement antifasciste," Institut d'Histoire du Temps Présent, "Colloque: Réfugiés et immigrés d'Europe Central," vol. I, p. 3; Grynberg, p. 79.

76. Berthoin, Secretary General, Ministry of the Interior, Circular, 9 October 1939, AN F7 14662; Ministry of the Interior, Sûreté Nationale, Telegram to Prefects,

slow," and according to an advisor to the Central Criblage Commission, aside from those internees who had French wives or children, no more than 100 persons had been released by early November.[77] To remedy this situation, the Interministerial Criblage Commission decided in early November that whole categories of refugees were to be released, except for those interned at Le Vernet and Rieucros. These categories included all refugees over the age of 40 who either were married to French citizens or had French children; were former Legionnaires; had applied for French citizenship before the war with favorable recommendations; or had received the Legion of Honor or the Médaille Militaire. Still other categories were to be released unconditionally regardless of age: refugees with sons currently serving in the army; those not medically fit; those who had acquired some citizenship other than German prior to the mobilization; and Saar refugees who had completed military service. In mid-December these lists were expanded to include all refugees with visas to emigrate abroad, plus Saar, Rhineland, and ex-Austrian refugees over 48 years of age. Refugees remaining in the camps were to be granted several options. Men between the ages of 17 and 48 judged physically fit were encouraged to join the Foreign Legion, and Saar refugees of military age were allowed to join the regular army. Refugees over 48 years of age, or those who refused to join the Legion, were to sign up for prestataire, or noncombatant labor service.[78] The government

---

received 8 October 1939, Archives départementales du Bas-Rhin, Strasbourg (ADBR) D 391/ 24 dos. 240; Colson, Army Chief of Staff for the Interior, Ministry of National Defence and War, President of the Council, to the Commanding Generals, 17 October 1939, ADBR D 391/ 24 dos. 240 [also in SHAT 7N 2475 dos. 1_2]; Lania, pp. 76-77.

77. J.C. Hyman, Memorandum to JDC Officers, 8 February 1940, JDC No. 617. See also Françoise Joly, et al., pp. 190-191; Koessler, pp. 116-118; Report of Heinz Soffner, former Secretary of the Federation of Austrian Emigrants in Paris, "The Internment of refugees in France during the War: Legal situation, facts, conclusions," JDC No. 618.

78. Ministry of the Interior, Sûreté Nationale, 7ème bureau, to the Prefect of Police, the Prefects, and the Governor General of Algeria, 11 November 1939, SHAT 7N 2475 dos. 1 (reproduced in Badia, et al., eds., Les Barbelés de l'exil, photos.) See also Badia, "Réfugiés et immigrés d'Europe Centrale dans le mouvement antifasciste," Institut d'Histoire du Temps Présent, "Colloque: Réfugiés et immigrés d'Europe Central," vol. I, p. 4; Fabian and Coulmas, p. 70. Ministry of Defense, EMA/1er bureau, and the Ministry of the Interior, 2ème bureau, to the Prefect of Police, the Prefects,

therefore seemed intent on fulfilling its promise to liquidate the existing camps, with one or two exceptions for those refugees still considered suspect.

Once the new criblage regulations went into effect, the pace at which internees were released accelerated tremendously. By February there were only 6,428 left in the camps, and only 29 camps remained in existence.[79] In April the Military declared the sifting process over for refugees being considered for prestataire service, and Jewish relief organizations reported their first drop in expenditures since the outbreak of the war.[80]

The administration's most significant reform, and the one on which the success of the criblage system depended, was the decision to utilize the internees, alongside foreigners in general, in the war effort. Yet this issue inspired the greatest ambivalence in administrative circles, and ultimately the General Staff allowed xenophobia and antisemitism to take precedence over military exigencies. That this would occur, however, was by no means immediately apparent, since during the winter the Ministry of Defense launched a concerted effort to encourage internees to sign up either for the Foreign Legion or prestataire service. In January prestataire service became compulsory not only for internees not yet enlisted in the Legion, but for all stateless refugees and beneficiaries of the right of asylum in the same situation. Those who signed up were transferred to special camps where living conditions were appreciably better. Most significantly, the Military declared that the prestataires who numbered about 5,000 in the spring of 1940, would be treated on par with French soldiers: they were to receive equivalent military allocations for themselves and

---

and the Governor General of Algeria, 21 December 1939, APP DA 783 Règlements; Morris Troper to M. Stephany, Central Council for Jewish Refugees, 12 January 1940, JDC No. 617; "France, Refugees, 1933-40," JDC No. 617.

79. "French Speed Aid for Enemy Aliens," *NYT*, 17 December 1939, p. 37; Foreign Ministry to Saint-Quentin, teleg. No. 2013, 14 December 1939, MAE Z 790; "Liste des camps d'internés prestataires et effectifs à réviser," 20 February 1940, SHAT 7N 2480; "Situation of the Refugees in France during the Year 1939," n.d., JDC No. 604.

80. Françoise Joly, et al., pp. 182-183; CAR, "Note on the Activity of the CAR from May 1, 1940," JDC No. 604. For those cases not yet settled by April, the government planned a second triage.

their families, in addition to pensions and regular leaves.[81] A few internees with specialized technical skills were even allowed to work in national defense industries.[82] The General Staff made an even greater effort to enlist refugees into the Foreign Legion. To accommodate these foreigners, the army created special units, the Régiments de Marche des Volontaires Etrangers, or RMVE. Although incorporated into the framework of the Legion proper, these regiments had their own command structure and differed from other Legion regiments with regard to personnel.[83] The majority of those who joined the RMVE were either Spanish refugees, stateless refugees – mostly Eastern and Central European Jews – or Polish Jews who had not been welcome into the Polish Legion.[84] To encourage foreigners to enlist in the RMVE, the government granted them special dispensations, such as exemption from having to carry the special identity card for foreigners, automatic and free extension of residence permits, and temporary amnesty from expulsion or depor-

81. On the overhaul of the prestataire service in the winter of 1939-1940, see Ministry of Defense, EMA/1er bureau, and the Ministry of the Interior, 2ème bureau, to the Prefect of Police, the Prefects, and the Governor General of Algeria, 21 December 1939, APP DA 783 Règlements; Morris Troper to M. Stephany, Central Council for Jewish Refugees, 12 January 1940, JDC No. 617; JDC report, "France, Refugees, 1933-40," JDC No. 617; *JOLD*, 18 January 1940, pp. 515-516; Ministry of National Defense, 1/EMA, to the Military Governor General of Paris and the Commanding Generals of the Paris regions, No. 1617, 23 January 1940, SHAT 7N 2480; Report of Heinz Soffner, "The Internment of Refugees in France during the War: Legal situation, facts, conclusions," JDC No. 618; Schramm and Vormeier, pp. 240, 256; Vormeier, "La situation des émigrés allemands," p. 159; Vormeier, "La situation des réfugiés," p. 91; André Fontaine, "L'internement au camp des Milles et dans ses annexes: Septembre 1939-Mars 1943," in Grandjonc, ed., *Les Camps en Provence*, p. 120; Grynberg, p. 77; Tartakower and Grossmann, pp. 150-151; Kempner, pp. 451-452.
82. "CAR Rapport de l'Exercice, 1940," Marseille, 13 January 1940, pp. 1, 5; J. Biélinky, "Le reclassement professionnel des immigrés," *L' Univers israélite*, 29 March 1940, p. 105.
83. Douglas Porch, *The French Foreign Legion: A Complete History of the Legendary Fighting Force* (New York, 1991), p.445; Koestler, *Scum of the Earth*, note, p. 186.
84. On the ethnic composition of the Legion, see L' Adjudant-Chef Mazzoni, Chef de l'Annexe de Barcarès, Camp de Barcarès, to M. le Capitaine, Chef du S.I.L. at Sathonay, No. 118/AB, 25 January 1940, in SHAT 7N 2475 (dos. 3). On anti-semitism in the Polish Legion, see "Nos lecteurs nous écrivent: 'Des volontaires,'" *L 'Ordre*, 25 September 1939, p. 4; Szajkowski, *Jews and the French Foreign Legion*, pp. 66-67.

tation orders. The one inducement not granted, however, was the promise of eventual naturalization.[85]

The fate of so-called "enemy aliens" interned in the camps was slightly different. While Czechs were quickly released so that they could join the newly formed Czech Legion, Germans and Austrians were initially barred from the Foreign Legion. The General Staff soon changed its mind on this issue, however. Already in September the internees were being recruited for five-year terms of duty, and in late October the Ministry of Defense issued a decree allowing Germans as well as Austrians to volunteer solely for the duration of the war. In November, the government promised to pay military allowances to the families of those internees who signed up for the Legion.[86] Recruitment nevertheless proceeded slowly during these initial weeks, largely because the majority of refugees, with the exception of diehard Communists, still nurtured the dream of serving in the regular army. Camp commandants frequently resorted to cajolery and coercion to persuade internees to sign up. According to Leo Lania, many refugees enlisted solely because they needed military allocations to support their now destitute families. Heinz Pol, too, claimed that some internees were told that their property would be confiscated if they did not sign up, while others were threatened with imprisonment or expulsion to Germany.[87]

Once the refugees realized they were not going to be permitted to join the regular army, and as the benefits extended to those serving in the Legion improved, the Legion became more attractive. According to Pol, 70 percent of the internees at his camp

85. A. Bussière, Director, Sûreté Nationale, Ministry of the Interior Circular, No. 419, 4 January 1940, AN F7 14662; Jean-L. Prim, "Paris en guerre, toujours les étrangers," L' Ordre, 14 October 1939, p. 1; Lania, pp. 79-80; Pol, p. 260.
86. E. Ricard, Ministry of National Defense and War, President of the Council, to the Commanding Generals [of the camps], No. 4.910, 1/EMA, (Urgent), 22 October 1939, SHAT 7N 2475, dos. 1$_2$; Army Chief of Staff, Overseas section, "Note sur l'utilisation des allemands, engagés volontaires pour la durée de la guerre," 9/EMA, 2 December 1939, SHAT 7N 2475, dos. 2; "Les allocations militaires seront accordées aux familles des étrangers combattants en France," Le Populaire, 2 November 1939, p. 3.
87. Lania, pp. 79-80; Pol, pp. 237-250. See also Palmier, vol. II, n. 6, pp. 120-121; W. Bein, "Digest of Letter dated October 24, 1939 from a lady in Paris who visited a concentration camp for German aliens in France," 27 November 1939, JDC No. 617.

ultimately volunteered, and many were so eager to serve that they finagled their way in even after failing their medical examinations.[88] By December the flood of volunteers had become so great that the Sûreté Nationale agreed to allow the LICA into the camps to assist with the registration process, and the *New York Times* reported that the Legion could not absorb all the internees who had signed up.[89] By the spring, no fewer than 9,000 internees had enlisted in the Legion.[90]

Despite the General Staff's zeal in getting foreigners and internees mobilized as quickly as possible, problems persisted. As we have seen, the General Staff lobbied vigorously to speed the naturalization process, at least for the thousands of foreigners who had applied for citizenship prior to the war's outbreak. On this issue, however, the Generals encountered staunch resistance from the new Minister of Justice, Georges Bonnet. Bonnet, it is true, attempted to appease them by issuing a circular on 22 October that ordered the prefects to accelerate naturalization procedures for foreigners whose applications were already in the pipeline, and especially for those between 18 and 45 who had resided in the country legally for at least five years. Bonnet, however, insisted these benefits be restricted to foreigners considered "assimilable," i.e., those with desirable professional skills, especially in agriculture and manual labor, and those from "countries bordering France, with the obvious exception of German nationals."[91]

Bonnet's concessions did not appease the Generals, however. In November, General Louis Colson, the Army Chief of Staff, complained to Bonnet that the government was not adequately publicizing the new naturalization procedures, and he insisted that all

88. Pol, p. 246; Lania, p. 80; Szajkowski, *Jews and the French Foreign Legion*, pp. 64-65.
89. Police report on LICA meeting, 17 December 1939, APP BA 1812 79.501-882-C; "French Speed Aid for Enemy Aliens," *NYT*, 17 December 1939, p. 37.
90. Schramm and Vormeier, p. 256; Vormeier, "La situation des réfugiés," p. 91; Tartakower and Grossmann, p. 150.
91. Bonnet, Ministry of Justice, Keeper of the Seals, to the Prefects, [22 October 1939], APP BA 407 P 200.263; "On décrète, on recommande, on communique, on suggère ...," *L'Oeuvre*, 27 October 1939, p. 5; "La naturalisation des étrangers qui veulent servir la France sera accélérée," *L'Epoque*, 29 October 1939, p. 4; Crémieux-Brilhac, vol. I, p. 489.

foreigners be included, not merely those from countries bordering France. It was urgent, he stressed, to remedy this problem in order not to dampen the fighting spirit of these foreigners and "to satisfy a public opinion impatient to see foreigners fulfill their obligations to the country."[92] During a parliamentary debate over the issue in December, Bonnet conceded that there were significant military reasons to quicken the naturalization process. He nevertheless argued for caution, since far too many undesirables had already been naturalized, and he again insisted that "racial affinities" and occupational skills had to be taken into account. On 26 December, Bonnet issued a circular that encompassed these new guidelines, but he refused to go any further.[93]

Even the Military was not immune to such prejudices, as its treatment of the refugees, and especially Jews, within the ranks of the Legion and the RMVE units shows. From the beginning the Legion commanders, with the complete support of the General Staff, insisted that former internees be treated differently than veteran Legionnaires. In October it was decided that the new recruits were to be stationed exclusively in North Africa or Indochina,[94] and in December, General Maurice Gamelin, Commander-in-Chief of the Army, declared that they would be kept in segregated units, contrary to long-standing Legion practice of creating units of mixed national backgrounds. This procedure was justified on the grounds that the army would have been remiss "to neglect the

92. Colson, Army Chief of Staff of the Interior, President of the Council, Ministry of National Defense and War, 1/EMA, to the Keeper of the Seals (Service des Naturalisations), 2 November 1939, SHAT 7N 2475, dos. 1. On public disgruntlement that the refugees were sitting idle in the camps while French citizens were dying, see the comments by Camille Blaisot during the Chamber of Deputies' debate over naturalization on 8 December 1939, *JODCD*, p. 2112 (cited also in Crémieux-Brilhac, vol. I, p. 497); *La Petite Gironde*, 2 December 1939, cited in Vormeier, Jean-Philippe Mathieu, and Claude Laharie, "Le Camp de Gurs," in Badia, et al., eds., *Les Barbelés de l'exil*, p. 242.

93. *JO, Débats, Sénat*, 7 December 1939, pp. 699-700; "Le problème des étrangers devant les Chambres," *Le Monde libre*, 16 December 1939, clipped in AIU Ms. 650 Boîte 13 (45). Keeper of the Seals, Ministry of Justice, Circular, 26 December 1939, APP DA 783 (Règlements).

94. Army Chief of Staff, Overseas Section, "Note sur l'utilisation des allemands, engagés volontaires pour la durée de la guerre," 9/EMA, 2 December 1939, SHAT 7N 2475, dos. 2.

security measures required by the regrouping of enemy subjects among whom dangerous elements may have slipped in."[95] Legion commanders were furthermore obsessed by the need to control the proportion of Germans among their ranks. Already in November the Commander of overseas operations began to worry that if the majority of German internees were eventually recruited into the Legion, they would constitute nearly a third of Legion troops, creating a "troublesome disequilibrium."[96] It was therefore decided as early as October that the proportion of Germans allowed to serve in North Africa be limited to 25 percent.[97] Ironically, this level was reached in May 1940, just at the time of the German invasion. According to an internal Defense Ministry memo, the proportion of Germans was now about 24 percent of all North African troops, and "it would be dangerous to increase it any further." "Under these conditions," the memo continued, "it seems desirable to put a definitive stop to enlistments of Germans in the Legion for the duration of the war." Hence, at the very moment the army most needed additional troops, the Legion Command actually began to ship German recruits back to the metropole, where they were either incorporated in prestataire formations or, if considered suspect, interned.[98]

Specifically antisemitic attitudes among Legion and RMVE commanders were even more pronounced. In his book, *Jews and*

95. Gamelin, "Annotation du Général Commandant en Chef les Forces Terrestres," 3 December 1939, SHAT 7N 2475 dos. 2; Ministry of National Defense and War, President of the Council, to the Commander in Chief of the North African Theater of Operations, No. 13091, 16 December 1939, SHAT 7N 2475, dos. 1$_2$.
96. Army Chief of Staff, Overseas Section, "Note sur l'utilisation des allemands, engagés volontaires pour la durée de la guerre," 9/EMA, 2 December 1939, SHAT 7N 2475, dos. 2. According to Pol, however, the refugees had been promised they would be put into special units when they arrived in North Africa; they were instead put into regular Legion units. Pol, p. 247.
97. Army Chief of Staff, Overseas Section, "Note sur l'utilisation des allemands, engagés volontaires pour la durée de la guerre," 9/EMA, 2 December 1939, SHAT 7N 2475, dos. 2. See also Crémieux-Brilhac, vol. I, p. 490.
98. Ministry of National Defense, EMA, n.d. [sometime after 10 May 1940], "Note pour M. le Général Ménard, chargé de l'utilisation des étrangers pour la Défense Nationale," SHAT 7N 2475 dos. 1$_2$. See also "Anti-Nazis Herded Back into Germany," NYT, 21 August 1940, p. 3. Crémieux-Brilhac claims this quota was never implemented, but this does not seem to be the case (vol. 1, p. 491).

– 155 –

the French Foreign Legion, the historian Zosa Szajkowski, himself an East European Jew who served in one of the RMVE units, wrote, "The attitude toward Jews was not exactly friendly," and that Jewish Legionnaires were convinced that the officers "did not want an almost completely Jewish regiment," a concern that stemmed from the fact that Jews constituted as much as three-quarters of the troops in several RMVE units.[99] Documentation from the French military archives bears out Szajkowski's claims. In evaluating the caliber of the different nationalities under his command, Adjutant-chef Mazzoni, commander of the Legion training camp at Barcarès in southern France, ranked stateless East European Jews at the bottom of the camp hierarchy. "With a few exceptions," he noted, "I do not think we can nurture great hopes for this category of enlistees."[100] Captain Pierre-Olivier Lapie, commander of the 13th demi-brigade, often referred to as "the troop of intellectuals" because of the high proportion of Jews, commented that his soldiers, while "excellent in study, in application, in calculations ... were detestable in drill, in marching, in fatigue duties, and in discipline, always complaining."[101] Szajkowski, too, recounts that Colonel Besson, commander of the 12th regiment, informed his troops that other officers had refused to work with them because of the large number of Jews.[102]

These attitudes filtered up to the highest levels of the Legion and ultimately influenced recruitment policies. On 10 January the Legion Command issued secret orders "to refuse from now on the enlistment of Jews in the Legion under a variety of pretexts." Future troop reinforcements from the RMVE to the Legion proper were "not to include any Jews." As for the 900 Jews already in the Legion, they were to be transferred into the less prestigious RMVE, together with "a hundred non-Jews (the least skilled, so as to

99. Szajkowski, *Jews and the Foreign Legion,* pp. 61, 70-71. See also Szajkowski, *Analytical Franco-Jewish Gazeteer,* 1939-45 (New York, 1966), pp. 22-25.
100. Adjudant-Chef Mazzoni, Chef de l'Annexe de Barcarès, Camp de Barcarès, to M. le Capitaine, Chef du S.I.L. at Sathonay, 25 January 1940, No. 118/AB, SHAT 7N 2475 (dos. 3); Porch, pp. 452-453.
101. Porch, p. 451.
102. Szajkowski, *Jews and the Foreign Legion,* p. 71. See also Crémieux-Brilhac, vol. I, p. 495.

remove from this operation any taint of being a measure targeted exclusively at Jews.)"[103] In February, the Commander-in-Chief in North Africa, General Charles Noguès, who subsequently threw in his lot with Pétain, reaffirmed these orders, declaring that he wanted "to see the Jewish candidates categorically kept out of the Legion."[104] The impact of these decisions was discernible immediately, since, as Szajkowski describes, when new Legion units were being assembled at the training camp at La Valbonne, near Lyons, Jews were systematically separated from the other new recruits and sent away, leaving "a terrible impression on the remaining Jews."[105]

Such attitudes may well have reflected military considerations rather than antisemitism per se, as Douglas Porch has recently speculated in his history of the Foreign Legion. That Legion commanders perceived the largely middle class, highly educated, and generally older Jewish recruits as poor fighting material is not surprising. The Jewish recruits, Porch notes, "were deeply out of sympathy with the culture of the barracks in which social acceptance was earned after a novitiate of bullying, brawling, drinking and womanizing." Furthermore, many Legion officers looked askance at the ideological motivations that had impelled these Jews to join the Legion. From their perspective, the Legion was supposed to be a strictly mercenary army, aloof from the political fray. These officers may also have feared rivalries between these refugees and veteran Legionnaires, whose politics often veered toward fascism.[106] Yet, while discrimination against Jewish recruits may have stemmed in part from antibourgeois and anti-intellectual biases, it is difficult to dismiss as anything other than antisemitism the constant barrage of insults suffered by Jewish Legionnaires. Szajkowski's sergeant, for example, referred to all the Jewish volunteers as "Salomon" and frequently shouted: "This is the Legion, not a synagogue!" In light of this evidence, as well as the

103. Note verbale (Secret), "Israélites de la Légion," 10 January 1940, SHAT 7N 2475 (dos. 3).
104. Perisse, Battalion Chief, 1er Bureau, Army Chief of Staff, to the Army Chief of Staff, Overseas Section, "Note pour information," 13 February 1940, SHAT 7N 2475, dos. 1$_2$.
105. Szajkowski, *Jews and the Foreign Legion*, p. 70.
106. Porch, pp. 442-443, 446-447; Koestler, *Scum of the Earth*, p. 186 note; Szajkowski, *Jews and the French Foreign Legion*, p. 83.

harsh treatment meted out to Jewish Legionnaires after the fall of France, Porch, too, admits that "it is difficult to escape the conclusion that antisemitism was the principal motivation in the Legion's desire to exclude Jews."[107]

These problems were not readily apparent to the public, however, and even the administration's most severe critics, such as Moutet, were willing to concede by the spring of 1940 that considerable progress had been made toward speeding up the criblage process, incorporating the refugees into the prestataire units and the Legion, and liquidating the camps.[108] These efforts, however, came to an abrupt halt on 10 May when the Wehrmacht invaded the Low Countries. As German troops headed toward France, a wave of fifth column hysteria swept the country that far exceeded anything that had surfaced in September, and the government again resorted to mass internments. On 13 May, General Pierre Héring, Military Governor of the Paris region, ordered the reinternment of all "Greater German" subjects between the ages of 17 and 55; two weeks later this age limit was extended to 65. Moreover, women up to the age of 55 were, for the first time, also included.[109] On 14 May posters went up throughout the metropolitan area ordering all men from "Greater Germany" to report to the Buffalo Stadium with a two-day supply of food, cutlery, and a maximum of 30 kilograms of baggage, while women were ordered to report to the Vélodrome d'Hiver on 15 May.[110] In the course of

107. Porch, p. 454.
108. Moutet, "Le sort des réfugiés politiques: Le régime imposé à de nombreux amis de notre pays a pu être amelioré: il n'est pas encore satisfaisant," *La Lumière*, 1 March 1940, pp. 1, 2. As the title of this article suggests, Moutet believed many problems still persisted.
109. Feuchtwanger, p. 77.
110. "Note de la Sûreté Nationale: Mesures à prendre au sujet des étrangers ressortissants allemands," 15 May 1940, MAE Z 791, pp. 90-91; Colson, Ministry of National Defense and War, 1/EMA, to the Military Governor General of Paris and the Commanding Generals of the Paris regions, No. 121. III 1/EMA, (Very Urgent), 15 May 1940, APP DA 784, Règlements (also in MAE Z 791, pp. 93-94); Bussière and Colson, Ministry of National Defense, 2/EMA, 2ème bureau, no. 12.207-I/EMA, and Ministry of the Interior, Sûreté Nationale, 7ème bureau, to the Prefects and Commanding Generals of the Paris regions, No. 46, 17 May 1940, APP DA 784 Règlements (also in SHAT 7N 2462 dos. 3); CAR, "Note on the Activity of the CAR from May 1, 1940," trans. in JDC No. 604; "L'internement des allemands," *Le Matin*, 15 May 1940,

these roundups it was estimated that some 8,000 "Greater German" subjects were apprehended in the Paris region, of whom at least 5,000 were Jews.[111] By the end of the month, these internment orders were extended to the provinces. Furthermore, the 10,000 refugees from Belgium, Holland and Luxembourg, who had streamed across the French border in flight from Hitler's armies, were also directed to the internment camps.[112]

Why the administration of Paul Reynaud, which had just come to power in March, resorted to this second round of internments can be explained only by the wave of fifth column hysteria that swept the country following the German invasion. This time, however, France was not acting alone. Even Great Britain interned its "enemy alien" population in May in response to fifth column fears, which had been raised to fever pitch by rumors that the Netherlands' defeat had been brought about in part by internal German subversion.[113] The French decision may nevertheless seem somewhat puzzling in that nearly all the refugees, with the exception of recent arrivals from Belgium, Holland and Luxembourg, had supposedly been screened by the criblage commissions. On the other hand, most of the refugees had been released only because they belonged to one of the categories fixed by the government in November, and the vast

---

p. 2; "Contre la cinquième colonne," Le Matin, 18 May 1940, pp. 1-2; "Les Allemands au Vélodrome d'Hiv," Le Matin, 24 May 1940, p. 2; "Les mesures de sécurité à l'égard des réfugiés étrangers sont renforcées," Le Matin, 25 May 1940, p. 2; "France Interns Germans," NYT, 16 May 1940; "Paris will Check on Refugees," NYT, 25 May 1940, p. 3; Kempner, pp. 456-457; Koessler, p. 119; Schramm and Vormeier, pp. 271-272; Hans-Albert Walter, pp. 300-302; Fabian and Coulmas, pp. 75-76; Grynberg, pp. 81-83; Tartakower and Grossmann, p. 152.

111. Grynberg, p. 83.

112. Although the French agreed to take German, Czech and Austrian refugees from the Low Countries on condition that they register with the police and ultimately go to the camps, every effort was made to prevent East European and stateless refugees among them, nearly all of whom were Jews, from entering the country. *American Jewish Year Book 5701*, 3 October 1940 to 21 September 1941, vol. XLII, p. 450; Belgian refugee committee member, "Report on the events from May 10th to July 30, 1940," 26 September 1940, JDC No. 618.

113. Koessler, pp. 104-114; Kempner, pp. 455-457; *American Jewish Year Book 5701*, 3 October 1940 to 21 September 1941, vol. XLII, p. 452; Louis de Jong, *The German Fifth Column in the Second World War*, trans. C. M. Geyl (Chicago, 1956), pp. 87-88; Cesarani, p. 45; Wasserstein, p. 88.

majority had never been screened individually. The government may also have wanted to appease popular apprehensions regarding the refugees, who were increasingly identified with their Nazi victimizers. All refugee memoirs attest to the depth of anti-German sentiment that surfaced in May. As trains transported refugees to internment camps in the south, crowds of onlookers threw stones and branded the refugees as Nazi spies.[114] One refugee actually expressed relief at being sent to a camp, claiming "It's our only defense against the popular indignation."[115] After a nightmarish journey to St. Cyprien, during which Belgian refugees traveled for three days in sealed cars without food or water, one Belgian refugee reported that "I have never seen such a fear of spies, no, not even in 1914."[116] French officers, too, now treated the refugees as outright criminals. According to Koestler, while being escorted to the Buffalo Stadium, he was told by one French officer that "we're going to line you up and shoot you ourselves before the Germans come."[117]

Yet the decision to go ahead with the internments was motivated not only by the need to appease public opinion. Rather, Georges Mandel, a staunch conservative of Jewish background who became Minister of the Interior on 18 May, was dead-set on weeding out potential fifth columnists, including those who had infiltrated the émigré population. Hence, although many historians and even some refugees have minimized Mandel's responsibility for the crackdown in May, the action must be seen as an integral aspect of his anti-fifth column crusade in general. Unlike his predecessors, Mandel for the first time energetically pursued potential traitors on the extreme right as well as the Communist left, and among the notorious right-wing Nazi sympathizers he arrested were Charles Lesca, director of *Je suis partout*, his collaborator Alain Laubreaux, and the Baron Robert de Fabre-Luce.[118]

---

114. Letter from St. Cyprien, 16 September 1940, JDC No. 618; Fittko, pp. 11, 17, 32; Schramm and Vormeier, p. 10; Lania, pp. 129-130.
115. Lania, p. 131.
116. Letter from St. Cyprien, 16 September 1940, JDC No. 618. On the odyssey of the Belgian refugees see also Feuchtwanger, p. 96.
117. Koestler, *Scum of the Earth*, p. 176. See also de Jong, pp. 90-93.
118. Pol, pp. 171, 175; John M. Sherwood, *Georges Mandel and the Third Republic* (Stanford, CA, 1970), pp. 234-236; Kempner, pp. 454-455; Lazareff, p. 303. On

Despite this focus on the extreme right, Mandel gave no respite to the Communist left or the foreign population. On 26 May the *New York Times* reported that Mandel had just arrested the wives of two missing Communist Party leaders, André Marty and Gabriel Péri, for having engaged in defeatist propaganda, and it added,

> Under M. Mandel's direction, raids have been multiplied in the Paris region. More than 2,000 cafés and public establishments were visited and 62,000 persons questioned in these raids or on the streets. This resulted in the arrest of 500 individuals and 334 foreigners have been sent to concentration camps.[119]

By pursuing this antileftist campaign, Mandel furthermore sent a clear signal that he concurred fully with the conclusions of an internal Sûreté Nationale memorandum issued on 14 May, just prior to his taking office. In this memorandum, entitled "German efforts to weaken French morale," the director of the Sûreté proclaimed that, "The defeatism borne of German inspiration and Communist propaganda is, in reality, two forms of a vast demoralization campaign which must be repressed with equal attention and equal rigor," and he recommended that certain groups be placed under heightened surveillance, including "the foreign colonies, among whom the intelligence services from across the Rhine may easily have found contacts, and in particular German women who, for the most part, have not been interned."[120] Interestingly, Mandel's fifth column fears did not extend to the Italian immigrant population. Despite pre-existing orders that Italians, too, were to be interned *en masse* if Italy declared war, which occurred on 10 June, these orders were canceled due to the economic "perturbations" that were expected to ensue. In the end only individual Italians considered suspect were sent to the camps.[121]

---

these right-wing collaborators see Pascal Ory, *Les Collaborateurs*, 1940-45 (Paris, 1976), ch. 2, pp. 11-35.

119. "Communists' Wives Seized in France," *NYT*, 26 May 1940, p. 33. See also de Jong, p. 93.

120. Ministry of the Interior, Sûreté Nationale, to the Prefects, P.A. 7.364/I, "Efforts allemands pour atteindre le moral français," 14 May 1940, AN F7 14713.

121. Colson, Ministry of National Defense, to the Military Governor General of Paris and the Commanding Generals of the Paris regions, EMA, 1er Bureau, 7 and 13 May 1940, SHAT 7N 2462 dos. 3; Fabian and Coulmas, pp. 68-69; Koessler, p. 120.

As the Germans advanced southward, capturing Paris on 14 June, the fate of the refugees became a living hell. For those in the camps, living conditions deteriorated sharply. The two major camps, St. Cyprien for men and Gurs for women, were disease ridden and overcrowded, and became even more so as they absorbed growing numbers of refugees evacuated from camps in the north. St. Cyprien, nicknamed the "hell of Perpignan" by its former Spanish inmates, was the worst. Lacking vegetation, the place was regularly besieged by sandstorms. During the day the heat and sun were intolerable, while at night temperatures dropped close to freezing. Sanitary conditions were abysmal: toilet paper was unknown, and the water infected with typhoid. As one refugee reported, "Dysentery is raging to the point of insanity." The barracks remained unlit, and there were no mattresses.[122] Moreover, there was now no hope of release. When a delegation of former premiers and left-wing members of Parliament petitioned Reynaud on 16 May to release the anti-Nazi refugees in the camps, the Prime Minister allegedly "received the delegation ungraciously and replied that he had far more important things to attend to."[123]

As Nazi victory seemed imminent, a veritable panic seized those refugees trapped in the camps and who now faced the nightmarish prospect of being turned over wholesale to their German persecutors. Not surprisingly, German advances emboldened some refugees to reveal themselves as Nazi sympathizers. "Hitlerites," Feuchtwanger commented, "seemed to sprout more numerously the nearer Hitler's armies came."[124] The overwhelming majority of refugees were petrified, however, and pleaded with camp commanders to be released. Astonishingly, the government had made no provisions for the internees in the advent of a German victory, and camp commanders were left to their own devices. Most ultimately followed the dictates of their consciences, and complied

---

122. For descriptions of St. Cyprien from May through the fall of 1940, see Member of the Belgian refugee committee, "Report on the events from May 10th to July 30, 1940," 26 September 1940, JDC No. 618; Letter from St. Cyprien, 16 September 1940, JDC No. 618; "The Plight of Jewish Refugees in French Camps," excerpt from *Jewish Daily Forward*, 31 October 1940, JDC No. 618.
123. Lazareff, diary entry, 16 May 1940, p. 288.
124. Feuchtwanger, p. 110. See also Lania, pp. 157-158.

with refugee demands, but others refused, claiming that they could not disobey orders.[125] When the armistice was finally announced on 22 June, the refugees initially reacted with relief, but this sentiment soon gave way to despair as the terms, particularly of article 19, became known. This article stated that "The French Government is obliged to surrender upon demand all Germans named by the German Government in France, as well as in French possessions, Colonies, Protectorate Territories and Mandates."[126] The terror inspired by article 19 as well as the hopelessness caused by Hitler's triumph sparked a wave of suicides. Among the most prominent refugees who took their lives were the literary critic, Walter Benjamin; the writer and art historian, Carl Einstein; and the playwright, Walter Hasenclever.[127]

Paradoxically, many refugees chose to remain in the camps, calculating that they were safer there than roaming the countryside without resources and contacts.[128] For those who escaped, however, the logical solution, after having located their families, was to get out of France as quickly as possible. A fortunate few were able to board the last British ships departing from Bordeaux.[129] The vast majority flocked to Marseille where they tried desperately to procure overseas, and especially American, visas, with which they were then able to obtain transit visas for Spain and Portugal. In

125. Hans-Albert Walter, pp. 302-303, 305-307; Tartakower and Grossmann, pp. 153-154; Fittko, p. 51; Grynberg, p. 138; Feuchtwanger, pp. 100-126; A. Herenroth to M. Troper, [15] July 1940, JDC No. 618, pp. 121-122; Herbert Zivi, I. Kampf and Moise Torczyner, Camp de St. Cyprien, to Morris Troper of the JDC, 17 July 1940, JDC No. 618. International organizations also appealed to the French government to release the refugees from the camps. See "Asks France to Free Refugees," *NYT*, 21 June 1940, p. 13.

126. Varian Fry, *Surrender on Demand* (New York, 1945), pp. ix-x; Palmier, vol. II, pp. 129-130; Fabian and Coulmas, p. 77; Schramm and Vormeier, p. 265; Tartakower and Grossmann, p. 154; Hans-Albert Walter, p. 309; Koestler, *Scum of the Earth*, p. 151.

127. Tartakower and Grossmann, pp. 156-157; Feuchtwanger, pp. 131, 171-174; Lania, p. 160; Koestler, *Scum of the Earth*, pp. 205-206, 238, 260-261; A. Herenroth to M. Troper, [15] July 1940, JDC No. 618, pp. 121-122. Benjamin tried to escape over the Pyrenees; when this failed he committed suicide. Fittko, ch. 7, pp. 103-115. Koestler suggests that many of those who committed suicide may not have done so had they believed that Great Britain would fight on.

128. Feuchtwanger, p. 129.

129. Lazareff, p. 342; Koestler, *Scum of the Earth*, pp. 206-207.

those days, as relief worker Varian Fry noted, the U.S. consulate was generally cooperative, and visas were not particularly difficult to come by. A more significant problem was securing a French exit visa, without which it was impossible to leave the country legally. Fortunately, for many refugees this requirement was rarely enforced.[130] Still, the process of securing these papers usually took several weeks, and in the meantime a cloud of uncertainty hung over the refugees. As Fry observed, so great was the tension that refugees trapped in the south "believed that every ring of the doorbell, every step on the stair, every knock on the door might be the police come to get them and deliver them to the Gestapo."[131]

Refugees who served in the prestataire service, the RMVE, or the Legion proper, although exempted from reinternment, did not fare significantly better. While some prestataires succeeded in escaping to Great Britain, the majority fled south, often with assistance from the British, where they joined the masses of other foreigners.[132] And, although the Legion proper did not fight on French soil, RMVE units ultimately did. At first it seemed that the antisemitism and xenophobia most refugees had previously encountered vanished with their arrival at the front. For the first time, Szajkowski noted, Jewish recruits were treated as human beings.[133] Nevertheless, once the military situation began to deteriorate, antisemitism resurfaced with a vengeance. According to Hans Habe, who served in the 21st RMVE, the response of one general to the news that 500 soldiers had been lost in the battle of Ste. Menehould, was simply, "Five hundred Jews the less." Habe also argued that the Army Command deliberately used the RMVE troops as cannon fodder to protect French forces. As he states in his memoir, *A Thousand Shall Fall*, the Generals deliberately blew up the lines of retreat "to keep the Germans busy massacring us, in

130. On problems getting exit visas in the summer of 1940, see Fry, pp. 6-7, 14-19; Fittko, p. 96.
131. Fry, p. 13. See also Tartakower and Grossmann, pp. 156-157; Kempner, pp. 449-450. For other descriptions of this period, see Koestler, *Scum of the Earth*, pp. 155-264; Feuchtwanger, pp. 169-261; Alfred Döblin, *Destiny's Journey*, trans. Edna Passler (New York, 1992), pp. 150-210; Fittko, pp. 55-101.
132. Lazareff, p. 342; Koestler, *Scum of the Earth*, pp. 276-277.
133. Szajkowski, *Jews and the Foreign Legion*, p. 72; Porch, pp. 454-455.

order to gain as much time as possible for the troops retreating southward."[134] That there was a massacre is beyond dispute; unofficial sources after the war testified that as many as 80 percent of the 21st regiment had been declared missing in action.[135] Whether this massacre was deliberately planned remains unclear even today. What is certain, however, is that these troops were sent into battle with badly outdated equipment and with no logistical support. Szajkowski states that his regiment wore World War I uniforms and carried antiquated guns dating back to 1907 or earlier, while Habe was issued an 1891 Remington.[136] According to Porch, the equipment of the 12th REI (Régiment Etranger d'Infanterie) was in such paltry shape that it had to be held together with string – hence the Germans nicknamed it the "string regiment." Moreover, these troops were never provided with adequate air, artillery or tank support.[137]

Despite the abysmal quality of their armaments and munitions, these troops fought with courage and fortitude. Habe, who himself was not Jewish, claimed that the East European Jews with whom he fought were the most heroic of the lot. From his perspective the French Army was thoroughly demoralized, from top to bottom, and the soldiers in the field had not a clue what they were fighting for. French soldiers, according to Habe, were amazed that anyone would have volunteered to fight, and their favorite slogan, he claimed, was "run for your lives!"[138] Jewish recruits, on the other hand, knew precisely what they were fighting for, and they fought with a vengeance that surprised many of their commanders.[139] In

---

134. Hans Habe, *A Thousand Shall Fall*, trans. Norbert Guterman (New York, 1941), pp. 165, 137. According to Koestler, one army colonel maintained that his troops had been attacked not by the Germans, but by "a column of Jewish refugees" near Longwy, and his troops found this claim entirely credible. Koestler, *Scum of the Earth*, p. 232.

135. Tartakower and Grossmann, pp. 145-146; Porch, pp. 458-461. According to Porch, losses in other regiments were similarly high. The 11th REI lost 75 percent of its men and the 12th over 90 percent.

136. Szajkowski, *Jews and the Foreign Legion*, pp. 72-73; Habe, p. 199.

137. Porch, p. 457, see also p. 461.

138. Habe, p. 46.

139. Habe, pp. 54-55, 130. According to Koestler, even left-wing soldiers, although they knew what they were fighting against, no longer knew what they were

a report issued after the armistice, the commander of the 12th REI commented that "the Polish Jews, who by nature are not very courageous, have performed their duty; one of the wounded refused to allow himself to be evacuated."[140] Years later, General Brothier remarked: "In observing the behavior of our Jewish volunteers, later I better understood why, in the Israeli army, familiarity and slovenliness went so well with courage and a redoubtable efficiency."[141] To be sure, these assessments were still riddled with ambivalence toward Jews. Nevertheless, precisely because of this ambivalence, the praise is that much more compelling.

France's military defeat, however, brought an end to any prospect that the situation of the refugees might improve. Indeed, as we know, under the Vichy regime their prospects declined sharply. Nevertheless, it is essential to remember that nothing was determined until May, and even then the administration's policy was more one of confusion than deliberate persecution. As we have seen, those countervailing forces that had characterized French refugee policy throughout the 1930s continued to operate even during the "phony war." To be sure, fifth column fears, heightened by the Nazi-Soviet non-aggression pact, resulted in the mass internments of September and May. Nevertheless, in between those dates powerful counter pressures, including military demands for more manpower as well as international and domestic criticism of the internments and the seizures of refugees at sea, persuaded the administration to release the majority of refugees and to utilize them either in the Foreign Legion or the prestataire service. As a result, the situation of the refugees improved dramatically by the spring of 1940, and relief organizations had every reason to expect that the camps, with one or two exceptions, would be liquidated in the near future. Only in May, when Mandel inaugurated the second wave of mass internments, did it become clear that fifth column fears would prevail over efforts to utilize the refugees constructively in the war effort. Hence,

---

fighting for since they, too, had lost faith in democracy. See Koestler, *Scum of the Earth*, pp. 48, 273.

140. "Extraits de fiches de renseignements établis après l'armistice de 1940 par le commandant Jacquot," n.d., SHAT 7N 2475 (dos. 3).

141. Porch, p. 454. See also Crémieux-Brilhac, vol. I, p. 491.

although Reynaud ultimately opted for a hard-line position, it is essential to remember that the situation between September and May remained one of considerable fluidity.[142]

In the long run, however, there is also no doubt that by having failed to implement a more complete mobilization of the refugee population for the war effort, France wasted an enormous reservoir of manpower, talent and professional skills. Whether a more farsighted use of foreigners in general and refugees in particular might have enabled France to win the war will obviously never be known. There can be no question, though, that France's chances of victory would have been improved had she made better use of the millions of foreigners residing on French soil, many of whom were eager to serve and often possessed valuable technical and professional skills. Instances such as that cited by Porch, in which a French intelligence officer was forbidden from using immigrant cryptographers until they had enlisted in the Legion, or another case in which a German refugee industrialist released from the camps was barred from returning to his factory since it was engaged in defense work, could only have weakened French military preparedness. Similarly, as Porch has suggested, French defenses might have been bolstered had the army allowed regular Legion regiments to fight on French soil.[143] That xenophobia and anti-semitism were allowed to obstruct military efficiency in these ways strongly suggests that the administration was not prepared to mobilize every available resource for the sake of winning the war. To have done so would ultimately have entailed a radical liberalization of naturalization procedures, a proposition the administration was not ready to countenance, despite some support for such a measure in parliament and the press.

142. Crémieux-Brilhac also stresses the distinction between the treatment of foreigners during the "phoney war" and their subsequent treatment under the Vichy regime (vol. I, ch. 9, pp. 484-499).
143. Porch, pp. 444-446; "Report on the Visit to the Camp of St. Juste en Chaussée," 21 December 1939, attached to "Minutes of plenary meeting of Commission des Centres de Rassemblement de l'Intercomité des Oeuvres Françaises," 1 December 1939, JDC No. 617. See also Report of Heinz Soffner, former Secretary of the Federation of Austrian Emigrants in Paris, "The Internment of refugees in France during the War: Legal situation, facts, conclusions," JDC No. 618; Feuchtwanger, p. 4.

But aside from the issue of manpower and talent, it is also necessary to ask whether the internments and the persistence of xenophobia and antisemitism tell us anything about the larger causes for France's defeat. As the rich memoir literature from this period suggests, many refugees perceived their experiences to be emblematic of larger problems that ultimately brought about the country's demise. For Lion Feuchtwanger, for example, the internments were due not to deliberate malice or persecutory zeal on the part of the government. In speaking of his experiences at the camp of Les Milles, he repeatedly stressed that, "There was never a case of beating, of punching, of verbal abuse." Rather, as he saw it, it was the very muddledness of French policy, the fact that French statesmen did not have their priorities straight, that led to the internments and ultimately to the defeat. Even if the initial internments were justified, the fact that the refugees were allowed to languish in the camps for months afterwards, despite the fact that they could have been put to use for the war effort, was, Feuchtwanger believed, the result of "pure thoughtlessness, a lack of talent for organization." Whereas the German devil was one of sadism, the French devil assumed a more congenial, but no less pernicious form – that of bureaucratic ineptitude, irresponsibility, and a "genteel indifference to the sufferings of others," summed up by the motto, *"je m'en fous,"* or "I don't give a damn." For Feuchtwanger, this *"je m'en foutist"* attitude was responsible not only for the ill-conceived refugee policies of the Daladier administration, but for the military debacle as well.[144]

While Feuchtwanger put the primary blame on bureaucratic ineptitude, others saw the internments as sign of the deep defeatist mentality that had penetrated the bureaucracy, the population at large, and perhaps most significantly, the army command. According to Koestler, the internment of the anti-Nazi refugees was only one of many signs that the government hated its enemies on the left, particularly the foreigners, far more than its enemies on the right. As Koestler explained, military officers frequently blamed the war not on Hitler, but on Léon Blum & Co. – the Socialists and Communists, the refugees, and the Jews – and no one believed any

---

144. Feuchtwanger, pp. 40-42, 48-49, 85.

longer in fighting to save democracy and freedom. Rather, the prevailing sentiment among the population as a whole, and the troops as well, was *"Il faillait en finir"* – "Let's get it over with," a slogan that Koestler maintained summed up the tragedy of France. A desire to preserve the status quo and be left in peace, together with the failure to see fascism and Nazism as significant threats to democracy, especially in comparison to Communism, ultimately brought about what Koestler, together with Heinz Pol, referred to as the "suicide" of France.[145] Hans Habe, too, perceived defeatism to be rampant among the ranks of the military. While his own commander, Lieutenant Saint-Brice, did his utmost to fight the Germans, Saint-Brice's superiors, according to Habe, wanted peace at any price and simply delivered their country over to the Germans. As one captain allegedly told Saint-Brice, "he loved France more than he loved Hitler, but … he loved Hitler more than Léon Blum." On another occasion Saint-Brice explained that the real reason for France's defeat was not the state of her weaponry or munitions, but rather that "this was a war of Frenchmen against Frenchmen. And no one told us …."[146]

Despite the subjectivity of these accounts, the extent to which they concur in their assessments of administrative and military weaknesses, as well as on the pervasiveness of a defeatist mentality, is striking, and there is no doubt that the refugee experience afforded these writers a unique vantage point with which to survey the larger historical forces at work. Yet, these accounts would also agree that the experience of refugees during the thirties, while perhaps a prelude to what was to come during the Vichy era, nevertheless remained distinct from that experience. Just as Feuchtwanger claimed that the nature of French refugee policy from September 1939 through June 1940 was not one of deliberate malice, in contrast to the situation in Germany, the same could also be said when comparing the refugee policies of the Daladier and Reynaud administrations to those of the Vichy regime. While xenophobia and antisemitism colored some of the policies under

---

145. Koestler, *Scum of the Earth*, pp. 67, 141-143, 159, 193. Pol, p. 273, claims the motto that summed up the mentality that led to debacle was *"tout s'arrangera."*
146. Habe, pp. 151, 153.

Daladier and Reynaud, these forces generally remained submerged. Under Vichy, however, deliberate malice and outright antisemitism surfaced almost immediately, and all notions that there might still be constructive solutions to the refugee crisis, solutions that would allow at least a portion of the refugees to live freely in France, were shelved once and for all. Under Vichy, in contrast to the situation at the end of the 1930s, there was simply no one left to argue the liberal line. Given the sharp deterioration of the economy following the defeat as well as the psychological need to find scapegoats, it is not surprising that the refugee population, which had so enthusiastically endorsed the war, became a principal target of popular indignation and administrative wrath. Already in September 1940 one Belgian refugee trapped in southern France lamented that, "The democratic ideal, which seemed to be the essence of France itself, has yielded to xenophobia, [and] to poorly understood totalitarianism ...."[147]

---

* This article is based on a chapter in the forthcoming book *Uneasy Asylum: France and the Jewish Refugee Crisis of the 1930s*. The author would like to thank the National Endowment for the Humanities, the Institute for Advanced Study, the Memorial Foundation for Jewish Culture, and Brown University for their generous support of this project.

147. Member of the Belgian refugee committee, "Report on the events from May 10th to July 30, 1940," 26 September 1940, JDC No. 618.

VII
PRELUDE TO DEFEAT
Franco-Soviet Relations, 1919-1939[1]

Michael Jabara Carley

Since the fall of France in May-June 1940 historians and others have advanced various explanations to account for the sudden, shocking collapse of the once powerful French army. Such reasons range from the "decadence" and corruption of the Third Republic to the ineptitude and cowardice of the French high command. "The French have no blood left in their veins ... the French are funks," spat out Jean-Paul Sartre's fictional characters in *Le Sursis*.

There is, nevertheless, another aspect of the French collapse in 1940 to which historians have devoted little attention. Franco-Russian relations were vital to French security before the First World War; in 1914 the Russian army diverted German divisions to the Eastern Front, contributing to the French victory on the Marne. Although Franco-Soviet relations should have been equally important to French security in 1940, France then had no Russian ally to draw off German divisions to the east.

During the interwar years Franco-Soviet relations were nearly always difficult and nasty, having been poisoned by the Bolshevik

---

1. I wish to thank the Social Sciences and Humanities Research Council of Canada for financial support and the Humanities and Social Sciences Federation of Canada for leaves of absence to do continuing research.

revolution in November 1917. Anti-Bolshevik ideologues rejected any accommodation with the Soviet and held the upper hand over Realists, who said that judgments about Soviet communism should not affect questions of national security and trade. The debate between Realist and Ideologue continued throughout the interwar years: it pivoted ultimately on the question of who was France's paramount enemy: Nazi Germany or Soviet Russia?

Immediately after the Bolshevik seizure of power in 1917 Franco-Soviet relations were overtly belligerent. The Bolshevik revolution offended and angered the French government. The Soviet annulled the Russian state debt, nationalized banks and industries, summoned the European proletariat to socialist revolution, and withdrew from the war against Germany. In response, the French and Allied governments blockaded Soviet Russia and sent troops to overthrow Soviet authority.

The French government shuddered at the prospect of Bolshevik revolution in Europe and sought to eradicate it in Russia before the "virus" could spread. "The Bolshevik question has ceased to be solely a Russian affair, and has become an international problem," said the Quai d'Orsay, the French foreign ministry, in November 1918.[2] The "Bolshies," no longer the *Boche*, preoccupied the French government. In December 1918 France sent troops to southern Russia. But it could not intervene in sufficient strength and withdrew French forces precipitously in April 1919, jeered by choirs of mutinous sailors singing the *Internationale*.[3]

In self-defence, as much as by principle, the Bolsheviks organized the Communist International, the Comintern, sending out agents to promote world revolution. The French government fell back on a strategy of containment, the *cordon sanitaire*, to build up a ring of anti-Bolshevik states on Russia's western frontier – led by Poland and Rumania – to stop the spread of revolutionary Bolshevism and to keep Germany and Russia apart. In 1920 France condoned a Pol-

---

2. Stephen Pichon, French foreign minister, to P. Dutasta, French minister in Berne, 14 Nov. 1918, Ministère des Affaires étrangères, Paris [MAÉ], ancienne série Z- Europe, 1918-40, followed by the geographic subheading, volume and folio numbers, thus Z-Russie/1144, 282-283.

3. M. J. Carley, *Revolution and Intervention: The French Government and the Russian Civil War, 1917-19* (Montréal and Kingston, Ont., 1983).

ish offensive in Belorussia and the Ukraine to throw back Russia's western frontiers and to destabilize the Soviet in Moscow. Polish Marshal Jozef Pilsudski sent intermediaries to Paris to ask French premier Alexandre Millerand for at least a blind eye to a spring offensive against the Red Army. Poland counted on French material support, said Pilsudski, to conduct its military operations. Millerand obliged by sending powder and shell to the Polish army.[4]

Pilsudski's offensive failed disastrously and led to a Red Army counter-offensive which in turn failed calamitously before Warsaw in August 1920. It was a near-run thing, but the French government still grasped at hope of reversing Soviet power. Death's rattle was the anti-Bolshevik rebellion at the Soviet fortress of Kronstadt in March 1921. The French government declared that it would not intervene in Russian internal affairs, but it suggested to the British Foreign Office that the Allies provide the Kronstadt insurgents with victuals and medical supplies. It was a "very disingenuous" position, noted a Foreign Office clerk, but the British government itself was tempted.[5] Supplies began to reach Kronstadt, with the Finnish government's connivance, but the Red Army soon crushed the rebellion and with it, the last French hopes of downing the Bolsheviks.[6]

France would have to learn to live with Soviet Russia – not easy when Bolshevism was infectious and 12 billions in "stolen" investments rankled the French *grande bourgeoisie*, the so-called "two hundred families." Already in 1920 while president Millerand ignored Polish preparations for a spring offensive, pressure mounted for a resumption of trade with Russia. Soviet Russia, though victorious in

---

4. Untitled note by E. Petit, Millerand's *chef du cabinet*, nd [but March 1920]; B. V. Savinkov to Petit [?], 28 Jan. 1920, and enclosed untitled, confidential note, Archives nationales, Paris [AN], Papiers Millerand, 470AP/63; also M. J. Carley, "The Politics of Anti-Bolshevism: The French Government and the Russo-Polish War, December 1919 to May 1920," *Historical Journal* 19 (1976): 172; and Carley, "Anti-Bolshevism in French Foreign Policy: The Crisis in Poland in 1920," *International History Review* 2 (1980): 410-431.

5. Jacket nº N3377/4/38, 16 March 1921, Public Record Office, London [PRO], Foreign Office [FO] 371 6847; various papers in Jacket nº N2962/2/38, 7 March 1921, PRO FO 371 6845; and Philippe Berthelot, secretary-general, Quai d'Orsay (in London), to Aristide Briand, French foreign minister, nº 190, 8 March 1921, MAÉ Z-Russie/97, 194.

6. Jean Fabre, French minister in Helsingfors, nº 72, 24 March 1921, MAÉ Z-Russie/98, 57ff.

the civil war, was ruined and needed to buy and borrow in the west to rebuild. Scoundrels and adventurers first, more respectable merchants later, were willing to risk the business and lobbied the French government to lift trade restrictions. They feared being left behind by American, British, and other competitors.[7] In March 1920 M.M. Litvinov, deputy commissar for foreign affairs, told a French intermediary that the Soviet government wanted trade relations and would "pay its debts" when war with Poland had ended. Just as importantly, Litvinov stressed that France, unlike Great Britain, had an interest in a strong Russian state. The implicit reference to French security against Germany was not the last time Litvinov would draw French attention to their common security interests.[8]

In 1920 the French government ignored Litvinov's plea for negotiations. But in 1921-1922 circumstances changed. Trade prospects in Soviet Russia became increasingly attractive, and nearly united business opposition to trade relations with Soviet Russia slowly broke down. Nonetheless, "stolen" investments and fears that trade would finance Bolshevik propaganda deadened the French profit motive. Soviet policy wanted to revive it, seeking to encourage trade and political relations with France and the West. At the same time, the Bolsheviks refused western demands for recognition of tsarist debts and for compensation of foreign nationals for property expropriated in Russia. The appetite for profit gradually divided the western powers and reduced the danger of a capitalist *bloc* against the USSR. "Gold will not jingle less in French pockets than in those of your competitors," observed maliciously Soviet commissar for foreign trade, L. B. Krasin. French officials recognized the strategy: Get businessmen "to bite" at attractive contract offers, but link them to the establishment of diplomatic relations.[9] This was a dupe's game, thought the French, and they would not play – anyway, not at first.

7. Auguste Isaac, commerce minister, to Millerand, 29 March 1920, MAÉ Z-Russie/514, 39-40.
8. M. A. Mikhailov, agent of the French trading firm SOCIFROS (Copenhagen), to SOCIFROS, Paris, 2 March 1920, MAÉ Z-Russie/69, 83-91; and Henri Martin, French minister in Copenhagen, nºs 109-112, 13 March 1920, *ibid.*, 106-109.
9. "Note de M. [Fernand] Grenard pour le directeur des Affaires politiques," 22 July 1922, MAÉ Z-Russie/582, 256-260; "Note sur les relations commerciales entre la

Other considerations began to affect French policy. France became increasingly embroiled with Germany over reparations and security issues, culminating in the Ruhr crisis in January 1923. These circumstances led some French officials and politicians to favour a rapprochement with Soviet Russia. Edouard Herriot, president of the Radical party, was the first important politician to urge a Franco-Soviet rapprochement. In September 1922 Herriot made a much publicized visit to Russia. He met with Soviet officials and returned to Paris as an advocate of better Franco-Soviet relations. He wrote a series of articles on his trip in the Paris daily, *Le Petit Parisien*, and met with then President Millerand and the premier and foreign minister, Raymond Poincaré. Herriot also wrote privately to G. V. Chicherin, the Soviet commissar for foreign affairs, marking his determination to bring about an improvement in Franco-Soviet relations. "I have encountered opposition," he wrote, "but I am persistent and I will succeed ..."[10] Even Radical Gaston Doumergue, who soon succeeded Millerand as president, wrote in the press in favour of better relations. The British ambassador in Paris, Lord Crewe, noticed Doumergue's article and commented that, "Although France has excellent reasons for disliking the present regime in Russia, she has still better reasons for disliking and mistrusting Germany."[11] The French would not want to drive Russia into waiting German arms.

Apart from the politicians, some French officials in the Quai d'Orsay, motivated by the traditional French need for an eastern counter-balance to Germany, advocated better relations with Soviet Russia. The Ruhr crisis made it imperative "to resume a policy of entente with Russia as soon as possible," said Emmanuel Peretti de la Rocca, political director at the Quai d'Orsay.[12] Peretti went to see Marshal Ferdinand Foch, who had once favoured coop-

---

Russie soviétique et les citoyens français," Sous-direction d'Europe [Europe], 25 Aug. 1921, MAÉ, ancienne série C - Relations commerciales [RC], 1920-40, Russie/2044 (not paginated); and "Declaration of the official representative of the RSFSR in Great Britain L. B. Krasin ...," Sept. 1921, Kommissiia po izdaniiu diplomaticheskikh dokumentov, *Dokumenty vneshnei politiki SSSR [DVP]*, 22 vols. (Moscow, 1959-) IV, 384-385.

10. Herriot to Chicherin, 26 Oct. 1922, DVP, V, 667.
11. Crewe, nº 3032 (C.), 29 Dec. 1922, N76/62/38, PRO FO 371 9343.
12. "Conversations avec Peretti et [René] Sicard [chief, Bureau du contrôle des étrangers]," by Alfred Vignon, deputy secretary-general to president Millerand, 5 Jan. 1923, MAÉ, Papiers Millerand/70, 13.

eration with the Bolsheviks against Germany. Not any more, and Foch sent Peretti away. But the political director did not give up so easily. "An alliance with the Russian people is necessary to France," he said. "We need a point of support in Europe which only the Russian land mass can offer us and with which we have no conflict of interest." Peretti did not like Bolshevism any more than his colleagues, but he drew a distinction between the Bolsheviks and "the Russian people" with whom France needed to resume contact.[13]

Peretti promoted this view throughout 1923, but Millerand blocked any change in policy. The French president's anti-Bolshevism did not soften with time. "The truth is," Millerand said, "that there is nothing to be done with anarchy, and it is anarchy which has implanted itself in forsaken Russia."[14] In answer to French merchants who wanted to trade in Russia, he remarked, that they "are building on sand."[15] In October, Alfred Vignon, Millerand's deputy secretary-general, advised Peretti that the president "has not changed his mind." And in December 1923, when Peretti wanted to pursue informal contacts with Soviet representatives, Millerand signaled that nothing should be done without his consent. Uneasy about such contacts, Millerand did not want them to go further.[16] Poincaré appears to have been somewhat more open to Soviet overtures, but his terms for agreement – formal Soviet recognition of all tsarist debts, resumption of interest payments, and compensation to French nationals – were unacceptable to the Soviet government. "Let's 'live and let live,'" said the commissar for foreign affairs, G.V. Chicherin, "but don't ask us to give up first principles."[17]

13. "France-Russie," Vignon, 22 Feb. 1923, MAÉ Papiers Millerand/70, 31; and "De l'opportunité d'une représentation économique officielle en Russie soviétique," MAÉ, 23 Feb. 1923, ibid., 42-49 (Peretti's handwritten minute is on folio 49).
14. Millerand to Aimé de Fleuriau, French minister in Peking, 25 April 1923, AN Papiers Millerand, 470AP/69.
15. "Envoi de M. [Paul-François] de Chevilly ... extrait des Izvestia ...," 27 Aug. 1923, quoting a French businessman, Antoine Semidei, MAÉ Z-Russie/82, 87.
16. "Conversation avec Peretti, Russie," Vignon, 10 Oct. 1923, MAÉ Papiers Millerand/70, 144; "Conversation avec Peretti, France-Soviets," Vignon, 22 Dec. 1923, ibid., 197; and "France-Soviets," Vignon, 29 Dec. 1923, ibid., 210-212.
17. Poincaré to Fernand Couget, French minister in Prague, nºs 26-35; and elsewhere, secret, 31 Jan. 1924, MAÉ Z-Russie/353, 104-108; "Report of a conversation with Czech foreign minister Eduard Benes," by K. K. Iurenev, Soviet representative in Prague, 3 January 1924, DVP, VII, 11-13; "Interview of People's commissar for foreign

French officials had not the slightest doubt that the USSR wanted better relations. Soviet overtures were repeated and exasperating. According to a briefing paper for Millerand, "the efforts which, in every form and by every means, the Soviets have multiplied during the last three years ... to shake [French] resolution, demonstrate what price they attach" to better relations with France.[18] But the French government would not budge, not anyway, until after national elections in the spring of 1924.

As was often to happen, French elections affected Franco-Soviet relations – and the political calculations of Herriot's *Cartel des gauches* and Millerand's *Bloc national*. Even in 1922, Herriot thought that public debate on resumption of Franco-Soviet relations would be useful in winning political power. A rapprochement, leading to a debt settlement and increased trade, would win support from bondholders as well as from workers and merchants and manufacturers engaged in the Russian trade.[19] Millerand's advisors calculated that improved Franco-Soviet relations could help the *Cartel* by gaining French Communist votes in the upcoming elections. But the Poincaré government was not above passing a law in Parliament, making small concessions to bondholders, to counter the *Cartel*'s strategy.[20]

Whatever these opposing calculations, the *Cartel* won the 1924 elections. Millerand was forced to resign, and Herriot became premier. In October 1924 the French government recognized the USSR. Herriot told the British in December 1924 that France had recognized the USSR because it feared an isolated Russia would "combine" with Germany.[21] But no sooner had the French recog-

---

affairs, G. V. Chicherin, with the correspondent of the French newspaper *Temps*, Rollin," 26 Jan. 1924, *ibid.*, 46-49.

18. "Note à consulter," ns, nd (but Dec. 1923), MAÉ Papiers Millerand/70, 213-217.

19. Joseph Wielowieyski, Polish counsellor in Paris, to Jules Laroche, deputy political director, which covered a note, *strictement confidentiel*, 6 Oct. 1922, MAÉ Z-Russie/350, 37-38; "Note pour le Président du Conseil," Europe, ns, 3 Dec. 1923, MAÉ Z-Russie/424, 146-147; and "Le paiement des rentes russes et la responsabilité du Bloc national," Armand Charpentier, *Ère nouvelle*, 27 Feb. 1924, *ibid.*, 162.

20. See n. 18 above; and Note by Jacques Seydoux, deputy director, Relations commerciales, 19 Jan. 1924, MAÉ RC, Russie/2090.

21. "Memorandum of conversation between [foreign secretary] Austen Chamberlain and Herriot at the Quai d'Orsay, 5 December 1924," N9233/44/38, PRO FO 371 10471.

nized the Soviet government then events started going wrong. The *Cartel* of Radicals and Socialists weakened as soon as the elections were over. The new government could not cope with the stresses caused by grave financial difficulties and the end of the Ruhr crisis. The generally troubled state of French affairs was aggravated by matters bearing more directly on Franco-Soviet relations. In Great Britain the Conservatives defeated Ramsay Macdonald's minority Labour government in national elections in October 1924. The "Zinoviev letter," an alleged directive from the Comintern to British Communists, caused a tumult on the right, facilitating Labour's loss. In France, the Tory victory encouraged the *Bloc national*. In late 1924 the Parisian right-wing press began to whip up anti-Communist fears. Communist street demonstrations during the procession of Jean Jaurès' remains to the Panthéon, and the return from Moscow of the renegade Captain Jacques Sadoul stoked right-wing discontent. Nor was the Soviet government wise to celebrate the opening of its embassy in Paris by raising the red flag and playing the Internationale. In Paris "Communist Peril" became a familiar leader in newspapers of the right.[22]

These developments were not lost on either Herriot or the Soviet ambassador in Paris, Krasin. In December 1924 Herriot told Krasin that if the Soviet pressed him too hard for concessions, his government could fall. Coincidently, Austen Chamberlain, the new Tory foreign secretary, made the same observation after a visit with Herriot in Paris.[23] Krasin reported to Moscow that the suddenly rotten political atmosphere would not lead to a quick settlement of Franco-Soviet differences. "We had better wait awhile before starting negotiations," one French official told Krasin, until hostile public opinion had quieted down. Herriot denied that there was any Communist danger in France. He told the U.S. ambassador in Paris, Myron T. Herrick, that he had recently ordered his secret police chief to break up a Communist meeting "in order to calm public opinion" on the right. Unfortunately, remarked Herriot, the police could not find a meeting to raid. Herriot added that

---

22. For example, see various articles and editorials in *Le Temps*, in December 1924.
23. Krasin to Narkomindel, 20 Dec. 1924, *DVP*, VII, 580-583; and minute by Chamberlain, 19 Dec. 1924, PRO FO 371 10480.

he would not make the same mistake as the Labour government in London and rush into negotiations with the USSR.[24] Herriot was probably trying to calm his own jagged nerves. Ambassador Herrick reported a few days later that the right and even some of Herriot's own supporters did not share the view that French Communists were harmless.[25] And Aimé de Fleuriau, the new French ambassador in London, told a Foreign Office official that "the French ... now bitterly regretted their recent recognition of the Soviet government. There had been an outcry all over France against the Soviets and their open instigation of Communist revolution ..."[26]

The debate over Franco-Soviet relations was far from over. Jean Herbette, a well-known journalist, became the French ambassador in Moscow, and was an important advocate of a Franco-Soviet rapprochement. Krasin played a similar role on the Soviet side. Herbette arrived in Moscow in early January 1925 and met with Chicherin, Litvinov and Krasin, among other Soviet officials. They discussed a debts settlement in exchange for French credits and a cessation of Comintern propaganda and subversive activities.

Herbette cabled to Paris that Soviet officials were anxious for better relations, but were concerned by the anti-Communist press campaign in Paris and doubtful of the prospects for improved relations. Why the sudden outburst of hostility in the French press?, asked Chicherin. Herbette replied that French Communist activities were causing strained relations, and that Krasin's arrival in Paris had been ill-timed with Jaurès' interment in the Panthéon and Sadoul's return to Paris. But the clamour would pass, said Herbette. In the meantime, the Soviet government should take care to control the Comintern; its activities prompted general mistrust against anything associated with Soviet Russia. Herbette said a debts settlement was vital, but Chicherin replied that no settlement was possible without credits in return. Herbette

24. Krasin to Chicherin, 7 Dec. 1924, DVP, VII, 568-571; and Herrick to Secretary of State, nº 613, 30 Dec. 1924, 751.61/34, National Archives, Washington [NA], M[icrofilm] – 569/[reel] 3.
25. Herrick, nº 4733, 7 Jan. 1925, 751.61/36, NA M-569/3.
26. "Monsieur de Fleuriau, conversation," by Sir Eyre Crowe, permanent undersecretary, 15 Dec. 1924, N9296/44/38, PRO FO 371 10471.

remained optimistic: he had come to Moscow, he said, to work for better relations. [27]

Soviet officials remained skeptical. Will France end its hostility toward us?, asked Litvinov. And if we make concessions to France, what concessions will we obtain in return? Or will France simply make further demands? The Soviet government was divided: some favoured making concessions; others argued that it was not worth the sacrifice, and that France would only find other pretexts for hostility.[28] In response to these early discussions, Herriot replied frankly both to Herbette and to Krasin in Paris that he was up against opposition on all sides, and that concessions to the USSR would bring down his government.[29]

Behind the issues of a debts settlement and an end to Comintern subversion lay a more important matter for Herbette – traditional French security concerns about Germany. Peace in Europe would not be assured without breaking up the German-Soviet relationship, consummated in the 1922 Rapallo treaty. To achieve this objective France had to demonstrate to the USSR that it foresaw a "legitimate" Soviet diplomatic role and had no intention of excluding Russia from European affairs. "This is exactly my view," Herriot scribbled on Herbette's report.[30] If Herriot was convinced, it hardly mattered because he fell from power in April 1925. Herbette kept up the argument with Aristide Briand, Herriot's successor, repeatedly making the case that France needed Russia as an eastern counter-weight against Germany. If the USSR industrialized and rebuilt on its own, or with the help of France's adversaries, the Soviet government would have no reason to respect French interests in time of crisis. Some Soviet officials feared iso-

---

27. "Record of a conversation of the people's commissar for foreign affairs with the French ambassador to the USSR, Herbette," Chicherin, 11 Jan. 1925, *DVP*, VIII, 39-45; and Herbette, nºs 2-7, 12 Jan. 1925, MAÉ Z-Russie/357, 124-129.

28. "Record of a conversation of the deputy commissar for foreign affairs with the French ambassador in the USSR Herbette," Litvinov, 26 Jan. 1925, *DVP*, VIII, 99-102; and Herbette, nºs 97-107, 26 Jan. 1925, MAÉ Z-Russie/357, 180-190.

29. Herriot to Herbette, nºs 18-20, 25 Jan. 1925, MAÉ Z-Russie/357, 175-177; Krasin to Narkomindel, 16 March 1925, *DVP*, VIII, 183-186; and Krasin to Narkomindel, 23 March 1925, *ibid.*, 189-191.

30. Herbette, nº 35, 26 March 1925, MAÉ Z-Russie/141, 54-58; see also Herbette to Berthelot, 25 Sept. 1925, *ibid.*, 123-128.

lation and wanted "friends," but this situation would not last indefinitely if France failed to respond. Good relations with the USSR, said Herbette, were an important factor in French security on the Rhine.[31] In a personal letter to Herriot a few months after the fall of his government, Herbette praised his political courage in recognizing the Soviet government: "You reopened a door through which the destiny of France must pass, or risk mortal peril for its integrity and its independence."[32]

Whatever Herriot thought, Quai d'Orsay officials did not entirely share his view of Franco-Soviet relations. Even before Herriot fell the *Sous-direction d'Europe* challenged Herbette's policy recommendations. Overly friendly Franco-Soviet relations would arouse Polish and Rumanian anxieties. France could not pursue a rapprochement with the USSR without provoking Polish hostility and prompting adverse public opinion at home. The USSR was not "stable enough" to provide a "serious counter-weight" to Germany; for the time being Poland was the "stronger element of force." Even if the French government cared to ignore Comintern propaganda, these other considerations would impede practical cooperation with the USSR. Moreover, "our relations with England must ... induce us to maintain a certain reserve in our relations with the Soviet government." The Conservative return to power, the new government's refusal to ratify the Anglo-Soviet treaty, negotiated by Labour, and British concerns about Soviet propaganda, dictated prudence. "At a time when we are engaged in difficult negotiations ... with London on security issues, we risk arousing its mistrust if we give the impression of seeking support in Moscow." France might at times be obliged to pursue policies in contradiction with those of the Foreign Office, but this should not include French relations with the USSR. It would be too risky. All this being said, Quai d'Orsay officials conceded that French recognition of the USSR had certain advantages: it permitted the disruption of Soviet-German relations and it thwarted the German aim of securing Russia as a potential ally against Poland. In these circum-

---

31. Herbette, nºs 318-322, 20 April 1925, MAÉ Z-Russie/358, 68-72; and Herbette nºs 490-494, 29 June 1925, *ibid.*, 103-107.
32. Herbette to Herriot, 24 Oct. 1925, MAÉ Papiers Herriot/16, 65-66.

stances, France should maintain a reserved attitude toward the USSR, neither overly cordial, nor excessively hostile. When Russia had regained its power, the French government could reexamine the situation.[33]

In the meantime the French government sought security through conciliation of Germany. In 1925 Anglo-Franco-German negotiations led to the conclusion of the Locarno accords. This settlement assured French security on the Rhine, but worried Krasin who thought it would end French interest in improved relations with the USSR.[34] Krasin also complained about the western "credit boycott" which held the USSR in a "half-besieged state." The west would not take down the "blockade" until the Soviet government had agreed to a satisfactory debts settlement. Krasin surmised that the French government would not risk the anger of domestic public opinion or of Great Britain for the strictly limited settlement to which the USSR could afford to agree.[35] On the other hand, Herbette saw Locarno and worsening Anglo-Soviet relations as a French opportunity, since the Soviet government appeared anxious to conclude political and economic agreements. However, he warned against trying to drive too hard a bargain with the Soviet government, which would not settle at any price.[36]

In the course of the spring-summer of 1925 Franco-Soviet discussions moved slowly forward: French policy drifted between mild interest in Soviet overtures for negotiations and hostile acts which would have confirmed the worst Soviet suspicions. On 10 July Briand signaled to Herbette that Soviet fears of a "Holy alliance against Bolshevism" were "a morbid exaggeration"; on 31 July he authorized discussions with the British about the formation of an Anglo-Franco-American embargo against Soviet oil exports. No one would be able to obtain "regular and advantageous contracts," reckoned the Quai d'Orsay, without a common oil policy toward

---

33. "Note pour M. le Président du conseil," Europe, 28 March 1925, MAÉ Z-Russie/358, 43-49.
34. Krasin to Narkomindel, 23 March 1925, DVP, VIII, 189-191.
35. Krasin to Narkomindel, 22 Jan. 1925, DVP, VIII, 85-86; Krasin to Narkomindel, 16 March 1925, ibid., 183-186; and Krasin to Narkomindel, 30 April 1925, ibid., 256-265.
36. Herbette, nº 219, 23 Oct. 1925, MAÉ Z-Russie/358, 178-185.

the USSR. And the money raised through Soviet oil sales would be used "solely" to fund "dangerous" Bolshevik propaganda.[37] French concerns about propaganda increased because of the Rif rebellion in Morocco and the spreading revolutionary movement in China. The Soviet government appeared to be unaware of this abortive western oil embargo, and it continued to press for negotiations. Chicherin publicly challenged the French government to cease its "dilatory tactics" and negotiate.[38] The French finally agreed, and a Franco-Soviet conference began in February 1926.

As preparations were being made for the conference, Herbette sent good advice to Paris. Most western information on the USSR, he said, was false or tendentious. "The Soviet regime is depicted as a sort of irrational organization of rogues ..., the government is portrayed as completely incompetent, as profoundly corrupt, and as hopelessly divided. Perhaps this system of denigration has for a time served certain electoral, financial, or diplomatic interests." But it could also be counter-productive: "French diplomacy cannot retain its freedom of action if the French public is continually excited against Russia by spurious reports or by erroneous analysis, since the French government will be inhibited in its relations with the USSR by domestic political campaigns."[39]

Herbette urged Paris to conclude an agreement with the USSR. "If others reproach us later for having allowed a new war and a new invasion to be prepared because we could not find the necessary solutions to settle the Russian debt and because we did not anticipate inevitable future changes in eastern Europe, what responsibility will we bear?"[40] In May 1927, when the Foreign Office broke

---

37. Briand to Herbette, nº 238; and elsewhere, 10 July 1925, MAÉ Z-Russie/358, 138; Berthelot to Fleuriau, nºs 1045-1053, 31 July 1925, MAÉ RC, Pétroles de Russie/100, 100-105; "Note pour M. Berthelot," RC, ns, 24 Sept. 1925, with Berthelot's minute, *ibid.*, 123; and Fleuriau to FO, 2 Aug. 1925, N4491/1247/38, PRO FO 371 11023.

38. Pierre de Margerie, French ambassador in Berlin, nº 120^s, 6 Oct. 1926, enclosing the text of a Chicherin interview in the *Berliner Tageblatt*, MAÉ Z-Russie/141, 140-145.

39. Herbette, nº 20, 28 Jan. 1926, MAÉ Z-Russie/1168, 328-330.

40. Herbette to Eirik Labonne, secretary-general of the French delegation to the Franco-Soviet conference, 24 March 1926, Fondation Nationale des Sciences Politiques, Paris [FNSP] Papiers Anatole de Monzie/1. The papers in this collection are not the originals, but are old, faded copies of which some are partially illegible.

off diplomatic relations with the Soviet government, Herbette warned against a rupture and the "encirclement" of the USSR. Such policy would not lessen the "internal troubles" of other countries, but would increase the possibility of war in Europe. And a European war, said Herbette, would lead to social revolution.[41]

These reflections have an eerie quality, as portents of the 1930s, but few French officials or politicians listened to Herbette when it might have counted. French policy towards the USSR could not escape domestic policy considerations. In 1925-1927 the Rif rebellion in Morocco, the general strike in Great Britain, the revolution in China, and French Communist agitation in the army contributed to a growing anti-Communist tumult. And the *Bloc national*'s determination to split the *Cartel des gauches* led to further agitation. The right branded the Socialists as revolutionaries and pseudo-Communists, and invited Radicals not to be duped and to join the *Bloc national*.

At first, the French government may have taken seriously Herbette's advice; the Paris press was relatively circumspect in reporting the proceedings of the Franco-Soviet conference in the spring of 1926. On the day after the opening of negotiations, *Izvestiia* urged the French to accept the USSR "as we are," just as the Soviet government would also have to accept France as it is. Like Herbette a few months earlier, *Izvestiia* asked the French government not to load negotiations with demands which a much weaker Soviet government had rejected in previous years.[42] The USSR could not fund a debts settlement without credits in return. Soviet officials applied the Roman law *do ut des*, "I give, that you may give." The French understood the concept, and had their own expression, *donnant, donnant*; they just did not want to apply the principle.

In July 1926 Raymond Poincaré returned to power as premier and finance minister. When he turned his mind to Franco-Soviet negotiations, he loaded them with fresh demands on war debts and compensation for French property losses during the revolution, which the Soviet government had earlier said it would not

41. Herbette, nº 289-294, 21 May 1927, MAÉ Z-Grande-Bretagne/65, 107-112.
42. "La reconstruction des 'Ponts coupés'," *Izvestiia*, (translation) 26 Feb. 1926, Ministère des Finances, Paris [MF], B32012.

accept. Whenever K. G. Rakovskii, the chief Soviet negotiator, wanted to consign points of agreement to paper, Poincaré or his officials discouraged it. And when agreement on a partial settlement seemed possible in May 1927, finance official Jean-Jacques Bizot wrote that if Chicherin accepted all French demands, two more would be raised.[43]

These developments took place before a back-drop of increasing anti-Communist agitation in the press. Lurid articles and editorials condemning Communist subversion in the armed forces and Communist activities in China and elsewhere flooded the papers. *Le communisme, voilà l'ennemi!*, trumpeted the interior minister, Albert Sarraut, in a widely publicized speech in April 1927.

A month later the word "elections" began to crop up as a factor in Franco-Soviet negotiations. Poincaré was determined to block any agreement that could help the *Cartel* regain power in the 1928 elections. On 29 May a political cartoon appeared in the Paris daily *L' Oeuvre* which depicted Poincaré discussing with Sarraut the celebrated 1919 poster of a hirsute, fearsome Bolshevik clenching a knife in his teeth. "Hm, do you think it will work again?," read the caption. Poincaré apparently thought so; earlier in May his officials had raised the problem of "elections" as an impediment to a Franco-Soviet agreement.[44] By the autumn of 1927 the Paris papers were full of such speculations. Anti-Communist rhetoric in the papers culminated in a successful press campaign against Soviet ambassador Rakovskii, which drove him out of Paris in October 1927. British sources heard that Sarraut had inspired the campaign, and that the anti-Communist oil magnate Sir Henri Deterding had paid for it.[45]

Philippe Berthelot, secretary general of the Quai d'Orsay, explained to the British chargé in Paris that the French govern-

43. Personal notes by Jean-Jacques Bizot, finance ministry representative at the Franco-Soviet conference, 13 May 1927, MF B32013; for a fuller account of Franco-Soviet negotiations, see M. J. Carley and R. K. Debo, "Always in Need of Credit: the USSR and Franco-German Economic Cooperation, 1926-29," *French Historical Studies* 20,3 (Summer 1997): 315-356.

44. Personal notes by Bizot, 13 May 1927, *ibid.*; and also K. G. Rakovskii, Soviet ambassador in Paris, to Litvinov, 7 May 1927, *DVP*, X, 188-191.

45. Sir Eric Phipps, British chargé d'affaires in Paris, nº 1893, 5 Sept. 1927, N4218/47/38, PRO FO 371 12584; and Phipps, nº 190, 14 Sept. 1927, N4376/47/38, *ibid.*

ment no longer feared a rupture with Moscow would drive the USSR and Germany into a closer embrace, "so long as the Anglo-French Entente remains solid ...."[46] And Herbette, who had long stressed the importance of a Franco-Soviet rapprochement against an eventual German *revanche*, gave up the fight. He came home on leave for the first time in the spring of 1927. According to Parisian wags, Herbette had been "Bolshevized"; he was a mere minion of Moscow.[47] The jibes of being a Soviet soft-touch in the anti-Communist delirium of Paris were too much for Herbette. He adjusted his position when he returned to Moscow, railing against the Soviet trade surplus with France. Soviet profits would pay for Communist propaganda to promote "social revolution" and military desertion. In 1928 he recommended French cooperation with other western countries in trading with the USSR – so that the Bolsheviks could not play off western merchants against each other; he also recommended joint western action to curb Communist propaganda. These ideas, though hardly new, were floated in the press. Litvinov, who noticed, warned Herbette that the USSR would resist any such combinations. And Berthelot, chastened by earlier failures, conceded that western cooperation against the USSR would not work and would only serve Soviet interests.[48]

In the late 1920s French policy toward the USSR languished in passive hostility. In October 1930, however, the government launched an ill-advised trade war against the USSR, from which it had to retreat in the following spring. At the same time, disquieting events in Germany attracted attention at the Quai d'Orsay. In September 1930 the Nazi party made startling gains in national elections. The previously insignificant Nazis now had to be reckoned with. In March 1931 the French government blocked a German-Austrian customs union. In the summer of 1931 the French and Soviet governments initialled a nonaggression pact, something the Soviet government had wanted since 1926. For the French, the pact was bait to win economic concessions, but by the autumn of 1931 the Quai d'Orsay saw in it intrinsic advantages

46. Phipps, nº 118, 13 June 1927, N2852/47/38, *ibid*.
47. Carley and Debo, "Always in Need of Credit."
48. Herbette, nºs 247-249, 3 March 1928, MAÉ RC, Russie/2059; and "Note," Europe, 25 Aug. 1928, with Berthelot's minute, MAÉ Z-Russie/1173, 88-89.

for French security. The old idea of loosening Soviet-German ties re-emerged.[49] But the right still opposed better Franco-Soviet relations, and its press raised a hue and cry when news of the nonaggression pact leaked out. The French government dropped the pact like a hot stone and foisted off on the Soviet the responsibility for initiating the negotiations.[50] A British diplomat observed a few years later that there was an "after you Alphonse" quality to Franco-Soviet relations, where each side attributed to the other any initiative for rapprochement.[51]

In the spring of 1932 French elections returned the old *Cartel* of Radicals and Socialists with an important gain in seats. Herriot came back as premier and foreign minister, and he resumed his earlier policy – his *idée fixe* – of better relations with the USSR. The Franco-Soviet non-aggression pact was signed in November 1932. It was none too soon: Hitler became German chancellor in January 1933. Herriot had fallen from power in December 1932, but his successors at the Quai d'Orsay, Socialist Joseph Paul-Boncour and conservative Louis Barthou, continued and deepened Herriot's policy. The Soviet government was anxious for better relations also, and Litvinov, fearing Nazi Germany, took the lead in negotiating with the West. He had no trouble in persuading Paul-Boncour, who presided over the signing of a trade agreement in January 1934. He and Litvinov also began to talk of mutual security against Nazi Germany which Louis Barthou continued when he became foreign minister in February 1934.[52] In the meantime Colonel Edmond Mendras and Charles Alphand had gone to Moscow as French mil-

49. Briand to Jules Laroche, French ambassador in Warsaw, n° 914; and elsewhere, 21 Oct. 1931, MAÉ Z-URSS/1007, 44-47.
50. M. J. Carley, "Five Kopecks for Five Kopecks: Franco-Soviet Trade Negotiations, 1928-39," *Cahiers du monde russe et soviétique* 33 (1992): 23-58.
51. Lord Chilston, British ambassador in Moscow, n° 391, 18 Aug. 1934, N4836/2/38, PRO FO 371 18299; for earlier accounts of Franco-Soviet relations in the 1930s, see William E. Scott, *Alliance Against Hitler: The Origins of the Franco-Soviet Pact* (Durham, NC, 1962); and Jonathan Haslam, *Soviet Foreign Policy, 1930-33: The Impact of the Depression* (London, 1983), and *The Soviet Union and the Struggle for Collective Security in Europe, 1933-39* (New York, 1984).
52. V. S. Dovgalevskii, Soviet ambassador in Paris, to Narkomindel, 1 Nov. 1933, DVP, XVI, 602-603; and M. I. Rozenberg, Soviet chargé d'affaires in Paris, to Narkomindel, 28 April 1934, *ibid.*, XVII, 309-311.

itary attaché and ambassador respectively. Both men worked for better relations, and these improved significantly. Mendras reported that he was treated with great cordiality and relative openness by the Soviet high command, and that the French government should hasten to establish its presence in the USSR.[53] Alphand was equally positive, reporting the strong Soviet desire for closer relations: the USSR was "for anything which would strengthen France and for anything which would weaken Germany." To the Soviet government he advised perseverance in seeking better relations; to his own government, he urged a prompt response to Soviet initiatives.[54]

"I have just re-read," wrote Alphand, "Jean Herbette's correspondence to the department, at the time of the resumption of Franco-Soviet relations, in which he advised a general settlement. He was not listened to, [and] the negotiations failed ... A new opportunity for a Franco-Soviet rapprochement has arisen ..." The message Alphand repeatedly sent home was that France should not lose this second chance.[55]

The French government seemed intent on taking such advice – until October 1934, when foreign minister Barthou was killed during the assassination of King Alexander of Yugoslavia. Pierre Laval, a long lapsed Socialist, succeeded Barthou as foreign minister. He was not a partisan of a Franco-Soviet rapprochement; indeed, he had opposed it in Cabinet during Barthou's tenure at the Quai d'Orsay. Better relations with the USSR, he said, would bring to France "the International and the red flag." And if there were a European war, it would lead to an "invasion" of Bolshevism. Laval preferred an agreement with Nazi Germany, an inclination well known to Litvinov, who at once became mistrustful.[56] So did Ambassador Alp-

---

53. See Mendras' various reports in 1933-34 at the Château de Vincennes, Service Historique de l'Armée de Terre [SHAT], 7N 3121.
54. "Record of a conversation ... with the ambassador of France in the USSR Alphand," by Litvinov, 22 Sept. 1933, DVP, XVI, 527-529; "Record of conversation ... with ... Alphand," by B. S. Stomoniakov (Narkomindel, Moscow), 13 Feb. 1934, DVP, XVII, 140-142; and Alphand, nºs 535-537, 12 Dec. 1933, Documents diplomatiques français [DDF], 1re série, 13 vols. (Paris, 1964-84), V, 214.
55. Alphand, nº 311, 5 Nov. 1933, MAÉ Z-URSS/988, 1-7; and Alphand, nº 275, 2 July 1935, MAÉ Z-URSS/1059, 122-5.
56. Edouard Herriot, Jadis: D'une guerre à l'autre, 1914-36 (Paris, 1952), 437-438; and Jean Szembek, Journal, 1933-39 (Paris, 1952), 85-86.

hand; he warned that if the Soviet government came to fear a reversal of French policy, it would not hesitate to steal a march on France. Such warnings were often heard over the next few years, but were not heeded. The Soviet chargé in Paris reported rumours that Laval would step back from Barthou's policy, and that he was surrounded by officials pushing for an agreement with Germany. While giving assurances about the stability of French policy, Laval admitted to Litvinov that he wanted better relations with Germany, though not at the expense of Soviet interests. Litvinov, hardly persuaded, often tried to rely on Herriot, still a minister of state, to thwart Laval. Germany was making offers, Litvinov warned, and seeking to sow mistrust between the USSR and France.[57]

In 1934 Litvinov stated repeatedly that the only way to assure European security was for France, Great Britain, the USSR, and the Little Entente to confront Nazi Germany with a strong coalition of states determined to preserve the peace. So long as it was controlled by the Nazis, Germany would be a "mad dog that can't be trusted, with whom no agreements can be made, and whose ambition can only be checked by a ring of determined neighbors." War, he said, was inevitable if Nazi Germany was not reined in.[58]

The message was lost on Laval who only allowed the dead Barthou's inertia to lead to the conclusion of a Franco-Soviet pact of mutual assistance in May 1935, after Nazi intransigence left no other option. The Quai d'Orsay made sure the pact had little meaning; Alexis Léger, Berthelot's successor as secretary-general, supervised the gutting of the agreement. It was "largely due" to me, Léger told the British ambassador in Paris, that the French government resisted "pressure from M. Litvinov."[59] Léger had help from Paul Bargeton, the political director, who argued that a bilateral Franco-Soviet pact would play into German hands. France

57. Rozenberg to Narkomindel, 19 Oct. 1934, DVP, XVII, 647-649; Litvinov to Rozenberg, 19 Oct. 1934, ibid., 824; Litvinov to Rozenberg, 6 Nov. 1934, ibid., 666-667; and Litvinov (Geneva) to Narkomindel, 5 Dec. 1934, ibid. 725.
58. William C. Bullitt, US ambassador in Moscow, nº 340, strictly confidential, 5 Oct. 1934, 500.A15A4/2588, NA RG59 (1930-39), box 2396; and "Memorandum of Conversation with Litvinov," by Hugh R. Wilson, US representative in Geneva, 21 Nov. 1934, 500.A15A4/2618, ibid.
59. G. R. Clerk, nº 493, 28 March 1935, C2656/55/18, PRO FO 371 18833.

should leave open the option of responding to a more conciliatory German position, and it should therefore avoid, as "the permanent basis" of French policy, the conclusion of a pact openly directed against Germany.[60]

Léger may have wondered if he could hold out against pressure from "the Herriot faction"; the British ambassador, Sir George Clerk, certainly pondered whether he could. Laval warned Clerk against the "violently anti-German" Herriot, who was a strong advocate of a Franco-Soviet alliance and still retained influence in the French government. Some Foreign Office officials saw Herriot as an evil influence. The Nazi danger had transformed him, "from a kindly, but academic patron of the Soviets into a fiery apostle with a mission ..."[61]

Laval also faced pressure from the Little Entente for tighter security arrangements in eastern Europe. The British ambassador reported having seen Laval just after a meeting with the Rumanian foreign minister: "I got the impression," he said, "of catching a school boy who had just banged the door of the store cupboard but had not yet got hold of the jam."[62] Léger and Bargeton stiffened Laval's back, if he needed it. Litvinov tried on several occasions to strengthen the terms of the accord, but French officials resisted. Laval's tactics raised doubts in Soviet minds as to French commitment to an agreement. The Soviet ambassador, V. P. Potemkin, accused Laval of double-talk and playing hard to get, as though France was making a sacrifice in concluding a mutual assistance pact with the USSR.[63] Litvinov eventually settled for what he could get – fearful he might get nothing – and Laval went to Moscow in May 1935 to consummate the agreement.[64]

After promising speedy ratification of the pact, Laval returned home to delay ratification for the rest of the year. "I signed it. All

60. "Note, directeur politique," 19 March 1935, MAÉ Z-URSS/973, 107-110.
61. See n. 59 above; Clerk, nº 62 confidential, 23 March 1935, C2458/55/18, PRO FO 371 18832; and FO minutes, 1-2 Jan. 1936, C1/1/17, *Documents on British Foreign Policy*, [DBFP], 2nd series, 19 vols. (London, 1947-84), XV, 531.
62. Clerk, nº 70, 31 March 1935, C2692/55/18, PRO FO 371 18833.
63. V. P. Potemkin, Soviet ambassador in Paris, to N. N. Krestinskii, deputy commissar for foreign affairs, 23 Feb. 1935, DVP, XVIII, 130-133; Litvinov to Potemkin, 2 April 1935, *ibid.*, 259; and Potemkin to Narkomindel, 10 April 1935, *ibid.*, 282-283.
64. Chilston, nºs 5-6, 10 Jan. 1935, DBFP, 2nd, XII, 366-367.

right, I signed it," he said. "But I won't keep my promises and that's that. Why get sore, my boy?"[65] Litvinov was very sore, and he was disquieted to learn of unofficial Franco-German discussions in Berlin in the autumn of 1935. A settlement with Germany was Laval's *grande idée*, according to the Polish ambassador in Paris. Laval admitted as much to Potemkin: "My Germanophilia," he said, "... is the pacifism of the French people; without an improvement of relations between France and Germany, peace would be impossible."[66] A Foreign Office official surmised that Laval was trying to ride two horses at the same time; it was more like four, commented I. M. Maiskii, the Soviet ambassador in London.[67]

Litvinov reckoned that if Laval remained in power, he would refuse to ratify the pact, or would turn it into a "scrap of paper."[68] The British ambassador in Berlin was of a similar opinion: "M. Laval is wriggling like a devil in holy water and keeps postponing ..." the evil day of ratification.[69] Alphand saw the wriggling and was angry. Fearing another lost opportunity, he criticized the intransigent Poincaré for having missed the chance of a settlement in 1926-27, but the bolt was really aimed at Laval.[70] Litvinov launched some also: he was discouraged at the delays, but his despair was mixed with cynicism and worry over the weakness and duplicity of French policy.[71]

Although Laval fell from power in January 1936, there was no improvement in Franco-Soviet relations. The French Parliament finally ratified, with little enthusiasm, the mutual assistance pact in March 1936, just after the Nazi reoccupation of the Rhineland.

65. Henry Torrès, *Pierre Laval* (New York, 1941), 217.
66. Szembek, *Journal*, 141-142; and Potemkin to Narkomindel, 22 Nov. 1935, *DVP*, XVIII, 562-564.
67. Memo by Robert Vansittart, permanent under secretary of state, Foreign Office, 18 Nov. 1935, N5966/17/38, PRO FO 371 19452.
68. Litvinov to Potemkin, 29 Oct. 1935, *DVP*, XVIII, 541; and Litvinov to Potemkin, 4 Nov. 1935, *ibid.*, 667.
69. Phipps, nº 307 saving, 31 Dec. 1935, *DBFP*, 2nd, XV, 531; and Clerk, nº 2 saving, 3 Jan. 1936, *ibid.*, 537-538.
70. Alphand, nºs 671-672, 8 Dec. 1935, MAÉ Z-URSS/980, 137-138.
71. Litvinov to Potemkin, 13 Jan. 1936, *DVP*, XIX 26-27; "Record of a conversation ... with ... Alphand," Litvinov, 14 Jan. 1936, *ibid.*, 27-28; and Litvinov to Potemkin, 23 Feb. 1936, *ibid.*, 38-39.

The deputy commissar for foreign affairs, N. N. Krestinskii, wisecracked that if Hitler had only wanted to block passage of the pact, he would merely have had to *threaten* the Rhineland occupation, and the pact would have failed in Parliament.[72] The French government had lost its nerve in face of the Nazi threat, and the Franco-Soviet pact was destined to languish.

"It is not hard to understand the reasons explaining the indecisiveness and trepidation of French policy," wrote Potemkin in March 1936. France feared losing British support, while its other allies and friends, not to mention the neutral countries, were wavering before the increasing danger of war with Germany. This mood was best reflected in Léger, said Potemkin: "I must say that I have never seen [him] in such a state of dark and desperate pessimism, as during these last days." The USSR was far away, and the Red Army not ready for an offensive war. And then there were insinuations that the USSR was attempting to push Europe into war in order to prepare the way for world revolution. It was in "this atmosphere of self-doubt, peril, distrust, and hesitation that the French government had to function ..." The government had to face elections in the spring, said Potemkin, and no one could stand for election as a partisan of war and implacable resistance to Nazi Germany. "The elections will take place under the ill-omen of pacifism."[73]

Although Potemkin did not say it, national elections also intruded directly into Franco-Soviet relations. A centre-left coalition, the Popular Front, had been formed the previous year and seemed certain to win the elections. The right parties fulminated against this prospect, and to combat it, renewed their polemics against Moscow.

After the conclusion of the Franco-Soviet trade agreement in January 1934, further negotiations focused on the provision of a large French loan to the Soviet government, underwritten by a French or Anglo-French consortium. The anti-Communist finance ministry disliked the loan project, and the Banque de France would not cooperate. The loan collapsed in January 1936, amidst the clamouring of the right-wing press. Alphand angrily recalled simi-

72. Krestinskii to Potemkin, 22 March 1936, *ibid.*, 182-183.
73. Potemkin to Krestinskii, 26 March 1936, *ibid.*, 189-195.

lar campaigns in 1927 and 1931 which had blocked better Franco-Soviet relations. The Franco-Soviet rapprochement had butted into the "wall of money."[74]

The right also fulminated against the ratification of the mutual assistance pact, hawking anti-Communism with a bill sticker's effrontery. France, said the right, was becoming a "brilliant second for Bolshevism"; it should take care not to get dragged into a war by the USSR, which could lead to Communist revolution in Europe.[75] Such opinion troubled Alphand. The Soviet government had so far taken it in stride, he reported, "but I hardly need signal the danger to French interests if this unprecedented press campaign continues." Alphand, Herriot, and cabinet ministers Pierre Cot, Georges Mandel, and later Paul Reynaud, argued that different political systems should not prevent France and the USSR from recognizing their common security interests.[76] If France could ally itself with the white tsar before 1914, they said, it could now ally with the red tsar, Stalin, against Nazi Germany.

Strikes and demonstrations following the Popular Front election victory further unsettled the right, and the outbreak of civil war in Spain in July 1936 unhinged it. The Quai d'Orsay had no thought of consolidating the French relationship with the USSR, though the Soviet government asked for military staff talks. The French general staff refused, not wanting to provoke Nazi Germany or to alienate Poland, France's unreliable ally. Nor did the generals want too close a contact with Russian Communists, fearing subversion in the army and the spread of Communism in France. And Great Britain would disapprove. In any event, the Red Army could not take the offensive for months after the start of hostilities, observed the French generals, who were already thinking about a defensive war behind the Maginot line of fortifications.[77] On staff talks, chief

74. Alphand, nºs 12-14, 13 January 1936, MAÉ RC, Russie/2057; "Note sur le financement de commandes russes en France," Alphand, 3 Sept. 1936, ibid.; and Carley, "Five Kopecks," 45-48.
75. Charles A. Micaud, *The French Right and Nazi Germany, 1933-39: A Study of Public Opinion* (New York, 1964), 79-83.
76. Alphand, nºs 36-40, 25 Jan. 1936, MAÉ, Bureau du chiffre [BC], télégrammes, à l'arrivée de Moscou, 1936; and Alphand, nºs 91-92, 28 Feb. 1936, ibid.
77. "Note, directeur politique [Bargeton]," 24 June 1935, MAÉ Z-URSS/1004, 172-174; and Alistair Horne, *To Lose A Battle, France 1940* (London, 1990), pp. 80-81.

of staff General Maurice Gamelin's orders were unambiguous: Do not offend the Soviet, but stall, stall, stall.[78]

The French cabinet was divided about staff talks, and some initial soundings did take place in early 1937, but the government could not overcome opposition from within. Moreover, the Foreign Office was dead opposed to talks and applied heavy pressure to stop them. Staff talks were moribund when Stalin launched the purge of the Red Army in May-June 1937, offering to the French general staff a suitable pretext to administer the finishing stroke.[79]

Litvinov often warned the French and British against the failure of collective security. Soviet cooperation was worth having, he said, but it should not be taken for granted. The USSR would strengthen the Red Army and take care of itself. If the French and British governments rejected collective security and sought agreements with Nazi Germany, the USSR could do the same, trusting to the Red Army and staying out of harm's way.

French officials who wanted Franco-Soviet cooperation were worried by the prospect of a German-Soviet rapprochement. At the highest levels of the government, however, Litvinov's warnings were, if troubling, not sufficiently so, to cause a change in French policy. Some British officials, who disliked close Franco-Soviet relations, were even a little blithe. "The argument which Litvinov has used all along in order to bring the French Government up to the scratch is the threat that if France won't give him an alliance he will go and get one from Hitler." But everyone knew that as long as Hitler remains in power, there would be no rapprochement with the USSR. Litvinov's hollow "threats" are a "bluff ... [and] ought to be challenged whenever possible."[80]

The Spanish civil war and the Stalinist purges of old Bolsheviks, which began in the summer of 1936, did not help to improve Franco-Soviet relations. But both of these developments, occur-

---

78. M. J. Carley, "End of the 'Low, Dishonest Decade': Failure of the Anglo-Franco-Soviet Alliance in 1939," *Europe-Asia Studies*, vol. 45, nº 2 (1993), 303-341.

79. "Note, directeur politique," 24 June 1935, cited above and Carley, "Low, Dishonest Decade," passim.

80. Minute by Orme Garton Sargent, assistant permanent under secretary, FO, 1 April 1935, PRO FO 371 18833; and "Memorandum by Mr. Sargent ...," 7 Feb. 1935, *DBFP*, 2ⁿᵈ, XII, 501-502.

ring well after Barthou's death and Laval's hostility toward the USSR, merely hardened opponents and inhibited partisans of better relations. Ambassador Alphand was one of the latter. Although he did not abandon his support for a Franco-Soviet alliance, he had had enough of Stalinist Moscow and asked to be relieved in the summer of 1936.[81]

Alphand was replaced by Robert Coulondre, who had considerable experience of Russian affairs. He was a partisan of better relations, but he left France in early November 1936 as anti-Communist hysteria was reaching its heights. Coulondre warned Litvinov of the danger in their first meetings. Strikes, plant occupations, and rumours that the Communists were ready to seize power had disquieted the French middle class and even elements within the Popular Front. Coulondre said that he had seen Herriot before leaving for Moscow: Herriot thought that Franco-Soviet relations had been "poisoned."[82]

And so they were. In October 1936 Léger advised the Soviet chargé that relations would suffer if the USSR did not pursue a less aggressive policy in Spain. At the same time, he was smug about General Francisco Franco's advance toward Madrid, which, if successful, would mark the beginning of the ebb tide of Bolshevism.[83] Léger held this position in spite of the negative strategic consequences for France of having another fascist state established on its borders. But as one Foreign Office official noted in 1937, "People ... seem to lose all consideration for the interests of their country, as opposed to those of their church or of their class, when they deal with affairs in Spain ...."[84]

81. Sir G. Warner, British ambassador in Berne, nº 532 confidential, 18 Dec. 1936, N362/136/38, PRO FO 371 20346.
82. "Record of a conversation of the People's commissar for foreign affairs ... with the ambassador of France to the USSR, Coulondre," Litvinov, 10 Nov. 1936, *DVP*, XIX, 550-551; and Coulondre, nºs 507-520, 12 Nov. 1936, *DDF*, 2ᵉ, 18 vols. (Paris, 1963-), III, 748-751.
83. "Compte-rendu du général [Victor-Henri] Schweisguth sur un entretien avec M. Léger," 9 Oct. 1936, SHAT 7N 3143; and N. Lloyd Thomas, British chargé d'affaires in Paris, to Vansittart, private and confidential, 26 Oct. 1936, W14793/9549/41, PRO FO 371 20583.
84. Minute by Laurence Collier, head of the Northern department, 5 Nov. 1937, N4924/272/38, PRO FO 371 21103.

Litvinov heaped scorn on the British and French governments, " ... who believe that preparations to resist openly-planned aggression can only be made with the consent and participation of the instigators of that aggression ..." Litvinov challenged the West to choose between collective security "and falling in meekly with the wishes of these aggressors." The latter course, he warned, could only be "a rapprochement of the lobster with the shark."[85] In January 1937 Potemkin made virtually the same observation to French cabinet minister, Camille Chautemps. It was a mistake, he said, always to peer over one's shoulder at Germany waiting for its next hostile outburst or to subordinate French foreign policy to British "direction."[86]

Such comments only irritated French officials. In 1937-38 Franco-Soviet relations entered a doldrums. Stalin pursued his bloody purges, while surviving Soviet officials contemplated continuing Anglo-French efforts to come to terms with Hitler. At the end of 1937 Soviet officials were grim: the French feared tomorrow, said Ia. Z. Surits, the new Soviet ambassador in Paris, and seemed destined to make a "complete capitulation to Hitler and Mussolini."[87] Coulondre reported at the same time that Litvinov was bitter and discouraged, but that the Soviet government still wished to work with France and Great Britain.[88] A Soviet-German rapprochement remained a possibility, however, if the French government forgot the reasons why it had sought better relations with the USSR.

The year 1938 brought no change in Anglo-French policy toward the USSR, though Austria was annexed in March, and Czechoslovakia dismembered at Munich in September. Ambassador Surits reported that French public opinion had become entranced by German virility and "power."[89] On such rotten foundations, Soviet policy collapsed. After the long "Calvary" of appeasement, observed

    85. Chilston, nº 648, 20 Nov. 1936, N5722/307/38, PRO FO 371 20349.
    86. "Record of a conversation of the plenipotentiary representative of the USSR in France with minister of state ... Chautemps," 19 Jan. 1937, *DVP*, XX, 43-46.
    87. Surits to Litvinov, 27 Nov. 1937, *ibid.*, 630-634.
    88. Coulondre, nº 288, 29 Nov. 1937, *DDF*, 2ᵉ, VII, 550-552; and Coulondre, nº 306, 15 Dec. 1937, *ibid.*, 715-719.
    89. Surits to Litvinov, 27 July 1938, *DVP*, XXI, 392-402.

Coulondre, the Soviet government had lost all confidence in collective security, even if not openly denouncing it. "For now, the USSR expected nothing more" from France. Coulondre warned again of a Soviet-German rapprochement, the costs of which would be paid by Polish dismemberment.[90] And yet two weeks after Coulondre wrote these lines, he was somewhat more positive, having seen Litvinov, to say good-bye, as he prepared to move to the French embassy in Berlin. Litvinov still held out the possibility of Soviet cooperation if the French and British governments would "make a penultimate effort" to contain Nazi Germany. "But instructed by experience," noted Coulondre, "[the USSR] would undoubtedly demand precise guarantees of assistance" before making further security agreements. There will be a last chance "to reestablish a European equilibrium," and it would no doubt come soon. "We must know who we can count on, and for whom, in return, we are ready to fight. But I should tell you," reported Coulondre, that the Franco-Soviet pact is now "null and void." For France it offered merely disadvantages; for the USSR, it will serve only to mask Soviet isolation, or to pay the price of a Soviet-German rapprochement.[91]

After Munich the French government was like a predator's mesmerized prey, and it paid Coulondre little mind. Georges Bonnet, the French foreign minister, contemplated the abandonment of remaining French commitments in the east. The French general staff calculated that the Red Army could not fight, and would only do so to spread communism "on the ruins of a civilization devastated by war."[92] French generals had seen Red and turned yellow about war with Nazi Germany – but not about civil war against French Communism, if necessary.[93] Litvinov had no illusions; he

90. Coulondre, n⁰ 235, 4 Oct. 1938, MAÉ Cabinet [Georges] Bonnet/16, 327-333.
91. Coulondre, n⁰ 283, 18 Oct. 1938, AN Papiers [Édouard] Daladier, 496AP/11.
92. "Note sur la situation actuelle," General Louis-Antoine Colson, deputy chief of staff, nd, but covered by Gamelin to Daladier, n⁰ 936/DN.3, 26 Oct. 1938, SHAT 5N 579. My thanks to Joel Blatt for a copy of this document.
93. Memorandum by Lloyd Thomas, of a record of conversation with former head of the French 2ᵉ Bureau, 17 June 1937, C4517/18/17, PRO FO 371 20686.

expected the Anglo-French to turn to the USSR only as a last resort: if appeasement of Nazi Germany failed.[94]

These attitudes were not favourable to negotiations for an anti-Nazi alliance, which started after the German occupation of rump Czechoslovakia in March 1939. In the circumstances, one might have supposed that the French government would become more accommodating to the USSR, and superficially it did. The new French ambassador in Moscow, Paul-Emile Naggiar, warned of the danger of a Soviet-German rapprochement if western-Soviet relations did not improve.[95] Such warnings, of course, were not startling; the French embassy in Moscow had been issuing them since 1934. Nor did French subservience to British policy cease, though superficially the French government became more insistent on negotiations with the USSR. When Poland objected in March 1939 to a joint declaration of intent to cooperate against further German aggression, the British and French governments demurred. The French would not pressure recalcitrant Poland because, as Bonnet told the British, care had to be taken not to give the Poles or Rumanians a pretext "for running out on account of Russia."

The British prime minister, Neville Chamberlain, agreed: "If bringing Russia in meant their [Poland and Rumania] running out I should think the change was a very disastrous one."[96] Léger, whose tune had changed somewhat, said that Anglo-French policy should not be subordinated to its Polish or Rumanian "corollaries." In ordinary great power politics, "the cart did not go before the horse," as Léger put it, but these were not ordinary great power politics. Litvinov made the same point to Ambassador Maiskii in London: "... it is up to Chamberlain and [French premier Edouard] Daladier, not [Polish foreign minister Jozef] Beck, to have the last word. This is not the first time England is addressing to us proposals for co-oper-

---

94. "Record of a Conversation of the people's commissar for foreign affairs of the USSR with the ambassador of France to the USSR, Coulondre," Litvinov, 16 Oct. 1938, *DVP*, XXI, 589-590; Litvinov to Surits, 19 Oct. 1938, *ibid.*, 600.

95. Unless otherwise noted, the following is taken from Carley, "Low, Dishonest Decade."

96. N. Chamberlain to his sister Hilda, 29 April 1939, NC18/1/1096, University of Birmingham, N. Chamberlain Papers; and Chamberlain to his sister Ida, 21 May 1939, NC18/1/1101, *ibid.*

ation and then taking them back, pointing to the real or possible objections of first Germany, then Japan, and now Poland."[97]

The problem for Chamberlain was that "the Bolshies" could not be trusted: their "... motives ... seem to me to have little connection with our ideas of liberty and to be concerned only with getting every one else by the ears."[98] "I cannot believe" he noted, "that she [Russia] has the same aims and objects that we have or any sympathy with democracy as such."[99]

Bonnet thought the Soviet government could "drag us into a war." Chamberlain concurred: Soviet efforts were "devoted to egging on others." "... I cannot rid myself of the suspicion that they are chiefly concerned to see the 'capitalist' powers tear each other to pieces while they stay out themselves." He acknowledged that there was the chance "... that if we don't agree Russia and Germany will come to an understanding which to my mind is a pretty sinister commentary on Russian reliability."[100] Such an observation might now be considered paradoxical from a prime minister who had spent much of his time trying to achieve "an understanding" with Nazi Germany.

Chamberlain's ideological position contrasted with Litvinov's "realism" and persistence in seeking agreement with France and Great Britain. "If we want to gain something from [the Anglo-French]," he said, "we also must disclose a little our own position ... We ought not to wait for the other side to propose to us the very thing which we want." It was thus Litvinov who took the initiative in mid-April 1939 to lay out the "minimal" Soviet position for an Anglo-Franco-Soviet alliance, guaranteeing the security of all neighbouring states of the USSR.[101] Eventually, Litvinov also recommended Soviet acceptance of security guarantees for Belgium, Holland and Switzerland requested by France.[102] To Litvinov's for-

---

97. Litvinov to Maiskii, 4 April 1939, V. M. Falin, et al., *Soviet Peace Efforts on the Eve of World War II (September 1938-August 1939)* 2 vols. (Moscow, 1973), I, 311-313.

98. N. Chamberlain to Ida, 26 March 1939, NC18/1/1091, U. of Birmingham, N. Chamberlain papers; and Chamberlain to Ida, 10 June 1939, NC18/1/1102, *ibid*.

99. Chamberlain to Hilda, 29 April 1939, NC18/1/1096, *ibid*.

100. Chamberlain to Ida, 21 May 1939, NC18/1/1100, *ibid*.

101. Litvinov to Stalin, secret, 15 April 1939, DVP, XXII, book 1, 277-278.

102. Litvinov to Stalin, secret, 3 May 1939, *ibid*., 325-326; for a different view of Litvinov, see Geoffrey Roberts, "The Fall of Litvinov: A Revisionist View," *Journal of Contemporary History* 27 (1992): 639-657.

mal proposals the British responded with disdain and hostility, while the French prevaricated and eventually deferred to their British allies.

The French position continued to be funk-ridden and weak; Bonnet was willing to let the British "do the running" in negotiating with the Soviet government. And the British did, though with only one leg. In the meantime, Litvinov was sacked on 3 May, the same day Litvinov sent to Stalin a pessimistic but accurate assessment of Anglo-French policy.[103] The French embassy in Moscow reported – it would appear correctly – that British stalling on Litvinov's proposals had precipitated his fall.

V. M. Molotov, chair of the Soviet of people's commissars, took over the Narkomindel. The Soviet government stuck to a basic position throughout the negotiations, though it haggled obstinately on apparently secondary matters. Molotov wanted a binding political and military alliance with security guarantees to all the east European states bordering on the USSR; the British, especially Chamberlain, sought to avoid such obligations. The French remained largely clamorous bystanders. Ambassador Naggiar thought an agreement could have been achieved in June, if the British and French had accepted Soviet proposals based on those advanced by Litvinov in April.[104] Weaker Anglo-French counter-proposals had only prompted the Soviets to make their own. At the end of July an agreement, nevertheless, seemed close enough to prompt Anglo-Franco-Soviet military discussions in Moscow, which took place in August.

British instructions were to go "very slowly"; French instructions were similar. The Soviet government knew of these dispositions, and Soviet instructions took them into account: If the Anglo-French delegations do not have plenipotentiary powers, "…express astonishment, take them by the hands and 'respectfully' ask for what purposes did their governments send them to the USSR."[105]

103. Litvinov to Stalin, 3 May 1939, as quoted above.
104. Naggiar, nºs 686-691, 13 July 1939, MAÉ Papiers Naggiar/10.
105. "Instructions to the people's commissar for defence of the USSR, K. E. Voroshilov …," 7 Aug. 1939, DVP, XXII, book 1, 584.

The issue of Red Army passage across parts of Poland and Rumania to meet the enemy was crucial to the Soviet government; it would be the sign of Anglo-French good faith. The Poles had long resisted such conditions; in fact, Daladier had given verbal instructions to his chief delegate not to agree to Red Army passage across Poland. Soviet instructions anticipated this also: "If it is clear that free passage of our troops across the territory of Poland and Rumania is excluded, then declare that without [acceptance of] this condition an agreement is impossible ..." Defensive operations against German aggression would be unsuccessful, "... and we do not intend to participate in an undertaking destined from the outset to failure."[106] Each side followed its instructions, and the talks failed. At the last minute the French and British governments half-heartedly moved toward the Soviet position and attempted to persuade Poland to accept the Soviet demand. The Poles adamantly refused. They would prefer defeat, the Soviet military attaché in Warsaw had predicted in January 1939, to an alliance with the USSR.

During the summer of 1939, as the Soviet government became further convinced of Anglo-French bad faith, it decided to indulge in its own, becoming progressively more interested in a nonaggression pact with Nazi Germany. The threat of a reversal of Soviet policy, against which Litvinov – and the French embassy in Moscow – had warned for many years, came to pass on 23 August 1939.[107] The Anglo-French military delegations in Moscow were left beached on the dilatory instructions of their governments. The delegations left Moscow quietly, humiliated and offended by what they perceived to be Soviet treachery.

The double-dealing was, of course, reciprocal, though Molotov thought that the Soviet government had only paid back the British and French in their own coin. This was hardly a statesman-like position, as Russian historians have noted, and it had calamitous consequences for Europe. The French paid the price earlier than the USSR when in 1940 there was no Red Army to threaten Germany's eastern border. The French debacle undoubtedly had many

106. Ibid.
107. Geoffrey Roberts, "The Soviet Decision for a Pact with Nazi Germany," *Soviet Studies* 44 (1992): 57-78.

causes, but one of these was the failure to conclude a military alliance with the USSR. One is tempted to say that France had "lost opportunities" to settle with the Soviet government; certainly, some French officials, like Ambassadors Alphand and Coulondre, thought so. The years 1926, 1934 and 1939 were fateful in this sad story of failure. But it is doubtful whether there were real opportunities lost. The French government was too hostile to Bolshevism and too much hostage of the wealthy, powerful *grande bourgeoisie*, most of whom opposed any dealings with Soviet Russia. All too frequently the right shabbily exploited the Red bogeyman for electoral gain, sacrificing traditional French policy of alliance with Russia. Right-wing press campaigns often unnerved the weak, unstable French governments of the interwar years, making them afraid of closer relations with the USSR. In the 1920s Poincaré seemed a short-sighted, mean-spirited politician, determined to down the Radical-Socialist *Cartel*. In the 1930s Laval and Daladier played equally short-sighted roles.

And then there was the British factor. Even in the 1920s the French government to some degree subordinated its Russian policy to Tory anti-Communism. In the 1930s, French policy became more subservient. In 1939, when a last chance for cooperation appeared to arise, the French government deferred again to the British when Chamberlain contemplated negotiations with the Soviet only because – as he freely admitted – the pressure of public opinion and from the House of Commons forced him into it.

In such conditions Realists never had a chance against the Ideologues, who repeatedly hampered or blocked Franco-Soviet relations. "What responsibility will we bear?," Ambassador Herbette asked prophetically in 1926, if the failure of a Franco-Soviet rapprochement led to a new German invasion. The "grave-diggers" of France, as the French journalist Pertinax would later describe them, included those who feared Communist revolution; they could not forget their "stolen" billions in investments, and ultimately they put their class interests before those of their country. Such an assertion is hardly new; on the contrary, it is an old idea which stands discredited by many contemporary historians. The evidence of Franco-Soviet relations in the inter-war years, however, suggests that the death of this old idea is premature. Anti-

Bolshevism obsessed France's government and society, perverted the calculation of French national interests, and by impeding a Franco-Soviet rapprochement and later an alliance, contributed to the fall of France in 1940.

VIII
FRANCE AND THE ILLUSION OF AMERICAN SUPPORT, 1919-1940

William R. Keylor

"We can do France no worse disservice today than to allow her to base her security on an illusion of American support."
                    William C. Bullitt to Franklin D. Roosevelt, 29 November 1936

"Can you stretch a hand across the ocean to help us save civilization? It could reverse the course of history."
                    Paul Reynaud to Franklin D. Roosevelt, 5 June 1940

"We shall always be a mirage to the French."
                    Durand Echeverria

Some Counterfactual Conjectures About the Catastrophe of 1940

France's military collapse in May-June 1940 has prompted much retrospective speculation about both the short-term and long-term causes of that critical turning point in the history of the twentieth-century. From Marc Bloch to Eugen Weber the historiographical literature has focused on causal agents of a domestic character, notably the ideological polarization of French society in the 1930s.[1]

---

1. Marc Bloch, *Etrange Défaite* (Paris, 1957); Eugen Weber, *The Hollow Years: France in the 1930s* (New York, 1994).

It is now widely accepted that the Third Republic was gravely undermined by a host of political conflicts and social tensions in the decade before its ignominious demise. Robert Soucy has refuted René Rémond's long-standing assertion that France lacked an indigenous fascist tradition in the interwar period by demonstrating that the Croix de Feu and other anti-parliamentary groups on the Right were both fascist in character and immensely popular in the eyes of a French public profoundly alienated from the regime.[2] Zeev Sternhell and Philippe Burrin have shown how fascism also appealed to politicians and intellectuals on the Left who, disillusioned both with the bourgeois republic and with the conventional Marxist critique of capitalism, looked across the Alps or the Rhine for inspiration.[3]

But as important as these and other signs of the disintegration of the republican consensus may have been, the argument that they represented decisive factors in the fall of France merits the Scotch verdict "not proven." As William Irvine cautions, the historian must take care not to seek an explanation of the *causes* of the French defeat through the lenses of its political *consequences*. To trace the roots of the authoritarian, collaborationist policies of the Vichy regime to the proliferation of anti-republican groups and sentiments in the 1930s is one thing; to attribute the military debacle of 1940 to those earlier developments is quite another.[4]

To elaborate on Irvine's fleeting allusion to the cultural pessimism and political polarization in France before World War I as a point of comparison: In the years before 1914, the term "decadence" had become the watchword on the French cultural scene. Writers of diverse political tendencies bemoaned the decline of French civilization in the face of various cultural threats from within and abroad.[5] The Republic sustained vigorous challenges to

---

2. René Rémond, *La Droite en France de la première restauration à la Ve République* (Paris, 1963); Robert Soucy, *French Fascism: The Second Wave, 1933-1939* (New Haven, 1996).
3. Zeev Sternhell, *Ni droite ni gauche: L'Idéologie fasciste en France* (Paris, 1983); Philippe Burrin, *La Dérive fasciste: Doriot, Déat, Bergery* (Paris, 1986).
4. William D. Irvine, "Domestic Politics and the Fall of France in 1940," pp. 85-89
5. K.W. Swart, *The Sense of Decadence in Nineteenth-Century France* (The Hague, 1964); Claude Digeon, *La crise allemande de la pensée française, 1870-1914* (Paris, 1959).

its legitimacy from both extremes of the political spectrum: The revolutionary syndicalists adopted the tactic of the general strike to prevent a war initiated by the bourgeois state. This strategy was officially adopted in 1908 and 1912 by the Confédération Général du Travail, the country's only nationwide labor organization, amid the worst labor unrest that France had ever known.[6] The newly unified Socialist party enthusiastically endorsed the principles of proletarian internationalism and antimilitarism that emanated from the annual congresses of the Second International.[7] The officer corps reeled from the purges of its clerical-monarchist members in the aftermath of the French military's sordid role in the Dreyfus Affair, producing what David Ralston has called "a grave crisis in morale" in the army that "seriously impaired its military effectiveness."[8] The Catholic Church was locked in bitter conflict with the staunchly anticlerical state as thousands of monks and nuns fled France into exile.[9] Militants from the Action Française invaded the Sorbonne to disrupt the lectures of republican professors, shut down plays deemed ideologically offensive, and descended into the streets of Paris and other large cities to wage war against the detested regime.[10]

With the wisdom of hindsight we know that the domestic enemies of the republican regime postponed their ideological grievances and embraced the cause of national defense once war with Germany had broken out in August 1914. The pleasant surprise of the *union sacrée* relieved the government of the necessity to round up the thousand-odd suspected subversives who had been ear-

---

6. Frederick F. Ridley, *Revolutionary Syndicalism in France: The Direct Action of Its Time* (Cambridge, 1970), pp. 135-139.
7. James Joll, *The Second International, 1889-1914* (London, 1974), pp. 135-144, 151.
8. David Ralston, *The Army of the Republic: The Place of the Military in the Political Evolution of France, 1871-1914* (Cambridge, Mass., 1967), p. 252.
9. John McManners, *Church and State in France, 1870-1914* (London, 1972).
10. Zeev Sternhell, *La Droite Révolutionnaire: Les Origines françaises du fascisme* (Paris, 1978); on the French royalist movement's plans for and acts of violence against the republican regime and its defenders, see Eugen Weber, *Action Française: Royalism and Reaction in Twentieth-Century France* (Stanford, 1962), chapter 2; William R. Keylor, *Jacques Bainville and the Renaissance of Royalist History in Twentieth-Century France* (Baton Rouge, 1979), pp. 46-48.

marked for preventive detention by the Ministry of Interior.[11] The French intellectual elite miraculously recovered from its prewar bout of cultural despair to close ranks in defense of France's superior *civilisation* against Germany's barbaric *Kultur*.[12] But the broad-based consensus in support of the wartime governments of the Third Republic represented a fragile truce that concealed deep divisions within French politics, society, and culture that would reappear as soon as the war came to an end.[13] The divisive and corrosive trends that recent scholarship has diagnosed in interwar France were not spawned in that era. They were inherited, *mutatis mutandis*, from the halcyon days of *La Belle Epoque*. Had the German army penetrated the French defenses during the great offensives of September 1914 and March 1918 – and it came close to doing so on both occasions – historians in search of causal connections would have had ample justification for attributing the French defeat in the Great War to the "decadence" of French society in the "hollow years" from 1905 to 1914.

But to challenge the conventional view that the internal political and social crises of the Third Republic during the 1930s "caused" the military collapse of 1940 obliges the skeptic to propose an alternative interpretation. The application of Occam's razor to the question yields a straightforward military explanation that requires no reference to broader trends in French politics, culture, or society: The defective strategy pursued by the French high command, exacerbated by the faulty tactics employed by tank commanders in the field, has been exhaustively examined by competent specialists on the subject. The scholarly consensus is succinctly summarized in the blunt assertion by Nicole Jordan elsewhere in this volume that "Strategy lay at the heart of the French military collapse and prepared the way for the armistice in

---

11. Jean-Jacques Becker, *Le Carnet B: Les pouvoirs publics et l'antimilitarisme avant la guerre de 1914* (Paris, 1973). On the background to the formation of the *union sacrée*, see the same author's *1914, Comment les Français sont entrés dans la guerre* (Paris, 1977).
12. Martha Hanna, *The Mobilization of Intellect: French Scholars and Writers During the Great War* (Cambridge, Mass., 1996), especially the introduction and Chapter 3.
13. *Ibid.*, pp. 13-14.

1940."[14] Most specialists in military history are now in agreement that the comparative strength of the armies that faced each other on the western front in the spring of 1940 did not foreordain France's defeat. That outcome was due not to the quantitative or qualitative inferiority of French manpower and weaponry but rather to the manner in which they were deployed. Once again, an exercise in counterfactual speculation illustrates the argument: Had Charles de Gaulle replaced Maurice Gamelin as commander-in-chief of the French army at the beginning of the war and been able to assemble a coterie of like-minded disciples to manage the spring campaign, this book might well have been entitled *The French Victory of 1940: Reassessments.*

The case for a purely military explanation of France's collapse is a compelling one. Yet it seems to me incomplete without a consideration of the severe constraints that had been imposed on French policy makers by the deterioration of relations with France's potential allies in the two decades after the Great War. The disadvantageous diplomatic position that France found herself in as she faced a rearmed, aggressive Germany at the end of the 1930s played a role in the debacle of 1940 at least as important as the notorious blunders of the French high command.[15] A comparison with the previous confrontation with the German army once again proves instructive: Joffre's forces had been able to repulse von Kluck's offensive in the autumn of 1914 in part because of the unexpectedly rapid Russian offensive in East Prussia (which drew off units from the right wing of the advancing German army in France) and the decisive intervention of the British Expeditionary Force. The French were able to withstand the second great German bid for a breakthrough in the spring of 1918 – after their erstwhile Russian allies had left the war and

---

14. Nicole Jordan, "Strategy and Scapegoatism: Reflections on the French National Catastrophe, 1940," pp. 13-38. See also Don W. Alexander, "Repercussions of the Breda Variant," *French Historical Studies*, Vol. 8 (1974), pp. 459-488.

15. It is ironic that Jean-Baptiste Duroselle, the late doyen of diplomatic historians in France who has written so extensively on France's relations with other powers, is perhaps best remembered for his study of the domestic influences on that country's disastrous foreign policies during the 1930s. Jean-Baptiste Duroselle, *La Décadence* (Paris, 1979).

their British allies seriously contemplated evacuating Dunkirk and the other channel ports[16] – because of the influx of American supplies, money, and, eventually, military manpower.

At the beginning of the Second World War, France enjoyed none of the diplomatic advantages that had saved her army from disaster and defeat in the Great War. Had the Tsar signed a separate peace with the Kaiser in the summer of 1914 as Stalin would do in the summer of 1939, and had the Liberal government in London made as half-hearted a commitment of British forces to the defense of France as the Conservative government did in 1940, the Battle of the Marne might well have resulted in some version of Bethmann-Hollweg's "September Program" for the reduction of France to the status of a servile satellite of the Reich.[17] In the absence of the lavish financial assistance that flowed from Washington after the American declaration of war, and of the American Expeditionary Force that belatedly but decisively replenished the depleted Anglo-French forces in the summer of 1918, the Ludendorff offensive might well have resulted in a Carthaginian settlement with France modeled on the one recently imposed on Russia.

In the years before both world wars, French governments had to rely on skillful diplomacy to compensate for their country's demographic and economic inferiority to Germany. Philippe Berthelot, who as secretary general of the Quai d'Orsay would exercise enormous influence on French foreign policy during the 1920s, wrote his patron Aristide Briand as early as 1923 that France's thirty-eight million people had no hope of opposing the seventy million people of Germany and Austria alone.[18] The governments of interwar France were condemned to the unpleasant but inescapable fate of dependence on foreign powers for the containment of Germany and the preservation of the peace settlement. France's inability to ensure that two of the three great powers that had intervened to prevent her from being overwhelmed by the advanc-

16. John Toland, *No Man's Land: 1918-The Last Year of the Great War* (Garden City, 1980), p. 157.

17. On the *Mitteleuropa* plan see the still reliable analysis by Fritz Fischer, *Germany's Aims in the First World War* (New York, 1967), pp. 98-106.

18. Edward D. Keeton, *Briand's Locarno Policy: French Economics, Politics, and Diplomacy, 1925-1929* (New York, 1987),pp. 89-90.

ing enemy during the First World War would be at her side again in 1939-1940 had two crucial consequences. The first was that Germany would not be deterred from revising the Versailles settlement, by diplomatic pressure if possible, by military force if necessary. The second was that once war began in the West, Germany stood a much greater chance to achieve the decisive breakthrough in France that had eluded her twice in the Great War.

The failure of the Third Republic to resurrect the alliance with Russia that had helped to prevent a national catastrophe in 1914 represents the most conspicuous shortcoming of French diplomacy in the interwar period. The deterioration of Franco-Russian relations, for the reasons cited by Michael Carley,[19] led to a frantic search for alternatives to the Soviet Union as an eastern counterweight to German power on the continent. The strategic value to France of the small successor states of the Habsburg, Hohenzollern, and Romanov empires in East Central Europe has become the subject of spirited dispute among specialists.[20] Whatever the usefulness of France's ties to Poland and the countries of the Petite Entente, Carley has convincingly argued elsewhere that Paris exploited these eastern commitments as a pretext for avoiding a serious approach to Moscow because of the French political and military elites' ideological antipathy for the Soviet regime.[21]

19. Michael Jabara Carley, "Prelude to Defeat: Franco-Soviet Relations, 1919-1939," pp. 171-203.
20. Nicole Jordan, *The Popular Front and Central Europe: The Dilemmas of French Impotence, 1918-1940* (New York, 1992), and Piotr S. Wandycz, *France and her Eastern Allies, 1919-1925* (Minneapolis, 1962), and *The Twilight of French Eastern Alliances, 1926-1936* (Princeton, 1988) attribute great importance to the eastern alliances in France's comprehensive strategy to contain Germany. Stephen A. Schuker disputes this interpretation, claiming that French policy makers had little faith in either the Polish or the Czechoslovak army and concluding that "the alliances in East-Central Europe had no great significance at all, at least outside the perfervid imagination of such scholars as Piotr Wandycz and Nicole Jordan." Stephen A. Schuker, "Two Cheers for Appeasement," paper presented at the annual conference of the Society for French Historical Studies, Boston, Mass., 21 March 1996. Keeton concludes that "France's eastern allies were a welcome stop-gap, but Briand did not consider them a permanent substitute for British and American support." Keeton, *Briand's Locarno Policy*, p. 86.
21. Michael Jabara Carley, "Appeasement in the 1930s: Was There an Alternative?," paper presented at the annual conference of the Society for French Historical Studies, Boston, Mass., 21 March 1996.

Stalin's separate peace with Hitler in August 1939, like Lenin's with the Kaiser in March 1918, liberated Germany from Bismarck's old nightmare of a war on two fronts and enabled Hitler to concentrate the bulk of his military power against France. In the meantime, for all of the reasons adduced by Martin Alexander, Great Britain was ill prepared in 1939-1940 to endure the enormous sacrifices in the defense of France that it had stoically borne in 1914-1918.[22] The hesitant, half-hearted character of the British continental commitment was obviously influenced by the traumatic memories of Passchendaele and the Somme. But it also reflected the persistence of that profound British ambivalence toward the Franco-German rivalry on the continent that had surfaced shortly after the peace conference and remained an obstacle to Anglo-French cooperation throughout the interwar period.[23] French political leaders were perfectly aware of this reluctance on the part of their past and present ally, but the absence of obvious alternatives had kept France rigidly dependent on British support against Germany right up to the outbreak of hostilities in 1939.[24]

The Disappearance of the American Guarantee

Was there an alternative to the "impossible" alliance with Russia that might have supplemented the "insufficient" alliance with Great Britain to afford France adequate protection against German aggression after the Great War? At the end of the Paris Peace Conference of 1919, Georges Clemenceau thought there was. The system for the preservation of postwar French security that "the Tiger" had devised in the spring of 1919 was based on the active participation of the United States in preventing a resurgent Germany

---

22. Martin Alexander, "Fighting to the Last Frenchman"?: Reflections on the BEF Deployment to France and the Strains in the Franco-British Alliance, 1939-1940," pp. 296-326.
23. Alan Sharp, "Standard-bearers in a Tangle: British Perceptions of France after the First World War," in David Dutton, *Statecraft and Diplomacy in the Twentieth Century* (Liverpool, 1995), pp. 56-73.
24. F. Bédarida, "La gouvernante anglaise," in R. Rémond and J. Bourdin, eds., *Edouard Daladier, Chef de Gouvernement* (Paris, 1977), pp. 228-240.

from reversing the allied military triumph of 1918. Then the very power whose money and men had enabled France to win the Great War, and whose president had pledged to guarantee the postwar security of France, promptly disengaged from Europe and retracted its continental commitments. The unavailability of financial assistance and military protection from the United States at the beginning of the Second World War must be counted, along with the defection of Russia and the inadequate support from Great Britain, as a significant factor in the deterioration of France's power position in Europe that paved the way for the debacle of 1940.

The Franco-American wartime partnership of 1917-1918 – it had, of course, never acquired the formal designation of an "alliance" because of President Wilson's obdurate insistence on preserving his country's separate and unique status as a belligerent – had been severely tested at the Paris Peace Conference. The acrimonious struggle between Clemenceau and Wilson over reparations, the Rhineland, the Saar, and other provisions of the peace settlement has received extensive scholarly treatment and needs no recapitulation here.[25] Suffice it to say that the French prime minister was obliged to sacrifice a number of desiderata (most notably Marshal Ferdinand Foch's pet scheme for an independent Rhineland Republic as a buffer against German military power) in order to ensure American support for the postwar European security system that was being fashioned. The *quid pro quo* that Clemenceau wrested from Wilson and Lloyd George was a set of compensatory security arrangements that would have adequately protected France. The cornerstone of this postwar security system – which included the permanent demilitarization of the Rhineland and its temporary occupation by an interallied military force – were the unprecedented commitments by the United States and Great Britain to intervene on France's behalf in the event of unprovoked aggression from Germany. André Tardieu, Clemenceau's right-

---

25. The most comprehensive treatment is to be found in Arthur Walworth, *Wilson and his Peacemakers: American Diplomacy at the Paris Peace Conference, 1919* (New York, 1986), esp. pp. 255-276, 321-334. A blow-by-blow record of the sparring between the two leaders appears in Paul Mantoux, *The Deliberations of the Council of Four (24 March – 28 June 1919): Notes of the Official Interpreter*, 2 vols. (Trans. Arthur S. Link, Princeton, 1992).

hand man who was instrumental in negotiating the two guarantee pacts, accurately described them as "the key factor in making possible the Versailles treaty" and "the crowning achievement of M. Clemenceau's policy" at the peace conference.[26]

The American security guarantee never entered into force because of the failure of the U.S. Senate to consent to the agreement signed by Wilson at Versailles, while the British guarantee lapsed because Lloyd George had shrewdly made its application contingent on the legislative ratification of the American pact.[27] It has long been assumed that the failure of the United States Senate to ratify both the Franco-American guarantee treaty and the peace treaty with Germany reflected the unwillingness of the Republican legislative majority to endorse such an expansion of America's foreign entanglements. But the archival record reveals a willingness on the part of the Republican leaders in the Senate, who abhorred the limitless global commitments implied by article ten of the League Covenant, to contemplate the more precise obligation to defend France against unprovoked aggression from Germany.[28]

Had the campaign to ratify the Versailles treaty and the French security pact taken a different turn, the position of France would have been much stronger than it turned out to be after the entire peace settlement went down the drain on Capitol Hill. Seldom

26. André Tardieu, *La Paix* (Paris, 1921), p. 237.
27. On the fate of the Franco-American security treaty, see Louis A. R. Yates, *The United States and French Security, 1917-1921* (New York, 1957) (which is based excusively on American sources); William R. Keylor, "The Rise and Demise of the Franco-American Guarantee Pact, 1919-21," *Proceedings of the Annual Meeting of the Western Society for French History*, vol. 15 (1988), pp. 367-377 (which exploits the French archival sources opened in the 1970s). The best analysis of the Anglo-French security treaty is Antony Lentin, "The Treaty That Never Was: Lloyd George and the Abortive Anglo-French Alliance of 1919," in Judith Loades, ed., *The Life and Times of David Lloyd George* (Bangor, 1991), pp. 115-128, and Lentin, "Une Aberration Inexplicable?": Clemenceau and the Abortive Anglo-French Guarantee Treaty of 1919," Paper presented at the annual meeting of the Society for French Historical Studies, Boston, 23 March 1996.
28. William R. Keylor, "France's Futile Quest for American Military Protection, 1919-1922," in Marta Petricioli, ed., *A Missed Opportunity? 1922: The Reconstruction of Europe* (Berne, 1995), pp. 68-71. Republican support for the French security treaty and the Versailles treaty apart from the League is discussed in Lloyd E. Ambrosius, "Wilson, the Republicans, and French Security after World War I," *Journal of American History*, LIX, No. 2 (September 1972), pp. 341-352.

can the role of a single individual be said to have altered the course of history. But the behavior of the ill, incommunicado American president during the treaty fight in Washington throughout the autumn and winter of 1919-1920 is one such instance. On learning of Wilson's stubborn refusal to compromise with the Republican majority in the Senate in spite of urgent appeals from friends and admirers, Clemenceau exploded to the British ambassador: "What on earth is the Lord Almighty doing that he does not take him to his bosom at once?"[29] A speech by Vice President Thomas R. Marshall to a fraternal organization in Atlanta on 15 November 1919 was interrupted by a report that Wilson had just died in the White House.[30] These two incidents afford me the opportunity to indulge in a final exercise in counterfactual speculation: What if Clemenceau's wish had been granted and the premature report of Wilson's demise been accurate?

The German peace treaty, as modified by the Lodge reservations, failed by only seven votes to obtain the requisite two-thirds majority in the Senate on 19 March 1920 because twenty-three Wilsonian Democrats had reluctantly obeyed their party leader's command to join with the twelve "irreconcilable" isolationists to kill it. With Wilson out of the picture, the treaty with the Lodge reservations would have been approved by the Senate with plenty of votes to spare. The Franco-American security treaty, which obliged the United States to defend France in the event of unprovoked German aggression, would have passed with the strong support of prominent Republican leaders including Henry Cabot Lodge, Philander K. Knox, Frank Brandegee, Elihu Root, and other Republican leaders (who, as noted above, had favored it as a much more precise and practical commitment than the open-ended, utopian pledge of global collective security in article ten of the League Covenant). Both the German peace treaty with the Lodge reservations and the guarantee pact with France would have been promptly signed by the new president, who – along with Secretary of State Robert Lansing and Senate Minority Leader Gilbert

29. Derby to Curzon, 5 December 1919; Papers of Marquis Curzon of Kedleston, India House Library, Mss. Eur. F112/196.
30. *New York Times*, 16 Nov. 1919.

Hitchcock – had endorsed them both in confidential discussions with French ambassador Jules Jusserand.[31] The U.S. commitment to the Versailles peace settlement in general and French security in particular would have represented a formidable deterrent to German revisionism. The presence of American officials on the various treaty commissions would have lent U.S. prestige to the enforcement machinery. The principal bone of contention between Wilson and his Republican antagonists on Capitol Hill, the League of Nations Covenant, would have been discussed and debated at leisure while the Versailles treaty entered into force.[32]

Ah, the irresistible temptation of counterfactual historical speculation! In fact, Wilson lived out the rest of his presidency, indeed long enough to admit, in response to Poincaré's occupation of the Ruhr in 1923, that "I would like to see Germany clean up France, and I would like to meet [French Ambassador Jules] Jusserand and tell him that to his face."[33] The Harding administration had concluded a separate peace agreement with Germany that freed the United States of all obligations specified in the Versailles treaty. Neither Harding nor his successor, Calvin Coolidge, displayed any interest in resurrecting the old pledge to defend France that lay forgotten in a congressional pigeonhole. Aristide Briand's artful attempt in 1927 to lure Coolidge's Secretary of State, Frank Kellogg, into a privileged bilateral relationship with France represented the last serious bid to lay the groundwork for a security commitment from Washington. Kellogg shrewdly deflected Briand's

31. Jusserand to Foreign Minister, rec. 8 and 10 Dec. 1919, rec. 12 and 31 Jan. 1920, Service Historique de l'Armée de Terre (Vincennes), Fonds Clemenceau, carton 6N139; Jusserand to Foreign Minister, rec. 24 Nov., rec. 30 Nov., rec. 1 Dec., rec. 6 Dec., 1919, Archives du Ministère des Affaires Etrangères (hereafter MAE), Série A, Paix, vol. 213; Jusserand to Foreign Minister, 30 Nov. 1919, MAE, Série Amérique, 1918-29, sous-série Etats-Unis, (hereafter Etats-Unis), vol. 38; Keylor, "France's Futile Quest for American Military Protection," p. 71.

32. William R. Keylor, "'Lafayette, We Have Quit!': Wilsonian Policy and French Security After Versailles," in Nancy L. Roelker and Charles K. Warner, eds., *Two Hundred Years of Franco-American Relations* (Worcester, Mass., 1981), pp. 44-75.

33. The remark was made to James Kerney, the editor of the *Trenton Evening Times*, as he was interviewing Wilson on the porch of his Washington D.C. residence on 7 December 1923. In the same conversation Wilson denounced Poincaré as a "bully" and Foch as a "militarist." James Kerney, *The Political Evolution of Woodrow Wilson* (New York, 1926), p. 476.

overture by transforming it into an innocuous multilateral renunciation of war that Wilson would surely have applauded.[34] French statesmen thereafter abandoned – at least for the moment – all hope of securing an American role in upholding the Versailles settlement and in defending France against a future attempt by Germany to dismantle it. In the meantime, French attitudes toward the United States had taken a turn for the worse.

America the Menace

By the end of the nineteen twenties, the French image of the United States had acquired a set of negative stereotypes that emphasized the putative economic and cultural threat posed by American civilization to the French way of life.[35] The French critique of American civilization was based partly on impressions gathered during fleeting visits to the devil's lair, partly on more sustained encounters acquired during extended residence. The most devastating literary portrait of American culture and society was painted by a misanthropic Parisian writer whose familiarity with his subject was confined to a miserable three-week sojourn. The memorable collection of images of American life that Georges Duhamel brought back with him to France would set the tone for French anti-Americanism for generations to come: the soulless assembly line of the industrial cities, the vulgarity and philistinism of what passed for American culture, the moral absurdities of puritanism and prohibition, the fetid stockyards and machine-gun-toting gangsters of Chicago, the masters of deception and manipulation on Madison Avenue. Every familiar cliché about American culture and society reverberated throughout Duhamel's indictment in *Scènes de la vie future*, which became a best seller in France and was more accurately translated into English as *America the Menace*.[36]

    34. Robert H. Ferrell, *Peace in Their Time: The Origins of the Kellogg-Briand Pact* (New Haven: Yale University Press, 1952), pp. 194-200. Keeton, *Briand's Locarno Policy*, p. 230.
    35. For a comprehensive analysis of this phenomenon, see David Strauss, *Menace in the West: The Rise of French Anti-Americanism in Modern Times* (Westport, CT, 1978).
    36. Georges Duhamel, *Scènes de la vie future* (Paris, 1930); *America the Menace* (trans. Charles M. Thompson, Boston, 1931); Strauss, *Menace in the West*, pp. 73-75.

Duhamel's vehement denunciation of America as the nest of a pernicious brand of cutthroat capitalism that threatened to engulf France established a cottage industry that would subsequently employ the most eminent members of the Parisian intelligentsia during the Cold War.[37] This critique was not confined to critics on the Socialist or Communist Left. Some of the most vituperative assaults on American economic imperialism emanated from French observers without an identifiable ax to grind. There was a profound irony in this French outburst against American economic hegemony: Works by Octave Homberg, Jean Bonnefon-Craponne, Pierre Laurent, and Charles Pomeret all raised the specter of an American economic takeover of Europe in general and France in particular just as the world depression deepened and American lending and investment in Europe dwindled.[38]

Some French intellectuals worried less about domination by American corporations and banks than about the invasion by American cultural and social values. Two youthful devotées of the new doctrine of personalism, Robert Aron and Arnaud Dandieu, sounded the alarm in 1931 about the insidious extension of the conformity, monotony, and materialism of American life to Europe.[39] The Maurrasian Henri Massis's lament about the decline of European civilization, though directed primarily at the threat from the East, also decried the spread of the dehumanizing values from the society across the Atlantic.[40] After chiding the Catholic Massis for his excessively parochial definition of Western culture, the Jewish writer Kadmi-Cohen echoed the mounting *angst* about American cultural hegemony in an outburst of defiant wrath.[41]

37. David Caute, *Communism and the French Intellectuals, 1914-1960* (New York, 1964), pp. 173-175, 190-196; Tony Judt, *Past Imperfect: French Intellectuals, 1944-1956* (Berkeley, 1992), chapter 10; Richard Kuisel, *Seducing the French: The Dilemma of Americanization* (Berkeley, 1993), esp. chapter 3; Irwin Wall, *L'influence américaine sur la politique française, 1945-1954* (Paris, 1989), pp. 170-187, 188-228.

38. Octave Homberg, *L'Impérialisme américain* (Paris, 1929); Jean Bonnefon-Craponne, *La pénétration économique et financière des capitaux américains en Europe* (Paris, 1930); Pierre Laurent, *L'Impérialisme économique américain* (Paris, 1931); Charles Pomeret, *L'Amérique et la conquête de l'Europe* (1931).

39. Robert Aron and Arnaud Dandieu, *Le Cancer américain* (Paris, 1931).

40. Henri Massis, *La Défense de l'Occident* (Paris, 1927).

41. "Out with the Yankees! Out with their people and their products, their methods and their lessons, their dances and their jazz! Let them take back their Fords

Such sentiments extended beyond the drawing rooms of the disaffected intelligentsia in France. Apprehension about American economic domination and cultural hegemony influenced French foreign policy during Aristide Briand's long tenure at the Quai d'Orsay in the second half of the twenties. Briand's two major initiatives in this period, his bid for a Franco-German rapprochement with Stresemann and his ill-fated proposal for a European Union, were inspired in part by a determination to counter American economic power by harnessing the industrial dynamism of the Weimar Republic to a continental bloc dominated by France. Even Poincaré, the preeminent symbol of harshness toward Germany who served as Prime Minister in 1926-1929, fully supported Briand's courtship of Stresemann (even at the cost of an early French evacuation of the Rhineland) because of his own fears of American financial power and commercial aggressiveness.[42] Since "Americanization" threatened not only France but also Germany and the other states of Europe, the ideology of anti-Americanism reinforced the Franco-German rapprochement of 1925-1929 as well as the early movement of "Europeanism" that Briand sought, prematurely as it turned out, to launch at the end of his career.[43]

This acrimony between Paris and Washington was exacerbated by the persistence of controversies inherited from the war and the peace

---

and their chewing gum." Kadmi-Cohen, L'Abomination américain: essai politique (Paris, 1930), p. 264.

42. Keeton, Briand's Locarno Diplomacy, esp. pp. 247-248, 298-304. On Briand's European Union scheme, see Walter Lipgens, "Europäische Einigungsidee 1923-30 und Briands Europaplan im Urteil der deutschen Akten, "Historische Zeitschrift, vol. 203 (1966), pp. 46-89, 316-363; Georges Suarez, Briand, vol. VI (Paris, 1952), pp. 325-344. For a skeptical assessment, see Ellinor von Puttkamer, "Der Briand-Plan, Verbote der europäischen Integration?," in W. Hallstein, ed., Festschrift für L. Bergsträsser (Dusseldorf, 1954), pp. 153-166.

43. On the connections between anti-Americanism and the movement for European unity in the twenties, see Strauss, Menace in the West, pp. 214-220 and Keeton, Briand's Locarno Diplomacy, pp. 300-301, 314-315, 320-324. Kadmi-Cohen established the link with his customary flair. "The Franco-German entente is a European necessity," he declared. "The United States of Europe! These words are on everyone's lips, in everyone's heart, in everyone's imagination! Enough of the intolerable oppression by America. We will put an end to the unimaginable insolence of the United States toward the old and noble nations of Europe." Kadmi-Cohen, L'Abomination américaine, pp. 230, 263. For similar sentiments predating Briand's proposal for European union in the summer of 1929, see Lucien Romier, Qui sera le maître, Europe ou Amérique (Paris, 1927).

settlement. The disputes over German reparations and the French war debt – the two *causes célèbres* of Franco-American relations in the nineteen twenties – were blown far out of proportion to their actual economic significance by rhetorical excesses on both sides of the Atlantic. The widespread claim in the United States that France's exigent reparations demands imposed an intolerable financial burden on Germany, inhibited its industrial recovery, and undermined the economic structure of postwar Europe has been disproved by subsequent scholarship. Marc Trachtenberg and Sally Marks have demonstrated how moderate France's reparation policy at the peace conference actually was.[44] Marks and Charles Maier have shown how the Weimar Republic succeeded, with timely support from London and Washington, in reducing the reparation bill from the original inflated sums to an amount well within Germany's capacity to pay.[45] Stephen Schuker has assembled data that reveal how Germany ended up paying no net reparations at all, since American commercial loans (on which Germany later defaulted during the Great Depression) more than covered Germany's reparation payments after the Dawes Plan had opened the German capital market to foreign (and primarily American) lending.[46] Yet Keynes's early indictment became and remained the bible of American critics of the financial provisions of the peace settlement and France's efforts to enforce them.[47]

The issue of the $3.4 billion French war debt to the United States treasury likewise developed a life of its own that was entirely unre-

44. Marc Trachtenberg, *Reparation in World Politics: France and European Economic Diplomacy, 1916-1923* (New York, 1980), chapter 2; Sally Marks, "Smoke and Mirrors in Smoke Filled Rooms in the Galerie des Glaces: Reparations at the Paris Peace Conference," paper presented at the conference marking the 75th anniversary of the Versailles treaty sponsored by the German Historical Institute, Berkeley, Calif., June 1994.
45. Sally Marks, The Myths of Reparations," *Central European History*, 17 (1978), pp. 231-255; Charles Maier, *Recasting Bourgeois Europe: Stabilization in France, Germany, and Italy in the Decade After World War I* (Princeton, 1975), 249-53.
46. "Not only did the Reich entirely avoid paying net reparations to its wartime opponents; it actually extracted the equivalent of reparations from the allied powers, and principally from the United States". Stephen A. Schuker, *American "Reparations" to Germany, 1919-1933* (Princeton, 1988), p. 10.
47. On Keynes's legacy, see William R. Keylor, "A Reevaluation of the Versailles Peace," *Relevance: The Quarterly Journal of the Great War Society*, Vol. V, No. 2 (Summer 1996), pp. 12-17.

lated to its actual economic effects on creditor and debtor country alike. Though the liberty bond legislation had rendered the allied war debt theoretically payable on demand, the U.S. treasury department granted the allied debtor governments a three-year extension after the armistice to afford them breathing space to recover from the devastation of the war. At the expiration of the moratorium in 1922, Washington increased the pressure on the debtor governments to conclude refunding agreements. But despite the rhetorical posturing to satisfy public opinion, the Harding and Coolidge administrations treated the European debtors in general and the French in particular with remarkable forbearance and generosity. After dispatching the head of its permanent staff to Washington to demonstrate with facts and figures France's inability to pay,[48] the French Finance Ministry waged a skillful campaign of procrastination that postponed the day of reckoning. By the time the State Department's imposition of an informal loan embargo finally induced the French to sign the Mellon-Bérenger funding agreement on 29 April 1926, the debtor government had obtained an average interest rate of 1.6 per cent over a 62-year period (compared to the 5 per cent minimum specified by Congress and the 3.3 per cent obtained by the British three years earlier). This sleight-of-hand erased 60 per cent of the total obligation, or, to put it another way, effectively canceled the entire amount that had been borrowed during the war, leaving payment for only the sums received after the armistice.[49]

Notwithstanding this magnanimous gesture from Washington, the French Chamber of Deputies delayed ratification of the pact for another three years, until it received assurances under the Young Plan of 1929 that German reparations would be forthcoming.[50]

48. The correspondence concerning the mission of the French treasury official Jean Parmentier to testify before the World War Foreign Debt Commission in 1922 is located in MAE, Etats-Unis, cartons 229 and 230.
49. Of this total roughly $2 billion had been borrowed prior to the armistice, another billion had been borrowed after the armistice for reconstruction purposes, and $400 million was owed in payment for surplus American war stocks. The best treatments of the war debt controversy are Ellen Schrecker, *The Hired Money: The French Debt to the United States, 1917-1929* (New York, 1979), and Denise Artaud, *La Question des dettes interalliés et la reconstruction de l'Europe, 1917-1929*, 2 vols. (Lille, 1987).
50. Artaud, *La Question des dettes interalliés*, pp. 908-910.

Then, after only two years of French payments on the debt, the Hoover Moratorium of 20 June 1931, postponed payments for a year. Rebuffing Prime Minister Edouard Herriot's request for an appropriation to pay the installment of roughly $19 million that came due on 15 December 1932, the Chamber of Deputies opted for default rather than suffer the wrath of a public aroused by the French press campaign against France's tightfisted creditors across the Atlantic. A few months after pleading penury as a justification for the default, the French Finance Ministry withdrew for other purposes enough gold from the New York Federal Reserve Bank to prepay its entire war debt for the next ten years.[51]

Domestic political considerations also dictated the vindictive response of the United States to the European debt defaults. This is revealed in the congressional debates preceding the passage in April 1934 of the Johnson Act, which prohibited American citizens or corporations from purchasing the securities of governments in default to the United States treasury. In Washington as in Paris, the official reaction to the breakdown of the debt agreements was determined not by careful calculations of national interest or financial exigency but by the fear of an outraged public opinion. Just as the bill mandating the default on the war debt had passed the French Chamber despite opposition from the Herriot government, the Johnson Act was approved by the U.S. Congress over the confidentially communicated objections of the State and Treasury Departments. In keeping with the public mood, Roosevelt repeatedly resorted to his Republican predecessors' ritualistic rhetoric about the solemn obligation for the European governments to pay their "debts of honor."[52]

Keynes's devastating portrait of a vengeful France driving Germany to economic ruin through excessive reparation demands while it constructed an enormous military force, juxtaposed against

---

51. Schuker, *American "Reparations" to Germany*, p. 69. The texts of most of the relevant agreements, including the Mellon-Bérenger Accord, the Hoover Moratorium, the Final Act of the Lausanne Conference, are conveniently assembled as appendices in Roger Picard and Paul Hugon, *Le Problème des dettes interalliés: Nécessité d'une révision* (Paris, 1934).

52. Selig Adler, *The Isolationist Impulse: Its Twentieth-Century Reaction* (New York, 1957), p. 232.

the equally sinister (and distorted) image of "Uncle Shylock" extracting his pound of flesh from impoverished France, poisoned Franco-American relations throughout the interwar period.[53] The growth of American isolationism in the 1930s was a complex phenomenon that reflected a number of influences. But one of its important sources was mounting public disillusionment with and resentment of the country "over there" that seemed to display a lack of gratitude for the American money spent and American lives lost in the Great War. To the perennial contretemps over reparations and war debts was added the growing perception of the "war to end all wars" as a senseless waste of life that was nurtured by Hollywood films such as King Vidor's *The Big Parade* (1925) and Lewis Milestone's cinematic version of Erich Maria Remarque's *All Quiet on the Western Front* (1930).[54] This spreading disillusionment hindered French attempts to keep alive the memory of the joint crusade against Germany in order to win American support in the future.[55]

The public reaction against America's participation in the Great War intensified as Hitler consolidated his absolute power in Germany. The liberal journalist Helmuth C. Englebrecht's best-seller *Merchants of Death*, published in 1934, exposed the world's munitions industries as the culprits responsible for causing the catastrophe of 1914-1918 in order to market their wares. Later in the same year, legislative hearings conducted by Senator Gerald P. Nye of North Dakota added to the expanding rogues' gallery a conspiratorial coterie of Wall street bankers who had duped Wilson into

---

53. Jacques Chastenet, *L' Oncle Shylock, ou l'impérialisme américain à la conquête du monde* (Paris, 1927); Octave Homberg, *La grande injustice: La question des dettes interalliés* (Paris, 1926). A more balanced French critique is to be found in Picard and Hugon, *Le Problème des dettes interalliés*.

54. Though Milestone's depiction of the absurdity of the war became a classic, Vidor's earlier silent film enjoyed a phenomenal success as well. After the opening burst of enthusiasm for America's transatlantic crusade, the sordid reality becomes evident as doughboys march in the "big parade" to the battlefield in Northern France as the unseen machine gun thins their ranks.

55. For a treatment of the early phase of these efforts, see William R. Keylor, "'How They Advertised France': The French Propaganda Campaign in the United States during the Breakup of the Franco-American Entente After the Great War, 1918-1923," *Diplomatic History*, Vol. 17, No. 3 (Summer 1993), pp. 351-373.

intervening on the side of the allies in order to recoup their loans. The Nye Committee revelations inspired a torrent of "revisionist" histories of the Great War detailing the machinations of America's former wartime associates in dragging America into war. These works all bore the implied warning that it should never be allowed to happen again.[56] Isolationists such as Senator William Borah inveighed against French foot-dragging on a war debt settlement as a scheme to trick American taxpayers into footing the bill for France's bloated military budget.[57] In short, the virulent anti-Americanism that had begun to spread in France during the interwar period was paralleled by the growth of an ill-tempered strain of Francophobia in the United States. The issue of the debt hanging over from the last war served as a potent and enduring symbol of the parting of ways by the two former partners in the coalition that had defeated Germany.

America the Savior

Notwithstanding the myriad of Franco-American tensions after the dissolution of the wartime entente, the United States remained for many Parisian policy makers the ultimate source of security for France in its increasingly dangerous international environment. The vivid memory of America's decisive intervention in the Great War and of Wilson's extensive (if unfulfilled) commitments to France at the peace conference had never entirely disappeared from French consciousness. The abrupt termination of U.S. government financial assistance to France, the rapid repatriation of American military forces after the armistice, and the disappearance of the American security guarantee for which Clemenceau had sacrificed the Rhine frontier, had not effaced the indelible impression that this intensive encounter with America had left on the French political elite and the public at large.

    56. Walter Millis, *Road to War: America, 1914-1917* (Boston, 1935); Charles A. Beard, *The Devil Theory of War* (New York, 1936). The most intemperate assault on France as the principal villain had appeared several years earlier. See Harry Elmer Barnes, *The Genesis of the World War* (New York, 1927), esp. pp. 96-151.
    57. *Congressional Record*, 67th Congress, 2nd session, pp. 1684-85.

Durand Echeverria entitled his classic study of French attitudes toward America in the eighteenth century "Mirage in the West."[58] That arresting metaphor for the distorted French vision of the United States applies just as accurately to the period between the two world wars of the twentieth century. A large section of French public opinion had never adapted to the sudden and unexpected disengagement of the United States from the European scene. Paul Monaco has explored the traumatic psychological consequences for France of this American withdrawal, identifying in the postwar French cinema a recurrent theme of the orphan representing the nation cruelly abandoned by its former purveyor and protector.[59] In its wistful yearning for the old wartime partnership, French public opinion seemed impervious to the ubiquitous signs of America's disinterest in Europe's postwar quarrels. The illusion that France could expect to receive American financial and military support if a resurgent Germany ever tried to destroy the peace settlement lingered on right up to the bitter end.

This misconception played a role in the decision to establish the continuous fortified line along France's frontier with Germany after Briand consented at the end of the 1920s to the premature termination of the interallied military occupation of the Rhineland. One of the critical strategic assumptions that led to the construction of the Maginot Line was the expectation that the economic and military resources of the United States would eventually be placed at France's disposal in the event of the long war of attrition that all French strategists had been anticipating since the conclusion of the last one. In light of France's demographic and economic inferiority to Germany, her only hope seemed to lie in a strategy designed to conserve France's precious manpower and resources behind an impenetrable barrier until the arrival of American assistance could again, as in the last war, tip the balance against the German invader.[60]

58. Durand Echeverria, *Mirage in the West: A History of the French Image of American Society to 1815* (Princeton, 1957).
59. Paul Monaco, *Cinema and Society: France and Germany During the Twenties* (New York, 1976), pp. 84-103.
60. Jacques Néré, The Foreign Policy of France from 1914 to 1945 (London, 1975), p. 98.

The almost simultaneous accession of Hitler in Germany and Roosevelt in the United States in early 1933 introduced a new dimension to France's quest for American support in its effort to preserve the Versailles system. At the end of Herbert Hoover's presidential term, French Ambassador Paul Claudel had lamented to his superiors in Paris that after years of Franco-American squabbles over debts, tariffs, and other matters, "the state of American opinion [toward France] is worse now than it has been for a long time." But his anxiety was promptly alleviated after conversations with the president-elect, who was fluent in the French language and had acquired an intimate familiarity with French culture during regular summer sojourns as a youth, and whose mother was an annual visitor to Paris. Claudel remarked that Roosevelt's "friendly attitude with his open and cheerful countenance was a pleasant contrast to the hostile and cold approach of President Hoover who of late hardly bothered to conceal his feelings toward our country." In early April 1933 Roosevelt warmed the heart of the French ambassador with the observation that "The situation in Europe is alarming. Hitler is a madman and his advisers, some of whom I know personally, are even crazier than he is."[61]

But the actual policies of the Roosevelt administration toward the impending Franco-German showdown in Europe would not confirm these initial indications of American opposition to German revisionism. As the new leader in Berlin launched his assault on the disarmament and territorial provisions of the Versailles treaty, the new president in Washington would acquiesce in the Nazi campaign in such a way as to strengthen the hand of those in France who favored rapprochement with, rather than resistance to, the new regime across the Rhine.

The spirit of Woodrow Wilson would reappear in the foreign policy of his former assistant secretary of the navy as Roosevelt sought to promote a peaceful resolution of Germany's grievances against a peace settlement that many prominent officials in his administration considered to be unjust and indefensible. Though declining to pay his former chief the ultimate compliment of bringing the United States into the League of Nations, Roosevelt resur-

---

61. Cited in Mario Rossi, *Roosevelt and the French* (Westport, Conn., 1993), pp. 2-3, 16-17.

rected another salient feature of the Wilsonian program in a determined effort to preserve the peace in Europe. This was the principle of national self-determination, which had been enunciated in Wilson's wartime addresses before succumbing to political, economic, and strategic necessities at the peace conference. Hitler's shrewd exploitation of this hallowed Wilsonian precept to justify Germany's challenges to the territorial provisions of the Versailles treaty would strike a responsive chord in Washington.[62]

The Roosevelt administration's role, as what Julian Hurstfield has called "a copartner in the Anglo-French appeasement of Germany,"[63] was facilitated by the strong-willed, impetuous individual who occupied the American embassy in Paris during the last four years of the Third Republic. William C. Bullitt, a close personal friend of the president who promptly developed a more intimate relationship with key French political leaders than any representative of a foreign power had ever enjoyed,[64] was gripped by two obsessions that colored his behavior as Roosevelt's man in Paris during this critical period in the Franco-American relationship. The first was a concern bordering on paranoia that the Soviet Union, which he had come to despise after three years' residence in the American embassy in Moscow, would profit from a war between Germany and the Western democracies to achieve its goal of European hegemony. The second was the belief that the peace settlement after the Great War was fundamentally flawed, a conviction that he had held since his resignation from the American peace delegation in the spring of 1919 in protest against what he deemed to be the excessively harsh provisions of the peace treaty.[65]

62. William R. Keylor, "The Principle of National Self-Determination as a Factor in the Creation of Postwar Frontiers in Europe, 1919 and 1945," in Carole Fink, ed., *National Frontiers in the Two World Wars* (Berne, 1996), pp. 37-54. Arnold A. Offner, *American Appeasement: United States Foreign Policy Toward Germany, 1933-1938* (Cambridge, Mass., 1969), p. 261; Julian G.Hurstfield, *America and the French Nation, 1939-1945* (Chapel Hill, 1986), p. 3.
63. Hurstfeld, *America and the French Nation*, p.3.
64. Roosevelt's Secretary of the Interior, Harold Ickes, remarked that "Bullitt practically sleeps with the French cabinet." Harold Ickes, *The Secret Diary of Harold Ickes* (New York, 1954), p. 124.
65. For the letter of resignation, see Bullitt to Wilson, 17 May 1919, in Arthur S. Link, ed., *The Papers of Woodrow Wilson*, vol. 59 (Princeton, 1988), pp. 232-233.

These two sentiments – fear of the Soviet Union and hatred of Versailles – had produced in Bullitt an unswerving determination to promote a rapprochement between France and Germany based on a peaceful revision of the postwar territorial settlement. "If there is a chance to maintain peace in Europe during your next administration" he wrote Roosevelt shortly after his reelection in November 1936, "that chance lies in the small possibility that it may be possible to draw the French government and the German government closer together." In pursuit of this objective, Bullitt urged the recall of William E. Dodd as Ambassador to Germany because Dodd "hates the Nazis too much to be able to do anything with them."[66] He rejoiced at Dodd's replacement in late 1937 by the more pragmatic diplomat Hugh Wilson, remarking that "it is not difficult to establish good conversational relations with the Nazi leaders" and expressing the confidence that the United States could broker a satisfactory arrangement between Paris and Berlin. "The Germans are anxious to get together with the French and the French are even more anxious to get together with the Germans," he observed, "and Hugh and I, without seeming to move hand or foot, ought to be able to pour a lot of useful oil on the troubled waters."[67]

Bullitt was convinced that the basis for such a Franco-German rapprochement rested in a peaceful revision of the Versailles treaty whereby France would acknowledge German domination of Central Europe. "If you believe, as I believe, that it is not in the interest either of the United States or of civilization as a whole to have the Continent of Europe devastated," he wrote Roosevelt as Hitler's pressure on Czechoslovakia began to intensify in 1938, "I think we should attempt to find some way which will let the French out of their moral commitment" to the Prague government. The unacceptable alternative, he periodically reminded his chief, was "the complete destruction of western Europe and Bolshevism from one end of the continent to the other."[68]

66. Bullitt to Roosevelt, 7 December 1936, in Orville H. Bullitt, ed., *For The President Personal and Secret: Correspondence Between Franklin D. Roosevelt and William C. Bullitt* (Boston, 1972), pp. 195, 233-234.
67. Bullitt to Roosevelt, 7 December 1937, in *ibid.*, p. 242.
68. Bullitt to Roosevelt, 20 May 1938, in *ibid.*, p. 262-263.

In line with Bullitt's suggestions, Roosevelt played an active role in promoting a peaceful resolution of the dispute between Germany and Czechoslovakia when it reached its crescendo in the autumn of 1938. On 26 September, when it appeared that Great Britain and France might reluctantly go to war with Germany over the unresolved details of the Sudetenland settlement, the American president insistently urged the parties concerned not to break off negotiations.[69] The next day his direct appeal to Hitler paved the way for the Munich conference.[70] When Chamberlain eagerly accepted Hitler's invitation to the high-level meeting, Roosevelt cabled his hearty congratulations to the British prime minister with the famous (or infamous) exclamation "good man!"[71] A few weeks later the president assured the American ambassador to Rome that he was "not one bit upset over the final result."[72] Czech President

69. The September 26 message is printed in Samuel I Rosenman, ed., *The Public Papers and Addresses of Franklin D. Roosevelt*, 38 vols. (New York, 1938-1950), vol. VII, pp. 531-532.
70. Roosevelt to Hitler, 27 Sept. 1938, *Papers Relating to the Foreign Relations of the United States*, (hereafter FRUS), 1938, vol. 1, pp. 686-688. Bullitt had suggested to Under Secretary of State Sumner Welles during a transatlantic telephone conversation on 27 September that Roosevelt propose the convocation of representatives of England, France, Germany, Poland, Czechoslovakia, and Hungary – explicitly omitting Italy and the Soviet Union – at a conference in The Hague on 29 September at which an American representative would be present. Memorandum of Telephone Conversation between Ambassador Bullitt and Under Secretary Welles, 27 September, 1938, in Bullitt, *For the President Personal and Secret*, pp. 293-294.
71. Hull to Kennedy, 28 Sept. 1938, FRUS, 1938, vol. I, p. 688. When Bullitt heard the news that Roosevelt's proposal for a conference had prompted Hitler's invitation to Munich, he wrote the president that he was "so relieved this evening that I feel like embracing everyone and I wish I were in the White House to give you a large kiss on your bald spot." Bullitt to Roosevelt, 28 September 1938, in Bullitt, *For The President Personal and Secret*, pp. 297-298.
72. Roosevelt to Phillips, 17 Oct. 1938, in Elliott Roosevelt, ed., *F.D.R.: His Personal Letters, 1928-1945*, 2 vols. (New York, 1950), vol. II, pp. 816-819; Offner, *American Appeasement*, pp. 268-269. On learning of the peaceful transfer of the Sudetenland to Germany, Under Secretary of State Sumner Welles confided to French Ambassador Saint-Quentin "his hope that the psychology created by the Munich conference would be put to good use by the great European powers in order to settle as soon as possible the most dangerous question: that of colonies, obviously through concessions by us to Germany." Saint-Quentin (Washington) to Bonnet (Foreign Minister), 1 October 1938, *Documents Diplomatiques Français, 1932-1939*, 2e série (1936-1939)(Paris, 1972 –) [hereafter DDF] Vol. XI, pp. 753-754.

Edvard Benes, who had allowed himself to imagine the possibility of some type of American diplomatic support,[73] complained bitterly in his memoirs that Daladier had frequently hinted to him that his appeasement policy had the full support of the American ambassador and therefore of the American government.[74] Benes regarded Roosevelt's intervention during the crisis of September 1938 as a stab in the back and "the last heavy blow."[75]

Bullitt's views in Paris were complemented in Washington by those of Assistant Secretary of State Adolf A. Berle, another disenchanted alumnus of the American peace delegation who had resigned in disgust at the Versailles Treaty. During the *Anschluss* crisis of March 1938, Berle reminded his superiors that the "Union of German-Austria with Germany was regarded as a legitimate aspiration of both countries" in 1919 and had been "blocked by the peace treaties ... solely to maintain France in a superior military position." He also complained that "the splitting up of Central Europe into a series of highly nationalistic small states tends to paralyze commerce and development" and noted that the formation of a larger economic unit (presumably under German domination) would promote a more efficient economic development of the region. As the German-Czech crisis heated up in the autumn of 1938 Berle drafted a memorandum to Roosevelt employing historical arguments to justify the expansion of German territory eastward. He predicted that the newly enlarged Reich would be preoccupied with fending off the "Slavs" rather than threatening America's friends in Western Europe, and counseled vigilance against Anglo-French efforts to lure the United States into perpetuating the untenable territorial arrangements established by the treaties of Versailles and Saint-Germain.[76]

73. Lacroix (French Minister in Prague) to Bonnet (Foreign Minister), 26 September 1938, *DDF*, Vol. VIII, p. 560.
74. Edvard Benes, *Memoirs: From Munich to New War and New Victory* (Trans. Godfrey Lias, Boston, 1954), p. 173.
75. Igor Lukes, *Czechoslovakia Between Stalin and Hitler: The Diplomacy of Edvard Benes in the 1930s* (New York, 1996), p. 242.
76. Beatrice Bishop Berle and Travis Beal Jacobs, eds., *Navigating the Rapids, 1918-1971: From the Papers of Adolf A. Berle* (New York, 1973), pp. 13-14. Berle to Hull and Welles, 16 March 1938; Berle to Roosevelt, 1 Sept. 1938; quoted in Henry Blumenthal, *Illusion and Reality in Franco-American Diplomacy, 1914-1945* (Baton Rouge, 1986), pp. 240-241.

The advent of the European war in the early autumn of 1939 enabled another prominent member of Roosevelt's foreign policy team to try his hand at conciliating Nazi Germany. Ever since his appointment as Under-Secretary of State in the spring of 1937, Sumner Welles had conveyed to the French embassy in Washington his enthusiasm for the policy of appeasement that the British government was assiduously pursuing.[77] He persuaded his old family friend in the White House to send him to Europe in February 1940 on a last-ditch mission to seek a negotiated settlement of the war. Welles's round of conferences with officials in London, Paris, Rome, and Berlin (which was reminiscent of House's efforts on Wilson's behalf before America's intervention in the last war), enraged French officials by raising the prospect of peace through Italian mediation and by appearing to reward German territorial expansion in the interest of restoring peace.[78] Intensely jealous of Welles's friendship with Roosevelt and offended that the interloper from Washington had been allowed to poach on his European preserve, Bullitt gleefully reported the French government's resentment at Welles's glorification of Mussolini as arbiter of the European crisis, his barely concealed opinion of Nazi Germany's invincibility, and his eagerness for a compromise peace that would leave Germany supreme on the continent.[79]

The official policy of the United States toward the European crisis was that of strict neutrality. Bullitt scrupulously warned his friends in the French government on a number of occasions that

---

77. After a chat with Welles during the *Anschluss* crisis of 1938, the French chargé informed the Quai that the State Department "appears to adopt the same indifference [to the fate of Austria] that characterizes the British government." A week later Welles informed the French chargé that he was not dismayed at the resignation of Anthony Eden as British Foreign Secretary since he considered Chamberlain's foreign policy "much more realistic, open to interesting possibilities for the establishment of European peace." Henry (French chargé, Washington) to Delbos (French Foreign Minister), 18, 24 February 1938, DDF, Vol. VIII, pp. 408, 517.

78. Hurstfeld, *America and the French Nation*, p. 7; Arnold A. Offner, "Appeasement Revisited: The United States, Great Britain, and Germany, 1933-1940, *Journal of American History*, Vol. 64, No. 2 (September 1977), pp. 384-393; Blumenthal, *Illusion and Reality*, pp. 256-257.

79. Bullitt to Roosevelt, 18 April 1940, in Bullitt, *For the President Personal and Secret*, p. 410.

they could not count on American support in the event of war with Germany. "Blum lunched with me alone today," he cabled Hull at the beginning of December 1936, "and I had the opportunity to repeat to him everything that I had said to [Foreign Minister Yvon] Delbos with regard to the absolute determination of the United States to stay out not only of any wars on the continent of Europe but out of any engagements or commitments that might possibly lead to our involvement in wars."[80] Notwithstanding these unmistakable warnings, French officials tenaciously clung to the illusory expectation that massive American assistance would somehow arrive in time to cope with the threat from the east. "Day in and day out I say to the French that, if war should come, the United States would declare immediate neutrality," Bullitt reported in the summer of 1938. "The answer invariably is, 'Yes, we know that; but the Germans will behave in such a way that you will soon be drawn in.'"[81]

Such hopes for an American rescue operation were nurtured by inadvertent words of encouragement that periodically emanated from the mouths of prominent American officials. When the American delegate to the Geneva Disarmament Conference, Norman Davis, suggested in March 1933 that the United States would be willing to consult with other states in the event of a threat to peace, the French interpretation of this offhanded speculation as a concrete commitment to collective security obliged Davis to beat a hasty retreat.[82]

When Davis mentioned to Bullitt during a visit to Paris that Roosevelt was considering a more interventionist foreign policy, the horrified ambassador complained to his chief that his guest had "made it sound as if you thought God had laid Woodrow Wilson's mantle upon you, and that you were about to take on your shoulders, or rather those of the people of the United States, all the pains of the world." Bullitt implored Roosevelt to remember that Wilson "used to lie in bed thinking of the text, 'By their fruits ye shall know them,'" while lamenting that "the fruits he could report to St. Peter were war and the Treaty of Versailles."[83]

80. Bullitt cable to Hull, 1 December 1936, in *ibid*., pp. 196-197.
81. Bullitt to Roosevelt, 13 June 1938, in *ibid*., pp. 269-270.
82. Blumenthal, *Illusion and Reality*, p. 183.
83. Bullitt to Roosevelt, 2 November 1937, in *ibid*., p. 228.

The ambassador himself was prone to committing the occasional indiscretion that kindled false hopes in his French friends. Speaking at an emotion-filled ceremony in September 1938 to commemorate the arrival of the first contingent of American soldiers in the Great War, Bullitt announced that "if war breaks out in Europe, no one can say or predict whether the United States would be drawn into such a war."[84] With the threat of armed conflict over the German-Czech crisis looming, Roosevelt hastily assured the American press that "Ambassador Bullitt's speech does not constitute a moral engagement on the part of the United States toward the democracies .... To include the United States in an alliance [with] France-Great Britain against Hitler" was an interpretation that was "one hundred per cent false."[85]

Roosevelt himself was not immune to the foot-in-mouth disease that occasionally afflicted members of his administration on the matter of French security. Secretary of the Treasury Henry Morgenthau reported to his staff in December 1938 that "The President of the United States says that we consider the Maginot Line our first line of defense."[86] In early February 1939, Roosevelt invited members of the Senate Military Affairs Committee to the White House to discuss America's position concerning the impending crisis in Europe. "The safety of the Rhine frontier does necessarily interest us," he informed his startled listeners. "[I]f the Rhine frontier is threatened by Hitler, the rest of the world is too." Obliged to backtrack at a hastily convened press conference, he indignantly denounced as a "deliberate lie" the report attributing to him the statement that America's frontier was on the Rhine and reiterated the familiar refrain that disarmament and world trade were the keys to peace.[87] In spite of such occasional lapses, the Roosevelt administration was at pains to put the French govern-

84. Georges Bonnet, *Défense de la Paix: De Washington au Quai d'Orsay* (Geneva, 1946), p. 261.
85. Truelle (French chargé in Washington) to Bonnet (Foreign Minister), 10 September 1938, in DDF, Vol. XI, pp. 126-128. Bullitt, *For the President Personal and Secret*, p. 285.
86. John Morton Blum, *From the Morgenthau Diaries: Years of Urgency, 1938-1941* (Boston, 1965), pp. 68-69.
87. Rossi, *Roosevelt and the French*, p. 32. Jean Monnet claimed that reliable witnesses at the meeting recalled Roosevelt uttering the phrase "The frontiers of the

ment on notice that it could count on no diplomatic, let alone economic or military, support from the United States in its dispute with Nazi Germany.

"Clouds of Planes" to Deter or Defeat Hitler

The French high command's strategy of excluding the German army from the national territory through the combination of the Maginot Line and the planned offensive into Belgium and Holland was jeopardized in many eyes by one critical source of vulnerability: the overwhelming superiority in air power that Germany had achieved after Hitler began to construct a German air force in violation of the disarmament clauses of the Versailles Treaty in 1935. The French air force had been the largest in Europe from the end of the war to the mid-1930s, when a technological breakthrough in aircraft construction suddenly enabled Germany to acquire a substantial qualitative advantage. By late November 1937 British Prime Minister Neville Chamberlain was complaining to French Premier Camille Chautemps that French air power was in a "lamentable" state. "You have no modern planes and are not ready to produce any," Chamberlain remarked. "This is a great danger to your country."[88] No matter how impenetrable the static fortifications on the German frontier or how successful the plan for forward defense in the Low Countries, the bomber (as Chamberlain's predecessor, Stanley Baldwin, had bluntly put it) would always get through.

The prospect of massive aerial bombardment of France's major cities not only represented a deplorable loophole in the French defenses in the west. It also undermined the French government's determination to honor its treaty commitments in Eastern Europe. Three days before the Munich Conference, the French Air Ministry had received a report from the air force chief of staff revealing that the French air force possessed a grand total of 600 battle ready

---

United States are on the Rhine." Jean Monnet, *Memoirs* (Trans. Richard Mayne, Garden City, 1978), pp. 122-123.

88. Bonnet, *Défense de la Paix: De Washington au Quai d'Orsay*, pp. 49-50; John McVickar Haight, Jr., *American Aid to France, 1938-1940* (New York, 1970), pp. 4-5.

planes (fighters and bombers) compared to the Luftwaffe's alleged 6,500. Minister of Air Guy La Chambre promptly shared the alarming report with Ambassador Bullitt, noting that "the German planes would be able to bomb Paris at will" in light of the insufficient numbers of French pursuit planes and that in the event of war "the destruction in Paris would pass all imagination." La Chambre contended that the only conceivable means for France to overcome German superiority in the air was the purchase of aircraft manufactured by American aeronautics firms.[89]

The French Air Minister realized that the Neutrality Act of 1935 included an embargo on arms sales to all belligerents that would preclude the manufacture of such planes in the United States if war were to break out between France and Germany. He therefore suggested that assembly plants be constructed in Canada opposite Detroit and Buffalo to which American airplane parts, instruments, machine tools, and skilled labor could be readily transported. Bullitt passed the proposal on to Roosevelt with his enthusiastic endorsement and urged La Chambre to ask his friend Jean Monnet, who had distinguished himself as an effective French representative on interallied economic organizations during the First World War, to undertake an exploratory mission to the United States.[90]

On returning from his meeting with Hitler and Chamberlain, Daladier grumbled that "If I had had three or four thousand aircraft Munich would never have happened." That remark was made three days after the conference at an intimate luncheon with La Chambre, Bullitt, and Monnet, at which it was decided to send the latter to the United States to explore the prospects for a major purchasing operation that would provide France with the air power

---

89. An earlier mission had been sent by the French Air Ministry to the United States in January 1938. After consulting with various government officials, it discovered a great deficiency in American military aircraft production. But a top secret test flight of the Curtiss P-36 fighter plane by a French pilot on 20 March revealed that the American-built aircraft was equal to both France's latest fighter and Germany's Meserschmitt-109. Haight, *American Aid to France, 1938-1940*, pp. 6-9, 11-13; Bullitt to Hull, 24, 25 Jan. 1938; Hull to Bullitt, 27 Jan. 1938; Bullitt to Hull for Roosevelt, 23 Feb. 1938, FRUS, 1938, vol. II, pp. 300-303.

90. Bullitt cable to Roosevelt, 28 September 1938, in Bullitt, *For the President Personal and Secret*, pp. 297-299.

she would require to prevent future Munichs. Bullitt offered his services to set up appointments for his French friend with key decision makers on the other side of the Atlantic.[91] With the ambassador making the necessary arrangements, the French representative wasted no time after his arrival in the United States in going right to the top. At a meeting at Hyde Park on 19 October, Roosevelt agreed with Monnet that air power was the key to deterring Hitler and endorsed the scheme to circumvent the neutrality act by utilizing Canadian production facilities.[92] Like Bullitt, the President appeared to have been jolted into a change of heart in the months after the Munich Conference that he had played such an important role in promoting. "I am not sure that I am proud of what I wrote to Hitler [on] 27 September 1938 in urging that he sit down around the table to make peace," he confessed to a high-level conference at the White House on 14 November. "That may have saved many, many lives now, but that may ultimately result in the loss of many times that number of lives later."[93]

At the end of his conference with Monnet at Hyde Park, Roosevelt telephoned Secretary of the Treasury Henry Morgenthau in Washington to arrange a dinner with Monnet and Bullitt on 22 October. At this gathering Morgenthau, who considered France "a bankrupt, fourth-rate power,"[94] warned Monnet that his information indicated that the French treasury would never be able to raise the $85 million required to purchase the 1,700 aircraft that the Frenchman sought. Morgenthau and Bullitt put their heads together and came up with an imaginative solution to the financial conundrum: The Treasury Secretary suggested that the French government requisition the dollar holdings of French citizens on deposit in American banks, even if it had "to put 1,000 people in jail" to obtain the necessary foreign exchange.[95]

91. Monnet, *Memoirs*, pp. 117-118; Elizabeth du Réau, *Edouard Daladier, 1884-1970* (Paris, 1993), p. 305.
92. Monnet, *Memoirs*, pp. 118-119.
93. Blum, *From the Morgenthau Diaries: Years of Crisis, 1928-1938* (Boston, 1959), pp. 48-49; Haight, *American Aid to France, 1938-40*, p. 59.
94. Blum, *From the Morgenthau Diaries: Years of Crisis, 1928-1938*, p. 460.
95. A hasty investigation by the Treasury Department revealed about $500 million worth of liquid capital held by French nationals in American banks. Monnet, *Memoirs*, pp. 118-120; Haight, *American Aid to France, 1938-1940*, p. 33.

After receiving Monnet's report on 4 November, Daladier steamrollered over most of the domestic political obstacles to the proposed purchases in America: Minister of Finance Paul Reynaud's reluctance to deplete France's gold reserves and weaken the franc to pay for the planes; the French Air Force's refusal to concede that American models were superior to its own; organized labor's dismay that American aircraft workers would reap the benefits from orders paid for with French funds. The one battle that Daladier lost was over Morgenthau's plan for the seizure of private French assets in American banks to finance the imports, which clashed with Reynaud's liberal economic principles. Undaunted, the bull-headed French premier pressed on. "The purchase of American airplanes is possible and it must be done," he decreed. On 9 December, after obtaining the approval of the Comité Permanent de la Défense Nationale, Daladier ordered Monnet back to Washington to place an order for 1,000 aircraft for delivery by July 1939.[96]

When the French negotiator arrived in the United States, he learned that the only American airplanes that met the stringent specifications of the French military's technical experts were prototypes that remained on the Army Air Corps' secret list. When the Chief of the Army Air Corps', General H. H. Arnold, refused the French mission access to the Corps latest fighter just as it was to become operational in American squadrons, Monnet had to get Morgenthau to intercede with Roosevelt. "If it's your theory that Britain and France are our first line of defense," the Treasury Secretary declared, "let Monnet have what he needs." Five days after Roosevelt had ordered Arnold to cooperate with the French mission, the American press announced that a secret army prototype aircraft had crashed on a trial flight near Los Angeles with a French military officer on board. Forced to acknowledge publicly for the first time that the United States had been negotiating for the sale of combat aircraft to the French government, the president preempted the objections of the isolationists by invoking the needs of the American economy: "It's very good business for our

---

96. Monnet, *Memoirs*, pp. 120-121; Réau, *Edouard Daladier, 1884-1970*, p. 346; Haight, *American Aid to France, 1938-1940*, p. 37.

aircraft industry, which is in the doldrums and needs the stimulus that these orders will give." Morgenthau assured a Senate committee that the $65 million that the French government was prepared to spend in the next six months would put idle plants in production and "good hard dollars" in workers' pockets. In fact, the deal that Monnet closed at the end of January 1939 for the purchase of 555 modern aircraft for delivery by July 1939, with a firm option on 1,500 more for the beginning of 1940, enabled Roosevelt to keep alive his goal of expanding American aircraft production in preparation for the possibility that the United States would again be dragged into war.[97]

But the nagging problem of how France would finance the plane purchases continued to lurk beneath the surface. Though Monnet assured Morgenthau on 16 December that Daladier had allocated $65 million for the initial orders, he also mentioned plans to float loans in the United States for a French-controlled Canadian corporation to assemble the American aircraft. Morgenthau pointedly reminded Monnet that the Johnson Act of 1934 prohibited loans to governments in default on their war debts.[98] After authorizing gold shipments on 13 February 1939 to pay for a consignment of Martin and Douglas bombers, Reynaud and Daladier met with Bullitt on the same day to explore the possibility of arranging private American bank credits to finance future purchases of American aircraft. The Ambassador predictably invoked the Johnson Act to nip the French initiative in the bud. The two officials thereupon declared that France had acted with "extreme stupid-

---

97. Monnet was convinced that Roosevelt's desire to revive the stagnating American military aircraft industry was "one of his essential motives in taking such an interest in my mission." Monnet, *Memoirs*, pp. 121-122; Haight, *American Aid to France, 1938-1940*, pp. 68-70, 97. The correspondence between the American embassy in Paris and the State Department concerning the French attempts to purchase planes in 1939 may be found in *FRUS*, 1939, Vol. II, pp. 500-528.

98. Blum, *From the Morgenthau Diaries*, Vol II, p. 65; Haight, *American Aid to France, 1938-40*, p. 71. After the French default in 1932, the State Department would regularly notify the French Embassy as the date of each interest payment approached. The Quai would express its gratitude for the notification and express its eagerness to resume discussions leading to an agreement on the war debt. See, for example, Chautemps (foreign minister ad interim) to Henry (chargé, Washington), 4 December 1937, *DDF*, vol. VII, p. 601.

ity" in defaulting on the war debt in 1932, recalling that both of them had supported Herriot's abortive bid to win parliamentary approval for payment.[99] Once again the legacy of the Great War, and of the Franco-American dispute about how it should have been financed, returned to haunt the French government as it struggled to enlist American assistance in preparation for the next confrontation with Germany.

The French Ministry of Finance's apprehensions about the financial burden of paying for the aircraft orders finally prompted a desperate bid to gain access to the American money market. Reynaud approached Bullitt on 22 February with a proposal for an immediate lump sum payment of ten billion francs in gold against the war debt in order to release France from the restrictions of the Johnson Act. Acknowledging that the offer represented about ten per cent of the Bank of France's current gold reserve, Bullitt noted that it amounted to a paltry $300 million to settle a debt of over $3 billion and therefore would probably not appeal to Congress. The ambassador then suggested that the offer would appear much more attractive if it were sweetened with a few French overseas possessions "which we might desire for strategic reasons." Reynaud immediately offered Clipperton Island and the French interests in the Anglo-French condominium of the New Hebrides as well as "any other French possessions that we might fancy in either the Caribbean or the Pacific." At Reynaud's urgent request Bullitt transmitted the French proposal to Roosevelt with the observation that perhaps the president "might fancy French Guiana" as well.[100]

The decision to seek entrée to American capital markets in this desperate manner had been made at the highest level of the French government. Daladier informed Bullitt on 23 March that he had himself initiated the idea of ceding the French possessions, and offered to entrust Monnet with the negotiations.[101] At a lunch

---

99. Bullitt to Hull, 13 Feb. 1939, *FRUS*, 1939, vol. II, pp. 501-502. The Secretary of State warmly approved of his ambassador's warning to the French premier and finance minister that the Johnson Act would rule out commercial loans to finance the airplane purchases. Hull to Bullitt, 16 Feb. 1939, *ibid.*, pp. 504-505.

100. Bullitt to Roosevelt, 22 Feb. 1939, in Bullitt, *For the President Personal and Secret*, pp. 315-317.

101. Bullitt to Roosevelt, 24 March 1939, in *ibid.*, pp. 326-327.

with Reynaud, Monnet, and Bullitt on 4 April, Daladier boasted that he had the power to govern by decree and declared that "he did not care how many islands it might be necessary to turn over to the United States if only the question could be settled." Bullitt noted that both the prime minister and the finance minister were "anxious to act quickly" before war with Germany began, and he urged Roosevelt to meet with Monnet to consider the proposal.[102] In the course of a private interview on 3 May, Roosevelt informed Monnet that "it would be a mistake for his government to deplete a bettering [sic] cash condition for a little while" by offering the ten billion francs as a gesture of good faith. As far as the French possessions were concerned, some would be "a headache for us if we had to run them" while others were worth "a drop in the bucket compared with the total owed." A few days later Morgenthau informed Monnet that it was not an opportune moment to revive an issue that would serve as a red rag for the isolationist bulls in Congress just as the White House was hoping to line up votes for revision of the arms embargo.[103]

French expectations of obtaining credit for purchases of aircraft in the American market were therefore dashed just as the war clouds gathered as a result of Hitler's territorial claims against Poland. The "cash and carry" provision of the Neutrality Act had lapsed on 1 May 1939, thereby depriving the Allies of access to American arms in the event of war. Daladier expressed to Bullitt on 28 June 1939 his conviction that the only hope of dissuading Hitler from precipitating a European war by attacking Poland lay in the conclusion of an alliance with the Soviet Union *and* the revision of the Neutrality Act to give the allies access to American military supplies. Two days later Alexis Léger, the secretary general of the French Foreign Ministry, confirmed the official French view that the Russian alliance and American arms for Britain and France represented the last remaining constraints on the Führer.[104]

After the conclusion of the Nazi-Soviet non-aggression pact on 23 August 1939 and the German Blitzkrieg against Poland in Sep-

102. Bullitt to Roosevelt, 4 April 1939, in ibid., pp.334-336.
103. Roosevelt to Bullitt, 16 May 1939, in ibid., p. 353. Réau, *Edouard Daladier, 1884-1970*, p. 346.
104. Bullitt to State Department, 28, 30 June 1939, FRUS, 1939, Vol. I, pp. 277-280.

tember, France was again (as in the spring of 1918) left alone with Great Britain to face the full force of German military power in the west. As in 1918, she looked to the United States for assistance. The economic and military aid that the Wilson administration had furnished France in the later stages of the First World War was obviously an impossibility at the beginning of the Second. But the prospect of obtaining American-built bombers and fighters to offset Germany's aerial superiority had been kept alive by the signal success of the Monnet mission during the last year of peace.

By the beginning of the war, only two hundred pursuit planes had reached France from the United States. But the prewar orders had laid the groundwork for French access to the expanding American arsenal. With the full approval of the Roosevelt administration, Daladier dispatched Monnet to London to set up a joint Anglo-French purchasing board in anticipation of the day when the modification of the neutrality legislation would open the American market to the Allies.[105] The French premier campaigned vigorously to get the embargo lifted, informing Bullitt on 8 September that "If we are to win this war, we shall have to win it with supplies of every kind from the United States." In transmitting Daladier's message the ambassador bluntly warned Roosevelt that "if the Neutrality Act remains in its present form, France and England will be defeated rapidly"[106] and cabled Hull to the same effect on 20 September. The next day Roosevelt convened a special session of Congress that finally replaced the American embargo with the "cash and carry" provision on 3 November. Daladier declared to a luncheon meeting with La Chambre, Bullitt, and Monnet on 23 November that "We must have absolute superiority in the air, and to obtain it the Allies must buy 10,000 aircraft in the United States." Recognizing that the assembly lines of the American aircraft industries were already working at full capacity, he envisaged the conversion of the automobile industry to the production of such war-related items. When Reynaud reiterated his familiar concerns about depleting French reserves, Dal-

---

105. Bullitt to Hull for Roosevelt, 17 Oct. 1939; Hull to Bullitt, 18 Oct. 1939; *FRUS*, 1939, Vol. I, pp. 566-567.

106. Bullitt to Roosevelt, 8 September 1939, in Bullitt, *For the President, Personal and Secret*, pp. 368-369.

adier replied that he would "find the money to buy these planes, even if I have to sell Versailles."[107]

Once Monnet was formally approved as Chairman of the Anglo-French Coordinating Committee in early December, his assistant René Pleven rushed to the United States to open negotiations with an interdepartmental committee appointed by Roosevelt to act as liaison between the allied purchasing commission and American procurement agencies. He was able to negotiate a preliminary agreement in Washington in January 1940 for the purchase of 8,000 warplanes for delivery by October of that year, with the $1 billion cost to be borne equally by the French and the British treasuries. After overriding the inevitable objections on financial grounds from Reynaud in Paris[108] and Chancellor of the Exchequer Sir John Simon in London, Daladier sent Pleven back to Washington to complete the negotiations. After arriving on 4 March, Pleven was obliged to reenact the drama of Monnet's earlier mission as opposition to the sale reappeared in the American Army Air Corps. General Arnold attempted to withhold from the French mission the latest aircraft models (which were the only ones capable of matching the new Messerschmitt 109s), Morgenthau again appealed to the White House, and Roosevelt brought the chief of the army air corps to heel (this time by threatening to banish him to Guam).[109]

Contracts for 2,400 fighters, 2,160 bombers, and 13,000 engines were signed on 10 April with deliveries to begin in September 1940. In addition to the cost of the planes and engines, the Anglo-French Purchasing Commission had to agree to a $37 million capital investment in the American aircraft industry as well as $7 million as a "friendly gesture" to help finance the development of a new aircraft type for the Army Air Corps. Pleven considered the latter requirement unreasonable and unfair, but he was hardly in a position to object. In advising the Europeans to pay the extra

107. Monnet, Memoirs, pp. 125-131.
108. Reynaud mentions not one word in his self-serving memoirs about his opposition to the aircraft purchases before replacing Daladier as Prime Minister. Paul Reynaud, In the Thick of the Fight, 1930-1955 (Trans. James D. Lambert, New York, 1955).
109. Monnet, Memoirs, pp.132-135; Haight, American Aid to France, 1938-1940, pp. 171, 176, 185.

development costs, a major American aircraft manufacturer had tactlessly confirmed the old "Shylock" image by warning that "You might have to pay a pound of flesh."[110]

Since deliveries of the Anglo-French order placed in March 1940 would not begin until the following September, they did not play a role in the Battle of France. Of the 555 American combat aircraft that the French government had purchased in the spring of 1938 and January 1939, only 200 Curtiss P-36 Hawk fighters had been delivered by the outbreak of the war in early September 1939. After the repeal of the American arms embargo on 3 November, convoys carrying Martin and Douglas attack bombers began to arrive in Morocco for assembly. When the German offensive began on 10 May, the French Air Force had received only 137 fully assembled aircraft for use against the invaders.[111]

The French government's frantic search for salvation in the United States during the military collapse of May-June 1940 makes poignant reading. As the German army's western offensive gathered steam on 15 May, Reynaud (who had replaced Daladier as premier on 21 March) issued the first in a series of emotional appeals for American aircraft (which he knew were unavailable) in order to reduce what he described as Germany's ten-to-one advantage.[112] That nonsensical request was followed two days later by a pathetic plea for a thousand American pilots to be recruited in Canada for enlistment in the French air force (shades of the Lafayette Escadrille!).[113] Alexis Léger, the secretary general of the French Foreign Ministry, told Bullitt on 18 May that Reynaud intended to send a personal appeal to Roosevelt asking him if it might be possible to obtain from Congress a declaration of war against Germany.[114] On

---

110. Haight, *American Aid to France, 1938-1940*, pp. 225-228.
111. *Ibid.*, pp. 232, 238-239, 242-244.
112. Bullitt cable to Roosevelt, 15 May 1940, in Bullitt, *For the President Personal and Secret*, p. 419. French military and political leaders consistently overestimated the numerical strength of the Luftwaffe during the Battle of France. Though Germany did enjoy an advantage in bombers, the French air force possessed more fighters (which were particularly suitable for defense). In the event, the French managed to put into action only 418 of the 900 modern fighter planes they possessed during the German offensive. *Ibid.*, p. 424.
113. Bullitt cable to Roosevelt, 17 May 1940, in *ibid.*, p. 425.
114. Cordell Hull, *Memoirs of Cordell Hull*, vol I (New York, 1948), p. 767.

31 May came the suggestion, endorsed by Bullitt, that the American Atlantic fleet be transferred to the Mediterranean to protect French North Africa from anticipated aggression from Italy.[115] The same Reynaud who as Minister of Finance had tenaciously opposed Daladier's plan to purchase American planes petitioned Roosevelt on the evening of 3 June for "clouds of aircraft over the Atlantic to crush the demonic force that is dominating Europe."[116] Two days later, as the German armies turned south and began their drive toward Paris, he telephoned the president to ask if he could "stretch a hand across the ocean to help us save civilization" and "reverse the course of history." Just before leaving the capital for Bordeaux on 10 June, Reynaud beseeched Roosevelt "to state publicly that the United States will give the Allies all the moral and material support within their means, short of sending an expeditionary force. I beg you to do this before it is too late." In his last transatlantic message, cabled from Tours on 14 June as the Wehrmacht entered Paris, the last prime minister of the Third Republic pleaded with the president to "throw the weight of American strength into the scales" by issuing France "a positive assurance that the United States will come into the struggle within a short space of time."[117]

Roosevelt's response to what Hull called the "extraordinary, almost hysterical appeals" from Reynaud[118] was punctuated with the prescient remark that "Naval power in world affairs still carries the lesson of history." To Churchill, the former First Lord of the Admiralty, he confidently predicted that "command of the seas means in the long run the saving of democracy and the recovery of those suffering temporary reverses."[119] An avid reader of Mahan,

---

115. Bullitt cable to Roosevelt and Hull, 31 May 1940, in Bullitt, *For the President Personal and Secret*, pp. 444-445. Roosevelt replied testily that the request concerning the Atlantic fleet, which was concentrated in Central and South American waters in accordance with the Declaration of Panama, "reminds me of mother Alice who met the rabbit." Roosevelt handwritten note to Bullitt, 31 May 1940, in *ibid*., p. 447.
116. Hull, *Memoirs*, p. 769.
117. Reynaud, *In the Thick of the Fight*, pp. 461, 478-479, 508-509.
118. Hull, *Memoirs*, p. 767.
119. Rossi, *Roosevelt and the French*, p. 41. On 26 May Roosevelt had issued his first appeal to Reynaud to prevent the French fleet from falling into German hands by removing it from the Mediterranean and, if necessary, to French ports in the West

Wilson's former Assistant Secretary of the Navy fully endorsed his old chief's vision of the American fleet as the key to world peace.[120] But American naval power meant nothing to faltering France in the spring and summer of 1940. As for air power, Reynaud's "clouds of aircraft" did eventually arrive, but too late for the Third Republic. Great Britain, which had placed so many roadblocks in Daladier's path during the difficult negotiations for joint purchasing arrangements, became the paradoxical beneficiary of the French government's energetic campaign to counter Germany's superiority in the air with American assistance. On 17 June, as Marshal Pétain (who had replaced Reynaud the previous day) asked the German high command for an armistice, the French representatives on the Anglo-French Purchasing Commission in Washington signed over all of the French contracts for American planes and engines to the British government.[121] The American aircraft factories that had been cranked up to full capacity by the French orders would, along with the naval superiority of the United States that Roosevelt celebrated in the Third Republic's dying days, help to rescue Great Britain from military catastrophe and eventually liberate France from the scourge of Nazi domination. But not before the latter country had suffered a national trauma whose consequences are still evident in our own day.

Indies. Hull, *Memoirs*, p. 771. Hull cable to Bullitt, 26 May 1940, in Bullitt, *For the President Personal and Secret*, pp. 431-432.

120. William L. Neumann, "Franklin Delano Roosevelt: A Disciple of Admiral Mahan," *U.S. Naval Institute Proceedings* (July 1952), p. 719.

121. Haight, *American Aid to France, 1938-1940*, pp. 258-259.

IX

IN THE EYE OF THE BEHOLDER

The Cultural Representation of France and Germany
by The New York Times, 1939-1940

Robert J. Young*

The Franco-German military confrontation of May-June 1940 had been preceded by weeks, months, even years of guerrilla warfare between the image-makers of Paris and Berlin. In keeping with the dictates of their Führer, the latter had stressed their abhorrence of Communism, and the Nazi state's triumph over unemployment. They had worked as well on the familiar theme of rectifying the international injustice which – they said – had been perpetrated against Germany in 1919; and a corollary to this, subtle but unmistakable, had been the Reich's success in restoring Germany militarily to the ranks of a great power. Certainly from 1935 on, Berlin had made no secret of its new air force, its armorled land force, and its submarines. All of this was packaged for domestic as well as international consumption, along with the underlying idea that the Reich stood for order. The opposition had gone to ground, or worse, and the ensuing silence was held up as proof of national unity. To be sure, most foreign observers knew how it had been done, as did many Germans, and many were appalled by the dishonesty, cynicism, and ruthlessness of Hitler's regime. But when 1940 dawned, and the tanks were slashing across northern France, there seemed a cruel but seamless compatibility between this iron regime and its iron victory.

Compatible, too, at least in the eyes of many, was France's collapse in 1940 with its discerned pre-war wavering. Throughout the 1930s French and foreign observers alike had ruminated over the shortcomings of the Third Republic. Its executive was too weak, its political fractiousness too strong; its economy was at the mercy of outdated technology and the greediness of either its unions or the tiny class of employers. There was always a low-grade disorder in the streets – whether expressed by the capital's drivers or the "artist" quarter of Montmartre – and occasionally outright, violent disorder when mobs openly had threatened the people's representatives in Parliament. Discipline was not the watchword of Paris and neither, until the late 1930s, was rearmament. By far and away the most important, the most celebrated, feature of France's national defence system was the Maginot Line. Conceived in the 1920s, to defend a small if important area of eastern France, and built early in the following decade, the Line was a formidable but static defensive obstacle. When it failed to do the job in 1940 – or rather when it was improperly employed – it instantly assumed the status of a white elephant, the ultimate symbol of something out of place and out of sorts.

To this day these images remain little tarnished. However critical we may be of Hitler's brutal, prewar recklessness, or disgusted by the systematic atrocities of his war-time regime, we are hard pressed to deny its battlefield successes in 1939-1940. Conversely, no simple tinkering with the scenario of May-June 1940 would suffice to award victory to the French. And it is even more difficult to prevent the spell of their defeat from being cast all the way back through the 1930s. Even francophiles must face the question. Was it not true that the Third Republic was a spent force after 1919, that it lacked the energy, the will even, to take on the restless Third Reich?

The answer proposed here, not for the first time, is no. In the field of comparative cultural image-making, we find that the French were very successful in competing with the Germans. In fact, a careful survey of the *New York Times* in 1939-1940 suggests that the French were much more effective than the Germans in presenting themselves and their culture to readers of the United States' largest newspaper. At first glance, this may seem curious. The Nazi state, after all, still remains a twentieth-century frontrunner when it comes to the intensive use of government-sponsored propaganda. For their part, the French were quick – indeed too quick – to acknowledge the feeble and lacklustre nature of their own experiments in propaganda.[1] In particular, or so they claimed, when it came to the United States, they were fearful of offending a former ally through the crude manipulation of lies and half-truths.[2] In fact, so cautious were they said to have been about American sensibilities that they "tended to suppress news and information that were essential to the formation of a correct appreciation abroad ..."[3] But even this, written by P. J. Philip, a Paris-based and openly francophile correspondent for the Times, was in its own way spectacularly misleading. For one thing is clear, the French government certainly did nothing to suppress information on France's cultural achievements of past and present. Indeed, there is reason to believe that the dissemination of cultural propaganda – what one French statesman called the "propaganda of truth" – was central to the process of positive imaging which one detects so frequently in the pages of the New York Times.[4]

As a leading newspaper of an officially neutral country, the Times betrayed little editorial ambiguity. On 29 August 1939, it

1. Indeed that belief is widespread. Long after the war Jean-Marie Domenach suggested that the failure of the Third Republic to disseminate its ideas and values abroad was evidence of its lack of faith in itself and a premonitory sign of its coming collapse. See La Propagande politique (Paris, 1969), pp. 126-127.
2. These remarks were attributed to Professor André Siegfried. See New York Times (NYT), 24 February 1939, i, p. 7. There was, of course, some substance to that fear. Americans were said to have been deeply shocked when they learned of the liberties which had been taken with the truth by their own war-time propagandists in 1917-18. See Michael Schudson, Discovering the News. A Social History of the American Newspaper (New York, 1978), pp. 140-143. See also, Deborah E. Lipstadt, Beyond Belief. The American Press and the Coming of the Holocaust, 1933-45 (New York, 1986), pp. 8-9.
3. "France Hurt by Hostile Propaganda," NYT, 7 April 1940, iv, p. 5.
4. The statesman was Louis Barthou, whose biography I completed under the title Power and Pleasure: Louis Barthou and the Third French Republic (Montreal, 1991). Barthou's appreciation of the propagandistic value of France's cultural achievements inspired this essay, as well as my projected book-length study of French cultural propaganda and French foreign policy.

described the French premier's appeal for peace as "conciliatory" and "moving," unlike the sophistry-ridden, propagandistic reply of Hitler. On the following day the German Chancellor was characterized as "a man who does not know what it is to keep a solemn promise"; and the next day's issue spoke openly of his "reckless disregard of the truth," indeed it called him "a madman who will find himself destroyed by the process of his own folly." Leaving no room for doubt on the matter of responsibility, the editors pitted the whole of the rational world against Adolf Hitler: "if the whole world cannot outwit one man, then we are all defeated, war or no war."[5] Ten months later, as France collapsed, the *Times* experienced no change of heart. In an editorial entitled "Hitler's Way and Ours," it acknowledged that Hitler had won the battle of France, won it on the field, but also long before – by destroying the German economy, overturning traditional moral standards, and "infecting the youth of Germany with a fanaticism that has now stormed the barricades of the bravest democracy on the European Continent." But the struggle was far from over. Hitler's final success against democracy was by no means assured, for there was nothing supernatural, nothing miraculous, nothing inevitable about his victories so far. In fact, there was still room for hope. When Hitler had completed his visit to the fallen Paris and gazed on the tomb of Napoleon, was he not reminded of the tragedies that had befallen great conquerors like the Corsican, or Caesar, or Alexander? "Each has had a part of a generation, not one of a thousand years."[6]

At the beginning of the conflict the *Times* was no more neutral on the subject of France. On 4 September 1939 the paper offered a long editorial entitled "The Sword Unsheathed." It was not the American sword, to be sure, although "no scruples of strict neutrality can conscript the underlying sympathies of the American people." Rather, it was the newly forged sword of Britain and France – countries which had done "all that was humanly possible" to avert this war, which they were fighting now "only in self-

---

5. *NYT*, 29 August 1939, i, p. 20; 30 August, i, p. 16; 31 August, i, p. 18; 1 September, i, p. 16.
6. *NYT*, 16 June 1940, iv, p. 8; 30 June, iv, p. 8.

defence" and which, as democratic powers, were clearly "the outposts of our own kind of civilization."[7] Ten months later, at the defeat, the editors in New York offered up one lamentation upon another. No excitement here over the power of *blitzkrieg*, and no exercises in clever but belated prophecy. They called it a "Tragedy" and spoke of the "debt of gratitude that every surviving democracy in the world owes to the heroic nation that gave away its strength in a vain effort to check dictatorship and aggression."

> For France herself a terrible ordeal now begins. In this nightmare become real, this hideous perversion that seems still to be incredible, the most civilized people in the world, deprived of resistance, now stand at the mercy of a barbarian.[8]

It was strong and uncompromising language. Even more striking was the trip-wire vocabulary of civilization and barbarism. Not for the first time. When Paris was bombed from the air in early June, one editorial excoriated the regime that had unleashed the Luftwaffe. It was not simply that broken bodies were left behind, or broken buildings, it was the fact that Paris had been targeted! Cities such as Paris "are more than aggregations of men, women and children. They are the treasure-houses of the Western spirit." So let it be known, the editor raged, that "the anger of civilized peoples will burn so fiercely that it will consume the hateful German system which has loosed these horrors upon the world."[9] One week later, with the Germans at the gates of Paris, the *Times* carried an editorial entitled "The Citadel." That citadel was Paris, "a stronghold of the human spirit." The German guns, this column affirmed, "are battering at the hearts and minds of all of us who think of Paris when we try to define what we mean by civilization .... When Paris is bombed, the civilized world is bombed."[10]

7. NYT, 4 September 1939, i, p. 8.
8. NYT, 18 June 1940, i, p. 22.
9. NYT, 4 June 1940, i, p. 22. Upon learning of the aerial bombardment of Paris, the paper's publisher, Arthur Hays Sulzberger, privately commented to his editorial board: "Gentlemen, we have got to do more than we are doing. I cannot live with myself much longer unless we do." See Meyer Berger, *The Story of the New York Times, 1851-1951* (New York, 1951), p. 439.
10. NYT, 12 June 1940, i, p. 24.

* * *

To be sure, not everyone read the *New York Times*. In 1940 the average American of 25 years of age, or older, had less than a grade nine education, and was almost entirely uninformed about international issues. Indeed, only a quarter of this population was deemed to be "consistently" knowledgeable about foreign problems – a cadre which approximated the 15,000,000 who had high-school diplomas or college degrees. Indeed, there were only 1,000,000 degree holders, most of whom were males from white, affluent, east-or-west coast families.[11] Here, unmistakably, was the core of *Times'* readers in 1939-40, some 500,000 by day and over 800,000 on Sunday. These were the men and women who associated the paper's breadth of vision with its publisher, the Columbia-educated Arthur Hays Sulzberger, and his chief editor, the Yale-educated, Charles Merz. These, among America's readers, were the ones most likely to appreciate the paper's coverage of international news, to savour the quality of its book-review section, or to monitor the pulse of Europe's fashion industry. It was they, more than most, who could appreciate the weekly labours of its Sunday editor, Lester Markel, a graduate of the Columbia School of Journalism, and of his associate, Francis Brown, a man with a doctoral degree and teaching experience from Dartmouth and Columbia. Impressive for other reasons was the paper's managing editor, Edwin L. James, a former war correspondent with the American Expeditionary Force, a recipient of the Légion d'Honneur, and one whose Paris-tailored suits had earned him the sobriquet 'Dressy James'.[12] Together, readers and editors, they had made the *New York Times* what one writer has called "America's preeminent newspaper," a paper which spoke confidently of western culture and world civilization.[13]

On 15 June 1940 the *Times* reviewed a book by that renowned American expatriate, Gertrude Stein. Entitled *Paris France*, it con-

11. Martin Kriesberg, "Dark Areas of Ignorance," in *Public Opinion and Foreign Policy*, Lester Markel, ed. (New York, 1949), pp. 49-61.
12. Meyer Berger, *op. cit.*, 347; Gay Talese, *The Kingdom and the Power* (New York, 1969), pp. 43, 184-185, 257-258, 262, 264-265; Harrison Salisbury, *Without Fear of Favor. The New York Times and Its Times* (New York, 1980), p. 30.
13. Ronald Brownstein, "The New York Times on Nazism (1933-39)," *Midstream* 26 (1980): 14.

tained illustrations by Pablo Picasso. Markel's reviewer, Charles Poore, began as follows:

> The barbarians have reached Paris. They must feel strange there. It represents everything that civilized people admire. A Nazi standing at the gates of Paris must feel like a burglar in a treasure house.[14]

In the same issue, the editors spoke of "The Paris that Did Not Fall." Again, there was the language of barbarism and civilization, but also a resolution to deny Hitler the city he now occupied. The "true" Paris was, after all, "inviolate, forever."

> Paris of Voltaire, Rousseau, Victor Hugo, Balzac, Anatole France, Montaigne; Paris of Madame Roland, Layfayette, Danton, Zola, Chateaubriand; Paris of Racine, Molière, Corneille; Paris of Gautier, Daudet and Rabelais; Paris that taught the world to paint and build; Paris that laughed, Paris that used words for rapiers, Paris that turned the troops out to march with muffled drums in the funeral trains of poets; Paris of museums, libraries, universities in which the mind could range at will ...: this is not Hitler's Paris, not today, not ever .... They may parade the Champs Elysées. But the Elysian Fields of Paris, as of civilization itself, they cannot traverse or conquer.[15]

It is difficult to say what most catches the attention of a reader fifty years removed from the crisis. Is it the passion, or the form of expression, or rather the cultural polarity which seems to be implied here? If the latter, it requires a very important caveat. While it is true that the incidence of *Times'* war-time coverage of German cultural activity does not compare with that accorded to France, it is also true that editors and correspondents, as well as public opinion in general, strove to distinguish German from Nazi. The latter were "ruthless" and had "misled" the German people who, at heart, were "essentially peace loving." For that reason, therefore, no attempt was to be made to curtail German language instruction in the schools, or to prevent American orchestras from playing German music.[16] In other words there was no disposition

---

14. NYT, 15 June 1940, vi, p. 13.
15. NYT, 15 June 1940, i, p. 14.
16. See the poll results for December 1939 conducted by the American Institute of Public Opinion and reported in *Public Opinion Quarterly* 4 (1940): 96,99.

to discard Bach or Wagner simply because their descendants had fallen under the spell of some evil *Meistersinger*. The same was true of German literature.

In the case of books, three patterns can be discerned in the *Times*' coverage.[17] One concerned books openly critical of the Nazi regime – many of them by disgruntled exiles. And the reviewers, not unnaturally, followed suit. On 3 September, for example, there were reviews of Hermann Rauschning's *The Revolution of Nihilism* and Franz Borkenau's *The New German Empire*, both of which constituted "a damning indictment" of Hitler's state. A week later there was a sympathetic review of Toni Sender's autobiography, the work of a German, a socialist and a woman who had had no time for the Nazis. In December it was the turn of Heinrich Hauser and Karl Loewenstein, two more exiles from Hitler's Germany who were foretelling the eventual collapse of the Nazi state.[18] 1940 saw the pace maintained. In February, Rauschning published another book, this one based on conversations with Hitler whom he called *The Voice of Destruction*. In April the former Nazi, Eitel Wolf Dobert, by then an exile in the United States, released his book with Putnam, entitled *Convert to Freedom*.[19] Not all, of course, belonged to the category of German exile. Early in the war, Ethel Vance had set her novel *Escape* inside Nazi Germany, a work which the reviewer called a portrait of "Nazi sickness"; and in November Yale published a book by Stephen Raushenbush which urged early action against the threat of Fascism. Two months later the *Times* reviewed Michael Power's book on Nazi persecution of the Christian church; and the following month saw reviews of a book called *Within Germany* – in which the author characterized Hitler's state

17. It is worth drawing attention to a piece written shortly after the war by Lester Markel, the *Times*' Sunday editor. Markel, who had the reputation for reading and editing every line from his writers and contributors, publicly acknowledged that words could be used as "weapons", not as the Nazis had used them, when the "Word" became "lie", but in the interest of truth – through libraries of information, and teacher-student exchanges, and cultural exhibitions. See his "Opinion – A Neglected Instrument" and "Opportunity or Disaster?" in his edited volume, *Public Opinion and Foreign Policy*, 9-38, 214-218.

18. NYT, 3 September 1939, vi, p. 1; 10 September, vi, p. 15; 10 December, vi, p. 3.

19. NYT, 18 February 1940, vi, p. 4; 7 April, vi, p. 5.

as "utterly unhappy and depressed" and certain to lose the war – and of another on the Nazi leadership, in which the author casually referred to Hitler as the Antichrist.[20]

A second kind of book was that for which the reviewer declined comment beyond question of literary merit. Such, for example, was the case of new books on Shakespeare by German specialists, or new books by Germans about Germans – for instance Karl Brandi's biography of Charles V – or new books about Germans by non-Germans – for instance, John Burk's study of Clara Schumann.[21] In each case the reviewer dealt strictly with the book itself and made no special effort to either applaud or diminish the Germanic quality of the achievement. This was, however, clearly a minority category.

More eye-catching in war-time was the review of works by or about renowned German cultural figures, for that renown seemed to inspire not only celebrations of Germanic cultural achievement but attempts to divorce that culture from Hitler's bloodstained regime. An example of this pattern was the review of a volume of letters by Rainer Maria Rilke, in which the *Times*' reviewer ended with thanks that the poet had never lived to see the Nazi state.[22] But the most outspoken examples of this genre came from the family of the legendary Thomas Mann, himself an exile in the United States. When his newly translated novel, *Royal Highness*, appeared in late 1939, the reviewer made a point of associating Mann's political sympathies with those of the democracy in which he now lived. Two months later his son and daughter, Erika and Klaus, released their book, *The Other Germany*, in which they did what they could to repudiate the Nazi state. In the spring Erika undertook a new assault, this time in *The Lights Go Down*, in which she again distinguished between the German people and the "brutal minority" which ruled them. Her father added his voice that same month, May 1940, first in a new work entitled *This War*, and then in an attendant interview during which he referred to "the detestable forces of evil" in Germany. For him, as for so many

20. NYT, 24 September 1939, vi, p. 2; 5 November, vi, p. 20; 28 January 1940, vi, p. 12; 4 February, vi, p. 16; 18 February, vi, p. 6.
21. NYT, 8 October 1939, vi, p. 8; 21 January 1940, vi, p. 5; 7 April, vi, p. 7.
22. NYT, 2 June 1940, vi, p. 4.

others, there would be no real escape "until the enemies of mankind are driven out."[23]

Although German music attracted less attention than German books, there were similarities in the *Times'* coverage. That is to say, there was a tendency – again, not that surprisingly – to distinguish between Germans of genius and the uniformed thugs of the Führer. In the early months of the war the paper carried a number of articles about the lives and compositions of celebrated German composers, including Bach and Beethoven.[24] But unmistakably, the focus was on Richard Wagner, partly because of his musical brilliance, partly too because Hitler had long since elevated the composer to divine station. Therein lay the problem for anti-Nazi Germans and Germanophiles, to somehow spare Wagner from the guilt of association with Hitler. It was not an entirely simple task, for no amount of inventiveness could exempt Wagner from a fascination with destructive Germanic heroism or with flashes of anti-semitism. Indeed, his heroically-long, four-part operatic series, "Niebelungen Ring," now served as a kind of select hymnary for the Nazi state. And Bayreuth, where the annual Wagner festival had been held for years, had reached the status of shrine. Still, those who wrote for the *Times* did what they could to rescue Wagner from the Germans of the day. They drew attention to the public disavowal of antisemitism by Siegfried Wagner, the composer's son. They ran a feature article by Otto Tolischus in the weekend magazine, an article which made it clear that the Nazis did not really understand Wagner anymore than he would have understood the Nazis. A full-blown romanticist, he would never have understood, never mind approved, the manipulation of his art for political purposes. To this the editors rallied with their own piece on "Wagner and Hitler," fulminating over the Führer's cynical and dishonest recasting of the "Ring," and his deliberate attempts to conceal Wagner's truth:

> that only one thing is more destructive than greed of gold – namely, greed of power; that a state founded upon violence, terror and false-

23. *NYT*, 10 December 1939, vi, p. 1; 11 February 1940, vi, p. 9; 5 May, vi, p. 7; 18 May, i, p. 13; 19 May, vi, p. 12. See also Mann's eulogy to René Schickele, *NYT*, 26 May 1940, vi, p. 8.

24. *NYT*, 14 January 1940, ix, p. 9; 7 April, ix, p. 7.

hood is doomed to annihilation; that the greatest leaders, the very high gods themselves, are not immune to the dread penalties of those who transgress moral law.[25]

Comparatively speaking, the French were on the side of the angels, at least as far as the *Times* was concerned. Hindsight in 1939-1940 might suggest things the French could have done or said differently, things that would have warned Hitler off and thus helped avert war. And the editors did have misgivings about the apparently do-nothing strategy that characterized the so-called "phoney" war between September 1939 and the following May. But the simple, basic, inexpungable fact remained that France had not wanted this war and had done nothing, actively, to contribute to its outbreak. Now it stood as the Continent's premier democracy, a bastion of freedom and – emphatically – a bastion of civilization. In the collective mind of the *Times*, all were of a piece: democracy, freedom and civilization. It is in this connection that one detects just how important positively-couched book reviews can be, and reports on concerts, art exhibitions, fashion displays and new cinema releases. In each of these respects, France attracted far more interest than Germany and far more sympathy.

The problem, at least for the purposes of this space-restricted study, is the volume and diversity of the material on France. For this reason it seems judicious to conduct a survey of the *Times'* book reviews in a way comparable to that used in the case of Germany. At the same time, there is no reason to be hostage to symmetry. The volume of coverage of French music in 1939-1940 was comparable to that of Germany, but there was certainly no single French composer who could bear the weight Wagner bore in Germany. Another difference was the *Times'* apparent interest in French women, and its apparent confidence that American women shared that interest. This will be the second theme from which this paper will draw its images.

* * *

25. *NYT*, 17 December 1939, ix, p. 8; 25 February 1940, vii, pp. 6-7, 23; 3 March, x, p. 7. The 1921 disavowal by Siegfried Wagner was reprinted on 19 May, ix, p. 5.

When it comes to books, the first feature of note is the frequency with which the *Times* reviewed books of French subject matter and/or provenance. Certainly it would be closer to understatement than exaggeration to suggest that the incidence of such reviews was twice that addressed to German works. One difference was particularly striking, and that was the fortnightly article by Charles Cestre, entitled "The Literary Scene in France." It was here that Cestre, who had occupied the chair of American literature at the Sorbonne since 1918, kept American readers *au courant* with the latest offerings from such houses as Plon, Fayard or Flammarion. Typically, he reviewed several new releases at a time, many of them novels and most of which elicited no comment – beyond their purely, and assumed, artistic merits – except perhaps to remark on some occasion, with disarming innocence, that France's writers, even in war-time, were obliged "to be active and maintain the renown of French literature."[26] But Cestre found other, better, occasions to further educate the readers of the *New York Times*. For instance, in mid-September 1939 he terminated his review of Henri Berr's *Les Allemagnes* with the observation that this German-initiated war had arisen

> from a warping of the minds and an organized attempt to ruin Christianity, democracy and humane civilization by the rise of a new materialism, mustering for its advancement the world-old forces of superstition and military power.[27]

By contrast, upon reviewing André Rousseaux's *Littérature du vingtième siècle*, Cestre was blinded by the "brilliance" of the writers surveyed, including: Carco, Colette, Malraux, Claudel, Mauriac, Valéry. Only in his closing line did it occur to him that this literature of the twentieth century was, exclusively, the literature of France. [28]

26. *NYT*, 21 January 1940, vi, p. 8.
27. *NYT*, 17 September 1939, vi, p. 8. Cestre's association with the American section of the Maison de la Presse went back to at least October 1918. The Maison was the French government's principal office for propaganda in World War I and the precursor of the interwar department known as the Service des Oeuvres Françaises à l'Etranger. See Rapports généraux du commissariat général à l'information et à la propagande, juin -décembre 1918. Seventh report, October 1918, Maison de la Presse, Dossier 74, Ministère des Affaires Etrangères (MAE).
28. *NYT*, 31 December 1939, vi, p. 8.

Beyond Cestre and his regular, sympathetic column, there were many other reviews of works from and about war-time France. For our purposes, these may be framed in two categories. The first were the straightforward assessments of new books on French history – the vast majority of which were biographical in character. Of these, some were addressed to those familiar with power: Charlemagne, Colbert, the Comtesse de Ségur, the beautiful Mme Récamier, the perspicacious de Tocqueville.[29] But far more were inspired by art of diverse forms: Racine, Ronsard and Montaigne, the composers Berlioz and Ravel, the poets de Vigny and Rimbaud, the novelist Flaubert, even the ageing sculptor Aristide Maillol, and the ever-restless, Spanish-born artist Pablo Picasso.[30] To be sure, very, very few of the reviews attempted any clumsy equation between besieged France and Eternal Truth. They simply worked with the names and the art, and let readers, already well-primed, draw their own conclusions.

That was made easier by the attention which had been paid by the *Times* to the real *vedettes* of contemporary French literature, at least those whose latest publications coincided with the war. Take for example the long review of Jules Romains' translated *Verdun*, the eighth volume of *Men of Good Will*. Accompanied by a prominent photograph of the author, this review left no doubt but that this was a "masterpiece," and a model of "French clarity and scientific comprehensiveness."[31] Then it was the turn of Georges Duhamel and Jean Giono, the former for his translated *Cécile Pasquier* and the latter for his translated *Joy of Man's Desiring*. Giono, the reviewer acknowledged, was "the supreme poet-novelist of our time."[32] And there were others: André Maurois, for his *The Art of Living*, in which the reviewer found more evidence of "that quality for which the French are famous, the power of reasoning"; and Henri Troyat, whose "brilliant" success as a novelist

---

29. *NYT*, 17 September 1939, vi, p. 9; 1 October, vi, p. 9; 3 December, vi, p. 8; 24 March 1940, vi, p. 9; 5 May, vi, p. 9.

30. *NYT*, 17 September 1939, vi, p. 3; 15 October, ix, p. 8; 15 December, i, p. 23; 21 January 1940, vi, p. 4; 28 January, vi, p. 5; 25 February, vi, p. 16; 5 May, vi, p. 28; 12 May, vi, p. 2.

31. *NYT*, 31 December 1939, vi, p. 1.

32. *NYT*, 26 May 1940, vi, p. 2; 9 June, vi, p. 2; 10 June, i, p. 15.

had led him now to a volume of short stories which were, in turn, original, remarkable, vivid, startling, and wonderfully fanciful.[33] Finally, and of quite another order, there was the no less remarkable Georges Simenon, whose energies, like his appeal, seemed inexhaustible. In March 1940 the *Times* reviewed *The Patience of Maigret*, a single volume of two earlier novels: "A Battle of Nerves" and "A Face for a Clue." Two months later, there was another volume of similar format entitled *Maigret Travels South*. In the latter instance, one reviewer opened with a barely veiled allusion: "The invaders we can always welcome are those who come to bring books, not to burn them."[34]

It was true that Nazi Germany's recent treatment of books had been outrageous. But if there was an inclination to separate German from Nazi on cultural matters, what explains the evident difference in the *Times*' treatment of German and French women? It was not as if the former were in any way pilloried or held up for special disdain, it was more that the paper's commentators on France – several of whom were women – displayed a far more active interest in the condition of women in war-time France.[35]

Barely a month of hostilities had gone by when Winifred Boulter reported from Paris on the recruitment of women for military and civilian service. Some were pilots and parachute-experienced nurses, some were in a 500 strong corps of women cyclists employed for running messages between municipal offices. Women were harvesting the autumn crops, collecting money for refugees, serving in publicly funded food kitchens, driving ambulances and providing much of the uniformed personnel for the urban passive defence organizations. Most of this, Ms Boulter observed, was unpaid, strictly volunteer service; and yet for all that, "the number of volunteers far exceeds present requirements."[36] In early November the *Times* ran a long article, datelined Paris, and entitled "Women of France Take Up War Tasks." Those tasks were quickly being

---

33. NYT, 24 March 1940, vi, pp. 8,9.
34. NYT, 18 May 1940, i, p. 13; 19 May, vi, p. 22.
35. On the increased profile of women readers and journalists, see the remarks on "feminizing the newspaper" in James Melvin Lee, *History of American Journalism* (New York, 1923), p. 389.
36. NYT, 8 October 1939, vii, p. 5.

extended into the industrial area and specifically defence production. And to facilitate their return to war-time service and production, after an interval of twenty years, French women could count on the services of a new department within the Commissariat for Information. At its head was Mlle Eve Curie, daughter and biographer of France's scientific heroine, Marie Curie.[37] It was a fitting choice for a government resolved to underline the heroic nature of the contribution it expected from French women. As Mlle Curie told the *Times*, the nation's women had "faced the war with resolution and bravery and with that spirit of invention and ingenuity that is so acute among our people." [38]

By late January 1940 there were said to be nearly 300,000 women working in French munitions factories, an increase which was said to explain why production was up as much as ten times over the preceding months. In April one of the *Times*' regular correspondents in Paris, the Pulitzer-prize winner, Anne O'Hare McCormick, contributed another piece on French women, this time describing those in one state arsenal, hard at work "with carefully curled hair and fresh lipstick, working ten hours a day, sighting guns and polishing up the business end of cannon." In May, the newspaper's readers learned more of this "army in overalls," former stenographers and housewives, now expertly wielding rivet guns and carrying trays of cellulose explosive in gun-cotton factories.[39]

Of comparable, perhaps greater, interest to American women was the fashion industry, one that provided literally graphic illustration of the connection between the profits of modern advertising and those

---

37. The French foreign ministry took particular note of the fact that this biography, translated by Doubleday, had sold exceptionally well in the United States. Accordingly, in coming to the Commissariat, Eve Curie already enjoyed a considerable reputation among American readers. See Jean Marx to Washington Embassy, 8 February 1939, Série Oeuvres, carton 571, MAE (Nantes).

38. NYT, 5 November 1939, i, p. 37. In March 1940 Mlle Curie spoke, "en anglais impeccable," to an audience at Stanford University. Her subject was French women and the war, and her intent, clearly, was to underscore not only their sacrifices but also their unshakable determination to finish with the Hitler regime once and for all. See Consul General (San Francisco) to Foreign Ministry, 14 March 1940, Série Oeuvres, 571, MAE (Nantes).

39. NYT, 17 January 1940, i, p. 5; 27 January, i, p. 3; 13 April, i, p. 16; 19 May, iv, p. 6.

of modern propaganda.[40] For example, in September 1930 the French flyers Coste and Bellonte completed their 37 hour transatlantic flight from Paris to New York, a record in aviation history. What is less well known is that their small cargo included columns of advertising for the *New York Times*, in this case for a dress, designed by Callot of Paris, which was to go on display at Wanamaker's in New York City.[41] In less than a decade the *Times* was sending its own photographs and sketches on the same transatlantic clipper flights carrying the latest fashion articles to New York. Included in their promotion of this service was an assurance that the creations first displayed in Paris on one day, were being sold in New York on the next. Of greater interest still, ready-to-wear copies could be on sale within ten days.[42]

To satisfy that interest, and to promote its own readership, the *Times* paid a great deal of attention to the Paris fashion industry. In Kathleen Cannell, it had its Charles Cestre of haute couture; and there was nothing miserly about the way the newspaper embellished its fashion coverage with illustrations of the latest gowns and with prominent interviews with the reigning czars of fabric and design. Without a doubt, some readers would have been far more familiar with Chanel than Corneille, with Patou than Pascal. And no doubt some would have known that Molyneux was in fact English, not French, that Mainbocher was an American, Schiaparelli an Italian, and Balenciaga and Paquin both Spanish. The fact is that all were residents of Paris from which, it was said, they took their inspiration. And that made all the difference, a cachet which was seemingly irrefutable – even when Mme Schiaparelli could complain that American women, whose natural beauty was unrivaled, seemed intent on overdoing their makeup and their ensembles.[43]

40. This connection has attracted the attention of many students of propaganda, including the following: Garth S. Jowett and Victoria O'Donnell, *Propaganda and Persuasion* (London, 1986), p. 62; and Leonard W. Doob, *Public Opinion and Propaganda* (Camden, CT, 1966), pp. 440-445.
41. M. Berger, *op. cit.*, 358. He claims, as well, that by 1929 the *Times* "led the world's newspapers in advertising," p. 345.
42. *NYT*, 20 August 1939, viii, p. 5.
43. *NYT*, 24 December 1939, vii, p. 7. See also the feature article by Clair Price, "Makers of Fashion," *NYT*, 21 May 1939, viii, pp. 10-11,24; and Bruno Villien, "Schiaparelli," in *Entre Deux Guerres* edited by Olivier Barrot and Pascal Ory (Paris, 1990), pp. 489-497.

But fashion could not transcend the sober realities of 1939-40 any more than Mme Schiaparelli could forget that her own daughter was now an ambulance driver. The war intruded even here, sometimes only in the ephemeral ways of fashion: the "Polish" coat of autumn 1939, the "Finnish" belt of March 1940. Handbags were extra-large that year, so as to accommodate gas masks; and Molyneux produced what he called "a censored scarf," which featured a "Dear ..." in black script on a blue background. Deliberately ironic were the so-called "unconcerned" swagger coats and the "carefree" sweaters of spring 1940.[44] But whatever the lies, there was one overriding truth. Fashion was not frivolous; it was essential to the war economy of France. That is why, late in 1939, the government hurriedly returned to the fashion industry thousands of seamstresses, *midinettes*, who had been redeployed in the September mobilization. At the time, someone had seen fashion as peripheral to the war effort and essentially deprived it of the necessary labour and material resources. Within a month, when it was obvious that the virtual shutdown of the fashion industry would mean a large drop in foreign revenues, the first steps were taken to revive the world of Paris couture. As part of that campaign a number of prominent women were enlisted for publicity purposes – including the wife of Jean Giraudoux, celebrated dramatist and Commissioner for Information, and the wife of Edouard Bourdet, playwright-administrator of the Comédie Française.[45]

What is one to make of the significance of such things, the association between fashion and literature – to say nothing of art or cinema? Two conclusions suggest themselves from this limited and preliminary exploration of cultural imagery in the war-time pages of the *New York Times*. First, the affinity that was so often and so variously expressed between the elites of the French and American republics discount any chance of a momentary *amour de circonstances*. Indeed, so much deeper are its roots than the war itself, even than this century or the century before it, that tracing them lies far beyond the possibilities of this study. One can only suggest, with some confidence, that what is evidenced in the columns of

44. NYT, 31 December 1939, ii, p. 4; 10 March 1940, viii, p. 1; 24 March, ii, p. 4; 27 May, i, p. 21.
45. NYT, 26 November 1939, vii, p. 14-15; 31 December, ii, p. 4.

this paper, in 1939 and 1940, is consistent with the historical literature on the shared Franco-American cultural tradition.[46] That is to say it was no accident when editors of an erudite paper like the *Times* associated themselves with the history and literature, the art, the music, the architectural landmarks of France. It was no accident that its correspondents, like Eleanor Kittredge, could combat the reality of May 1940 by recalling Anatole France's funeral procession in 1924, when the French Republic had paid such "respect for things of the mind." And it was no accident that Janet Flanner wrote in 1940 of her memories of interwar Paris "when fresh intellectual opinion and new esthetic enjoyment were legitimate forms of civilized excitement," or that her reviewer should close with the remark: "this American in Paris has a French mind."[47] Neither was it accidental that in June 1940, with the German army less than a hundred miles away, the American ambassador found himself at Domrémy, the birthplace of Joan of Arc. William Bullitt was there to present a new altar to the village church, an altar purchased through private subscription by American donors who wanted to express "their faith that the spiritual forces of the earth will triumph over the forces of Satanism." [48]

Certainly by then there had been a coalescence of opinion in America. President Roosevelt had been maneuvering his way for years toward the eventual repeal of the country's neutrality legislation, legislation which would have denied Britain and France wartime access to American military supplies and hardware.[49]

46. See Edward Fecteau's older study, *French Contributions to America* (Methuen, MA, 1945), and the more recent Donald Roy Allen, *French Views of America in the 1930s* (New York, 1987); Julian G. Hurstfield, *America and the French Nation, 1939-45* (Chapel Hill, 1986); Annie Lacroix-Riz, *Le choix de Marianne. Les relations franco-américaines, 1944-48* (Paris, 1985); Jacques Portes, *Une fascination réticente: Les Etats-Unis dans l'opinion française, 1870-1914* (Nancy, 1990); Colin Nettleback, *Forever French: The French Exiles in the United States of America* (New York, 1991). Special note should also be made of Henry Blumenthal's important *America and French Culture, 1800-1900* (Baton Rouge, 1975) in which he treats at great length the affinities and the ambivalence between the two people and their two cultures.

47. *NYT*, 21 April 1940, vi, p. 17; 26 May, vii, p. 22.

48. *NYT*, 10 June 1940, i, p. 3.

49. See chapters 8 and 9 of Robert Dallek, *Franklin D. Roosevelt and American Foreign Policy, 1932-45* (New York, 1979); and Henry Blumenthal, *Illusion and Reality in Franco-American Diplomacy, 1914-45* (Baton Rouge, LA, 1986), pp. 244-245.

Sulzberger's *New York Times*, despite its frequent firefights with the Administration, had been working toward the same goal. Indeed, a year and a half before war had returned to Europe, Merz had written a provocative editorial reminding readers that the western European democracies were truly "the outposts of our own kind of civilization" – the very words which he was to use again in his editorial of 4 September 1939.[50] But by the latter date public opinion had almost caught up to the pace set by Roosevelt and the *Times*. Whereas in August 1937 only 30% of Gallup's respondents believed Germany to be the country most likely to start a war, by January 1939 that figure had risen to 62%. With the war's outbreak, 82% said Germany had caused it; and by the end of June 1940, 80% of the respondents had come round to approving Roosevelt's sale of military aircraft to Britain and France, although neither that public, nor the *Times*, nor Roosevelt expressed any desire to see active American military intervention.[51] The fact was that isolationism was still very much intact, whatever the gulf between public sympathy for Britain and France and public disgust with Germany.

This is not to say that cultural affinity was lacking between Americans and Germans. Indeed, the German-American community in the United States was substantially larger than the Franco-American one. But typically, at least in the pages of the *Times*, the distinction was drawn between all that German writers and artists had contributed to the world, and all the damage that the Nazi regime had inflicted upon that contribution. No such caveat was drawn in the case of France, whatever misgivings had been expressed through the 1930s about the vitality of the Third Republic. No doubt this was partly owing to the range of cultural affinities that had for so long been subject to remark on both sides of the Atlantic. But was this an entirely natural process between self-seen sophisticates, or did it involve something orchestrated? This raises a second and equally preliminary, "conclusion".

As suggested at the outset, this study is but an early and tiny part of a projected book on French cultural propaganda in the first

50. M. Berger, *op. cit.*, 431, 573. See also note 7 above.
51. George H. Gallup, *The Gallup Poll. Public Opinion, 1935-71*, 3 vols. (New York, 1972); vol. I, 1935-48, pp. 66, 137, 179, 230.

half of the twentieth century. For reasons associated with that larger work, it has been necessary to explore the efforts of the French government in the field of cultural propaganda, and notably those of the foreign ministry.[52] Clearly, this is not the time nor the place to raise the curtain on what is a theatre unto itself. But what can be done, and what is consistent with a study focused on the *Times*, is to provide a few sample illustrations of the role played by French officialdom in this positive imaging.[53]

It was in 1935 that a French Information Center opened in New York. Described officially as "privately" organized and financed, the reports of its operations in wartime nonetheless were received in May 1940 by a meeting chaired by General Chambrun, temporarily sitting in for Marshal Pétain, and attended by the French premier, the minister of armaments, the former governor of the Bank of France and the American ambassador. One of the reports was delivered by André Maurois, once visiting professor of French literature at Princeton, currently a member of the Académie Française but, for the occasion, dressed instead in the uniform of the French army. The Center, he said, was working well, providing information only on request, and – unlike the Germans – only "simple data and straightforward information," information that was not "misleading." What could be more fitting, he might have asked, for a country "fighting for civilization."[54] A similar message had been

---

52. In particular, see the collection of articles on culture and international relations in *Relations Internationales* (Spring, 1983), especially that of Antoine Marès, "Puissance et présence culturelle de la France. L'exemple du Service des Oeuvres françaises àl' étranger dans les années trente," 65-80. Also noteworthy are M.T. Chabord, "Les services français de l'information de 1936 à 1947," in *Revue d'histoire de la deuxième guerre mondiale* (Oct., 1966), 81-87; Maurice Mégret, "Les origines de la propagande de guerre française," RHDGM (Jan., 1961), 3-27; M.B. Palmer, "L' Office français d'Information, 1940-44," RHDGM (Jan., 1976), 19-40; Denis Rolland, *Vichy et la France libre au Mexique. Guerre, cultures et propagandes pendant la deuxième guerre mondiale* (Paris, 1990).

53. For earlier French efforts to cultivate American opinion, see William R. Keylor, "'How They Advertised France': The French Propaganda Campaign in the United States during the Breakup of the Franco-American Entente, 1918-23," *Diplomatic History* 17 (1993): 351-373.

54. NYT, 5 May 1940, i, 36. The Office Français de Renseignements had its address on the Place de la Concorde and its New York address on Fifth Avenue. See letter to Jean Marx (Oeuvres), 28 May 1935, Série Oeuvres, carton 569, MAE

imparted, a month earlier, to an American literary audience in New York. One of the leading participants had been Eve Curie, who had just completed a tour of 30 American towns and cities on behalf of the French Commissariat for Information. She was, she said, 'marvelously at home in America', partly because, like France, it was a democratic country, partly too because of the cultural connection. Her friends, she predicted, would be deluging her with questions about American books, American plays, and certainly whether she had seen "Gone With The Wind."[55]

The arts were central to it all, whatever was natural and unrehearsed, whatever was calculated. If Jules Romains was billed as a literary star in the United States in 1939, it had something to do with travel funds provided by the French foreign ministry.[56] The same was true of Maurois who was a founding member of the New York Information Office and, as of 1939, an executive member of the government-funded Association d'Expansion Artistique.[57] If Georges Duhamel attracted New York reviewers and readers in 1940, his renown owed something to the patriotic radio broadcasting he had been recruited to do by that celebrated playwright – now Commissar for Information – Jean Giraudoux.[58] Members of

---

(Nantes); also a letter from Pierre de Lanux to Marx, of 15 March 1937, carton 570. For Maurois' impressions of America in 1927 and 1931, see his *En Amérique*, a translated version of which appeared in 1933 through the American Book Company; and his *Memoirs, 1885-1967* (New York, 1970).

55. *NYT*, 10 April 1940, i, p. 23.

56. See Jules Romains to Jean Marx (Service des oeuvres), 18 March 1939, Série Oeuvres, carton 570, MAE (Nantes); and the "Arrêt" signed by Alexis Léger for 25,000 francs, carton 571, MAE (Nantes). Romains was well travelled in the United States, partly in his role as International President of P.E.N., and partly as a coveted university guest lecturer. See for example the account left by the Consul General in San Francisco following Romains' stay at Mills College. Méric de Bellefon, 6 August 1936, Série Oeuvres, carton 570, MAE (Nantes).

57. See letter to Jean Marx (Oeuvres), 28 May 1935, Série Oeuvres, carton 569, MAE (Nantes). The executive body was known as the Comité d'Action Artistique, through which funds were passed from the budgets of the Beaux-Arts department in the Education ministry and from that of the Service des Oeuvres department in the Foreign ministry. See in particular Série Oeuvres, carton 485, MAE (Nantes). For a brief account of his American lecture in the spring of 1939, see Maurois' *Memoirs, 1885-1967*, pp. 203-204.

58. See the audition of Giraudoux, 29 November 1939, by the Chamber's foreign affairs commission, dossier no. 9. p. 114, Archives Assemblée Nationale (ASN); and

the French elite, whether artists or *dirigeants*, saw culture as the country's finest export, something that could not fail to endear France to the rest of the world. Was it not self-evident that the works of French literature had "constantly enriched the legacy of all humanity," or that French art advertised to the world "la création continue de notre génie"?[59] Is it no less evident that the question was rhetorical, that the answer should be as obvious to us as it was to those who worked within the propaganda services of the French foreign ministry? Fifty years ago, one of them wrote the following *profession de foi*:

> L'Art Français, qui a toujours été à l'étranger un des plus défenseurs du prestige de notre pays, n'a pas cessé depuis la guerre d'accomplir cette haute mission. Jamais nos peintres, nos sculpteurs, nos musiciens, nos artistes dramatiques, nos orateurs, n'ont servi plus efficacement et avec plus d'éclat la cause du génie français hors de nos frontières.[60]

In January 1940 someone had arranged for a special performance of Charpentier's "Louise" at the Metropolitan Opera, the proceeds from which were to go to the French Benevolent Society and Hospital. And someone had arranged for the boxes to be draped with the American and French flags, and for the interval between the second and third acts to be filled with an orchestral rendition of "La Marseillaise" and "The Star-Spangled Banner."[61] The month before the French pianist, Magda Tagliafero, had arrived in New York on the "Dixie Clipper", and debuted with the Philharmonic-Symphony Orchestra in March 1940. She was there on the behest, and on the account, of two French ministries, Foreign Affairs and Education. In an interview with the *Times* she performed with all the skill of a great artist, nimbly demarcating an "intellectual and artistic" France from totalitarian states which "victimized" even their own creative artists. What a pity that Mendelssohn's music should

---

the thoughtful appraisal of his work by Jean-Louis Crémieux-Brilhac, Les Français de l'an 40, I, La Guerre oui ou non? (Paris, 1990), pp. 273-296.

59. Jean Marx (Oeuvres) to the Cour des Comptes, 27 May 1940, Série Oeuvres, carton 481, MAE (Nantes).

60. Unsigned note entitled "Depuis la guerre," from the Section littéraire et artistique, early 1940, Série Oeuvres, carton 481, MAE (Nantes)

61. *NYT*, 21 January 1940, i, p. 36.

be banned in Germany, or that of Paul Hindemith, or the art of George Grosz, or the literature of Thomas Mann. As for her, as befitted an instructor of the Conservatoire de Paris, she would continue to play in recital the work of Schumann, Mozart and Bach.[62] Who could not but applaud such artistry, that of the Germans, but also that of the woman determined to play it? Mlle Curie and the Commissariat for Information must have been delighted, for it was precisely the right message to leave with Americans.[63] In January 1940, Eve Curie herself had addressed an audience of 1500 people from the arts community assembled at the Hotel Astor.

> The most terrible condemnation of the regimes of oppression which today rule several countries of Europe is the sudden, the total disappearance of their art. This does not only come from the fact that many artists ... are persecuted or exiled .... Some have been given full powers to create, by order of the dictator of the moment, a totalitarian art which would leave the world breathless. And yet their creation amounts to nothing. Having been ordered to speak, artists have nothing more to say. [64]

In France they were not ordered to speak, merely urged; and therein lay part of the difference between dictatorship and democracy. But there is no mistaking the fact that they were urged, or that their skills and reputations were shrewdly promoted by American and French citizens on both sides of the Atlantic. What added to the effect was the subtlety with which these messages were delivered – French art exhibitions arranged through the French Institute in New York, celebrated author-lecturers speaking to local chapters of the government-funded Alliance Française, concert musicians whose travel costs were defrayed by the Quai d'Orsay in cooperation with a steamship company located in the Maison Française on Fifth Avenue.[65] What was being marketed was cul-

62. NYT, 17 March 1940, x, p. 8.
63. Mme Tagliaferro was warmly recommended to the French embassy in Washington and the French Institute in New York by Jean Marx, director of the foreign ministry's Service des oeuvres. She was to have received a monthly subsidy of 10,000 francs. See letters of 15 and 27 November 1939, Série Oeuvres, carton 577, MAE (Nantes)
64. NYT, 20 January 1940, i, p. 13.
65. This was the Compagnie Générale Transatlantique, known in New York simply as "The French Line."

ture and a certain idea of France; and its effectiveness rested on a single conviction. The propagation of beauty, things of the mind and spirit, was not "propaganda" at all, at least not in the sense that most people had learned the word from 1917 or 1918. And in *that* sense, the French were only too quick to admit their backwardness, their old-fashioned commitment to truth, their inexperience with the manipulation of opinion. And as remarkable as it now seems, that notion stuck. Despite all that we have seen, in April 1940 a *Times* correspondent could still lament that the French "have lagged behind other nations in their effort to stir sympathy," and that they were neophytes in the use of propaganda.[66] In point of fact, the French already had won the war of words and ideas, hands down; and cultural propaganda had been central to the victory. Hitler might enjoy early triumphs on the battlefield, and rejoice by marching his troops down the Champs Elysées, but to the *New York Times*, these were only the momentary victories of barbarism over humanity, of darkness over light.

---

* The author gratefully acknowledges the financial support provided for this project by the Social Sciences and Humanities Research Council of Canada.

---

66. *NYT*, 7 April 1940, iv, p. 5. In fact, the charge might have been more valid for the Nazi regime's propagandistic activity in the United States. It has been judged unrealistic in its goals, clumsy in its methods, and ineffective in its results. See for example O.J. Rogge, *The Official German Report* (New York, 1961), and Arthur L. Smith, *The Deutschtum of Nazi Germany and the United States* (The Hague, 1965).

X

REFLECTIONS ON FRANCE, BRITAIN AND THE WINTER WAR PRODROME, 1939-1940

John C. Cairns

"We have pooled everything. At the last Supreme War Council there was no friction, no differences. *Cette fois, ça y est.*"[1]

Historians with their "flickering lamp stumbling along the trail of the past" toward the European disaster of 1940 must pass through the thicket of the Russo-Finnish Winter War. Notoriously, the Finns fought almost alone. But the tangential Allied involvement had consequences for France and for the Franco-British alliance. In the course of three and a half months, this remote little war so focused and stressed French domestic, foreign and defence policies as to bring the government to the point of collapse. Overall, the intense political and military conflicts arising from a tangle of Allied promises to Finland and strategic commitments between themselves were harbingers of the subsequent general crisis of spring 1940.

The story of Franco-British attempts to assist the Finns subsequent to the Soviet attack of 30 November 1939, and the mori-

---

1. Brigadier E.L.Spears, quoted by Louis Gillet,*Paris-Soir*, 15 February 1940.

bund League of Nations' unwonted activity in expelling the aggressor, has been told many times.[2] The complex interplay of motivation – political, ideological, military, economic, and not least, personal – can only be hinted at here. How the Allies were brought soon after expulsion of the USSR from the League to see that they might do something for Finland is well known. With an almost inert, ruinously costly war on their hands in western Europe, they considered, first, how, under cover of aiding Finland, they could deprive Germany of its supposedly vital source of iron-ore from the mines in Sweden; second, how they might also, while arming for a great land and air battle with the enemy in 1941 (or before, should Hitler strike), move against Germany's de facto ally and so damage the USSR as to ruin its capacity to supply the German war machine. In France, though not in Great Britain, a noisy press campaign and a quieter but no less intense political campaign was mounted with a view to destroying the Soviet Union – an almost surrealistic counterpart to the government's war on domestic Communism, in progress since the signing of the Nazi-Soviet Pact.

In early February 1940, when the French had failed to get British agreement to land troops at Finland's ice-free Arctic port of Petsamo, the two governments decided to send an expedition to Marshal Mannerheim, transiting Scandinavia, subject to receiving a formal Finnish appeal. In the following month, while collecting forces for this purpose, they unsuccessfully solicited the naturally obdurate Scandinavians. The secret purpose of the allied plan, to seize the mines in the Gällivare-Kiruna region, was leaked and discussed in the European market place almost from the moment of its formulation. In the elaborate "game of blindman's buff"[3] conducted among the capitals, the dealings of all the states involved were characterized by *suppresio veri* and *suggestio falsi*. Meantime,

---

2. The following are particularly valuable: Jukka Nevakivi, *The Appeal That Was Never Made: The Allies, Scandinavia and the Finnish Winter War, 1939-40* (London 1976); Max Jakobson, *The Diplomacy of the Winter War* (London 1961); Väinö Tanner, *The Winter War* (Stanford 1957); François Bédarida, *La Stratégie secrète de la drôle de guerre: le Conseil Suprême Interallié, septembre 1939 - avril 1940* (Paris 1979), edited texts with a judicious analysis and commentary, to which should be added the excellent paper by R.A.C. Parker, and the ensuing discussion, in *Français et Britanniques dans la drôle de guerre* (Paris 1979), 561-97.

3. Jakobson, *Diplomacy*, 5.

however, such a tangle of extravagant promises was woven as finally convinced the Finns they must accept Moscow's terms, not only because they were exhausted and suffering extreme Swedish pressure to seek peace, but also lest they be swept into the war with Germany and wholly ruined. Still awaiting the Finnish appeal as their initial sailing date approached and with Scandinavian permission to transit still denied, the Allies were goaded by prime minister Edouard Daladier to try to land in Norway. At that moment, 12 March, the Finns signed the Treaty of Moscow and the Winter War suddenly ended.

The public consequences in London and Paris differed greatly.[4] Just before the signing was announced, Daladier electrified the Chamber of Deputies by giving some account of what had been done for Finland. He astounded them by saying 15,000 troops were ready to leave next day if the Finns appealed and by threatening that unless they did appeal France would not be responsible for recovery of their lost territory at the war's end. He recounted Scandinavian efforts to prevent the expedition transiting Norway and Sweden, even naming King Gustav. "It's your friends the Swedish Socialists," he flung at Léon Blum, "who have refused passage to our troops." His allusion to contacts with Scandinavian unions caused a sensation.[5] "A stupefying sitting," Marcel Déat noted. "Daladier makes madly imprudent revelations; 50,000 men ready to embark from Channel ports, reads out confidential Finnish diplomatic documents, appeals to Swedish railway workers against their government, tells about the possible pulling up of rails in the event they should try to go through without Sweden's approval, etc." As Daladier left the Chamber, apparently ready to resign, the Minister of Public Works, Anatole de Monzie, gestured that the prime minister had had too much to drink. "Daladier is alcoholic," Maurice Pelletier said in private, "– officially we put it out that he was 'tired,' [but] at the rostrum he was tight." Though the *Journal officiel* was censored, the press and diplomatic corps had been in the gallery,

---

4. On the play of French politics in general, see the careful analysis of Guy Rossi-Landi, *La Drôle de guerre* (Paris 1971); on Daladier, the recent study by Elisabeth du Réau, *Edouard Daladier* (Paris 1992).
5. 12 March 1940, *Journal officiel de la République française, Débats parlementaires, Chambre des Députés* (JOC), 507-510; 12 March 1940, ibid., *Sénat* (JOS), 222.

and some newspapers carried the scandalous passages. "For the first time," Déat observed, "the average Deputy has felt the twofold chill of defeat and internal revolution passing by."[6]

The British were horrified: "that hysterical Daladier has *fairly* spilled the beans," Sir Alexander Cadogan, Permanent Under-Secretary of State for Foreign Affairs, scribbled. "Don't know where we are."[7] But once the Russo-Finnish peace was confirmed, Neville Chamberlain dealt with the affair with some dispatch. On 19 March he faced down criticism in the House of Commons, let the Scandinavians take their lumps, and offered a summation bearing some – but not much – relation to the truth: "The plan was carefully thought out, ... the preparations were carried through without a hitch." In all, there were sharp attacks, few tears, and, after so many raging War Cabinet debates and explosive diary entries, a minimum of bitterness.[8]

In Paris, the affair had – as it had always had – other purposes, more practical uses. Five days earlier, Daladier had been mauled in the Senate; his tactic had been to demand an immediate secret session, hoping to repeat his success in the Chamber on 9 February, when the promise of the forthcoming expedition to Finland had been high. Now his critics, furious over accumulated grievances of his wartime "dictatorship," reproached him for isolating himself, for his protracted failure to remake his government, for the perceived inadequacy of Britain's war effort, for the almost public ongoing scandal of trouble in the High Command, and finally for

---

6. Marcel Déat, diary, 12 March 1940 Archives Nationales (AN) F7 15342; Jules Jeanneney, *Journal politique, septembre 1939 - juillet 1940*, Jean-Noël Jeanneney, ed. (Paris, 1972), p. 34; Georges Pernot, *Journal de guerre (1939-41)* (Paris, 1971), pp. 43-44; Pelletier quoted in Journal de Madame Decori, 15 March 1940, vol. 40, Bibliothèque Nationale NAF 14804; Murphy to Hull, 13 March 1940, National Archives, State Department (SD)121.5451/123. Raffaele Guarigilia thought Daladier safe because parliament had still less confidence in Reynaud, Herriot or Chautemps; Guarigilia to Ciano, 13 March 1940, *I Documenti Diplomatici Italiani* (Rome, 1959) 9:3, #540.

7 *The Diaries of Sir Alexander Cadogan 1938-45*, David Dilks, ed. (New York, 1972), p. 262; *The Diplomatic Diaries of Oliver Harvey 1937-40*, John Harvey, ed. (London, 1970), p. 340.

8. House of Commons, 19 March 1940, Hansard, cols. 1161-194. "He gave the impression of great obstinacy and has enhanced his reputation." Harold Nicolson, *Diaries and Letters*, 3 vols. (New York, 1966-68), II, 64.

the humiliation of the Allies in Finland's acceptance of defeat by the Soviet Union. "Twice we've given him full powers," declared Henri Laudier. "We've given him a free hand. What has been done with it?" A catalogue of failures, deficiencies, and general malaise was paraded. It was no good blaming the Swedes, said Charles Reibel; France had lost "a splendid opportunity" to engage the enemy – the unspoken message was: on a far distant battlefield. Declaring the situation far worse than in 1914, Pierre Laval recommended that diplomacy find a way out of this misbegotten war with Germany. The subliminal insinuations of Daladier's defence were not lost on his audience: the ritual applause for Britain was strikingly muted. The senators' formal vote of confidence (236 to 0, with 60 abstentions), urging more vigorous prosecution of the war, left unanswered the question he had put, "whether, yes or no, you think I have served [the country] well."[9]

In some doubt about his intentions (his cabinet colleagues, in whom he confided very little, did not know), the Chamber met in secret session over two days, 19-20 March. Caught in the bitter political conflict where aggressive pacifist *mous* confronted relatively moderate *belliciste durs*, he had done nothing to act on earlier, contradictory, demands that he reshape his ministry. A wave of ridicule and scathing charges over this new "Charleroi" rolled in, particularly from the "peace party." It was being said of any nation guaranteed by France and Britain, mocked Gaston Bergery, "that within three months this people will be wiped off the map." One after another, opponents of the war with Germany insinuated their message: the government had flinched before the USSR and was soft on Communism: Where, shouted René Dommange, were Maurice Thorez and other Communist party leaders? Their flight from France was "either incompetence or collusion." Pierre-Etienne Flandin's shaft was no less deadly for being smooth-tipped: "Our people is logical. It likes clarity, and I defy you to go before any popular audience at all, workers or peasants, to explain why on the one hand you make war on Germany, and on the other you

9. 14 March 1940, JOS, 242-45; and JOC.CS, 1-32; Jacques Bardoux, *Journal d'un témoin de la Troisième République: Paris – Bordeaux - Vichy, 1er septembre 1939 – 15 juillet 1940* (Paris, 1957), pp. 244-246; Camille Chautemps, *Cahiers secrets de l'Armistice (1939-40)* (Plon, 1963), pp. 63-64.

don't make war on Russia." Though he wrung routine applause from the *durs* by rejecting a "German peace, this so-called compromise peace," the question remained: "Well then," asked Alfred Margaine, "how does the prime minister think the war will end? For it must end, one day." Convinced that Britain had dragged them to war, deputies attacked Britain's refusal to confront Russia. All very well for Englishmen to say they were prepared for a five-year struggle, said Camille Fernand-Laurent, but France must seek "a war shortened by daring, by one of those brilliant strokes" peculiar to its genius. The Franco-British falling-out over attacking the USSR, Jean-Louis Tixier-Vignancour remarked, constituted "the drama" of the affair. The English press alone, said Ernest Pezet, showed beyond the shadow of a doubt "that Britain's lack of understanding of continental affairs was the root difficulty that has led us to where we are today."[10]

Bergery's bon mot went the rounds: "It takes genius, all the same, to have so positioned us that we can make neither war nor peace." This was the essential indictment: the prime minister had not broken the stalemate of an increasingly unpopular war.[11] It was not only the motley "peace-party" deputies, left, right and centre, who demonstrated their anger in what *Le Figaro*'s editor, Wladimir d'Ormesson, would call a "grotesque and perverted corruption of parliamentarism" where "intellectual poverty vied with incoherence." Sometime after 3:00 in the morning, by a vote of 239 to 1, with 300 abstentions ("*durs*" and "*mous*" together), the Deputies refused to sanction the past and declared their foreboding about the future. "It's the crack-up," wrote Déat.[12]

Many wanted Daladier gone; most had no clear idea how to do without him. Praised and derided in parliament and press, he was the most popular prime minister in years, entrusted with "plenary powers" and expected somehow to find a way out of the maze of domestic contradictions and "twilight war" in which the country now wandered. Worn out by the fruitless exertions of the Winter War dilemma, infuriated by Finance Minister Paul Reynaud's

10. 19 March 1940, JOC.CS, 50-91.
11. Bergery quoted by Alfred Fabre-Luce, *Journal de la France* (Paris 1940), 291; Jacques Kayser, interview, 12 June 1961.
12. Wladimir d'Ormesson, *Figaro*, 21, 23 March 1940 ; Déat, diary, 19 March 1940.

manoeuvring to take his place (backed by Blum's Socialists, whose newspaper *Le Populaire* Reynaud subventioned through his *directeur du cabinet*, Gaston Palewski), he chose to resign next day. The Chamber's vote, he wrote President Lebrun, had denied the government the authority necessary to fulfil its "wartime mission." Jules Jeanneney, president of the Senate, advised Lebrun that Daladier was finished. But since his popularity with the public was not exhausted, he could remain as head of government, *if* surrounded by an energetic small war cabinet; failing that, Reynaud should be called. Daladier finally refused to try. "His being physically weary is perfectly natural," Jacques Bardoux noted. "But he had suffered a moral collapse."[13] At 5 pm that same day, Reynaud was summoned to the Elysée.

In all this, the British had been bystanders. During the final days, amidst the wreckage of their common northern enterprise, Chamberlain was silent. He had several times made extraordinary flights to see Hitler; it did not occur to him to fly to Paris and talk with Daladier, unless in a brief formal Supreme War Council with a set agenda and, as the Councils showed, less to explore minds than to explain what was deemed right. A renewed French proposal for immediately landing in Norway with a view to forcing Germany out of what Generals Maurice Gamelin, Chef d'Etat-Major Général de la Défense Nationale, and Sir Edmund Ironside, Chief of the Imperial General Staff, among others, mistakenly thought to be its policy of "wait and see,"[14] was rejected out of hand in London as "not convincing." The Foreign Secretary, Lord Halifax, whose nerve had failed on the eve of the expedition's

13. Daladier to Lebrun, 20 March 1940 (Jean Daridan's draft), AN 496 AP Archives Edouard Daladier (AED) 3 DA 6/Dr 1; Jules Jeanneney, *Journal politique, septembre 1939 -juillet 1940*, Jean-Noël Jeanneney, ed. (Paris, 1972), pp. 37-38; Bardoux, *Journal*, 20 March, 251.

14. [Gen. Louis Koeltz], Note, 17 March 1940, [Gamelin], Note sur la Conduite de la Guerre, 16 March 1940 325 Cab/DN, [Darlan], Observations sur le projet de Note sur la Conduite de la Guerre, 16 March 1940, Service Historique de l'Armée de Terre (SHAT), 27 N 4/2, 27 N 5 (Gen. Jules Bührer, chief of staff for colonial forces, a man with strong, if imprecise, views about carrying the war to Germany, whom Gamelin kept at some distance and who had never been shown the February Plan de Guerre pour 1940, commented sharply on the draft); Paul de Villelume, *Journal d'une défaite, 23 Août 1939 -16 juin 1940* (Paris, 1976), p. 238.

scheduled departure, also dismissed French arguments against "Royal Marine," a plan to mine the Rhine and disrupt its traffic. He suggested, however, that a personal meeting might bring Daladier round; Chamberlain proposed writing a letter. A formal Supreme War Council would have to be set up. No one remarked that the last Council, 5 February, which Chamberlain had taken as a personal triumph, was so brief, ill-prepared and superficial, that it had become the source of wild confusion.[15]

Six months of war showed that much high-level interallied machinery was ignored. As late as 18 March, Gamelin's *chef de cabinet*, Col. Jean Petibon, "appeared to have forgotten that such a thing as the Chiefs of Staff Committee existed," reported Col. Harold Redman; he "certainly was not clear to whom the A[llied] M[ilitary] C[ommittee], which met in London] was responsible, individually or collectively." On the eve of war Gamelin had proposed that the AMC "should be so to speak the permanent secretariat of the Interallied High Military Committee," but no such organisation was developed. The French chiefs of staff did not always fully brief their representatives to the AMC, Gen. A. Lelong, Ad. J. Odend'hal and Col. Rozoy. At Vincennes, they dismissed the AMC as a "paper mill."[16]

This situation reflected, in great part, the unsatisfactory command machinery in France. The scandal of intrigue and feud in the High Command that winter had tongues wagging. Relations were strained when not poisoned by the cold war (between Gamelin and Gen. Alphonse Georges, commander-in-chief on the North-East front), by resentment and contempt (on the part of Admiral of the Fleet François Darlan for Gamelin), and, in the case of the Air Force, perhaps even by a sense of personal inade-

15. War Cabinet 12, 19 March, 1940 Public Record Office (PRO) WM(40)66, 72 and Confidential Annex CAB 65/6 and 12; *The Ironside Diaries 1937-40*, ed. Col. Roderick MacLeod and Denis Kelly (London 1962), 227; Corbin to Daladier, 21 March 1940, Ministère des Affaires Etrangères (MAE) 22 Papiers 1940, Londres A; Chamberlain to Hilda Chamberlain, 9 February 1940 (the correspondence was seen prior to its deposit in Birmingham University Library).

16. [R. H. Dewing], Memorandum [December 1939], PRO WO106/1701; [Redman], Representation in France of the British COS Organisation ... 18 March 1940, PRO CAB 21/1281; Gamelin to Daladier, 2 August 1939 #1,584 DN/3, Service Historique de la Marine (SHM) 1 BB2 201; Howard-Vyse Report, WO 202/2.

quacy added to personal dispute (between Gen. Joseph Vuillemin and Gen. H.E. Mouchard). Gamelin divided up the Grand Quartier Général, asserting his control of the army and air force, while leaving Darlan's command, of course, entirely independent. "He takes the G[rand] Q[quartier] G[énéral]," Georges pencilled on Gamelin's letter of notification, "and leaves me with [the responsibility]." This dispersal of "a very happy family" was deplored by the British. "However illogical the original [GQG] organisation may have been," ran a restrained secret memorandum from Gen. Sir John Swayne's mission at Georges' headquarters, "it had settled down and it was generally felt that it was not the time to break up the organisation and create difficulties of working."[17] Occasionally the ill-effects caused an interallied flap (as in the case of the uncertain dependency on Gamelin and/or Georges of General Viscount Gort, the British Expeditionary Force's commander: "I don't want to fall down between these two stools," Ironside remarked early on, though Gort said he "was careful to retain the confidence of both"). But a certain reserve characterised the British military missions' reporting on all this: they were guests, and they were in any case constantly short-circuited by initiatives taken helter-skelter at the top. At Vincennes, where Col. Olivier Poydenot charmed mission members with ribald tales and Col. Petibon guarded the secrets, Gen. Sir Richard Howard-Vyse reported, quite amazingly, hearing no criticism of Daladier's being overburdened until 15 March.[18]

The British civil-military apparatus, despite a leisurely pace and bureaucratic style, as the French were quick to charge, was infinitely better organised and more effective than the French. Despite years of parliamentary discussion, the higher direction of France's war machine was badly flawed. The Daladier-Gamelin relationship, in place since 1936, was marked by awkward periods of exasperation, school-masterly disapproval, and threats of

17. Gamelin to Georges, 6 December 1939, MS with Georges' annotation, SHAT Fonds Georges 1 K 95; Memorandum initialled by Swayne, 21 February 1940, WO 167/41.
18. Sir Edmund Ironside, privately-held diary (EID), 30 September 1939; Harvey, *Diplomatic Diaries*, p. 339; Memorandum by F.K. Roberts, 14 February 1940, PRO FO 371/24320 C2548/839/17; Howard-Vyse to DMO, 15 March 1940, WO106/1655.

resignation.[19] Gort, quoting Marshal Foch as saying "he had discovered two men – Weygand and Georges," thought "possibly Gamelin got on better with the politicians."[20] Gamelin had no elevated opinion of the political arena but, being mindful of the fate of his master, Joffre, he was careful to maintain his contacts. Experience, however, had given him a certain contempt for Daladier. "I need help," he would say when things went badly. "Really, I'm discouraged. For a whole month now I haven't been able to get him to listen to reason." In the last Winter War crisis, the general's calm vanished; on the morning of 13 March he fell into a tirade over Daladier's intervention in an appointment, spilling his anger and threats to Gen. Joseph Doumenc, the army's *Major-Général*, and to Georges: "This man is absolutely mad ... He's going to mess things up with the British .... He doesn't know what he's doing. Too much work! Where's he leading us? ... It's my duty. My resignation will rid France [of him]. I'll be doing the country a service. After all, I'm leaving a magnificent army, in first- rate condition."[21]

After more than four years Gamelin knew Daladier well and himself, of course, less well. With his eyes "glued on the North-East frontier," he was instinctively opposed to doing much but preparing for the battle there. While his principal activity during the Winter War was to buttress his control, he astonished Generals Maxime Weygand, commander-in-chief of French forces in the eastern Mediterranean, and Georges in April by telling them he wished to remove himself "to a higher level."[22] Gamelin's minister,

19. Martin Alexander, *The Republic in Danger: General Maurice Gamelin and the Politics of French Defence, 1933-40* (Cambridge, 1993) (the indispensable scholarly study of the subject); Pierre le Goyet, *Le Mystère Gamelin* (Paris, 1975) (an excellent work whose publication had regrettable consequences for the author).
20. Gort in conversation, 3 March 1940, Harvey, *Diplomatic Diaries*, p. 339.
21. Pertinax, *The Gravediggers of France* (New York, 1944), p. 36 (by a great journalist; flawed and sometimes misleading, for obvious reasons, but an irreplaceable contemporary account); Doumenc note, François Delpla, *Les Papiers secrets du Général Doumenc (1939-40)*, (Paris, 1992), pp. 153-154; Georges, diary, 13 March 1940 (he noted his own perfectly accurate disbelief) 1 K 95.
22. *Ironside Diaries*, 191; Extraits de conversations avec le Général Gamelin tirés du Journal de Marche du Général Georges ..., 10 April 1940, SHAT Fonds Gamelin 1 K 224.

impulsive and desperately in need of firm guidance, received from him neither clear recommendations nor forthright warnings. "He complains about Game[lin]'s negative attitude," Weygand noted after a talk with Daladier, 23 December. "If you had been there and I had jogged your elbow," Daladier had said to Weygand of the 19 December Supreme War Council, "you would not have hesitated, etc ..." Gamelin's papers, Daladier complained, were "impracticable, it is just sand running through your fingers. Yours have some solid structure to them ...." "I said nothing," Weygand added, " – indeed what could I have said that would not have been a charge against Gam[elin]?"[23] Silence, sulks, flaccid compliance, or lectures on the civil-military relationship – their relations had sometimes come to that. Moreover, Gamelin's discussion of the Scandinavian dilemma could run to fantasy, moving indifferently from speculation about troops in Lapland missing "their *pinard*" to RAF pilots easily bombing Moscow from Scottish and Finnish airfields – "and two days later," he said, "reversing along the same route, they would be back in Great Britain."[24] "How should poor Daladier understand anything of all this?," Gen. Émile Laure commented to Marshal Pétain. "... He's a *normalien*, who loves logic and Cartesian *clarté*, astonished to find so little of it around him." Certainly Daladier did not much care for Weygand – they had had their disputes – but he could understand what Weygand said. Gamelin baffled him. He knew how the general explained his reorganization of the High Command that winter. "What a Tartuffe Gamelin is!" he remarked to Darlan (an expression he sometimes scratched on his documents), "I should have bounced him before the war. But now? Because of the British ..."[25] Gamelin was indeed alive to the importance of the British connection as his conduct in the "Royal Marine" affair showed. Having sent Daladier a luke-

23. Weygand diary, 23 December 1939, SHAT Fonds Weygand 1 K 130, a conversation missing from his *Rappelé au service* (Paris, 1950), although a bowdlerized version, not naming Gamelin, is in his chief-of-staff's recollections, P.A. Bourget, "Une année à l'ombre de Weygand," *Revue des deux mondes*, 1 May 1965, p. 24.
24. Réunion des Commandants en Chef, 23 January 1940, SHAT 27 N 5.
25. Émile Laure to Pétain, 28 January 1940 AN AGII 3; Darlan conversation with Admiral Docteur, 13 January 1940, Amiral Docteur, *La Grand Énigme de la guerre: Darlan, amiral de la flotte* (Paris, 1949), p. 57; Daladier MS note, "Gamelin - Refonte du GQG" 4 DA 24/Dr 6/sdr d.

warm endorsement of it, he agreed in the Comité de Guerre meeting, 11 March, that the operation was not then "profitable." Upon which, he declared this outcome "lamentable – I was let down by everyone except Darlan. This meeting was a victory for Georges" – and wrote Churchill "to say again how dreadfully sorry" he was.[26]

Daladier was a difficult master to serve. The circumstances of the Winter War crisis were improvised and dramatic, France's decisions finally dependent on a foreign government, itself seeking a suitable wartime civil-military modus vivendi. Beyond the virtually inert institution of the *Comité de guerre*, no consultative organ brought government (meaning Daladier in his multiple roles, since his ministers of Air and Marine were virtual ciphers) and High Command together. Neither man, Gamelin nor Daladier, wanted it. Critically in need of an effective working relationship, they had unsatisfactory encounters, wrote documents for the record, and separately spoke their despair. Neither one had the character to confront the complications of their changing Scandinavian appreciations. They scattered misleading clues to the end: "He did not say so," Ironside noted, 21 March, "but I could see that [Gamelin] was unlikely to stay if Daladier did not stay. 'On ne peut changer de maître à mon âge.'"[27] But that is what, for their different reasons, they both did – with grievous consequences. Before many days were out Gamelin remarked to Ironside that the situation with the new prime minister was so bad that he would not tell him about it until the war was over. After April, Ironside and Gamelin never met again.

The British government – "a collection of old men without a vigorous leadership"[28] – were not closely briefed on the French defense establishment. The problem for the United Kingdom was that it was both the potential major partner and, given the burdens borne by France's civil population and huge army in the field, less than that in practice. So far as anyone could tell, the war was just

26. [Gamelin], Information du Président: Emploi des mines fluviales, n.d., 3 DA 6/Dr 3/sdr a; Réunion du Comité de Guerre, 11 March 1940, SHAT 2 N 26; Journal de marche du Général Gamelin, 11 March 1940, 1 K 224; Gamelin to Churchill 13 March 1940, PRO ADM 116/4240.
27. EID, 21 March 1940.
28. EID, 16 September 1939.

beginning. It behoved Britain, as Ironside was mindful, to be sensitive to French feelings. When the *Evening Standard* suggested something of the turmoil Gamelin had produced in the High Command that winter, the CIGS was quick to apologize for "the annoyance which such an ill-informed and mischievous statement must have caused you," and promised to get censorship "into proper working order." An ally having fewer than ten divisions in the field in France, he believed, must tread carefully. He was nevertheless dumfounded by the thirty-four page document Gamelin had sent him in late December concerning eventual operations on the North-East front. Provoked by Ironside's request for some indication of forward planning, and adopting the Deuxième Bureau's forecast of Germany's capacity to raise 300 divisions and likelihood of having 175 by spring 1940, Gamelin's "Etude" foresaw no French offensive until the spring of 1941. But it assumed Britain would by then have "some forty divisions" in France. As greatly preoccupied at that moment by the northern expedition as Gamelin was nonchalant, Ironside snapped at the warning: "No cry for support in men and materiel should jeopardize these [Scandinavian] operations … There must be no yielding to French propaganda about our not having a sufficient army in France and its effects on the people of France." "The French," Ironside told his diary, "have no intention of carrying out an offensive for years, if at all."[29] He had his reservations, but in a formal way he was sympathetic and, as Poydenot said, absolutely loyal to Gamelin; Weygand judged him, in those days, "the most intelligent" of the British chiefs of staff – ever a mark of French approval.

An ally with an impressively growing air force needed to exercise great tact in dealing with Vuillemin's nascent force. It is not clear that Air Chief Marshal Sir Cyril Newall saw this. Poydenot, arguably not the most objective witness, recalled that Newall "refused – very courteously, I may add – to admit that proposals not directly inspired by the RAF, or at least not specifically British,

---

29. Ironside to Gamelin, 3 December 1939, SHAT 27 N 16; [Gamelin], Etude sur les possibilités allemandes au printemps et les possibilités d'une reprise de l'offensive de notre part, 22 December 1939, 171 Cab/DN (General Georges' copy of the "Etude" is annotated in his characteristically lapidary manner) 27 N 3; EID, 30 December 1939 and memorandum, "Our War Strategy."

made the slightest sense." Of Newall's discourse at one meeting, Gamelin repeatedly said to Gen. Lelong, "Je ne comprends pas;" Ironside passed him a note: "ni moi non plus."[30] Certainly an ally with a navy much larger than the French Marine needed to be sensitive to the "inferiority complex" and prickliness emanating from Darlan and his staff at Maintenon ("an awful scrap," as Cadogan put it, ensued when the admiral refused a lesser decoration than those bestowed on Gamelin and Georges); this need for sensitivity perhaps escaped the First Sea Lord, Sir Dudley Pound, of whom Darlan had no great opinion (he thought of him as "le demi-kilo"). After a December 1939 visit to London, however, Darlan suggested that periodic meetings would be useful; there was no follow-up.[31] About nothing so much, in the course of the Winter War, did Darlan and Pound need to have discussion as about risking war with the USSR: "Does [Darlan] want war with Russia?" Pound asked Odend'hal, "That's the whole question. For my part, I do not."[32] It was never talked out. The naval attaché, Cmdr. Cedric Holland, blamed Darlan's staff: "They are always on the defensive and their natural and first reaction to any suggestion is a flat refusal." But Admiral Odend'hal saw that the means to overcome suspicion and find a common strategy were largely either rudimentary or nonexistent. The war was being improvised. And as *Candide* remarked, "Improvisation was no way to suffer war every twenty years."[33]

The British government was not well informed on the fragile state of the French polity, the conditions, cross-tides, and disaffections of a country threatened again by invasion – vulnerable to propaganda that Britain was not pulling its weight. Churchill believed they must raise 50 or 55 divisions in order to pre-empt perceptions that the French would pay most of the "blood tax on

---

30. Cadogan, *Diaries*, 248; Ironside to Gamelin, 3 February 1940 SHAT 27 N 5/2; Olivier Poydenot, unpublished memoirs and interview, 2 June 1982; EID, 9 November 1939.

31. Hervé Couthau-Bégarie and Claude Huan, *Darlan* (Paris, 1989), p. 163; Darlan to Pound, 24 December 1939, PRO ADM 205/4.

32. Odend'hal to Auphan, 25 January 1940, SHM II BB7 l.11.

33. [Cmdr. Cedric Holland], Notes on the Amirauté Française, n.d. [c. November 1939], ADM 199/1928; *Candide*, 13 March 1940.

land. Such an arrangement would certainly be agreeable to us," he cautioned Chamberlain at the outbreak of war; "but I do not like the idea of our having to continue the war single-handed." Two weeks later, he warned again: "When the peace offensive opens upon us, it will be necessary to sustain the French."[34] Early in the war Churchill's friend, Brigadier E.L. Spears, MP, francophile, and liaison officer in the previous war, observed "exasperation in the countryside at the fact that France and France alone appears to be bearing the main brunt ... Many French people ... argue ... that ... they have perhaps been duped and are fighting for England." It was not just the circles Spears frequented that harboured such feelings; ordinary people shared them, they turned up in the police reports. Daladier from time to time vented his displeasure: "If this goes on," he remarked in October, "I'll make peace with Hitler in a week, over the heads of the British ...." Spears, of course, was angling for a high-level mission, probably the post occupied by Howard-Vyse, but his observation held true: "there is far more going on beneath the surface than you are probably led to believe from official sources." [35]

On the other hand, direct French criticism was sometimes badly taken. Reynaud's accusation that Britain had mobilized only one in forty compared with France's one in eight annoyed people in London. In their view the war effort amounted to more than deploying troops to peel potatoes in the Maginot Line or the frozen villages and farmyards on the north-east frontier: "nothing in the way of facts," Ironside grumbled, "seems to make any difference to the French mind .... I had quite a passage of arms with [Reynaud] .... I told him that it was untrue and that I looked to him – a professional friend of England – not to repeat such obvious rot."[36] Nonetheless, the observations of Spears and Churchill – even Churchill's impassioned exhortations to act in Scandinavia – underlined the primordial fact haunting France: the bloodletting, 1914-1918, and, not

---

34. Churchill to Chamberlain, 18 September, 1 October 1939, *The Churchill War Papers*, Martin Gilbert, ed. (London, 1993), I, pp. 111-112, 188.

35. Spears to Hankey, 26 September 1939 PRO CAB63/83; Commissaire de Police to Préfet, Saint Brieuc, AD Côtes du Nord 1 M 265; Daladier in conversation with Col. de Villelume, 14 October 1939, Villelume, *Journal*, p. 65.

36. EID, 15, 17, 20 November 1939.

least, the orchestration of it into a national obsession.[37] The immensity of Britain's own losses notwithstanding, the essential difference between them was that for the French the "foreign fields" were, and seemed likely to be once again, mostly theirs.

As the intensely cold winter advanced, little turned up to raise French spirits beyond the mirage of a brave and apparently successful struggle in the snow-clad forests of Karelia. A scattering of warning signals reached London: Daladier's insistence to Chamberlain that this time France would not be ridden off its war aims of getting the Rhine frontier as "the material guarantee of French security"; his promise to the deputies that he would be "sparing of French blood above all else"; his telling Ambassador Sir Ronald Campbell, 20 February, that "Things were going from bad to worse" in the procedures of the state, "with the result that the simplest administrative actions were the subject of interminable delays." These were so many straws in the wind.[38] The Supreme War Council encounters, 19 December and 5 February, made little impress on the British; they went away much as they had arrived. They were slow to recognize the coming final crisis. Campbell – "our not very impressive ambassador," as Hugh Dalton observed somewhat unfairly[39] – was inclined to report the gathering storm almost as a personal quarrel (between Blum and Daladier, between Reynaud and Daladier), or a matter of reshuffling the cabinet and getting on with the war. London did not understand that Daladier was nearing the end of his tether, nor imagined the implications of his fall.

Halifax *had* realised that the 5 February Council was not the place to raise again a "no separate peace declaration," which he had unsuccessfully proposed earlier while rejecting the French

---

37. Cf. Sartre's dismissive comments, February 1940, on Pierre Drieu la Rochelle's *Gilles* (Paris 1939) ("The war killed France; she will not recover from it"), *The War Diaries of Jean-Paul Sartre, November 1939/March 1940*, trans. Quintin Hoare (New York, 1984), p. 174.

38. Daladier, Chamber Finance committee, 20 December 1939, quoted in Joseph Denais, "Le Parlement et les responsabilités militaires," *Revue politique et parlementaire*, 10 Oct. 1945, 38-39; Daladier, Chamber, 22 December 1939, JOC, 2315; Campbell to Halifax, 21 February 1940 no 142 Saving FO371/24308 C2812/65/17.

39. Hugh Dalton diary, 23 February 1940, Dalton Papers, London School of Economics.

condition of "positive material guarantees."⁴⁰ Some weeks later, however, the Foreign Office, dismissing Dominion doubts, sent a text to the Quai. Though Alexis Léger, the rather strange Secretary General, once more declared himself "emphatically in favour of going ahead," he knew Daladier's signature was unlikely. The Winter War disagreements were intensifying, the parliamentary "peace party" was biding its time. Hence the unusual move of Georges Mandel, Minister of Colonies, a curious man patiently awaiting his hour that never came round, who urged signature as soon as possible. "The reason he gave, couched in suitably camouflaged words," Campbell wrote Cadogan, "was that, whilst a government of which Daladier was the head ... was perfectly sound as regards no separate peace, [Mandel] would not put his hand in the fire for any other." Campbell, who mistakenly believed the antiwar people to be making no headway, seemed puzzled, but concluded it best not to sign lest in the circumstances the declaration be taken as a mark of mutual lack of confidence. He did not see that Daladier neither wished nor dared to sign such a paper. More presciently, he suggested that "expanding the declaration (which in itself is a little thing) into something of wider import," giving it "some contractual form" concerning postwar economic and military cooperation, might buck up the French.⁴¹ Campbell's germ of an idea, crossing discussions elsewhere about postwar Franco-British association, had no follow-up. In late March, Daladier's successor signed a simple declaration. The consequences proved finally pernicious.

Mandel's initiative suggested the problem: the disunited government presided over by Daladier in dubious tandem with Reynaud appeared to be central to France's stability. In November, when the wrangle over renewal of his plenary powers had again aroused the prime minister's suspicions that Reynaud, Mandel and

---

40. Daladier, 30 November 1939, JOC, 2012; 29 December 1939, JOS, 829; Lucien Lamoureux, Notes de guerre, 20 December 1939 [privately held], p. 122; SWC proceedings PRO CAB99/3; Bédarida, pp. 196-198, 221-223; Elie J. Bois, *Truth on the Tragedy of France* (London, 1941), pp. 168-172.

41. Dalton diary, 23 February 1940; Cadogan minute, 7 February, Foreign Office memorandum and text, Cadogan to Halifax 21 February FO371/24297 C2051, Campbell to Cadogan 23 February 1940 C2986/9/17.

Blum were seeking to unseat him, Mandel had told him point blank: "You are the only possible man under the circumstances."[42] For good or ill, this withdrawn, suspicious, irresolute but dictatorial man remained the key figure. "It is no exaggeration to say," Campbell commented afterwards, "that the conduct of the war, so far as France is concerned, was virtually confined to himself, General Gamelin and M. Léger with whom he had daily conferences morning and evening, to which Ministers were rarely bidden."[43] A man of Munich, breaker of strikes, and, recently, foe of the Communist party and trade unions, he was nonetheless popularly thought to be honest, "one of them." Notwithstanding his insistence on plenary powers, his distaste for explaining himself, his immobility and reluctance to share power, he retained a firm following among the Radicals. For all the country's grumbling, neither the press nor the prefectoral and police reports suggested loss of trust in his government – though Reynaud, awaiting the Chamber vote, 19 March, remarked, "That is because the country does not know him."[44] But during the Winter War Daladier had played a dangerous game, holding off parliamentary foes, *durs* and *mous*, with imprudent revelations, half-truths, and implausible promises. On 13 March, the roof of his house fell in.

The high-stakes game being played in Paris had not been generally understood in Britain, and few in high position there seemed to have any idea of the disconcerting effects on the French of their own attitudes cast in the guise of Britain's global responsibility. The world had moved on since the Ruhr crisis, but Sir Warren Fisher's approach still had a certain currency: "However intelligible the motives of the French may be," he had written Stanley Baldwin, "are we not bound to consider the world problem as a whole, and are we not in a better position to do so than France .... France is under the influence of emotion, our judgment is cooler and more detached ...."[45] Neville Chamberlain, Halifax and Cadogan sug-

42. Bois, *Truth*, pp. 160-161.
43. Campbell to Halifax, 27 March 1940 no 356 FO371/24309.
44. Conversation at André Maurois's house that evening, Maurois, *Tragedy in France* (New York, 1940), pp. 70-71.
45. Fisher to Baldwin, 12 June 1923, quoted in Eunan O'Halpin, *Head of the Civil Service: A Study of Sir Warren Fisher* (London, 1989), p. 125.

gested they thought so; Pound and Newall seemed sure of it; Ironside, more imaginative, was possibly less certain: he had, after all, come to think well of Daladier at the 5 February Supreme War Council ("If he were replaced by a little man like Paul Reynaud I should not have the same confidence in the French Cabinet"[46]).

This British approach may, in part, have been the consequence of a certain French deference in any *face à face*, no matter how sharply London's communications were received in Paris or how swiftly and often the long-suffering Ambassador Charles Corbin was returned to the charge in Whitehall. Gamelin knew how to get along with Ironside, leaving others to deliver hard truths and insinuate reproach. Chamberlain, a man of superabundant self-esteem, seems not to have suspected the deep resentment of him Daladier sometimes expressed in private. With his "hard and accurate mind," Sir Samuel Hoare commented, "[Chamberlain] was not half so good in dealing with foreigners and foreign questions. He could never understand them and they could never understand him." He had foreseen difficulty early on ("Our real trouble is much more likely to be with the French") and naturally found it.[47] Campbell would say that Chamberlain and Halifax had had "complete confidence" in Daladier. This was untrue. It was "a comfort," Chamberlain commented, with relief, after Reynaud took office, that he "speaks English fluently and perhaps he is more courageous than Daladier of whom it is said that he is 'a bull with snail's horns'. Certainly he collapsed very suddenly and unexpectedly but I fancy he had been rather undermined by the pain he had suffered in his foot after his riding accident."[48]

For his part, Daladier was no more appreciative of the ostensible equanimity with which, across the Channel, they viewed the prospects of a three to five-year war. Following the fall of Poland, he had been vulnerable to anti-British, pro-peace sentiment,

---

46. EID, 6 February 1940.
47. Chamberlain assessed in John Colville, *The Fringes of Power: Downing Street Diaries 1939-55* (London 1985), 79; Hoare to Brendan Bracken, 9 August 1940, Cambridge University Library, Templewood Papers, vol. 13, 17; Chamberlain to Ida Chamberlain, 5 November 1939.
48. Campbell to Halifax, 23 March 1940 PRO FO800/410; Chamberlain to Ida Chamberlain, 30 March 1940.

inclined to blame Chamberlain for precipitating war in 1939 ("[Daladier]'s fully capable of making peace!," Gamelin had remarked to Col. Paul de Villelume one day. "After 6 February [1934] and Munich, you can expect anything of him!"[49]). For a time, the perceived "golden opportunity" of the Winter War had masked his very real doubts. But by late March, his situation was ruined: scandalous details of the Allied northern enterprise were scattered before the world; the shadow of some immense Franco-German blood-letting hung over the nation. In his struggle to create an eccentric theatre in the "twilight war" with Germany, he had received minimal assistance from Gamelin and what seemed to him delay and opposition from Chamberlain. Daladier was probably comfortable with no foreigner as he was with Ambassador William C. Bullitt. Bullitt courted him, encouraged him, entertained him, and made him believe Franklin Roosevelt cared about him, would send him aircraft, and possibly more. Bullitt's anti-Soviet opinions were unbridled; he had "no use for Chamberlain and almost none for Churchill." Absent from Paris from 3 February to 10 April, for good or ill, he was undoubtedly missed.[50] Daladier was not hostile to the British, but he could see, hear and read: not so much their surprise (sometimes a kind of amusement, occasionally admiration) at how far this "baker's boy" had come, as their effortless projection of certainty that, all in all, they knew best. He told Léger "that what had really taken the stuffing out of him was his loss of faith in his ability ever to induce the British Government to take a prompt action or a strong line." Momentarily, at the very least, he despaired of finding a way out of the tunnel into which he had taken France. He suffered changes of mood, he clearly pondered the options. When he briefed them, 27 February, the Chamber Foreign Affairs Committee received a first "impression that he was beginning to contemplate a so-called com-

---

49. Villelume, *Journal*, pp. 41-42, 46-48, 65.
50. On Bullitt's views, Harold L. Ickes, *The Secret Diary of Harold Ickes*, 3 vols. (New York, 1954), III, p. 146; NA SD 123 Bullitt, Wm. C./593. "Daladier is still trying to find out who influenced him, notably W.C.B. Before Munich the US Government was for capitulation. Hence Munich. After Munich, reacting to public opinion, the American Government changes, and B. too. Influence in the opposite direction." Paul Reynaud, note [c. 1942] AN Papiers Reynaud 74 AP 23.

promise peace." Déat speculated that it might be the influence of the Sumner Welles mission (Roosevelt wanted "to prevent the Western Powers from coming into the war against the Russians").[51] But there was more to it than that.

The peace temptation was, of course, not peculiar to France. Less obvious in the United Kingdom, it was nevertheless observed among persons closer to power than David Lloyd George, G.B. Shaw or busybody peers of the realm. "He might be talking too much – he probably was," the Parliamentary Under-Secretary for Foreign Affairs, R.A. Butler, remarked to J.-P. Moffat, then in London as a member of the Sumner Welles' peace mission, 13 March, "but he was reaching the conviction that Germany would be sincere, but that no one in England or France at present would believe it."[52] Butler's passing thought was to wax and wane somewhat covertly in the months to come. In France, the temptation was more robust. Daladier's entourage, like his cabinet, was diverse; he was tugged by opposites. Talking with Weygand, 5 December, he had labelled Pierre Laval a "traitor." And yet, one day in the early spring, the young Radical deputy Gaston Riou, close to Jean Mistler and other *mous* conservatives in the Radical party, put out a feeler for a Daladier-Laval meeting. Though apt to refer to the prime minister as "a shit," Laval replied that his phone number was known to everyone: "Politics isn't kidding around, for God's sake. So tell your friends: have him call me!" It was not mere chance that in the Senate, 14 March, rehearsing the errors of French diplomacy since 1936 (as he felt compelled to rehearse them for the rest of his life), Laval remarked of Daladier that "except when he is in his [ministerial] seat and I am here [at the rostrum], our relations are more friendly." The two appear to have met at Guy La Chambre's house and talked of overthrowing Reynaud and securing Italian mediation to arrange peace. Laval almost certainly told Daladier that the new cabinet must be headed by Pétain. The condition was unacceptable (since the pre-

---

51. Campbell to Halifax, 23 March 1940, FO800/312/410; Déat diary, 28 February 1940; Roosevelt, quoted by Gunnar Hägglöf, *Diplomat: Memoirs of a Swedish Envoy in London – Paris – Berlin – Moscow – Washington* (London, 1972), p. 138.
52. Jay Pierpont Moffat, diary, 13 March 1940, Moffat Papers, Houghton Library, Cambridge, Mass.

vious spring, Daladier had kept the Marshal in exile as ambassador to Spain; Pétain's visiting Paris in the final days of the Winter War crisis had been one more cause of anxiety). That appears to have been the end of it. "Now that they've dragged us into one hell of a mess," Laval told a friend, "they don't know how to get themselves out of it. They'd like to cut the cost, but they haven't the guts. They see a catastrophe coming and they'd like other people to assume the liability in their place. Well, nothing doing! I don't want to take that on."[53] The episode, tentative, possibly portentous, passed into a hazy limbo of recrimination and silent denial, obscured possibly forever by the very different play of events thereafter, the closing of ranks by surviving witnesses, and an inability or unwillingness of succeeding generations to pursue this and other matters against the stern guardians of *secrets d'état*.

Whether rebuffed by Laval then or some weeks later, but certainly embittered by the winter's long struggle, Daladier was unwilling to stand down entirely. "He alerts all his Radical friends against ... Reynaud," Lucien Lamoureux noted, "to whom he nonetheless promises his support on condition that he keeps the Ministry of War." The price for permitting Reynaud to take office, it was also the measure of Daladier's refusal to let go. Successful at Finance, Reynaud had borne much of the criticism for suspending, in the name of national defence, certain Front Populaire reforms, and imposing new taxes. "He is of course a Parisian," Oliver Harvey noted, "a bourgeois and well-to-do, and not the type of French politician who easily becomes a President of the Council." He had no party, but he had Mandel on the right, Blum on the Left, a maverick army colonel at the front, the *patron* of *Paris-Soir* and Churchill. Above all, Reynaud had at least as many political foes as Daladier, and he had yet to make contact with the country. He was

---

53. SHAT 1 K 130; Jean Durtal, *Les Coulisses de la politique: une femme témoigne 1932-42* (Paris, 1966), pp. 308-309, 317; Fred Kupferman, *Laval* (Paris, 1987), p. 214, an account based on a speech by Laval, February 26, 1944; Maurice Gabolde, "Contribution à l'histoire de l'Etat Français," 32bis, AN Papiers Schweisguth 351 AP 8; Marcel Guillaume in *France during the German Occupation 1940-44*, 3 vols. (Stanford, 1957), III, p. 1083; Laval, 14 March 1940, JOC.CS, 10; Lamoureux, Notes de guerre, 22 March 1940, pp. 138-139. The timing of the meeting remains uncertain. On Pétain's movements, Agende du Col. Bonhomme, AN AGII 15.

prime minister not because he had "intrigued" and assembled a cabinet against the odds, but because Daladier yielded the Matignon. "At any rate," Daladier told Monzie, "it's better that we not leave him alone."[54]
The Reynaud-Daladier cabinet was not the Daladier-Reynaud cabinet. It was a very large mix of *durs* and *mous*: "They've tossed the salad," remarked a letter-writer to *Le Figaro*. "There are people," said one *chef de cabinet*, "that it's better to see inside the cabinet than out."[55] Its reception in the Chamber, 22 March, was marked by violent partisanship; Pierre Drieu la Rochelle thought the country "as divided as at the time of Munich." The vote (chiefly delivered by Blum and the Socialists and manipulated to produce a majority of one) led the Radical leader Albert Chichery to say to Reynaud: "The only thing left for you to do is resign."[56] Again, D'Ormesson was so disgusted by this "hysterical assembly" that, like many people of quite other persuasions, he thought it should be shut down. At that moment, Campbell attributed Reynaud's survival to Daladier's "high sense of public spirit." But shortly he was disabused by Daladier's vindictiveness in bedeviling the government and vetoing "Royal Marine": "I had thought better of him. But he is, after all, a peasant and has the peasant's faults, I suppose, as well as his qualities .... No doubt the influence of the ladies makes matters worse .... It is all very sordid and tragic."[57]
At the Foreign Office, Frank Roberts, perhaps influenced by Sir William Tyrell's opinion that Reynaud was "one of the least reliable

54. Campbell to Halifax, 11 March 1940, no 200 Saving FO371/24805 N3604/9/56; Lamoureux, Notes de guerre, 22 March 1940, 138-139; Harvey, *Diplomatic Diaries*, p. 341; Monzie, *Ci-devant* (Paris, 1941), p. 204.
55. Georges Vanier to Mackenzie King, 12 April 1940, National Archives of Canada, King Papers Mg 26 J1, vol 298.
56. JOC, 22 March 1940, pp. 596-616; Paul Reynaud, *Au Coeur de la mêlée* (Paris, 1951), p. 379; Bois, *Truth*, pp. 189-213. On the creative recording of the vote by Reynaud's friends and Chamber *boitiers*, see, *inter alia*, Louise Weiss, *Mémoires d'une européene*, 6 vols. (Paris, 1968-76), IV, pp. 146-147, Bardoux, *Journal*, pp. 252-254; Pierre Drieu la Rochelle, *Journal 1939-45* (Paris, 1992), p. 195.
57. D'Ormesson's note quoted in Jean-Louis Crémieux-Brilhac, *Les Français de l'an 40*, 2 vols. (Paris 1990), I, 251; Campbell to Halifax, 22, 23 March 1940, no 232 Saving FO371/24309 C4383, 4658/65/17; *idem*, 3, 7 April 1940, FO800/312/416, 418; Vanier to King, 12 April 1940, King Papers MG J1 vol 298.

French politicians with whom he ever had to deal," warned against taking sides. Daladier, he advised, was "much more representative of the real France, ... in the long run a much more reliable figure, and one likely to return to power." On 23 March, with a few cold words, Daladier surrendered the *présidence du conseil*, the Quai and his hold on Information and Propaganda, rather than lose everything. "The time may come," Campbell thought, "when the country will demand to hear again his familiar voice." But Daladier remained his irrresolute self, saying a few days later, "I was wrong. I ought not to have entered this government. I was tired, worn out. I allowed myself to be persuaded. Then I ought to have left it on the evening of its presentation before the Chamber. I must get out of it at the first opportunity."[58] No one gave Reynaud great odds. And though it seemed improbable, the question was, *if* Daladier returned, would it be – as he had so often warned in reference to the "peace party" – "with another policy"?; or, as Harvey hoped, "stronger and wiser"?[59]

The end of the Winter War convinced Daladier they had lost the only acceptable way through the dark woods. He had said many times that "even if the war [with Germany] went on without fighting, its prolongation would be a disaster for the country."[60] This now seemed to be the prospect before them: endless attrition, or some bloody calamity on the North-East front. Jean Picard, secretary of the Comité des Forges, a member of the French armaments mission in London, in close touch with the political right, remarked that everyone he knew blamed Britain for the Finnish imbroglio. He told Frank Roberts that without action soon, French morale would collapse. It was "essential for French internal unity," he argued, "that Germany and Russia should be associated as the enemies of the Allies." If this was not done, "then France would again be divided between Germanophil and Russophil elements

58. Campbell to Halifax, 27 March 1940, and F.K. Roberts, minute, 1 April 1940, FO371/24309 C4658/65/17; Villelume, *Journal*, p. 247; Bois, *Truth*, p. 213.

59. E.g., the warnings on one particularly frantic day: telephone call, Daladier to Corbin, 1 March 1940, 3 DA 7/Dr 4/sdr a, [Maurice Dejean], C.R. de la journée du 1er Mars 1940, MAE, Papiers Dejean, p. 5; Harvey, *Diplomatic Diaries*, p. 341; Murphy to Hull, 22 March 190, SD 851.00/1996.

60. Daladier, 14 October 1939, quoted in Villelume, *Journal*, p. 65.

with disastrous results for the Allied cause." Picard's warning elicited sympathy, impatience and disagreement. It sounded like the voice of the French "peace party". But the point was clear: the expected faltering of French morale "is the most serious aspect of the Finnish collapse." A still small British army was only just building, the French army was massively deployed "with no other result to show so far," Sir Orme Sargent noted, "except the continuing economic paralysis of the country."[61]

Others disagreed. The French, said Halifax, were "tiresome people." Having vetoed "Royal Marine" for fear of reprisal and being "desperately anxious to 'do something,'" said Ivone Kirkpatrick, the French wanted Britain to do it: "above all they want the war fought anywhere but in France." The French complaint was "unwarranted," but likely nevertheless to be "a cause of grievance for some time to come." R.A. Butler swept it aside ("M. Daladier has not impressed me with his impatience and home politics"), vaguely proposing "a great building of the Anglo-French 'Federation'." Only true believers in the Entente, like Sir Robert Vansittart, Chief Diplomatic Adviser to the government (in name only), tilted the other way: no one, he observed, "thinks we are really serious in any direction," and given the "lamentable and notorious" state of British war production, it was "hardly surprising." He believed "the French grievance is an amalgam. If they were satisfied with us in other directions ... they would be less dissatisfied with us over [Finland]. If we do not soon set our house in order in these respects, the *cumulative* grievance may become formidable .... We have now been at war for over six months and have had every opportunity to remedy [our war production]. We have failed to do so; and unless we can now do so *immediately*, a really serious situation will ensue." Few people in London saw that. Among them, however, were Ambassador Corbin and Admiral Odend'hal who had been at the centre of the Scandinavian storm. "What we must now avoid at all costs," Odend'hal wrote to the ever wary Capt. Auphan, stretching the truth to make the point, "is that the Franco-British alliance, which has worked in

---

61. F.K. Roberts, Memorandum 13 March 1940, and minutes, 13-20 March 1940, FO371/24298 C4408/9/17.

perfect harmony until this moment, should emerge diminished."[62] Perceptions, however, were formed, the damage was done, it would not be made good.

In the end, of course, it came down to this: that though Ironside, Chamberlain and others, even Cadogan, had waxed hot and cold, the British political and military establishment had finally soured on the "harebrained," possibly disastrous, Scandinavian adventure, expectations for which were so disproportionate to the means at hand.[63] French perceptions were more varied. Some six weeks earlier, Mannerheim had written Weygand, "indeed we are going to collaborate closely to defeat Bolshevist Russia." And he asked, Weygand later told René Massigli, "when I'm going to hit the Russians in the South, as he is doing in the North. I should certainly like to." That was now all over. "A final, not very brilliant page," he told René Massigli, "is being turned." Though a serving soldier, he issued a stinging general rebuke: "Never before has a peaceful people been so wronged and betrayed."[64] Cancellation of the Allied expedition, the presumed first step (dubiously sheltering under Article 16 of the League Covenant) in a strategy of indirect approach to cripple Germany and even destroy the Soviet Union, left only the grim prospect of the *"grande bagarre"* on the North-East front that Gamelin forecast for 1941. For Daladier, it meant failure of the government to pass to safety along some *via media* in a nation that thought of itself as hardly recovered from one war, while still arming for a second that had already broken out.

André Maurois had asked Reynaud "who would be the ideal man to replace Daladier?" The answer was, "Daladier as the

---

62 Halifax quoted in Harvey, *Diplomatic Diaries*, p. 345; Kirkpatrick minute on FO371/24298 C4408/9/17; Vansittart minute on N3131, minutes on 24805 N3064/9/56, 12-14 March 1940, and on 24298 C4408/9/17, 15-20 March 1940; Halifax to Campbell, 27 March 1940, FO 800/312/411; Odend'hal to Auphan, 13 March 1940, SHM II BB7.

63. On the Chiefs of Staff and the Downing Street disarray on the eve of the expedition's scheduled departure, COS(40)51 Confidential Annex PRO CAB79/85; COS(40)271(S) CAB80/105; *Ironside Diaries*, pp. 227-228; Sir John Kennedy, *The Business of War* (London, 1957), p. 48.

64. Mannerheim to Weygand, 31 January 1940, SHAT 1 K 130; Weygand to Massigli, 25 February, 21 March 1940, MAE Papiers Massigli, vol. 99; Weygand interview with *Le Journal de Genève*, quoted in *Le Temps*, 4 April 1940.

French people imagine him to be."⁶⁵ As it happened, that image had been all but destroyed, and the affair of the Winter War had irreparably weakened trust between French and British. For the Republic, a terminal period of rancour had begun; it ran from misfortune to misfortune to final disaster three months later.

---

65. Maurois, *Tragedy*, p. 65.

XI

"FIGHTING TO THE LAST FRENCHMAN"?

Reflections on the BEF Deployment to France and the Strains in the Franco-British Alliance, 1939-1940

Martin S. Alexander

"Between allies," argued Colonel Charles de Gaulle in 1938, "the only means of forming a true solidarity in time of conflict is to make them interdependent in their entire means of waging war ... to make them create an 'entente of the democracies' in the field of arms, not simply between general staff and general staff but between one government and the other."[1] Yet it has generally been said that France's military mood in the autumn of 1939 wedded strategic inactivity to a long-term confidence in the Anglo-French entente's prospects for 1940 and beyond. That mood has appeared ludicrously unwarranted in the light of the debacle that followed. France may, in Alfred Sauvy's vivid image, have crept into the new conflict with Germany like some reluctant swimmer inching into an icy sea for a mid-winter dip.[2] But it is habitually suggested that with Hitler's anticipated attack in the west failing to materialize after the conquest of Poland, France found it easier than expected

---

1. De Gaulle, letter to Paul Reynaud, 12 Jan. 1938, in E. Demey, *Paul Reynaud, mon père* (Paris, 1980), pp. 317-318.
2. See A. Sauvy, *De Paul Reynaud à Charles de Gaulle. Scènes, tableaux et souvenirs* (Paris, 1972), p. 97.

to adjust to the water temperature of war. So, it is asserted, France was deceived by the passivity of the phoney war and lulled into complacency about her military strength and moral resilience.³ This article re-examines some elements in the entente's condition during the last months of 1939. Convention casts this relationship like a semi-comic Laurel and Hardy mismatch – cocksure Frenchmen waddling nonchalantly toward a campaign they would lose catastrophically, cheerily counting their divisions and beaming smugly at their Maginot Line, with the British tagging along sad-mouthed, occasionally venturing an unheeded plea for caution. But this depiction now looks as dated as the black and white celluloid comedies from Hollywood or Pinewood, the melodramas such as "*Double Crime sur la Ligne Maginot*," or the newsreel clips of George Formby and Flanagan and Allen which entertained cinema-goers during 1939. A more complex, more nuanced, series of pictures, of impressions, spring from the archives of the French parliamentary defense commissions and service ministries and from private military papers which include the headquarters diary, for the phoney war, of General Maurice Gamelin, chief of the French national defense staff and supreme commander of the Allied land forces.

Sources such as these reveal a deep disquiet that pervaded the world of the French service professionals. For the military leaders in Paris were worrying constantly about the threat accepted by the entente in standing by Poland in September 1939 as Hitler's *blitzkrieg* finally rolled eastward. A new "authorised version" in the interpretation of war preparations and foreign policy in the late 1930s stresses France's essential need of a firm British alliance before she could challenge Third Reich expansion. The historiography embraces work by Robert Young and Anthony Adamthwaite as well as that by J.-B. Duroselle and François Bédarida. Perhaps the hand of an "English Governess" may have guided the making of the Franco-British coalition. However, the present article argues that a distinctively Gallic grip reasserted itself once the diplomats with-

---

3. On the condition of French opinion see J.-L. Crémieux-Brilhac, *Les Français de l'an 40*, 2 vols. (Paris, 1990). Cf. J.-B. Duroselle, *Politique étrangère de la France, 1871-1969: L'Abîme, 1939-45* (Paris, 1982), pp. 17-129.

drew and left the warriors center stage. The French, after 3 September 1939, assumed the leading role in the direction of Allied strategy in the west and in shaping the British part within it.[4]

Since the Anglo-French staff talks of March and April 1936, prompted by Hitler's remilitarisation of the Rhineland, French leaders had sought close British support against Germany. Though a part of the revived coordination arose from a wish to strengthen the hand of French diplomacy, French policy-makers also had specific strategic grounds for moving closer towards a military combination with the British. British resources, added to the French order of battle, would increase the solidarity of western defenses in general and those of France in particular. The authorities in Paris perceived specific and selfish benefits to their military position from a British military effort, especially on land. What is less familiar is the precise character, the technical composition, of the defensive contribution France sought from Britain.[5] Less familiar is the degree to which the BEF that was built up in France in 1939-1940 fell short of French aspirations. Less familiar, also, is the impact of the gulf between aspirations and achievement on French morale and Allied strategic thought.

Leaving aside the navies (where Allied preponderance offered justifiable reassurance so long as Germany was the only foe), French planners had always envisioned a distinctive British contribution to security in the west. UK participation was envisaged in the air as well as by deployments on land. In the former arena, warfare's new dimension since 1914, successive French ministers for war and air had, since 1935-1936, laboured to reduce the strategic vulnerability of Paris. Worryingly near Luftwaffe bomber bases in the Rhineland, moving ever closer as aircraft ranges and payloads increased, the French capital's weakness was an unalterable outcome of geog-

---

4. Cf. F. Bédarida, "La gouvernante anglaise," in R. Rémond and J. Bourdin, eds., *Edouard Daladier, Chef de Gouvernement* (Paris, 1977), pp. 228-240; R. J. Young, *In Command of France: French Foreign Policy and Military Planning, 1933-39* (Cambridge, MA, 1978); A. P. Adamthwaite, *France and the Coming of the Second World War* (London, 1977); J.-B. Duroselle, *Politique étrangère de la France, 1871-1969: La Décadence, 1932-39* (Paris, 1979).

5. See, however, M.S. Alexander, *The Republic in Danger: General Maurice Gamelin and the Politics of French Defence, 1933-40* (Cambridge, 1992), pp. 236-278.

raphy. Security specialists had to wrestle with the problem, as Paul Reynaud put it to the Chamber of Deputies in 1937, that "Our capital, alas, is not at Bourges nor Clermont Ferrand."[6]

Action, however, was taken in the 1930s to reduce the potentially calamitous concentration around Paris of armaments' manufacture, aviation plants, metallurgy, tank and truck assembly. At the behest of Pierre Cot, air minister in 1936-1938, Bordeaux, Marseille and particularly Toulouse became the chief production centers of French aviation. But Paris remained terribly exposed behind an air defense system, the *Défense Aérienne du Territoire*, which never achieved a high priority in the 1936-1939 rearmament programmes. Blackout and civil defense provision scarcely existed except on paper. The capital remained in 1939-1940 the most important part of the industrial base that supplied and armed the French ground forces. Decentralised production of land armaments had hardly begun in September 1939. Indeed an armaments' ministry was only formed on 13 September by the appointment of the former head of the *Chemins de Fer de L'Etat*, Raoul Dautry.[7]

From an early juncture this air defense issue caused strains between the French and the British. The latter refused even to discuss France's vulnerability from the air. In every planning paper and joint staff meeting, the British assumed that they alone – and usually London – would be the Luftwaffe's target. It has become axiomatic to acknowledge that in the 1930s a "shadow of the bomber" hung like a pall over British forecasts of the character of a new war. What has not been sufficiently underlined is that they failed to entertain any possibility that the Luftwaffe's main attacks might fall on Paris or at least generally on targets in France.

Rather, the British thought their contribution sufficient if they located on airfields near Laon and Rheims an Advanced Air Strik-

6. République Française: Chambre des Députés, *Journal Officiel: Débats*, 27 Jan. 1937, p. 169.

7. On French air programmes see P. Cot, *Triumph of Treason*, trans. Sybil and Morton Crane (New York, 1944); J.-H. Jauneaud, *J'accuse le Maréchal Pétain* (Paris, 1977); H. Chapman, *State Capitalism and Working-Class Radicalism in the French Aircraft Industry* (Berkeley, 1991), pp. 101-174. On Dautry and the creation of an armaments' ministry: M. Avril, *Raoul Dautry, 1880-1951. La Passion de servir* (Paris, 1993), pp. 111-145; R. Baudoui, *Raoul Dautry, 1880-1951. Le Technocrate de la République* (Paris, 1992), pp. 183-217; Crémieux-Brilhac, *Les Français de l'an 40*, vol. II, pp. 106-109, 113-114.

ing Force of ten RAF bomber squadrons in 1939-1940.[8] These aircraft were, however, deployed to raid targets inside Germany and were under a Royal Air Force command independent even of Lord Gort, the BEF commander. Of no more use to French air security was the BEF aviation component, eventually four fighter squadrons, five cooperation squadrons and four bomber squadrons. These were small numbers and understandably dedicated to protect and support tactically the BEF's ground units. Even for fighter cover over the disembarkation and supply ports reserved to British forces, from Cherbourg round Brittany to Nantes, France had to bully and beg before she secured RAF participation. Henry Pownall, BEF chief of staff, sympathised in his diary as early as September 1939 with French dissatisfaction:

> It is clear even now, from the operations in Poland, that we must have air support to an extent not catered for at present – and we must have operational control over that force – the present AASF arrangements are no good to us and we want a greatly expanded Air Contingent under our orders [...] I am just as puzzled as the French ... at our arrangements. It all comes from allowing the Air Force to have too free a hand ... But there must be centralized *operational* control by the Army. Of that there's no manner of doubt. We have swung ... in the other direction by allowing the Army to be the underdog and allowing the bright theorists of the Air Force too large a say.[9]

At bottom, Whitehall was obsessed with a vision of the onset of war that came straight from H. G. Wells. In the minds of the Chamberlain government and its officials, the shape of things to come admitted only the flattening of industries and cities – and *only British* ones at that. Here lie the origins of the bitterest and longest-lived of 1940's sad controversies, that over Winston Churchill's and Air Marshal Dowding's rebuff of Reynaud's pleas to throw RAF Fighter Command wholesale into the battle for France. Contemporary military men saw a glimpse of the acrimony ahead. "The

---

8. P. Fridenson and J. Lecuir, *La France et la Grande-Bretagne face aux problèmes aériens, 1935-39* (Vincennes, 1976). For British preoccupation with bombing of the UK, cf. U. Bialer, *The Shadow of the Bomber: The Fear of Air Attack and British Politics, 1932-39* (Woodbridge, 1980).

9. Entries for 20 Sept. and 30 Sept. 1939 in B.J. Bond, ed., *Chief of Staff. The Diaries of Lieutenant-General Sir Henry Pownall*, 2 vols. (London, 1972), vol. I, pp. 237, 241.

struggle as to what air forces should be maintained in this country and what in France," noted Pownall in mid-October 1939, "is going to be one of our major and perpetual difficulties all through the war ...."[10] General Albert Lelong, military attaché and chief of France's military mission in London during the phoney war, likewise identified air defense of the UK as a British preoccupation liable to split asunder the coalition's political and strategic unity. For the British choice struck at the root of France's interest in unequivocally committing *all* Anglo-French resources to defense on and in the skies above continental western Europe. But the September 1938 crisis above all had focused London's attention on its own vulnerability.[11] Thus, Lelong warned Gamelin and prime minister Edouard Daladier (also French defense minister), Britain looked "resolutely determined not to divert one single fighter plane from this principal mission of the defense of the British isles." Gamelin's ground forces were absolutely relied upon. "The French army, they think here, resting on the Maginot Line, should be able to hold its positions ... indefinitely." The perils in such a chasm of incomprehension were underlined by the Superior Council of National Defense late in 1938: "the policy which tends to affirm this purely defensive configuration to British rearmament is a menace because it restricts the support which we French will get from the RAF."[12]

French planners understandably deplored that rearmament priority was accorded to equipment and tactics destined never to leave British shores or air space. From first to last the British favoured a sword and buckler rather than a chainmail approach to

10. Bond, *Chief of Staff*, I, p. 244 (12 Oct. 1939). Cf. the similarly jaundiced view of the RAF held by another senior British soldier of the phoney war, the Chief of the Imperial General Staff, General Sir Edmund Ironside: R. Macleod and D. Kelly, eds., *The Ironside Diaries, 1937-40* (London, 1962), pp. 120-122, 140-147, 155-156, 158-159.
11. Cf. R.J. Minney, *The Private Papers of Hore-Belisha* (London, 1960), pp. 149-154; J.R. Colville, *Man of Valour: The Life of Field Marshal the Viscount Gort* (London, 1972), pp. 110-116; K. Feiling, *The Life of Neville Chamberlain* (London, 1947), p. 371ff.
12. Lelong: "Etude sur la participation de l'Angleterre dans l'éventualité d'une action commune franco-britannique en cas de guerre," 8 Nov. 1938, Archives Edouard Daladier, 4 DA 8, Dr. 3, sub-dr. b, Fondation Nationale des Sciences Politiques, Paris; CSDN Secretariat to Daladier, No. CU/1, 22 Nov. 1938, Cabinet du Ministre, Carton 5N 579, Dr. 2, Service Historique de L'Armée de Terre (hereafter SHAT), Vincennes. Cf. Young, *In Command of France*, pp. 218-219.

the alliance's security. Thus the partnership resembled a medieval warrior whose stabbing weapon was the British forces, especially her aviation, whilst France provided the protective shield to deflect or blunt the adversary's blows. Conceived in this fashion there was little doubt where the British authorities believed the warrior's heart and vital organs lay. The French strove to merge two military efforts, to render the defense of France indissolubly co-terminous with the defense of the coalition. But Britain retained a lurking if – until June 1940 – unspoken conviction that in the last resort her prosecution of the war could be dissociated from the alliance's fate on the mainland. This was well expressed by George Davy, in 1939-1940 a colonel serving at Nogent-sur-Marne in the British liaison mission attached to Gamelin's headquarters. "The French thought," according to Davy, "we ought to send more fighter squadrons to France; the British knew our shortage of fighters and did not dare to put all their eggs in the French basket when there might possibly be a need to defend England."[13] For the British the shield might shatter and need discarding; but they supposed that in "a certain eventuality" the warrior could duck the killer blow, retreat, and fight on with his own (British) limbs and at least some of his weapons intact.[14]

Gamelin, for his part, had proclaimed since December 1938 the urgency of a "considerable effort" on the ground, as well as in the air, to redress German military advantages. An "important British reinforcement" on land was required beyond the two divisions and ten RAF squadrons mentioned in Franco-British conversations in late 1938. Gamelin's reasoning rested on his post-Munich reassess-

---

13. Brig. G. Davy, Unpublished Memoirs, p. 1208 (consulted by kind permission of the late Brig. Davy). Cf. B.J. Bond, *Britain, France and Belgium, 1939-40* (Oxford, 1990), pp. 168-171.

14. See P.M.H. Bell, *A Certain Eventuality: Britain and the Fall of France in 1940* (Farnborough, 1974). Cf. E.M. Gates, *End of the Affair: The Collapse of the Anglo-French Alliance, 1939-40* (London, 1981), pp. 8-17, 61-68, 80-142; M. Gilbert, *Winston S. Churchill*, vol. VI, *Finest Hour, 1939-41* (London, 1983), pp. 194-196, 378-600; D. Dilks, "The Twilight War and the Fall of France: Chamberlain and Churchill in 1940," *Transactions of the Royal Historical Society*, 5th ser., 28 (1978): 61-86; D.W.J. Johnson, "Britain and France in 1940," idem, 22 (1972): 141-157; J.C. Cairns, "Great Britain and the Fall of France: A study in Allied disunity," *Journal of Modern History* 27 (1955): 365-409.

ment of the stakes for the western democracies. These were no less than "whether France wishes to remain a great power, indeed whether or not she wants to succumb sooner or later to the Nazi yoke." He did not doubt that responding militarily to this challenge was essential but would engage France in an "extended war of attrition on which will hinge the whole world's fate."[15] Hence Gamelin played his part in overcoming any hesitation in September 1939 about France committing herself to war over Poland. Britain had guaranteed Poland and so Hitler's attack combined the commitment of the UK to war with the obligation of Germany to fight simultaneously on two fronts. As Gamelin told Gort in July 1939, "we have every interest in the conflict beginning in the east and only generalising little by little. This way we shall enjoy the time we need to mobilise the totality of Franco-British forces."[16] Unaware of the secret protocol in the 23 August Molotov-Ribbentrop Pact, allowing Soviet invasion of eastern Poland, Gamelin judged the Poles able to survive attack for four to six months.[17]

Instead, Gamelin saw two sorts of danger – either one of which could undermine his grand strategy for a long haul to victory through the Franco-British empires' superior resources. First, in late 1939 Britain seemed inadequately alert to Gallic suspicion that she sought to fight on land to the last Frenchman. Second, Gamelin's own political superiors betrayed complacency which the soldiers seemed powerless to eradicate. They supposed the French army proof against all comers, and they deluded themselves that the war might be successfully prosecuted by economic stranglehold of Germany without bloody fighting.

The first of these hazards, the complacent British attitude, arose mainly because the UK had achieved so much more militarily in late 1939 than she thought possible only a year before. Consequently, some British ministers became intoxicated by their own success. This was most true of the secretary of state for war, Leslie

15. Gamelin to Daladier, No. 5494/S, 3 Dec. 1938 and No. 5705, 19 Dec. 1938, reproduced in M.-G. Gamelin, *Servir* 3 vols. (Paris, 1946-47), vol. I: *Les Armées françaises de 1940*, pp. 133-136.

16 "Conversations militaires franco-britanniques: résumé des conversations du 13 juillet 1939," Conseil Supérieur de la Défense Nationale, Carton CSDN/136, SHAT.

17. See Alexander, *The Republic in Danger*, pp. 311, 314-318.

Hore-Belisha. An authentic francophile, Hore-Belisha was handicapped by his superficial military knowledge (much of it acquired in 1937-1938 through informal tutorials from Liddell Hart).[18] Being strategically gauche, he persuaded himself to accept the misleading equation of numbers with strength. Being ambitious and publicity-conscious, he contributed to military policy after Germany's Prague coup of March 1939 by announcing the doubling of the Territorial Army, despite a dearth of equipment and instructors, to generate a British land force of thirty-two divisions. Intending these formations for service on the continent, he strove to obtain maximum political advantage for his personal standing from such beguiling statistical sleights-of-hand.[19]

Hore-Belisha's greater concern for political showmanship than strategic calculation alarmed the French. Charles Corbin, the highly experienced ambassador in London, recommended to Daladier from January 1939 that he remind the British ceaselessly about "the inequality of sacrifice to which our two populations would have to consent in time of war."[20] Markedly divergent objectives on the part of the British and French characterised the staff talks over BEF deployment in France as these progressed in four phases between late March and late August 1939. The British sought to concentrate on planning for the middle and distant future, to do with creating, training and deploying the later echelons of the big "Belisha army." Gamelin, in contrast, had a pressing short-term agenda. He placed greatest importance on expediting the arrival in France of the limited forces actually available in 1939: five regular divisions and the first four divisions of Territori-

18. See B.J. Bond, "Leslie Hore-Belisha at the War Office," in I.F.W. Beckett and J. Gooch, eds., *Politicians and Defence: Studies in the Formulation of British Defence Policy* (Manchester, 1981), pp. 110-131; and the same author's *Liddell Hart: A Study of His Military Thought* (London, 1977), pp. 91-106, 110-112.

19. Cabinet Conclusions, 16 (39), 30 March 1939, CAB 23/98, Public Record Office, Kew, London. Cf. P. J. Dennis, *Decision by Default: Peacetime Conscription and British Defence, 1919-39* (London, 1972), p. 188ff; B.J. Bond, *British Military Policy between the Wars* (Oxford, 1980), pp. 303-311. For contemporary displays of irritation within the General Staff at Belisha's manner, cf. Bond, *Chief of Staff*, I, p. 123ff; Macleod and Kelly, *Ironside Diaries*, pp. 105, 160-168.

20. Corbin to Daladier, 26 Jan. 1939, in Etat-Major de L'Armée: 2e Bureau – Grande-Bretagne, Carton 7N 2816, SHAT.

als. Gort, chief of the imperial general staff before his assumption of BEF command at war's outset, shared the French general's concern for speedier support with what Britain had to hand. However, Hore-Belisha was less concerned to do some practical good for Gort and the BEF field commanders than he was with calculating the political good for his ministerial career if he fathered a khaki-clad legion reminiscent of Kitchener's New Armies.

Winston Churchill also had an unhealthy obsession with raw numbers. Taking satisfaction from their new burden-sharing in French defense, he felt virtuous at the prospect of being able – though not until at least 1941 – to put a mass force into the field alongside the ally. "Thank God we've [now] got conscription or we wouldn't be able to look these people in the face" remarked Churchill at the 14 July 1939 Bastille Day parade in Paris.[21] British politicians appear to have been less exercised by the military utility of their plans than by the search for a flourish with which to ease consciences still troubled by the failure of appeasement.

In late September Churchill, restored to office as First Lord of the Admiralty, conceded in a chilling phrase to Corbin that "the English, too, will have to pay their tax in blood." Yet, although Churchill agreed to fight in cabinet to increase Britain's land contribution, he discounted any German attack westward that autumn. He too, like British ministers since Baldwin, judged more likely massive Luftwaffe raids on UK war industries and cities and even spoke of diverting Allied military equipment to the Balkans to shore up an anti-German front. Corbin with some dismay evident in his tone, concluded that:

> Churchill is the most open-minded and imaginative of British ministers ... but even he has trouble grasping that however effective the blockade, the war's final decision will always depend on armies on the ground ... and I need hardly add that Churchill's colleagues are even more inclined to relegate land operations to a secondary importance, relying on the Maginot Line's impregnable solidarity. The British gov-

21. Recorded by Pownall (see Bond, *Chief of Staff*, I, p. 213, diary entry of 10 July 1939). Cf. Churchill's later contention that "[Britain's] introduction of conscription ... did not give us an army ... It was, however, a symbolic gesture of the utmost consequence to France and Poland." W.S. Churchill, *The Second World War: The Gathering Storm* (London, 1948), pp. 318-319.

ernment's attitude will change only once hundreds of thousands of their men have crossed the Channel to fight in the front line and once it has clearly understood that it is on our frontiers that Britain's forward defences are located.[22]

From May 1939 Lelong was able to convey to Gamelin news of larger and faster British deployments, projected under the so-called "18 month plan" of Territorial expansion.[23] Altogether more pertinent to Gamelin's concerns, however, was the transport of the first and second echelons of the BEF. On this count, seaport facilities, railway track allocations and assembly accommodation had been meticulously prepared in the winter-spring-summer of 1938-39. These projected a BEF readiness timetable in forward areas in France for the first echelon (two divisions) after thirty-two days, followed by the second pair of divisions after fifty-four days. This schedule held out the prospect of earlier availability of British strength – but no increase in its total amount. Nor did it offer the first four supporting Territorial Army divisions until six months after mobilisation.[24] The implicit result was that the BEF could not afford to sustain heavy attrition and still remain in the defensive line. What would later enter the lexicon of strategic analysts as "sustainability" was startlingly lacking.

Furthermore, what Gamelin wanted above all since 1937 and since the appearance of industrial logjams impeding French mechanised-force expansion were British armoured divisions. Two of these divisions were projected, but the first was unusable for the

22. Corbin to Daladier: report on a conversation with Churchill, 25 Sept. 1939, in Fonds Gamelin, 1K 224, Carton 7, Dr. 1, SHAT. Neither Churchill's memoirs nor Gilbert's biography mentions this meeting.
23. Ministère de la Défense nationale et de la Guerre – Cabinet: "Note sur les conversations d'Etats-major franco-britanniques," 8 May 1939, Cabinet du Ministre, Carton 5N 579, SHAT. Cf. Lelong's two reports to Gamelin on the Anglo-French Staff Talks: No. 1, 5 April 1939 (First Phase: London, 29 March-4 April 1939); No. 2, 5 May 1939 (Second Phase, London, 24 April-4 May 1939), in EMA: 2e Bureau – Grande-Bretagne, Carton 7N 2816, SHAT.
24. Author's interview with Major-General L.A. Hawes, Petersfield, Hampshire, 19 July 1979. Cf. Hawes's account of his work: "The Story of the 'W' Plan – the Move of our Forces to France in 1939," *The Army Quarterly* (1971): 445-456; B. Fergusson, *The Business of War: The War Narrative of Major-General Sir John Kennedy* (London, 1957), pp. 5-9; Bond, *Chief of Staff*, I, pp. 171-172, 204-205.

opening eight or nine months of war and the second for at least fifteen months, owing to utterly insufficient British output of armoured vehicles.[25] Yet Gamelin's weakest area on the ground was the paucity of mechanised-manoeuvre divisions to serve as the Allied counterattack reserve.

More encouragingly, from May 1939, the Anglo-French army staffs were cooperating to good effect. General Sir John Dill, BEF First Corps commander-designate, along with Pownall, visited the future British deployment zone around Maubeuge and Cassell. Dill "got on well" with General Georges Blanchard, commander-designate of the neighbouring French First Army, leading Pownall to reckon it "a very useful trip." Gort then started giving Lelong confidential details on progress towards strengthening UK land forces and hastening their availability.[26] By war's outbreak the British had acquiesced in the role for the BEF in Flanders earmarked for it by Gamelin. Its nonmechanised character had, however, militated against Gamelin's prewar scheme to hold it back to constitute the Franco-British strategic reserve.[27] A rumoured German descent on Holland in January 1939 had convinced the government in London that the Low Countries were essential for British as well as French security. Because of the fears this scare aroused, the French had extracted Chamberlain's commitment to staff talks.[28] These

25. See Chiefs of Staff Paper No. 821: "The modification of the Army programme," 9 Jan. 1939, CAB 21/510, PRO. Cf. Macleod and Kelly, *Ironside Diaries*, pp. 134-5 (entry of 24 Oct. 1939 in which Ironside reflected: "It is all very well ordering the equipment ... it is a matter of getting it. We have to withstand an attack in the spring with what we have got ... You can only make war with actual trained divisions.")

26. Bond, *Chief of Staff*, I, pp. 204-205. Cf. Colville, *Man of Valour*, pp. 125-128; Lelong to Gamelin, 14 April, 11 May 1939 and Lelong to 2e Bureau, 18 April 1939, in EMA: 2e Bureau – Grande-Bretagne, Carton 7N 2816, SHAT; COS "Report on measures to accelerate despatch of the Field Force to the Continent," 17 Feb. 1939, CAB 21/511, PRO.

27. See Bond, *Chief of Staff*, I, pp. 206-208, 211-213.

28 See M.S. Alexander, "Les réactions à la menace stratégique allemande en Europe occidentale: la Grande-Bretagne, la Belgique et le 'cas Hollande', décembre 1938-février 1939," in *Cahiers d'histoire de la Seconde Guerre Mondiale*, no. 7, April 1982 (Brussels: Centre de Recherches et d'Etudes Historiques sur la Seconde Guerre Mondiale), pp. 5-38. Cf. D.C. Watt, *How War Came. The Immediate Origins of the Second World War, 1938-39* (New York, 1989), pp. 99-107; C.M. Andrew, *Secret Service: The Making of the British Intelligence Community* (London, 1985), pp. 412-419.

gradually spawned an alliance which, in the perspective of the long attritional haul, was developing promisingly by late 1939.[29]

Yet, if the Allies knew what their *grand strategy* involved – tightening the screw of economic blockade and deferring major military offensives till 1942-1943 – they did little detailed planning of operational strategy for the Franco-Belgian theatre. The British contribution to decisions was minimal. In part this was because Britain's diminutive military contribution in France left Gort deferential towards Gamelin and Georges – and arguably too embarrassed by the BEF's smallness to question French capabilities or plans. In Davy's words, the French "of all ranks enjoyed a superiority complex ... towards their British opposite numbers." The BEF's officers were commonly treated "as learners in the military arts."[30] But more than this, the British – and especially Gort – were reluctant to go beyond coordinating assembly, movement and concentration. The BEF staff retained an old War Office fear, discernible since at least 1936, of being sucked into irrevocable participation in French manoeuvres that British officers had not helped to determine and that they, as markedly the "junior partner," would be unable to modify.[31]

Once the BEF was in France, its autonomy was, in practice, severely limited. Its concentration area was settled in July 1939. Gort agreed that "British forces operating in France will be placed under the order of the general ... commanding the north-east theatre"

---

29. Cf. R. Frank, *La Hantise du déclin. La France, 1920-60: finances, défense et identité nationale* (Paris, 1994), pp. 193-195; Duroselle, *L'Abime*, pp. 31-32, 61-67, 94-98, 126-129; M. Gowing, "Anglo-French Economic Collaboration up to the Outbreak of the Second World War" and P. Le Goyet, "Les relations économiques franco-britanniques à la veille de la 2e guerre mondiale," both in *Les Relations franco-britanniques, 1935-39* (Paris, 1975), pp. 179-188, 189-200 respectively; also L.S. Pressnell, "Les finances de guerre britanniques et la coopération économique franco-britannique en 1939 et en 1940," in *Français et Britanniques dans la drôle de guerre* (Paris, 1979), pp. 489-516.

30. Brig. G. Davy, Unpublished Memoirs, p. 1209. This point was confirmed by remarks to the present author by Lieutenant-General Sir Harold Redman (Colonel and GSO 1, Number One British Military Mission, Nogent-sur-Marne, France, 1939-40), interview at Lulworth, Dorset, 24 Aug. 1983.

31. See War Office: "Memorandum on the despatch of a Field Force to the continent in the event of war with Germany," July 1936, esp. paragraphs 284-287, CAB 64/22, PRO.

(General Alphonse Georges).³² French suggestions that the BEF First Corps concentrate at St. Pol, between Arras and Boulogne, were rejected on grounds that this was too advanced and too exposed. Instead, the whole BEF was to concentrate around Picquigny, west of Amiens. As precise an operational role as possible in peacetime was identified, considering neutral Belgium's refusal of staff talks. The BEF would link with the Belgians if the latter were attacked by Germany. More probably it would fill a contingent mission, either covering the French First Army's left or remaining in Picardy as the Allied northern reserve. "The dispositions," admitted Gamelin, "will depend on the prevailing situation." Pownall's diary recorded British support for this, noting that "amateur strategists will proclaim that it is 'unimaginative' ... but our interests so demand the safety of the Channel ports that it is right ..."³³

On 8 August 1939 Sir John Kennedy told Lelong of British cabinet approval for subordination of the BEF to French command. Nonetheless, the British commander, before executing French orders which he judged to "imperil" the BEF, explicitly retained an emergency right of appeal. General Sir Edmund Ironside, who became Inspector-General of the Forces and Chief of the Imperial General Staff after Gort took the BEF to France, immediately noted a dangerous vagueness: "I at once asked [Belisha] ... to whom the British C. in C. could 'appeal'? – to the Cabinet, the Prime Minister, the War Office or what? Belisha said he didn't know ...." Here lay another source of ambiguity which would contribute to accusations of *sauve qui peut* in May 1940 and send the Allies their separate ways amidst bitter recriminations when their defenses disintegrated under the impact of the Wehrmacht's *blitzkrieg*.³⁴

  32. "Conversations militaires franco-britanniques du 13 juillet 1939," CSDN Carton 136, SHAT.
  33. Bond, *Chief of Staff*, I, pp. 211-213 (diary entry of 10 July 1939). Cf. Colville, *Man of Valour*, pp. 129-130; Macleod and Kelly, *Ironside Diaries*, pp. 79-80, 84-87.
  34. See Lelong to Gamelin, 9 Aug. 1939, EMA: 2e Bureau – Grande-Bretagne, Carton 7N 2817, SHAT; also Macleod and Kelly, *Ironside Diaries*, p. 77. On the rupture between the French and British after the Dunkirk evacuation of the BEF in June 1940, the extensive literature may perhaps best be approached through Gates, *End of the Affair*, pp. 80-168; J.C. Cairns, "A Nation of Shopkeepers in Search of a Suitable France, 1919-40," *American Historical Review* 79 (1974): 710-743; and Bell, *A Certain Eventuality*, passim.

In retrospect, what remains remarkable is the very uneven level of development of different parts of the Anglo-French effort at alliance coordination. On the encouraging side of the ledger or *bilan*, useful military liaison at several levels was working smoothly even before the war broke out. Both staffs succeeded in ensuring that wireless signal communication was much more secure than in 1914. Meanwhile, at the summit of strategic war policy-making an interallied Supreme War Council was constituted. This convened nine times during the phoney war, bringing together the French and British war cabinets and military chiefs. Permanent linkage between the two military administrations led to a mutual secondment of staff officers sanctioned by Daladier on 11 July 1939.[35] It was also agreed that British and French missions would join the reciprocal higher commands:

> Much of our time is taken up in "liaising" with French officers [Pownall recorded in his diary on 25 October 1939] … but I'm sure it's worth doing. The "moral front" is going to be vastly important in this war … In a small way good liaison here will help to that end. A bit more of that sort of thing on the part of GHQ in the last war would have smoothed over the difficulties which then cropped up. French and Haig were pretty bad at making contacts and friends – Gort is very good at it.[36]

On the other hand, joint operational planning hardly existed. By 18 September 1939 British troops and equipment were moving forward with near-clockwork precision, crowding their trains and billets from St Nazaire to Le Mans. This was the fruit garnered as a result of the efficient staff work of Hawes' GS (Plans) section

---

35. Daladier (Cabinet militaire du Ministre de la Défense nationale et de la Guerre): Note of 10 July 1939, Cabinet du Ministre, Carton 5N 579, SHAT. Cf. Lord Ismay, *The Memoirs of General the Lord Ismay* (London, 1960), pp. 87, 101-103. The Supreme War Council's records have been published, with commentary, in F. Bédarida, *La Stratégie secrète de la drôle de guerre: Le Conseil Suprême Interallié, septembre 1939-avril 1940* (Paris, 1979). Informative, too, are D. Dilks, ed., *The Diaries of Sir Alexander Cadogan, 1938-45* (London, 1971), pp. 211-273; J. R. Colville, *The Fringes of Power: Downing Street Diaries, 1939-55* (London, 1985), pp. 24-114; and F. Bédarida, "La rupture franco-britannique de 1940. Le Conseil Suprême Interallié, de l'invasion à la défaite de la France," *Vingtième Siècle* 25 (1990): 37-48.

36. Bond, *Chief of Staff*, I, p. 249.

with the *Quatrième Bureau*. Yet the immediate employment of the British was still undetermined. The BEF was living only on its assembly and concentration procedures, as a result of what Ironside had termed in late July "our lack of plan."[37] The overall French strategy, as the British knew from the staff talks, was wholly defensive, conserving resources whilst methodically mobilising militarily and economically for a long industrialised war. Ironside, exasperated that "Everything was hopelessly defensive everywhere," was further frustrated by the dashing of his expectation of commanding the BEF. From the start he found it hard to see where his CIGS duties ended. He irritated GHQ by tending to interfere and trying to act as a "super commander-in-chief," and upsetting Gamelin – whom GHQ then had to placate. Gort and Pownall for their part were content with the style and prudence of the French. They found Gamelin perfectly "amenable ... if he is taken the right way, but Ironside did not do so and put his back up."[38] The idea of gradually moving the BEF up and prolonging its time in a defensive role equally suited them, for this offered training opportunities which Pownall judged more realistic than those possible if the BEF remained in base areas. In the second half of September GHQ successfully but amicably resisted a French contingency plan to swing the BEF forward onto the Scheldt if Germany attacked Belgium. Gort and Pownall convinced the French that a manoeuvre of this order would jeopardize the British forces' railway communications, which ran parallel to their front in a zone only twenty five miles deep to the Channel coast, and which stretched five hundred miles back to the Brittany resupply ports.[39]

37. Macleod and Kelly, *Ironside Diaries*, p. 85 (entry of 26 July 1939). On the BEF's advance from the disembarkation ports to its concentration zones see Bond, *Chief of Staff*, I, pp. 232-237. Gort's biographer asserts that this first-ever deployment overseas of an all-motorised army "was flawlessly achieved" (Colville, *Man of Valour*, p. 148). Cf., however, the admission on 27 Sept. 1939 by Pownall that "things have been going wrong in the loading of the ships, and there have been many delays and some muddle" (Bond, *Chief of Staff*, I, p. 240).
38. Quotations from, respectively, Macleod and Kelly, *Ironside Diaries*, p. 85 (entry of 26 July 1939), and Bond, *Chief of Staff*, I, pp. 237-238 (Pownall diary entry of 21 Sept. 1939).
39. Lelong to Gamelin, 19 Sept. 1939: "Conversation avec le général Ironside et le général Howard-Vyse," in EMA: 2e Bureau – Grande-Bretagne, Carton 7N 2817, dr.

By 27 September French intelligence detected Wehrmacht units returning from Poland. Pownall, conferring at La Ferté with Georges, found the latter preoccupied by evidence of increasing German formations amassing west of the Rhine. Anglo-French discussions consequently focused on the entry of the BEF into the line, the British agreeing to move up and take over a sector of the front on 3 October. From noon on the following day, two BEF divisions were duly deployed along the border from Lille southeast to Maulde-sur-Escaut, with the third and fourth divisions arriving from 12 October, the latter forming the BEF reserve. On the 15th Georges visited British GHQ, again discussing what could and could not be done on the Scheldt if Belgium was attacked. The BEF learned that its left, on what it judged the dangerously shallow front up to Ghent, would be taken by XVIth corps under General Fagalde. Pownall rejoiced on 25 October that "All three divisions in the line are working very hard indeed and there's a lot of progress made. It's all excellent training for the troops, much more so than if we had stayed in a back area practising battles."[40]

In mid-November Gamelin undertook his decisive strategical alteration, issuing the Dyle manoeuvre directive. This, "Plan D", committed the French First Army, the French mechanised cavalry corps and XVIth corps, along with the BEF, to a forward bound to defend along the Antwerp-Dyle-Namur line if Belgium was violated. The British force was assigned a front from Louvain to Wavre and accepted without complaint. In the Supreme War Council of 17 November, the new strategic variant was accepted virtually by default, hardly discussed and certainly not disputed.[41]

---

labelled "Correspondance: juillet-octobre 1939," SHAT. Cf. Bond, *Chief of Staff*, I, pp. 235-236, 238-240. In the first of these diary entries, dated 18 Sept. 1939, Pownall highlighted the influence of bad memories on British thinking, noting: "we had a pretty fair bellyful last time of fighting in the Flanders plain with all its mud and slime."

40. Bond, *Chief of Staff*, I, pp. 240, 242-243, 246, 248-249. Cf. A. Bryant, *The Turn of the Tide, 1939-43. A Study based on the Diaries and Autobiographical Notes of Field Marshal the Viscount Alanbrooke* (London, 1957), pp. 43-56. Cf. D. Fraser, *Alanbrooke* (London, 1983), pp. 132-140; N. Hamilton, *Monty: The Making of a General, 1887-1942* (London, 1981), pp. 307-325.

41. Cf. Bédarida, *La Stratégie secrète de la drôle de guerre*, pp. 149-181; M.S. Alexander, "Maurice Gamelin and the Defeat of France, 1939-40," in B. Bond, ed., *Fallen Stars. Eleven Studies of Twentieth-Century Military Disasters* (Oxford, 1991), pp.

This was what "planning" amounted to as autumn stretched into winter. The British remained deferential, even subservient. They were the passive recipients of information on what the French command had decided for the alliance rather than partners in the joint planning of strategic operations.

Yet the mere engagement of BEF ground forces in France had not, of itself, endowed the alliance with strength and cohesiveness. To begin with, only the first four regular divisions would have been in the field if Germany had immediately attacked westward after over-running Poland. Britain's contribution to Franco-British defense would then have been weaker numerically, and arguably qualitatively, than it was at an earlier point in the 1914 "war of movement." It became clear that Britain's build-up in France would be slower than predicted in the over-optimistic projections made in the summer of 1939. By November Ironside judged that even a fifteen-division BEF could not be in place before September 1940. No more than two of those divisions could be armored.[42] Britain's impressive-looking pledges of the size of her forces to stand shoulder to shoulder with France by autumn 1940 also tacitly assumed that defeat was no danger in the interim.

The Franco-British alliance remained far short of converting the potential of the partners into resources in the field. Yet it was frontline and battle-ready strength that would be required to deny Germany a surprise success that might negate all the behind-the-scenes financial, commercial and industrial preparation to win a long war.[43] This weakness was particularly apparent with regard to Allied coordination over combined munitions and arms procurement, production and distribution. In these matters collaboration between the coalition partners remained embryonic. In the first round of the

---

107-40; D. W. Alexander, "Repercussions of the Breda Variant," *French Historical Studies* 8 (1974): 459-488.

42. Macleod and Kelly, *Ironside Diaries*, pp. 104-105 (entry of 7 Sept. 1939), and 136-137 (entry of 14 Nov. 1939). Cf. General Gamelin: Cabinet militaire, Journal de marche, 15-16 Oct. 1939, Fonds Gamelin 1K 224, Carton 9, SHAT.

43. On the idea of the "long war" as the theoretical underpinning of French grand strategy, see R.J. Young, "La guerre de longue durée: Some Reflections on French Strategy and Diplomacy in the 1930s," in A. Preston, *General Staffs and Diplomacy before the Second World War* (London and Totowa, NJ, 1978), pp. 41-64.

1939 staff talks the French were perturbed by Britain's warning that in enlarging the BEF she would have "less trouble recruiting men than in providing the indispensable quantities of extra equipment." Gort emphasised to Lelong that slow tank assembly would be the greatest obstacle.[44] The French proposed placing a permanent team of armaments' engineers in Britain to expedite joint munitions manufacture. But action occurred only after war began when Dautry, on becoming French minister of armaments, despatched René Mayer to London at the head of a munitions procurement mission. Inevitably such delays in taking action led to delays in seeing results.[45] Reluctance – mostly British – to undertake peacetime measures that would mesh the Franco-British defense industries was the economic corollary to unwillingness, until February 1939, to embroil British foreign policy in an alliance, or British military options in joint staff planning. These were serious technical weaknesses in the chain binding together the Allied partnership.

The linkage was further imperilled by attitudinal "blind spots." An important one of these was the near-universal British complacency about the impregnable shelter provided by the Maginot Line and French army. This was most rife inside Chamberlain's war cabinet where, besides the prime minister, Hore-Belisha, Admiral Lord Chatfield (minister for co-ordination of defense), and even Churchill harboured limitless faith in French military prowess. (In Churchill's case his confidence was especially high in the competence of General Georges, with whom he had toured French positions in Alsace in August 1939).[46]

---

44. Ministère de la Défense nationale et de la Guerre: Cabinet, Note dated 12 April 1939 in Cabinet du Ministre, Carton 5N 579; see also Lelong report to Gamelin, 14 April 1939, in EMA: 2e Bureau – Grande-Bretagne, Carton 7N 2816, SHAT.

45. Lelong report to Gamelin, 21 April 1939, in EMA: 2e Bureau – Grande-Bretagne, Carton 7N 2816, SHAT; testimony of Dautry on 11 and 18 Jan. 1949 before the post-war French National Assembly's inquiry into the causes and consequences of the Fall of France: *Commission chargée d'enquêter sur les événements survenus en France de 1933 à 1945: Annexes: Dépositions – Témoignages et documents recueillis*, 9 vols. (Paris, 1951-52), VII-VIII, pp. 1947-49, 1951-53, 1963-65, 1997-2004.

46. Churchill, *The Second World War: The Gathering Storm*, pp. 342-344. Cf. E. L. Spears, *Assignment to Catastrophe* (London, 1956), pp. 16-21. Spears, Conservative MP for Carlisle, was a retired major-general and former liaison officer between BEF headquarters and the French in 1914. He had become a leading figure in the Anglo-French

But faith in French ground forces was also the hallmark of most of Britain's service professionals. Ironside, who worried at French inertia during the autumn of 1939, had cast off his unease by March 1940. Pownall took a poor view of the French 51st division that undertook duties in the BEF sector. But this was exceptional: the BEF chief-of-staff's diaries for the phoney war indicate that he mostly took French military power and proficiency for granted. In any case, most of his time was consumed by the day-to-day administration of the BEF.[47] Gort, furthermore, scrupulously respected the view that, as an operational field commander, strategic high policy with a political as well as military aspect – such as the Dyle plan – was outside his remit. "My responsibilities," he wrote, "were confined to ensuring that the orders issued by the French for the employment of the British Expeditionary Force were capable of being carried out; and, indeed, events proved that the orders issued for this operation were well within the capacity of the Force." Alan Brooke, commanding British II Corps, voiced concern for the deficiencies that he noticed in the state of French troops and fortification systems. But for raising the issue, and for drawing attention openly to the BEF's difficulties, Brooke found himself branded at GHQ as a carping defeatist. Equally little notice was taken of some critical assessments of French troops behind the Ardennes made by the Duke of Windsor, who was attached to Howard-Vyse's liaison mission. The discredited ex-King was not taken seriously.[48]

For Gamelin, then, British self-satisfaction was a constant and considerable problem. With the war underway, he could not publicly undermine his own forces by making too clean a breast of deficiencies known to the French high command. Yet he privately

---

Parliamentary Association and accompanied Churchill to the meeting with Georges in August 1939, before being chosen by Churchill to act as liaison officer to the French prime minister, Paul Reynaud, in May-June 1940.

47. Macleod and Kelly, *Ironside Diaries*, pp. 107-108, 231-232; Bond, *Chief of Staff*, I, pp. 249, 251, 256-304.

48. M. Bloch, *The Duke of Windsor's War* (London, 1982), pp. 24-58; Unpublished Memoirs of Brig. G. Davy (who helped the Duke draft his reports), pp. 1215-1219; Gamelin, Journal de marche, 4 Oct. and 14 Oct. 1939, Fonds Gamelin, 1K 224 Carton 9, SHAT.

worried that the BEF, though expanding, remained overwhelmingly infantry-based (if motorised), contrary to the mechanisation sought since 1937. In early September 1939 Lelong warned that British estimated arrival dates for the planned two armored divisions might prove optimistic since their "arrival will be a function of a distinctly unpromising rate of delivery of their equipment." Prospects had not improved when Lelong reported a talk at the War Office on 3 October with General Laurence Carr, Director of Staff Duties. Stores and weapons would be the "deciding factor in the rate of formation of British divisions." Carr insisted "several times" that this "was dependent above all on factory output." The new divisions' training, as well as the build-up of stocks behind the BEF, would be hampered by these shortages. Another discussion at the War Office left Lelong reporting that the British Territorials would be deploying in the first instance supported by stop-gap First World War vintage artillery brought out of mothballs.[49]

A vast gulf yawned between the prospect of Belisha's thirty-two division army and the reality of the 1939-1940 BEF build-up. This dismayed French politicians and the French public, easily misled by Belisha's grandiose gestures, more than French commanders privy to an approximation of the truth through the 1939 staff talks. But Gamelin worried about the effects of such demoralising influences on French spirits. "It transpires that ... the British command at present possesses no further unit sufficiently trained and equipped to be sent to the front," complained Corbin to Daladier in October.[50] In the middle of that month Belisha told Corbin that the fifth and sixth divisions would be ready for France in December. Belisha confessed that Britain's ambassador in Paris,

49. See Lelong report to Gamelin No. 382/S, 1 Sept. 1939 and Lelong despatch to 2e Bureau No. 592/S, 5 Oct. 1939, both in EMA: 2e Bureau – Grande-Bretagne, Carton 7N 2817, Dr. labelled "Correspondance, 1 octobre-10 octobre 1939," SHAT. Ambassador Corbin judged the second of these reports from the attaché to be so alarming that he sent a personal copy directly to Daladier, the prime minister and minister for national defense. The copy is now located in Archives Daladier, 3 DA 2, Dr. 3, sub-dr. c, FNSP.

50. Corbin, letter to Daladier No. 744, 18 Oct. 1939, covering the copy for the prime minister of Lelong's 5 Oct. despatch (see above n. 49). Cf. Gamelin, Journal de marche, account of Gamelin's inspection of the BEF, French First Army, French XVIth Corps and 51st Inf. Divn., 15-16 Oct. 1939, Fonds Gamelin 1K 224, Carton 9, SHAT.

Sir Eric Phipps, had warned the War Office of French disillusion at hearing of this total BEF strength by the year's end. France in contrast, Corbin reminded Belisha, was a nation that had "put its entire disposable manpower on a war footing from the very first days of the conflict." Belisha retorted that Britain "could do no more" despite her good will. "One cannot compare the effectives of a country organised for war, like France, with those that can be raised at the start of hostilities by a country like ours which has only just reintroduced conscription ...."[51]

Belisha personified British complacency. In the Commons, on 11 October 1939, he pledged the government's determination to train and deploy the promised large army and spoke with satisfaction of the entry into line of the BEF's I Corps. Corbin directly alerted Daladier to how these declarations were "persuading the majority of the English that they had made a remarkable effort ... that they had done all that we [French] could expect of them and that it would come ill from us to complain ... !" The British remained "so far from our concept of the nation-in-arms that they hardly realise the disproportion between the strength with the colours in France and those they've just sent to our country." Most disquieting of all, the British betrayed "such confidence in the French army that they are tempted to consider their military contribution as [merely] a token of solidarity instead of as a vital necessity."[52]

No-one who mattered in the Franco-British leadership believed that they were running a real danger of an early, quick and complete defeat. Pownall, when organising the BEF's assembly, observed in his diary on 21 September 1939 that "only on the Western front can the war be lost on land – But it won't be!"[53]

51. Corbin, letter to Daladier No. 744, 18 Oct. 1939 (cited above n. 50). Reynaud, at this time French minister of finance, was also applying pressure on Britain for accelerated deployment to France of even semi-trained and partially-equipped British Territorial Army divisions. See Macleod and Kelly, *Ironside Diaries*, pp. 113-114, 133-134, 137, 155, 162-164. Pownall recorded in his diary on 24 Jan. 1940 that, "[the] French government and Gamelin are pushing the War Office hard to send out as many divisions as possible and as early as possible" (Bond, *Chief of Staff*, I, p. 278).

52. Corbin, letter to Daladier No. 744, 18 Oct. 1939 (cited above n. 50). For Belisha's House of Commons statement see Minney, *Private Papers of Hore-Belisha*, pp. 248-249.

53. Bond, *Chief of Staff*, I, p. 238.

Corbin in contrast urged that Britain be convinced of the need to deploy "a significant-sized army which will render French soil the extension of British national territory." He sought "rapid and radical decisions" to unify the resources of the Allies. He feared British optimism and the "facility with which they accept reverses, sure as they are of carrying the day at the last ...."[54] An example which would have been felt to justify this unease came in the same week in October when Pownall ventured in his diary, that "The Polish campaign has given us the time and immunity we needed ... [and] our own preparations all the time make [German] victory in the spring most improbable." As BEF entrenchments deepened, barbed wire thickened and minefields spread, this confident breeze began bearing along first Gort and then Ironside. By November the former had discounted any German westward offensive – just when it was in fact being averted only by sudden autumnal rains and hitches in German preparations.[55]

What Pownall called the "'moral' front" meanwhile continued to trouble Gamelin. October extended into November, the cold weather set in, and there was no major engagement. But Gamelin was uncovering disturbing trends in the reports of the devastation wrought in Poland by German tank-aviation tactics. On debriefing the head of the French air staff mission to the Poles, General Armengaud, Gamelin alerted his staff in September that after the misleadingly calm prelude "when the real war starts here it will come as a very rude awakening." By 19 October, with some dismay, he confided in his diary that "a great number of French people imagine this war will be easy."[56] And only a day before, from London, Corbin advised Daladier of the "interest, every time we see the chance, in representing strenuously to the British government that our destinies will be at stake in the approaching months ... in

54. Corbin, letter to Daladier, No. 744, 18 Oct. 1939 (cited above n. 50).
55. Bond, *Chief of Staff*, I, pp. 244-245 (Pownall diary, entry of 12 Oct. 1939). On the postponements of the German offensive in the West, see J. Vanwelkenhuyzen, *Les Avertissements qui venaient de Berlin, octobre 1939-10 mai 1940* (Paris and Gembloux, 1982); Alexander, *The Republic in Danger*, pp. 326-348.
56. Gamelin, Journal de marche, entries of 12, 17, 18, 21 Sept. 1939 and 19 Oct. 1939, Fonds Gamelin 1K 224, Carton 9, SHAT. J. Armengaud, *Batailles politiques et militaires sur l'Europe: Témoignages, 1932-40* (Paris, 1948), pp. 95-140, 209, 304-316. Pownall's phrase occurs in his diary entry of 25 Oct. 1939 (Bond, *Chief of Staff*, I, p. 249).

the face of the desperate assaults that Germany will be able to unleash on our front ...." The Allied forces had to brace themselves to take "massive and fearful blows," certain to land before they themselves attained peak combat efficiency.[57]

And behind military morale loomed the broader question of the state of mind of politicians and populace. Conditions in the 1939-1940 winter were disconcertingly un-warlike. The risks of complacency, and of calls for a compromise peace, troubled Gamelin. Memories of the trenches of the First World War remained so vivid among French families that there was no repeat of the enthusiastic response to mobilisation seen in 1914. War was greeted stoically, and at best with a resigned sense of the inevitable captured by the contemporary saying: *"Il faut en finir."* *L' Intransigeant*, a conservative Parisian paper, headlined on its 3 September evening edition that the Allied mobilisations were proceeding "with icy resolve." The British Foreign Office's political intelligence department (PID) similarly noted that France "entered the war in a spirit of cold determination." The vital thing, recorded Pownall on 25 October, was that the "French and British have got to hang together to defeat German efforts to separate them."[58] Certainly there was a danger at this time that politicians previously inclined towards appeasement might be tempted by Nazi peace feelers. Hitler extended several versions of his olive branch after Poland's defeat. Fraser, the British military attaché in Paris, remarked on the activity of German propaganda throughout October and noted that "their broadcast in French is often quite clever ...." He suffered misgivings about the dangers of the "worst thing ... a premature patched-up peace," reflecting how it was "extraordinary what silly stuff sometimes catches people."[59]

57. Corbin, letter to Daladier, No. 744, 18 Oct. 1939 (cited above n. 50).
58. *L'Intransigeant*, 3 Sept. 1939, 6e edition, p. 1; Foreign Office *Weekly Political Intelligence Summaries, 1939-46: Vol. I, October 1939-June 1940*, nos. 1-38, Introduction by Clifton Child (London, 1983), summary no. 1 (3 Oct. 1939), p. 4. For Pownall's view quoted, see Bond, *Chief of Staff*, I, p. 249.
59. W. Fraser, letter from Paris to his wife, 9 Oct. 1939 (correspondence consulted by kind permission of General Sir David Fraser, Isington, Hampshire, Sept. 1983). Cf. Colville, *The Fringes of Power*, pp. 27-48; Dilks, *Cadogan Diaries* pp. 220-30; G. Rossi-Landi, "Le pacifisme en France, 1939-40," in *Français et Britanniques dans la drôle de guerre*, pp. 123-152.

Probably most pernicious, most divisive, was the suspicion that the Allies were bearing unequal sacrifices. This was a charge to which Britain was vulnerable from the start. On 3 October 1939 the PID warned:

> The period of getting British troops into line with the French troops is being a trying one for French public opinion. There is belief in France in the strength of the British blockade ... but it is the presence of the British troops in the line that is being eagerly awaited. And it is during this intermediate period while the British army is being lined up and got into position that it is felt that German propaganda could best work on French defeatist elements.[60]

A week later, though broadly content with French spirit, the PID raised concern that "failure to understand the part played by Great Britain is noticeable" in Lyon and the south of France, where Britain's efforts were "not appreciated ... because nothing has been seen of the British troops."[61] Most worrying was an insidious whisper that the alliance might appear to be a distasteful revival of the British use of blood-money – a latter-day reversion to Pitt's eighteenth-century strategem of defending British interests on the Continent by subsidizing the armies of allies such as Frederick II and Catherine the Great. Nothing would be so corrosive of the still-fragile alliance as a Gallic suspicion that a "joint" war effort meant sweat and treasure in comparative safety on the one side and sweat and blood in constant danger on the other (in the expression of Henry Bérenger, chairman of the French Senate's foreign affairs commission, in late 1938).[62] On 24 October 1939 the Foreign Office noted "murmurings about the volume of the British effort have not wholly ceased," and that quoting the UK contribution at sea in counterpoint to France's in the land war "is not held to be wholly just." A week later the British discerned "still

---

60. Foreign Office *Weekly Political Intelligence Summaries*, Vol. I, no. 1 (3 Oct. 1939), p. 4.
61. Idem, no. 2 (10 Oct. 1939), p. 8.
62. Bérenger's remarks at a meeting of the French Senate's Commission des Affaires Etrangères, reported in British Embassy (Paris) to London, 7 Dec. 1938, Foreign Office General Correspondence: FO 371, 21597, C15175/36/17, PRO. Cf. Adamthwaite, *France and the Coming of the Second World War*, p. 251.

considerable doubt in many minds whether this country is bearing its full share of the burden."[63]

Just as disquieting for Gamelin and the British was the state of political spirit in Paris. Press censorship and suspension of the sitting of the Chamber initially curtailed party politics. France instituted a propaganda agency, the *Commissariat Général à l'Information*, under the playwright Jean Giraudoux. At first the British praised the agency for using "its control of publicity with vigour to combat German attempts to drive a wedge between the Allies ...." But by mid-October "behind this firm front" it became more noticeable that there were "timid politicians both in and outside the Cabinet."[64] The reopening of fault-lines whose shape came from party loyalties was directly proportional to the stagnation of military activity as the mists and mud of winter enveloped the front. As early as 20 September 1939 Gamelin complained to his staff that it was "not from the military operations that our burdens come, nor from the hard work, but from this government of hesitant nervous faintbearts. They are what weigh us down." He returned to the theme time and again that autumn, writing that, "The military operations are really as nothing; what's so hard to endure is the government, the politicians and their cliques."[65]

In particular, since the war's first days, Gamelin privately suspected Daladier of lacking the resolution to stand up firmly for the command. In the political arena, he thought, Daladier wore too many hats. Until March 1940 when Reynaud took his place as prime minister, he was head of the government and at the same time foreign minister and minister for national defense and war. Gamelin compared unfavourably his own influence with Daladier to that of fellow politicians: "with them what matters are friendships, factions, debts to pay, and ties from bygone days."[66] And Daladier's opponents were numerous and powerful. Besides the

63. Foreign Office *Weekly Political Intelligence Summaries* Vol. I, no. 5 (31 Oct. 1939), p. 8; no. 6 (7 Nov. 1939), p. 9.
64. Idem, no. 1 (3 Oct. 1939), p. 4; no. 3 (17 Oct. 1939), p. 7. Cf. P. Masson, "Morale et propagande," in *Français et Britanniques dans la drôle de guerre*, pp. 163-172.
65. Gamelin, Journal de marche, 20 Sept., 24 Sept. 1939, Fonds Gamelin, 1K 224, Carton 9, SHAT.
66. *Ibid.*, 11 Sept. 1939.

ambitious Reynaud at the finance ministry, manoeuvring constantly until he secured the premiership from Daladier, there was Georges Bonnet, a vigorous appeaser who had been foreign minister from April 1938 until 13 September 1939.

Also sniping from the sidelines were three former prime ministers – Camille Chautemps, Pierre Laval and Pierre-Etienne Flandin. By moving Bonnet away from charge of diplomacy to the justice ministry and introducing Dautry to take charge of armaments, Daladier, in his 13 September government reshuffle, had temporarily reinforced his own position.[67] But he continued to fear that a cabal was plotting to topple him, especially one composed of prewar *Munichois* appeasers who had regrouped after the outbreak of hostilities as a "peace party."[68]

As winter passed, Daladier's stock as a war leader progressively fell with Gamelin. The general grew exasperated by what he regarded as Daladier's insecure and inefficient accumulation of offices – as well as by Daladier's subordination of war policy to his prior regard for political weathervanes on the home front. In October Gamelin bemoaned the prime minister as a "waverer, changing his opinions according to whatever he has just heard from the last person to have had his ear." In March 1940 he heard that "Daladier has said there won't be a battle, that everyone can be released for duty in the interior." This appalled Gamelin – for it seemed to be a further sign that the highest level of Allied counsels were dominated by civilians hooked on the addictive and hallucinogenic narcotic of attaining an Allied victory without any hard fighting.[69]

---

67. Ibid., 3 Oct. 1939. Cf. J. Harvey, ed., *The Diplomatic Diaries of Oliver Harvey, 1937-40* (London, 1970), pp. 318-319 (entry of 11 Sept. 1939).

68. O. H. Bullitt, ed., *For the President: Personal and Secret. Correspondence between Franklin D. Roosevelt and William C. Bullitt* (London, 1973), p. 373; Gamelin, Journal de marche, 19 Sept. 1939, Fonds Gamelin, 1K 224, Carton 9, SHAT.

69. Gamelin, Journal de marche, 3 Oct. 1939, 11 March 1940, Fonds Gamelin, 1K 224, Carton 9, SHAT. In his diary Colville, private secretary to British prime minister Neville Chamberlain, similarly noted on 31 Dec. 1939: "Here at home ... people seem to be resigned to the war without fully realising the hardships which it must, and the physical terror which it may, imply." (*Fringes of Power*, p. 61.) Cf. J.-L. Crémieux-Brilhac, "L'opinion publique française, l'Angleterre et la guerre, septembre 1939-juin 1940"; P.M.H. Bell, "L'évolution de l'opinion publique anglaise à propos de la guerre et

Comprehending Gamelin's concern, and thus his caution, comes from appreciating that French civilian leaders were over-confident and lulled by the "funny sort of war." They increasingly planned to forestall a second "loss" of the eventual peace instead of striving to guarantee military safety in the meantime. The resistance of the minister of labour, Charles Pomaret, to training in order to expand skilled labour for war work in June 1939 (fearing later redundancy problems), was matched by the insistence of the minister of commerce, Fernand Gentin, that military production should not reduce output of luxury goods. Their sale, he argued in October, would offset war imports. Their export would help preserve a competitive trading position for France: "It is essential that we continue manufacturing export goods so that we hang on to our customers ... for when the war is over."[70] At bottom, French politicians trusted their military defenses much more than their economy, whereas for their service chiefs the anxieties were exactly the reverse. Ministerial and military conviction coincided on the correctness of an attritional grand strategy to overthrow Germany. But, unlike the civilians, the soldiers' professional knowledge permitted them only qualified confidence in the incomplete, tardily-constructed military foundation upon which Franco-British security had meanwhile to rely.

Planning the Franco-British operational strategy for defense in the west, Gamelin had no risk-free means of both securing Belgium – which offered shorter lines and twenty two more divisions for the Allies – whilst at the same time preserving a large reserve for maneuver.[71] The two capabilities together were beyond the het-

---

de l'alliance avec la France, septembre 1939-mai 1940"; and P. Ludlow, "Le débat sur les buts de paix en Grande-Bretagne durant l'hiver 1939-40," all in *Français et Britanniques dans la drôle de guerre*, pp. 1-50, 51-80, 93-122 respectively.

70. Chambre des Députés: Commission du Travail, "Séance du 28 juin 1939. Audience de M. Charles Pomaret, ministre du travail," 16th Legislature (1936-40), Folder B102, Dr. 2; Commission du commerce et de l'industrie, "Séance du 18 octobre 1939. Audience de M. Fernand Gentin, ministre du commerce et de l'industrie," procès-verbal, pp. 13-14, Carton 58, both in Archives de l'Assemblée Nationale, Paris. Cf. Présidence du Conseil, "Directives de la politique économique française: programmes de production et d'achat pour 1940," 24 Feb. 1940, in Archives Daladier, 3 DA 5, Dr. 2, sub-dr. c, FNSP.

71. See J.A. Gunsburg, *Divided and Conquered. The French High Command and the Defeat of the West, 1940* (Westport, CT, 1979), pp. 119-135.

erogeneous, partially-trained and semi-coordinated Franco-British ground and air forces of May 1940. The BEF, it must be re-emphasised, contained ten divisions and was forward deployed on the Franco-Belgian frontier when the German attack came. Yet it was not of the mechanised and armoured type – and thus unsuited for the reserve, counterattack role – which Gamelin had envisaged for it before the war. The caution engendered by these factors explains Gamelin's rebuff of requests between December 1939 and March 1940 to cede precious French tanks to General Sikorski's Poles or even to the BEF. Gamelin after all sought British ground units, it is well to recall, from the moment he first importuned Whitehall in 1936 and 1937, as *reinforcements* to French maneuver forces, not as subtractions *from* them.[72]

Finally, French commanders felt their strategic deployments in the west to be tightly constrained by Belgium's neutrality. This policy, Gamelin warned at the beginning of September, played straight into German hands.[73] Gamelin's responsibility was to defend France's integrity: in the contemporary formulation of the 1920s and 1930s, to secure "the inviolability of French territory." That was a challenging and ambitious objective even if the French political and military leadership had been united in focusing on it, to the exclusion of party quarrels and personal ambition.

Yet they were anything but. By April and early May 1940 Gamelin was deeply shocked at the fratricide and factionalism rife among the French *classe politique*. His *journal de marche* betrays his irritation; it also hints that he already sensed a premeditated iden-

72. Letter no. 509/G, 9 Dec. 1939: "Le général Sikorski, commandant-en-chef de L'Armée polonaise à M. le général Gamelin, Chef d'Etat-major de la défense nationale et commandant-en-chef des armées françaises," Archives of the Sikorski Museum and Polish Institute, London; Gamelin letter to Ironside, 17 Feb. 1940, Fonds Gamelin 1K 224, Carton 7, Dr. labelled "Correspondance avec les Britanniques," sub-dr. 6, SHAT; dossier by General Louis Keller, French Army Inspector of Tanks, Feb. 1940, recounting negotiations over cessions to the BEF of Hotchkiss H.39 tanks, in Archives Daladier, 4 DA 23, Dr. 1, sub-dr. b, FNSP; Macleod and Kelly, *Ironside Diaries*, p. 163.

73. *Documents diplomatiques français, 1919-39* (Paris, 1963 et seq), 2nd ser., vol. XIX, no. 353, pp. 357-358 ("Le général Gamelin, chef d'Etat-major de la Défense nationale, commandant-en-chef les forces terrestres, à M. Daladier, ministre de la Défense nationale et de la guerre," D. no. 4/Cab. F.T., 1 Sept. 1939. Cf. P. Le Goyet, *Le Mystère Gamelin* (Paris, 1976), pp. 229-231, 277-278; Alexander, *The Republic in Danger*, pp. 207-209.

tification of possible scapegoats under way in the *coulisses du pouvoir*, as the men of party instinctively sought insurance to cover their own responsibilities. In this noxious atmosphere of intrigue and back-stabbing, even Gamelin, supposedly the consummate "political general," drew back towards his fellow officers. They, he noted, "are on a different level, with clear ideas and firm decisions. But then, of course, *they've* all been trained for leadership."[74]

Increasingly isolated in the military's hermetic world, as winter stretched endlessly onward, Gamelin was finally overcome by an insidious complacency in the adequacy of his fellow generals, their British counterparts and his own troops. On the western front the ground froze and the troops froze. As if in a hibernation of military intellect, the commanders' thinking apparently also began to freeze. After March 1940, Gamelin paid no further personal visits to inspect preparations along the front. Indeed, with Reynaud's ousting of Daladier at the head of the government that month, Gamelin's main energies were required in Paris as he conducted a distracting fight to avert his own dismissal by the new prime minister. By late March, too, Ironside was increasingly confident about the situation of the Allies, reassured by a visit he made with Gamelin to the Third Army of General Condé at the west end of the Maginot Line as well as to General Huntziger's Second Army behind the Ardennes. Ironside concluded that "the Germans had missed their opportunity in not attacking when the French were concentrating."[75] After 9 April and Hitler's move north, the Allied leaders' gaze was further distracted from France by the hastily-assembled and ill-executed Franco-British expedition to Norway.

What augured worst of all for the Battle of France was that Allied planning – the November Dyle manoeuvre settled just before the freeze-up and the even riskier Breda dash to south Holland for the previously reserved French Seventh Army – never thawed out. Capture of the German plan in January 1940 had offered a strong suggestion that the Allied designs were frozen in

74. Gamelin, Journal de marche, 14 Sept. 1939, Fonds Gamelin 1K 224, Carton 9, SHAT.
75. Macleod and Kelly, *Ironside Diaries*, pp. 231-232 (entry of 22 March 1940).

the wrong shape.[76] Ironically – or in unwitting prophecy – the Anglo-French staff talks of spring 1939 had identified the need to "keep on French soil considerable reserves for ... resisting an invasion of the Low Countries or counter-attacking in order to re-establish the integrity of the original front."[77] By spring 1940 French and British commanders did not realise that they now needed to be capable of doing all of these things at the same time. Meanwhile, French and British politicians did not recognize that a decisive military defeat in France remained a possibility. Thus the rupture of June 1940 was all the more bitter for being unforeseen. As the debacle unfolded and the Dunkirk evacuation by the British commenced, the image of Britannia "fighting to the last Frenchman" ceased to be a cynical jibe between friends and allies. It became the twisted, treachery-tainted undercurrent to an ugly new bout of cross-Channel xenophobia, one with a ferocity – and with bloody and tragic consequences at Mers-el-Kébir and Dakar – not seen since "Boney" had fought the "nation of shopkeepers" a century and a quarter before.[78]

76. See D.W. Alexander, "Repercussions of the Breda Variant" (cited above., n. 41); Vanwelkenhuyzen, Les Avertissements, pp. 176-224; Gunsburg, Divided and Conquered, pp. 126-153.
77. Chiefs of Staff Paper no. COS 877: "Anglo-French Staff Conversations: U.K. Delegation Report on Stage One," 11 April 1939, CAB 53/47, PRO.
78. See P.M.H. Bell, "Prologue de Mers-el-Kébir," Revue d'histoire de la Deuxième Guerre Mondiale 9, no. 33 (Jan. 1959), pp. 15-36; idem, "Shooting the Rapids. British Reactions to the Fall of France, 1940," Modern and Contemporary France 42 (1990): 16-28.

XII

FRENCH DEFEAT IN 1940 AND ITS REVERSAL IN 1944-1945

The Deuxième Division Blindée

Philip Farwell Bankwitz[†]

Ces chevaliers de la Table ronde de l'aventure gaulliste – une des grandes aventures humaines – quêtant obstinément au prix de sang, de souffrance et de mort, au fond de l'Afrique, dans les déserts de la Cyrénaique ou au coeur du pays occupé, ce Graal qu'était pour eux la liberté. Et *"là où ils mouraient renaissait la patrie."*[1]

From the abundant literature on the catastrophe of May-June 1940 in France, certain themes have emerged. It is my intention in this article to reflect and elaborate upon these themes as a witness attached to the G-2 (Deuxième Bureau) of the Deuxième Blindée Française, the élite unit of the Free French forces that surged across France from Normandy to Paris to Strasbourg between early August 1944 and the middle of February 1945.

Certainly, the first theme in the defeat of 1940 is the strategic one. Due to appalling losses in French lives, property and monetary assets in the 1914-1918 conflict, the General Staff and the War Office – hand in hand with the French diplomatic service – quite

---

1. Claude Chevalier-Appert, "Anniversaire: Leclerc ou la vertu de désobéissance." *Le Monde*, n. 10211, 27-28 November 1977, 30. (Italics in text).

understandably devoted the greater part of their energies to fight a second war outside France itself. The corollary to this position was the almost untouchable principle of *la défense intégrale du territoire*. As potential French allies recognized that they were to be the battlefields of another apocalyptic war, they either backed away from compromising military and diplomatic ties to France or declared their neutrality: Italy, Yugoslavia, Rumania, Poland, Belgium and, at the very last minute, the Soviet Union, under the boot of that master of the double cross, Stalin. After the abandonment of Czechoslovakia at Munich in 1938, the only ally reclaimed in this fiasco of making "war on the cheap" to be fought with "the blood of others," was Great Britain, whose immense industrial and military power on land could not be fully attained until mid-1942, at the earliest.[2]

The French were now consigned to an all-out battle with German forces in the geographically constricted Low Countries, with their difficult terrain, seemingly uncommitted governments and people, apparently focused on internal problems and determined to live out their fantasy that a second war would not occur during their lifetimes. With the nightmare of another Verdun and the antimilitarism of the French public reaching a peak in the mid-thirties (the most popular novel-autobiography of the time was Céline's *Voyage au bout de la nuit*) who can wonder that the General Staff, led by Maurice Gamelin, designed a master one-time super-*bataille de conduite* as far away from France's northern frontier as possible? But there was no second line of defense nor scattered fortifications inside northern France itself.

Various reasons have been advanced for the adoption of this strategy of glaring omission. The most plausible, but least important, was that the second barrier of scattered *Strengpunkten* would cut across the French energy and industry resources in the Lille-Roubaix and Valenciennes area, where the high water table made an extension of the huge fortifications strung from Rouffach-Montmédy (popularly known as the "Maginot Line") impossible.

---

2. This is documented by Nicole Jordan in "The Cut-Price War on the Peripheries: The French Staff, the Rhineland and Czechoslovakia" in Robert Boyce and E.M. Robertson, *Paths to War* (New York, 1989) and again, in her prize-winning book, *The Popular Front and Central Europe. The Dilemmas of French Impotence, 1918-40* (Cambridge, 1992).

(These vast installations should really have been called the Pétain-Painlevé Line in memory of its major military and political mentors in the 1920s.) But what about situating the scattered strong points on the various outcroppings of rock just somewhat in the rear of the factories and mines? The resources and industrial plants sacrificed in the move could easily have been balanced by the output of the Paris region and the deliberately dispersed armaments factories in the Centre. War materiel from overseas could have maintained French strength in the same manner as in 1914-1918.

Defense in depth was never practicable: the alternative was a system of scattered strong points.[3] The lack of that "second system," so desperately needed after the German breakthrough at Sedan and Dinant in 1940, was certainly due to political opposition and what was deemed at the time "expert" advice. The *môles de résistance* project would indeed have violated the principle of *la défense intégrale du territoire*, that malevolent relic of the national trauma of 1914-1918; it would also have quite possibly enraged the Parliamentary majority which had challenged the General Staff over disarmament and effectives in the ranks in the time between the victory of the Left at the polls in May 1932 and its collapse in the riots of the 6 February 1934, and had lost on both counts.[4]

Finally, Marshal Philippe Pétain himself had ruled against the strong points in the Nord as militarily unnecessary in the most important inter-war meeting of France's Conseil Supérieur de la Guerre on 4 June 1932. Those rejecting the Nord system and supporting the Marshal numbered seven against an important minority of six, including Maxime Weygand and Gamelin, the chief of the French Army and the Chief of the General Staff.[5] (That they

---

3. General Victor-Henri Schweisguth, journal, 31 October 1936, cited in Jordan *Popular Front*, p. 268. The undermanned and underequipped Meuse sector (Mézières-Sedan-Stenay-Semoy) through which the Wehrmacht eventually poured in 1940, was largely ignored by Gamelin, who repeated Pétain's notorious reassurances in 1934 on the impenetrability of the Ardennes to the same Senate Army Commission in 1936 and 1937. See General Paul-Emile Tournoux, *Défense des frontières Haut commandement-Gouvernement 1919-39* (Paris, 1960), pp. 54, 57, 58, 61-63, 65-66, 68-69, 275.

4. See my work, *Maxime Weygand and Civil-Military Relations in Modern France* (Cambridge, MA, 1967), chapters 2 and 3, pp. 177-209.

5. For the session, which includes a hostile letter from an absent Pétain, see France. Service Historique de l'Armée de Terre (henceforth SHAT). Cartons 1N 20-

were outfoxed by the already aged Pétain, who staged an elaborate trial of the "guilty" at Riom a decade later, is certainly ironic.) It also indicated Pétain's early preference for defeat in the coming war to fighting on French soil and to reliance on overseas allies. The second theme is rearmament. Gamelin, Weygand's successor in January 1935, was freed of the burdens of his predecessor, disarmament and effectives (the number of men to enter the army as conscripts and additions to the professional ranks). Weygand had exercised what can be called the military veto on these two issues with his characteristic tempestuousness. Gamelin was now able to focus on rearmament as Germany broke article after article of the Versailles treaty after March 1935. Gamelin's rearmament policy coincided with the social explosion following the victory of the Popular Front in the elections of April-May 1936. The French factories were quickly occupied by an exploited work force, cruelly hurt by the deflationist policies of the Centre-Right governments following the sixth of February 1934. Gamelin's dilemma at the triumph of historically anti-military forces in French politics was solved by the Popular Front's new Defense Minister, none other than Edouard Daladier, the "man of the sixth of February," and Weygand's sworn enemy before the European military-diplomatic balance had shifted against France. Daladier was now an ardent believer in immediate and rapid rearmament. As a highly-decorated captain in the First War, Daladier also believed in a network of separate strong points inside France,[6] rather than the one-shot

---

22 (procès-verbaux des séances, 1921-39), "Séance du 4 juin 1932," Carton 1N-21, vol. 16, pp. 215-217. Political opposition to the extension is amply indicated in Martin Alexander, *The Republic in Danger. General Maurice Gamelin and the Politics of French Defence, 1933-40* (Cambridge, 1992), pp. 177-209.

6. See Alexander, *Gamelin*, pp. 196-209. Further material from the Riom trial records Daladier's exasperation that the sizable funds for strongpoints between Montmédy and Dunkerque were under used. To a befuddled general, who could not remember the credits given for those *môles de résistance* in what turned out to be the breakthrough point for the Germans in 1940, the Ardennes sector, Daladier remarked with some asperity, "Enfin, vous ne savez pas; c'est permis, même à un général!" France. Ministère de la Culture et de la Communication, Cour Suprême de Justice séant à Riom. Dossier de la Procédure contre MM. Daladier, Léon Blum, Général Gamelin et al., 14e. Audience du 17 mars 1942 (Confrontation avec les généraux Besson et Georges Blanchard, WII82, série VII, p. 17.) There is an excellent discussion

gamble in the Low Countries that the C.S.G. had so narrowly consented to in the critical meeting of June 1932.

It is alleged by both Gamelin and Martin Alexander that the costs of the Popular Front's social reform would allow only for the modernization of the future *force de frappe*.[7] There apparently was precious little left for the fortified strong-points between Montmédy and the North Sea. In point of fact, the Blum government gave the General Staff more money than was requested, notwithstanding its social reforms.[8] In truth, these separated fortresses loomed up against Gamelin's determination to use the Belgian *porte de sortie* as the masterpiece of his *guerre ailleurs* strategy. In any event, Daladier pushed through the first important program of the entire interwar period in September 1936, well aware of the grudging nature of the Chamber's support. As a man of the Left and a keen adherent of the turn-of-the-century *Solidarité* movement within the Radical party, he knew by heart the antiwar stanza of the *Ça ira* as well as that of the *Internationale* which exhorts the troops to fire on their own generals.[9] His options were thus dominated by executing the rearmament plan in and by itself, as his Jacobin handling of the strikes and work problems in 1937-38 would indicate, and by his appeasement of French investors with the appointment of fiscally reactionary Paul Reynaud as Minister of Finance in 1938.[10]

---

of the alternatives available at this time in Judith Hughes, *To the Maginot Line: The Politics of French Military Preparedness in the 1920s* (Cambridge, MA, 1971), pp. 228-229.

7. Testimony of Gamelin (9 & 23 Dec. 1947) in France, Assemblée Nationale, 1946-58. Session de 1947. Commission chargée d'enquêter sur les événements survenus en France de 1933 à 1945. No. 2344. Rapport ... Annexes (Dépositions). *Témoignages et documents recueillis par la Commission*, 9 vols. (Paris, 1951-52), II. pp. 405, 544; Alexander, *Gamelin*, pp. 196-198.

8. Jordan, *Popular Front and Central Europe*, pp. 138-139.

9. Elisabeth du Réau, *Daladier, 1884-1970* (Paris, 1993), pp. 180-203. Fourteen billion francs were allocated for the period 1936-41. Daladier's background as a *militant* of the Left is found in *ibid.*, first part, chs. 1-6, and second part, chs. 1-5.

10. Réau, *Daladier*, pp. 224-230, 381; Alexander, *Gamelin*, pp. 133-138; Robert Frankenstein, *Le Prix du réarmement français, 1935-39* (Paris, 1982), pp. 280-281, 249-299. Reynaud's efforts to reconstitute the French gold reserve led him to oppose credits to potential Eastern allies and to the purchase of critically-needed advanced fighter aircraft from the United States. See respectively, the procès-verbal of the crucial meeting of 30 Jan. 1939, contained in Jean-Baptiste Duroselle, *La Décadence, 1933-39*

The third theme involves the claim that France was not prepared for Germany's coordinated tank and assault aircraft attack despite constant warnings from the Ebro-to-the-sea offensive of Franco's forces in March 1939, the Polish collapse in September and the iconoclastic Charles de Gaulle. The maneuvering of the existing French armored forces had been canceled by the mobilizations of 1938 and 1939.[11] If the French tanks in 1940 were superior to those of the Germans in both design and numbers,[12] they lacked experience as a cohesive and autonomous force on the battlefield.[13] The first armored French unit, the *division cuirassée*, did not come into existence until January 1940; it and the three others created later totaled only one-sixth of the entire roster of French tanks; the remaining five-sixths were incapable of taking offensive action. The B-1 and the B-1 *bis* vehicles, the best tanks in the world according to armored experts, numbered only three hundred eighty-seven in May-June 1940, hardly enough to deal effectively with the German attack.[14]

The fourth theme concerns the strategic posture developed by Gamelin. He positioned his weakest troops (the so-called coverage "B" units) at the very point of the oncoming German rush, and radically displaced the "grande" or heavy reserve from its normal position athwart the Reims-Toul-Verdun axis in the center of the French disposition. He shifted this reserve, which included France's best tank commanders and heaviest vehicles, to a cockamamie mission of thrusting through Belgium in order to join up with Dutch forces at Breda.[15] There was little or no conception of

---

(Paris, 1979), pp. 377-380, and a book based on Jean Monnet's personal papers, John McV. Haight: *American Aid to France 1938-40* (New York, 1970), pp. 37, 45-46, 106-107.

11. Lt. Colonel Henry Dutailly, *Les Problèmes de l'Armée de Terre* (1935-39) (Paris, 1980), pp. 195-196.

12. Lt. Colonel (General) Charles de Cossé-Brissac, "Combien de chars français contre combien de chars allemands le 10 mai 1940?" *Revue de défense nationale* 5 (1947): 75-81; Generaloberst Heinz Guderian, "La campagne de France," *Revue historique de l'Armée* 3 (1947): 109-119.

13. Dutailly, *Problèmes*, p. 196.

14. Commission chargée d'enquêter, Bordereaux d'envoi, numéro 18: Note sur le nombre de chars reçus par l'Armée entre 1935 et 1940.

15. See the account using General Alphonse Georges's papers, Claude Paillat, *Le Désastre de 1940, 10 mai-24 juin* (Paris, 1985), pp. 88-103. The landmark article

the factor of speed: the Germans were well equipped with what specialists call today the C3I factor, control and communication, while most of even the best French tanks and units had either a transmitter or a receiver, not both.[16] Gamelin, now called Gagamelin by the troops, refused to use radio contact during that fatal second week in May 1940.

As a last theme, there were French elements and interest groups opposed to the war waiting in the wings. They not only included the Communists, dissenters because of the Stalin-Hitler pact, but also political factions close to the regimes in Italy, Spain and Germany herself. They were in close contact, as Mme du Réau's work has brilliantly shown, with the aged but still powerful apostle of abandoning Western Europe to German control, Joseph Caillaux.[17] Behind them was the equally potent corps of senior or over-age French officers, whose psychological preparation for a military defeat-cum-authoritarian regime had hardened during the Popular Front's reforms. Indications of officer alienation had confirmed, as if in advance, a willingness to acquiesce in antiregime subversion: the "Corvignolles" officer network, and above all the Comité (Organisation) Secret d'Action Révolutionnaire, known popularly as "La Cagoule", with its mixed brew of civilian and military plotters.[18]

---

uncovering the Breda maneuver, which Gamelin's subordinate, Georges, vigorously opposed, is Don Alexander, "Repercussions of the Breda Variant," *French Historical Studies* 8 (1974): 481-482. Also, N. Jordan, *Popular Front*, pp. 78-80; Paul de Villelume, *Journal d'une défaite août 1939-juin 1940* (Paris, 1976), pp. 426, 438-439; and Col. Jacques Minart, P.C. *Vincennes. Secteur 4*, 2 vols. (Paris, 1945) I, 92-93.

16. Martin Alexander, "The Fall of France, 1940," p. 35. Ten years later, General Weygand was still covering his rival's mistake, declaring only that an unspecified "over-rash" penetration into Belgium was the military cause of the defeat. Interview, General Maxime Weygand, 18 Sept. 1950.

17. Réau, *Daladier*, pp. 266, 307, 369, 410. The whole issue of French neopacifism is well analyzed in Jean-Pierre Cointet, *Pierre Laval* (Paris, 1993), p. 286. On its fringes were Pierre-Etienne Flandin, Georges Bonnet, Camille Chautemps *inter alia*.

18. Réau, *Daladier*, gives a full account of the "first" judicial procedure against the "Cagoule" in 1938-9. There is a popular rendition of both this investigation and the "second" one of 1946-8 in Philippe Bourdrel, *La Cagoule* (Paris, 1970). It does not contain the indispensable records of the trial itself, which are to be found in the Palais Rohan of the Archives Nationales. Alexander, *Gamelin*, gives a straightforward description of the uniquely military nature of "Corvignolles," pp. 101-102. See also the somewhat harebrained memoirs of its head, Col. Georges Loustaunau-Lacau, *Mémoires d'un Francais rebelle* (Paris, 1948).

Arching over all of these concerns was the impending collapse in French civil-military relations that began in earnest with Daladier's resignation as Premier on 20 March, 1940. It was an even more dangerous crisis than that between Daladier and Weygand in the weeks preceding the upheaval of 6 February 1934: the new Premier, Paul Reynaud, detested Gamelin as Daladier's man and determined to have his head.[19] Both men were oblivious to the facts that the victor in the earlier German civil-military crisis had been Hitler, who dismissed those opposed to war, Generaloberst Ludwig Beck and Baron von Fritsch, in 1938 and then imposed on his now submissive Generalstab the short, apocalyptic war, the *Blitzkrieg*. This abrupt departure from military orthodoxy and military knowledge substituted short-range contingency plans and expertise, and fundamentally changed the nature of the coming German offensive. It transformed the Reynaud-Gamelin crisis into a potential catastrophe in the entire equation of French national security.[20]

In the end, the hunch that was "Plan Gelb" paid out extravagantly rich profits to the inveterate Monte Carlo mountebank in charge of Germany's destinies. The French defeat, beginning with the entrapment of the best troops and armor in the Low Countries[21] and ending with the sacrifice of the remaining units in Weygand's suicidal Götterdämmerung on the Somme-Aisne-Marne line in the first week of June 1940, shattered the first coalition against Hitler.[22] But this victory of sheer chance also released the

---

19. SHAT 1 K224. Inventaire. Fonds Gamelin, Carton 9, no.5: Notes manuscrits du Général Gamelin: feuillets journaliers d'août 1939 au 17 mai 1940; SHAT 1 K130. Dépôt Weygand. Dossier numéro 15, carton 4, Cahiers de 1915 à 1941, tenus sous forme d'agendas, no. 4; SHAT, Conseil Supérieur de Guerre, séance du 18 décembre 1933, Carton IN-22, vol. 17, pp. 1-28.

20. Michael Geyer, "The crisis of military leadership in the 1930s," *Journal of Strategic Studies*, XIV, no. 4 (Dec. 1991), pp. 451-60; Martin Alexander, "The Fall of France, 1940," ibid. XII, no. 1 (March, 1990), pp. 27-30.

21. In the second week of May, Gamelin was frightened by Goebbel's noisy threat to invade via Switzerland; thus, he did not move his remaining troops behind the Maginot Line to proceed northwest to take in the rear the Germans who were now careening toward the Channel. Daladier calls this failure the fundamental cause for the defeat, in Edouard Daladier, *Journal de captivité, 1940-45* (Paris, 1991), entry for 3 Sept. 1943, p. 236.

22. "The kind of preparation made ... undercut the ability to resist – *and this may very well have been the goal, albeit unthought and implicit, all along.*" Michael Geyer, "The

overpowering narcissistic faith in his, Hitler's own personal military genius. Before the tide turned again, however, Europe would be ruled by the Caesar of a gigantic super-empire. While it held sway, fastidious attention to what had formerly been details took center-stage: the annihilation of European Jewry and the transfer of those inimitable South Tyrolese in Italy's Alto Adige across Europe to the Crimea, where they were to become permanently charming hosts and hostesses in the Empire's *Kraft durch Freude* playground.[23]

* * *

Into the wreckage of that summer of 1940 stepped a badly wounded cavalry and tank commander Captain Philippe de Hautecloque. After the disintegration of his unit at Lille, he had twice evaded capture, gone back to the line at the Marne with the Third Division Cuirassée until it, too, dissolved. Then he had clawed and hobbled his way through the great *Exode* to San Sebastian, slipping through the dreaded *guardias fronteras* at the Franco-Spanish border. Born into what General Weygand would later describe to me in 1950 as "a great military family,"[24] de Hautecloque had been first in his *promotion* at St. Cyr, first at the cavalry school at Saumur, and first in his class at the Ecole de Guerre. In Morocco during the 1930s he had become the most prominent *baroudeur* and leader of the most important military unit, the deadly Goumiers. He had first heard of de Gaulle and France Libre on 25 June 1940 and since then had made his way through catastrophe, bandaged, fed and helped throughout by ordinary people, few of whom had heard the 18 June broadcast from London and even fewer of whom were convinced that with the Armistice France would become a German satellite under a senile Pétain.

Crisis of military leadership in the 1930s," *Journal of Strategic Studies*, XIV (1991): 449. (Italics in text).

23. Nr. 165: 2.7.42 in Dr. Henry Picker, *Hitler's Tischgespräche im Führerhauptquartier 1941-42*, 2nd ed. (Stuttgart, 1965), pp. 429-430. There is an emphatic declaration of Hitler's belief that after the French victory, he was a military genius, to whom advice from his staff officers was totally unnecessary, in Helmuth Greiner, *Die Oberste Wehrmachtsführung 1939-43* (Weisbaden, 1951), pp. 108-109.

24. Interview, General Weygand, 12 Oct. 1950.

Under the grim circumstances prevailing at Carlton Gardens on the date of his arrival there, 25 July 1940, de Hautecloque's presence marked the beginning of Gaullism as a political and military reality: he was the modern Bayard, the *chevalier sans peur et sans reproches*, for whom de Gaulle had been impatiently waiting. Hautecloque was swiftly dispatched to rally the French colonies in mid-Africa to the cause. The Cameroons became Gaullist on 26 August, followed by Gabon on 10 November. Since the Tchad had already parted from Pétain under the inspiration of its black leader, Félix Eboué, Hautecloque saw his chance to exhibit to the world Free France's fighting capabilities. In December 1940 – January 1941, leading a motley crew of only one hundred Europeans and two hundred natives, Black and Arab, armed with primitive weapons and twenty vehicles, de Hautecloque led a seventeen-hundred kilometer assault on the southernmost Italian fort in Libya, the oasis of Koufra.[25] The fortress fell after a few hours of fighting on 1 March. Philippe Leclerc, as he was now known to the outside world to protect the Comtesse and their children tucked away in northern France,[26] became a hero to his troops, who called themselves the "Rats du Désert," and to the Free French movement across the globe.[27]

Philippe Leclerc de Hautecloque also made a solemn pledge called the "Serment de Koufra" shortly after his victory. It was that he and his men would not rest until the Tricolour flew again over the Cathedral of Strasbourg.[28] Franklin Roosevelt and Dwight Eisenhower dismissed this oath as romanticism redolent of Lawrence of Arabia. They came from a culture that viewed war in narrow, technical, logical terms. George Patton, foul-mouthed in public and a Boston Brahmin in private, did understand the *Serment*, sensing that a *baroudeur* quite like himself had appeared at last in the Allied Command.[29]

25. *Le Général Leclerc vu par ses compagnons de combat* (Paris, 1948), pp. 79-92.
26. His wife, the Comtesse de Hautecloque, first understood that the victor of Koufra was in truth her husband via a B.B.C. broadcast. "Leclerc" is almost as common a name in France as "Smith" in England.
27. See above all the work of Charles Bené of Séléstat (Bas-Rhin), one of the last three or four survivors of the expedition to Koufra, *Carnets de route d'un "Rat du Désert," 1ère. partie, 1940-42* (Raôn l'Etape, 1991.)
28. *Le Général Leclerc vu*, p. 115.
29. Interview, Charles Codman, Patton's Chief of Staff, Boston, 2 Feb. 1948.

After more thousand-kilometer raids in all directions from Koufra and the Tchad, the Fezzan was entirely conquered by the end of 1942. On 24 January 1943, Leclerc joined Field Marshal Bernard Montgomery at Tripoli. He and his men then fought the Tunisian campaign with British and French North African troops. Free France now had strong allies in a fully mobilized Britain and America, an enormous difference from the situation in 1940. Leclerc was now given the task of recruiting the best of the French forces to create an armored division, patterned along American lines and equipped with American materiel.[30] Roosevelt himself, despite his strong aversion to de Gaulle as another "Jeanne d'Arc," had promised the French Provisional Government sitting at Algiers, one major Free French unit to be sent into northern France in the forthcoming invasion of the Continent. Leclerc now accomplished by sheer force of will the amalgam of French troops caught up previously in a deadly civil war: Giraudists, Pétainists, refugees from all over the world with some connection to France, escapees from the corrupt, roach-infested jails of Franco's Spain, indeed an entire brigade of French and foreign volunteers from the recent Spanish Civil War.[31] His *grande unité* became the model of cohesion, so sadly lacking in 1940 and so difficult within France Libre, not to mention the Resistance inside the *métropole*. Leclerc proved himself a master of conciliation, an indispensable counterweight to de Gaulle's often hollow oratory and his vengeful Jansenist mentality. The social, political and ideological "racines

---

30. According to Raymond Muelle in his *Histoire de la 2e. D.B.* (Paris, 1990), p. 38, "troupes de couleur" were not to be included due to American demands.

31. *Le Général Leclerc vu*, pp. 177-189. The great Lt. Col. Putz and his company of Loyalist Spanish Civil War veterans ("le soviet des capitaines") were incorporated along with Paul de Langlade, who would probably have been on the Franco side. The General Staff was made up of officers from primarily conservative and moneyed backgrounds. There are nearly 90 who have the particule in a list given in Alain Aymard, *Album mémorial de la 2e. D.B.* (Paris, 1990). The G-2 and G-3 staffs had more than a hint of the Ancien Régime. Comte Robert de Ganay, a coworker in the G-2, was the lord of a vast estate in eastern Algeria, the Domaine des Lions. While he, I and Alberto Arregui y Alba were on a brief leave from the front to a frightened, starving and bitter Paris in late December 1944, we were invited to tea by Robert's mother, the Comtesse Douairière, in a stone-cold mansion in the XVIe. It was pure Proust: Odile de Guermantes on an ice-floe!

d'un malentendu" in Marc Bloch's terms,[32] had finally been dug up and thrown into Leclerc's fiery furnace.

At Témara in Morocco, Force "L" as it was now called, received American supplies, tanks and vehicles of all sorts, uniforms and the whole list of war materiel from nearby Casablanca in 1943-1944. Its name was changed to the Deuxième Division Blindée Française on 24 August 1943.[33] Leclerc trained it to work according to the lessons learned in the 1940 debacle: surprise, speed, attack, will power and above all an obsession with victory.[34] In strictly doctrinal terms, he was of course following the ideas first proposed in 1920-22 by the French General Jean Estienne.[35] His theories, long ignored by the interwar French General Staff, were eagerly embraced by younger officers in France and elsewhere. Estienne and J.F.C. Fuller of Britain had made possible the careers of de Gaulle, Heinz Guderian, Erwin Rommel and Erich von Manstein.

By the spring of 1944, Leclerc was known as a general who would refuse to obey orders he considered impossible to achieve.[36] Thus, whenever the 2e. D.B. attacked, it would do so convinced that victory was certain: its *furia francese* would erase the shameful memories of 1940. At no time did Leclerc view his men as "cannon-fodder," a phrase used only by de Gaulle.[37]

* * *

I was a member of a six-man Photographic Intelligence Team, attached to the G-2 (Intelligence) section of the General Staff. Such a team had been constantly demanded by Leclerc since the 2e. D.B. journeyed from North Africa in May 1944 to its final training area concentrated around the North Sea port of Hull. Its

32. Marc Bloch, L'Etrange Défaite; témoignage écrit en 1940, suivis des écrits clandestins 1942-44, rev. ed. introd. by Georges Altmann (Paris, 1957), pp. 182-183.
33. A great ceremony was held on this occasion, after the all-important American technical inspection. See Cdt. (General) Paul de Langlade, En Suivant Leclerc (Paris, 1964), p. 76.
34. Langlade, En Suivant, pp. 106-107; Le Général Leclerc vu, p. 200.
35. General Jean Estienne, "Les forces matérielles à la guerre," Revue de Paris 19, 15 January 1922, p. 238; idem. (ed.), Conférence faite le 15 février 1920 sur les chars d'assaut, Histoire technique, histoire tactique, rues d'avenir (Paris, 1920).
36. Le Général Leclerc vu, p. 16.
37. Jean Lacouture, De Gaulle, 3 vols. (Paris, 1984-85) vol. II, Le Politique, p. 38.

headquarters were at a local aristocratic manor house, named Dalton Holme (sic), owned by Lord Hottan.[38] I was picked to join the team because I had studied French history, culture and language. But I was a long way from being truly bilingual, a skill that the terrifying first ten days in Normandy would give me. I was subjected, I later learned, to the "direct method," to "total immersion." What a strange gift, I have always thought, wholly unintended, from a battle of total annihilation.

After four weeks at Dalton Holme, where the team was outfitted with a darkroom and laboratory in a much-modified Dodge $1\frac{1}{2}$-ton truck,[39] we were sent to the Channel ports for transport to the Normandy beachhead. On 25 July, I was taking a lunch-break from duty, quite alone, dangling my feet in the water at the end of a long pier on the deserted Bournemouth waterfront. Suddenly, I heard the familiar tapping of a cane coming up behind me. Looking over my shoulder, I saw a slim, elegant French officer with two stars on his képi: it was Leclerc himself, the "Patron" or "Oncle Philippe" to us. As I struggled to get to my feet, Leclerc said simply "reste assis, mon petit, ça serait mieux pour nous." He knew, of course, where I belonged in his division, so he asked me about my origins, where I had been educated, and how I felt now. A western Massachusetts mill town, Harvard, and "ready to go" were my answers. Then he gestured to the east with his cane, across the waters, saying "Moi aussi, j'habite loin d'où nous sommes, la Picardie. J'ai ma femme et six enfants qui m'attendent dans notre château de Tailly, quatre garçons et deux filles. L'aîné a ton âge, Henri, et sera bientôt avec nous dès le moment de la Libération, notre Libération de toute la France." After a few more remarks, he said goodbye and left, all alone, tapping his cane along the empty pier to the shore. I had just turned twenty and had beheld a god. The reality of that chance encounter with Leclerc was so overwhelming that for months thereafter I could remember it only in and as a dream.[40]

It was that very dream that emancipated me. I was now part of a curious amalgam which did not rest on the principle of "Führer

---

38. Langlade, *En Suivant*, p. 113.
39. "Diary", 10-22 July 1944, Dalton Holme.
40. *Ibid.*, 23-29 July 1944, Bournemouth, Dorset. Vicomte Henri de Hautecloque joined his father's division when the Nord was liberated in August-September 1944. He was killed in action in Indochina in 1951.

befehl, wir folgen Dich." French irreverence, earthiness and *rouspéteurs* effectively assured that there was to be no caesarism in the 2e. D.B. I felt free, first of all because I was now functioning in a military atmosphere devoid of the resentfulness and horrible "chicken-shit" of American units. Here were informality, camaraderie and a universal, calm and powerful indifference to protocol and rank (*catégories*). The intelligence, skill and creativity unleashed in each member of the 2e. D.B. thus worked together to reach our goals in the shortest possible time. Without any strain on his part Leclerc had reproduced the fraternity and informality of the earliest de Gaulle days at Carlton Gardens, an ambiance that would occur again in what the General's best biographer, Jean Lacouture, calls "Le printemps de Matignon" in May through August 1958.[41] We in 1944 were not surprised at all, but hugely proud of the fact, that in the first mad days of the *ralliement* of Central Africa in 1940-1941, Colonel Leclerc had quickly and simply pasted two stars on his képi just before his meeting with a British colonel at a local France Libre headquarters.

That chance meeting with the *Patron* came just five days before we were thrown into the mêlée in Normandy where I was forced to become bilingual. Why learning, desperately, their language from my French comrades and Norman farmers worked on me, but not on the others in my team, remains a mystery to me. It was true that I was much younger than they, had spent years in perfecting the liquid sounds of French (especially the back-of-the-throat, "gargled" "r"). But I was thrown off for weeks by the Norman peasant dialect where "si ney" stood for "ça y est." The little Canadian French I had picked up as a boy in infrequent visits to family property at Lac Mégantic in southeastern Québec was of no use. In any case, really learning to speak French via the "direct method" gave me another kind of liberation as a bonus, so perfectly described in Alice Kaplan's *French Lessons*. Simply because it contains fewer words, linguistic convention, clichés and small talk are reduced, permitting deeper ideas and feelings to enter.[42] French, or any other language for that matter, may well become a kind of retreat

---

41. Lacouture, *De Gaulle*, II, *Le Politique*, pp. 548-550.
42. Alice Kaplan, *French Lessons* (Chicago, 1993), pp. 210, 216.

for the frightened of this world, but it gave me a sacred metaphor, a prized skill and a career.

* * *

The 2e. D.B. landed on Utah beach on 30-31 July 1944, at the precise moment when Patton had breached a huge gap at Avranches, the western part of the Cotentin peninsula's base. Beyond the hideous *bocage* that had taken so many lives since D-Day stood relatively open, rolling terrain, ideal for armored combat. Brushing aside the last German attempt to cut off the Allied advance at Mortain, Leclerc turned east behind the German lines to take Alençon, the capital of Upper Normandy. As a *baroudeur* without equal, Leclerc simply left his Poste de Commandement Avancé during the night of 11 August, alone with his jeep driver, his pistol and a machine-gun mounted on the rear of the chassis. He returned to an anxious Poste at six in the morning, fresh and intact, with a master-plan to take the city that very day. He had thus somehow become a French Henry V before Agincourt, substituting action for declamation. His *baraka* was now legendary: in this act of defiance there was the Command's *présence* on the battlefield, rather than the *absence* of 1940. It mattered little that the Luftwaffe bombed and heavily strafed headquarters on the night of 12 August. We occupied the *préfecture* in the city's center, a perfect target with its dark bulk and darker surrounding vegetation in a sea of moon-washed white dwellings. What I subsequently named "La Vierge du Mur" prevented the teetering, five-meter outside wall, just above my half-dug foxhole, from toppling over and crushing me. W.A.S.P. that I was, I joined that night the multitudes that seek safety in Her protection. Twenty percent of headquarters personnel were either killed or badly wounded that fatal night.[43]

The next objective was Argentan to the northeast, the southern anchor of that corridor stretching fifteen kilometers north to Falaise. Through this gap the débris of four shattered German armies were trying to escape to the safety of the Seine, sixty kilometers to the east. Again, Leclerc's rapidity and skill worked their magic: Argentan was taken on August 18. What stretched north

---

43. "Diary," *Alençon* (Orne), 12 August 1944.

to the Poles and Canadians from Falaise was the horrifying, compacted mass of dead bodies, horses, wrecked tanks and vehicles, the immense field of death, putrefying under the blazing sun, that Eisenhower writes so movingly about in his memoirs.[44] Nothing had ever approached that dreadful carnage in 1940.

Immediately, the problem of Paris emerged. An insurrection begun on August 18 by a general strike of the city's police force, was sputtering badly and slipping hourly under Communist control.[45] Leclerc, *fonceur* that he was, "disobeyed" by going over the heads of his corps commanders, a minuscule, tight-lipped Gerow and an uncharacteristically unsympathetic Patton. The American commanders regarded Paris as a secondary objective, to be bypassed via Melun and Mantes in pursuit of the fleeing Germans. But de Gaulle, and finally a reluctant Eisenhower, intervened in Leclerc's favor.[46] A blast of the wild African-tuned trumpet of the "Douxième Cuir" awakened us at four a.m. at Montmerré, a village northeast of Argentan. Despite battle fatigue and the downpour of rain, never were seventeen-thousand men so quickly in their jeeps, trucks, tanks, tank-destroyers, half-tracks and command cars: four minutes, by one count. The shout went up: "A Paris! A Paris!"[47]

* * *

Thursday, 24 August 1944. From the heights of the Bois de Saint-Cloud, Paris shimmered in the clear light of early evening. We had come that day from Rambouillet, nowhere as far away as Montmerré the day before, our progress impeded every five kilometers by the local population celebrating their liberation. The rain had

---

44. Dwight D. Eisenhower, *Crusade in Europe* (Garden City, 1948), p. 279.

45. The entire historiography of the French Communists and their goals in the Liberation of Paris are deftly summed up in Lacouture, *De Gaulle*, vol I, *Le Rebelle*, pp. 805-808. General Pierre Koenig, hero of Bir Hakeim, did exclaim at dinner in Paris on 26 August 1944: "'Paris has just barely escaped another Commune.'"*Ibid.*, II 30. Lacouture also contributes valuable knowledge about Pétain's last-minute attempt to achieve a reconciliation with de Gaulle. Laval's attempt to circumnavigate de Gaulle by using an aged Edouard Herriot to recall the Assemblée Nationale, which he had broken on 9-10, 12 July 1940, is ably recounted in Cointet, *Laval*, pp. 484-494.

46. Dominique Lapierre and Larry Collins, *Paris, brûle-t-il?* (Paris, 1969), pp. 128-200.

47. "Diary," 22 August 1944, Montmerré (Orne).

long since disappeared into the fog of Normandy and the sun shone brightly.

In the Bois de Saint-Cloud, echoing to the sound of distant explosions, gunfire and, later on, the ringing of church bells, stood a huge, sleek, black Packard limousine. It seemed so incongruous there, beneath the towering beeches, a poignantly sharp reminder of the vanished civilian world of luxury on the other side of the ocean. "C'est pour de Gaulle," murmured our comrades. A whole new order was emerging before my eyes in the shadows of the Bois: de Gaulle, the Spirit become flesh, the pulsating reality of what had by now become "our" 2e. D.B., Paris, the prize of our lifetimes. It all came together in a flash.[48]

At nine the next day, Friday 25 August, we passed over the Pont de Saint-Cloud to the right of Langlade's Groupement Tactique, through Boulogne to the Trocadéro and then across another bridge, the Pont des Invalides, to the great pile itself. It was late by the soldiers' clock, but the pajama-clad Parisians waving to us from their apartment balconies looked as if they had just awakened. Another reminder of the comfort of peace-time. Here and there fluttered hand-made American flags amongst the Tricolours.

Our destination, the west (La Tour Maubourg) wing of the Invalides, had just been taken by a detachment of Spahis attacking from the rear, up the avenues de Villars and de Breteuil. (The German garrison still held the Gare Montparnasse, the Luxembourg, and the rue de Rivoli from the Meurice to the Naval Office.)[49] By the time we crossed the Esplanade des Invalides to La Tour Maubourg, its courtyard was jammed with German prisoners of all ranks. Some of the enlisted men were hardly more than children, all of them Fabrices del Dongo marooned on the battlefield of a latter-day Waterloo. Many of them were shaking with terror and weeping as screams from the mob outside grew ever louder. My heart went out to them: I too had volunteered for the army at the age of seventeen. Summoning up my broken high-school German, I tried to reassure those German adolescents nearest me that my French soldier-comrades simply would not allow the mob to tear

48. *Ibid.*, 24 August 1944, Sèvres (Seine-et-Oise).
49. Lapierre and Collins, *Paris*, pp. 201-452.

them apart, that their lives were not in danger. Some of them swallowed hard and wiped away their tears. Almost at once, they were led out in single file between two double ranks of Spahis. The mob redoubled its screaming, its curses and its spitting at their erstwhile oppressors, but they were held back as far as I could see from the crowded courtyard. Years later, I saw a film that portrayed this exit. Fortunately, I had been right in my reassurances to those terrified youngsters: the French guards never gave way under mob pressure.

As we retreated from the heat of the day into the cool interior of the Invalides, the 2e. D.B. was mopping up "Gross-Paris", every building of which was etched into the minds of the many Parisians in our units. American and British correspondents were breaking into the west, or rue Cambon, side of the Ritz (which had the celebrated bar), as German officers were jumping into their automobiles on the east (Place Vendôme) side to escape capture.[50] And the formal surrender was taking place at the Gare Montparnasse with Leclerc, Dietrich von Choltitz (the German commander), the Resistance commanders and our beloved G-2, Colonel Repiton-Préneuf on hand. De Gaulle, furious that the formal surrender should take place in a mere train station, gave his most faithful follower, Leclerc, a horridly cruel tongue-lashing in public for the latter's allowing Colonel Rol-Tanguy, leader of the Resistance in Paris, to cosign the second of the two surrender documents.[51] Among the witnesses to this humiliating *algarade* was Commandant Jacques Massu, who, twenty-four years later, would effectively terminate the career of de Gaulle.[52] De Gaulle at this point was determined to present himself as the embodiment of the French State, of the Republic which had never ceased to exist despite the

50. Alan Moorehead, an eyewitness account, in his *Eclipse* (New York, 1945), pp. 163-164.
51. An abridged account of this *camouflet*, with all the venom carefully removed, is found in Charles de Gaulle, *Mémoires de guerre*, II, *L'Unité 1942-44* (Paris, 1956), pp. 305-307. Cf. the much more accurate and full account in Lacouture, *De Gaulle*, I, p. 830.
52. This concerns the *crise de régime* of April-May 1968 discussed in a chapter on the post-1945 French Army by Martin Alexander and myself in "From Politiques en Képi to Military Technocrats: De Gaulle and the Recovery of the French Army after Indochina and Algeria," in George Andreopoulos and Harold Selesky (eds.), *The Aftermath of Defeat* (New Haven, 1994), pp. 80, 171.

dishonour of the armistice of 1940 and the illegal coup engineered by Pétain, Weygand and Laval at Vichy on 9-10-12 July 1940. That Leclerc had delivered Paris to de Gaulle intact by his sheer speed and skill, outracing massive German reinforcements by thirty-six hours, was simply ignored by the leader of France Libre.[53]

Upon returning to the Esplanade des Invalides, where our vehicles and equipment had been left in the rush to reach La Tour Maubourg, a crowd of Parisians surrounded us, drawn by our American stripes as well as our gold insignia of the 2e. D.B. As I turned to go back to the Invalides, a short, elderly man with white hair and a ginger moustache stepped forward to lock me in a tight embrace. His whiskers and stubble scratched my face. Overcome by emotion, he murmured, "1916, Verdun, la Seconde Marne et Château-Thierry," tears running down his cheeks. I was young enough to feel embarrassed. I was mortified by this impromptu explosion of sentiment from a strange man who reeked of garlic, sweat, smoke and Pastis. It was only much later that I recognized this encounter to be a universal act: at that very moment, all over France, old and middle-aged men were hugging their American liberators.

As my discomfiture evaporated, I had a presentiment that I would somehow have to pay for being an American infatuated with the 2e. D.B. I knew nothing about the passionate intrigue that de Gaulle had to use with Eisenhower to liberate Paris in the first place, let alone the epic battles he had had to wage with Churchill and, above all, with Roosevelt since he had begun France Libre four long years ago.[54] Twenty years later, with

53. De Gaulle claimed that he and his movement inherited the "legitimacy" of the Third Republic because the Armistice – the "capitulation" – delivered France into the hands of the enemy. There can be, de Gaulle asserted, no "legitimate French government which has ceased to be independent." De Gaulle, *Mémoires*, II, p. 321. Pétain's counter-move, that he alone was France's "incarnation", is best discussed in a sardonic treatment of the "mythe Pétain", including photographs of what it led to in Marc-Pierre, marquis d'Argenson, *Pétain et le Pétinisme* (sic) (Paris, 1953). The whole notion of "incarnation" gets an hilarious treatment in Céline (pseud. of Louis-Ferdinand Destouches), *D'un château à l'autre. Romans*, II (Paris, 1974), pp. 124-126. The last point is made in the most recent and comprehensive treatment of Leclerc by Gen. Jean Compagnon, *Leclerc, Maréchal de France* (Paris, 1994), p. 604.

54. The American president refused to give de Gaulle the date and time of the Normandy invasion, alleging that France Libre security was too lax in both London

Gaullism and anti-Americanism running high, I was taunted by an unfamiliar commandant at the anniversary luncheon given by the city of Paris on my double loyalty, my wisp of an American accent. I remained silent, knowing that refusal to take the bait disorients one's antagonist, especially if he be French. As I, my great Franco-British friend Bernard Foulquiès and the commandant left the banquet hall, my adversary apologetically confessed that he had many American friends in N.A.T.O. exiled from France that year by de Gaulle. I realized instantly that the boozy adulation of that noon on 25 August 1944 on the Esplanade had run its historical course. My would-be tormentor was not an *ancien combattant* of the 2e. D.B., which never again allowed interlopers to disturb the real fraternity that united it to America. At the fortieth anniversary of the liberation of Strasbourg in November 1984, the President of the Association des Anciens opened the glorious Alsatian meal before us with the words: "Sans les Américains, nous n'aurions été rien!" Thunderous applause broke loose and I was hoisted to stand on my chair to symbolize the celebrated *amalgame* which had been built by Leclerc.[55]

It was now Saturday, 26 August, the day on which de Gaulle, risking assassination,[56] made his triumphal march from the Etoile, down the Champs-Elysées to the Concorde and then, (using the great black Packard) to Notre Dame for the Te Deum. As by far the youngest member of the team, I was ordered to stay in our minuscule *bureau* at La Tour Maubourg. From noon on a distant

---

and Algiers. Then Roosevelt had Eisenhower go through the cruel hoax of pretending to include de Gaulle's additions to the Invasion Proclamation which, without a single reference to Free France, had already been distributed to the troops 48 hours earlier. The famous shouting-match between an angry de Gaulle and an enraged Churchill took place at Portsmouth on 11 June 1944, where the latter roared: "'Any time I have to choose between Roosevelt and you, I'll choose Roosevelt!'" It comes as no surprise, therefore, to have de Gaulle, according to his principal private secretary, bursting out against his Allies on 5 September 1944 as "salauds ... Ils me le paieront!" Claude Mauriac, *Un Autre de Gaulle. Journal, 1944-54* (Paris, 1970), p. 23.

55. "Diary," 25 November 1984, Strasbourg and Sélestat (Bas-Rhin). The cordiality towards me, as an American survivor, was repeated on the fiftieth anniversary of the Liberation of Paris. *Ibid.*, 24-27 August 1994.

56. Two assassins, both Miliciens and the killers of Georges Mandel, had been arrested on 25 August 1944 at the Hôtel de Ville. Lacouture, *De Gaulle*, I, p. 883.

roar arose to the north across the Esplanade and the Seine. It grew ever louder and more distinct: about 1500 hours there was a tremendous sound wave of exclamation, applause and gunfire in the Concorde. Then it died away to the north. In three hours I had experienced the defining moment of my life as a man and as an historian, although I had gone through it like a blind person at the cinema, hearing only the sound-track of the film. Only Orson Welles, in his recording of the event brings out the furor at the Concorde and at Notre Dame as the so-called *tireurs des toits*, elite sharpshooters left behind by the dreaded Milice under Joseph Darnand, sowed their terror. As shots echoed throughout the Cathedral, a young priest literally taken off a nearby street and the terrified choir-boys went through the Te Deum at double-time.[57] (De Gaulle prevented Cardinal Archbishop Suhard, head of the Paris diocese, from officiating because he had participated in Pétain's visit in April and in the funeral of Philippe Henriot, Vichy's Minister of Information, assassinated on 28 June, 1944.)

There it was, "Paris, ivre de joie et d'amour, magnifique et fou," according to Paul de Langlade, one of our best commanders.[58] I had the evening off and was determined that I should see some of this Paris *en liesse*. As darkness fell, I and a Spahi friend named Raoul ambled down to a noisy *bal du quartier* on the rue Duvivier where, not far away, there were, in order of their importance to us, women, wine and music. Around 10 p.m. Luftwaffe bombs began falling, extinguishing the lights as the screaming crowd crammed itself into a nearby bomb-shelter. When the air-raid stopped one half-hour later, the same *tireurs des toits* of the killing earlier in the day reappeared, murdering the first unlucky twenty who climbed out of the shelter. Raoul and I crept up the stairs, turning away to the north to avoid the *tireurs*. Bullets sounding like a million angry bees buzzed past my right ear as I dropped to the pavement stones of Paris. We crawled north to an F.F.I. machine-gun nest which was firing at an upward angle to flush out the snipers. They agreed to take us out of the killing zone.

57. Alan Moorehead, an eyewitness, in his *Eclipse*, pp. 166-168.
58. Langlade, *En suivant*, p. 210, which also includes his indignation at the Luffwaffe raid.

Four of us eventually reached a huge underground garage, located under the present-day Place de la Résistance and the rue Cognacq-Jay. We were taken to the commander of the depot which housed hundreds of German and collaborationist vehicles captured or taken during the fighting of the previous week. Raoul and I had to return immediately to La Tour Maubourg, for our leave time expired at dawn. A huge, shining, armor-plated four-door Mercedes convertible appeared out of nowhere. Convinced that this was Charon's bark, Raoul and I huddled in the wells of the rear seats, as four armed Resistance men, including the chauffeur, climbed in. To our utter horror as veterans of the Normandy campaign, they all lit up cigarettes and switched on the powerful headlights as the Mercedes leaped up the ramp and roared down the street. At each junction where several streets or avenues converged, the driver raced to the center of the open space, then quickly turned an abrupt 45-degree angle, wheels spinning in the air as rifle and machine-gun fire crackled around us. Neither of us knew where we were but agreed that this was our death-ride, straight out of something Raoul had read all about: Chicago under Al Capone. When we finally arrived in the grey dawn at the east (avenue des Invalides) wing, our four rescuers waved a cheerful farewell and disappeared into the mist. Raoul and I were too terrified to utter a single word, let alone one of thanks. My seven-hour tour of rejoicing Paris had turned out to be a turkey-shoot with me as the potential victim – victim of the French who were "on the other side." It was also the beginning of a professional lifetime of ambivalence toward and fascination with French fascism and Nazism which had already torn so many French families apart.[59]

* * *

The all-time classic operation of tanks with air support was achieved shortly after the 2e. D.B. left the *bordel* that the Esplanade had become. Thirty kilometers north of Epinal in eastern Lorraine are the villages of Dompaire, Damas and Ville-sur-

---

59. A prime example is the de la Mazière family, whose son became an enthusiastic officer in the anti-Bolshevist Légion des Volontaires Français and then the Waffen S.S. Division Charlemagne, some of whose members defended Hitler's bunker in Berlin to the very last. See Christian de la Mazière, *Le Rêveur casqué* (Paris, 1972).

Illon. Two of our Groupement Tactiques, one headed by the fiery Massu, the other by Minjonnet, lured the 112th Panzerbrigade, itself heading for Patton's Third Army flank, into a trap. Infantry, artillery, Sherman tanks, tank destroyers and above all Eighth Air Force Thunderbolt fighter-bombers, all coordinated by Major John Tower of the 2e. D.B. air support liaison, wrecked 59 brand-new Panther tanks. The Panther was the most formidable armored vehicle in the world at that time. Six air-strikes homed in by Tower's tank radio had sufficed to reduce the Panzerbrigade's Panthers to 30 in number, all of which failed to reach their target in the next engagement: the brigade disappeared from the German Order of Battle. The few disoriented Germans left alive at what is called today "Dompaire" dismounted and fled into the neighboring forests.[60] The date was 13 September 1944. What a sweet revenge for what had occurred at the Bois-de-la-Marfée on the Meuse on 12 May 1940!

After the Dompaire victory, the whole Allied offensive line from Beveland in the north to Rouffach in the south slowly congealed into the autumnal mud, slowed down by difficult terrain (for us, it was the Vosges mountains). Shortages of fuel, materiel and supplies of all kinds also contributed to the stagnation. But in the small town of Gerbévillers, now our headquarters on the swollen Mortagne about 50 kilometers from Nancy, Leclerc was planning an audacious coup. He would break the stalemate on his front by infiltrating the two elaborately constructed German defense lines, the Vorvogesen and Vogesen Stellungen. Leclerc counted on the fact that when his tank units reached the crest of the Vosges mountains, the Rhine would become the next target and the Serment de Koufra – the tricolour should fly above Strasbourg's Cathedral – would be fulfilled. Our "team photo" had a run of luck: peering down through our stereopticon lenses at the photographs rushed to us by our liaison with the Eighth Air Force, we discovered that the numerous winding trails in the Vosges north of one objective, Phalsbourg, and south of the other, Saverne, had just enough width to allow our Sherman tanks to slip up unnoticed to the crest of the Vosges and then descend the eastern slope to the Rhine plain. Sav-

---

60. Langlade, *En Suivant*, pp. 239-246.

erne and Phalsbourg could thus be outflanked and enveloped from the rear. It was the most important work we had done for the 2e. D.B.: the discovery of a tank commander's dream operation. Repiton-Préneuf was ecstatic, and Leclerc upon receiving our news is reported to have exclaimed, "Ça y est! On les aura!"[61]

With Baccarat liberated on 4 November, all was ready for a jump-off from Cirey-sur-Vesouze, well inside the outer German wall, the Vorvogesen Line. Thanks to the quick liberation of Badonvillers, the signal was given to the subordinate Groupements Tactiques: "Pousser comme une brute!"[62] The northernmost G.T. under Quilinchi shortly enveloped Phalsbourg, while Massu's G.T. was by noon over the most formidable obstacle of the inner Vogesenstellung, the great Col de Dabo, following the forest trails our team had marked out. The German military and civilian personnel, illegally introduced into Alsace in violation of the 1940 Armistice, were in a state of panic, bewilderment and shock, mirroring the fleeing French armies and hordes of refugees in May and June of that year.

Far worse was to come. At dawn on 23 November Leclerc launched five Groupements Tactiques on defenseless Strasbourg, aiming for the vital bridge, the Pont de Kehl, connecting Strasbourg with its suburb in Baden. At Leclerc's Poste de Commandement Avancé, the key code message arrived at 10:30 a.m., "tissu est dans iode," which meant that the northernmost G.T., commanded by Rouvillois, was already inside Strasbourg and headed for the Rhine bridge. The other four Groupements Tactiques, led by Massu, Cantarel, Putz and Debray, were at the fortresses surrounding Strasbourg and ready to enter the city. Life in this much-coveted and utterly safe garrison haven suddenly became a giant mouse-trap. Street-cars were emptied as Germans and Alsatian collaborators fled for the Rhine, officers struggling to their automobiles with four and one-half years of booty taken from all of Europe: they and their drivers were shot and the booty "liberated."

The Tricolour did indeed float over Strasbourg Cathedral again: the Serment de Koufra had been kept. The commandant of "Gross-

---

61. "Diary," 20 October 1944, Gerbévillers (Meurthe-et-Moselle).
62. Repiton-Préneuf et al. *La 2e. D.B. Le Général Leclerc en France. Combats et combattants* (Paris, 1945), p. 114.

Strassburg", Walter von Vaterrodt, surrendered to Leclerc in the fortress of Ney, leaving masses of unarmed German civilians, who did not have the luxury of a deluxe escape as did their hated Gauleiter, Robert Wagner (né Backfisch) to flee across the Rhine at Neuf-Brisach. They huddled around the largest and ugliest building in the city's centre, the pre-1914 Kaiserpalast. At the dessert course of Leclerc's luncheon there on 25 November, G.T. leader Dio walked in to be cheerfully greeted, "Hein, mon vieux Dio, on y est, cette fois! Maintenant, on peut crever tous les deux!" At that precise moment, the German artillery east of Kehl had found the Palast's range, dropping a shell that sent the overhead chandelier, a masterpiece of Wilhelmine kitsch, crashing to the floor on Leclerc, Dio and the other guests.[63] Leclerc's reaction was uproarious laughter as he struggled to his feet, entirely encased in the crystal that Goering had so long coveted from Baccarat.[64]

We, on the other hand, as part of Massu's column from the Col de Dabo, were ensconced in the most prosperous farmer's house just 12 kilometers to the west, in a tiny village with the cuckooclock name of Dingsheim-an-der-Souffel.[65] The master bedroom, which we occupied, was entirely decorated with incredibly coloured and detailed frescoes, done in the time of the apogée of Alsatian folk art, the early 18th century. The effect was quite like that of the Amore e Psiche room at the Palazzo Te in Mantova. And we too had a surprise the morning after Leclerc's encounter with the chandelier. At 7:00 a.m. I was nudged awake by the proprietor who handed me from a silver tray a small glass of kirsch. "Ça vous fera du bien," he said as my body began to throw off the stiffness of a frosty night spent sleeping on the floor. It was the beginning of my love affair with Alsace and Alsatians, open and sincere as no other frontier people in Europe. And joyous too, as indicated at the end of the formal military ceremony held in the Place Kléber, given back its real name after four years' indignity as the Platz Karl Roos, the Alsatian autonomist spy executed

---

63. Repiton-Préneuf et al. *La 2e. D.B.*, p. 118.
64. Goering had ordered a complete setting of Baccarat crystal for 100 guests in 1940, but the local workers deliberately sabotaged its completion over four years until their liberation by the 2e. D.B. on 4 November 1944.
65. "Diary," Dingsheim-an-der-Souffel (Bas Rhin), 26 November 1944.

for treason by the French at Champigneulles, near Nancy, on 7 February 1940.[66]

* * *

The subsequent history of the 2e. D.B. is beyond the range of this essay. Suffice it to say it was shuffled back and forth between the Upper Saar, during Hitler's Ardennes offensive, and the northern edge of the Colmar pocket, midway between Strasbourg and Mulhouse, which it cracked open by a daring attack from the rear on Grussenheim on 29 January 1945.[67] The great Colonel Putz, commander of the Regiment de Marche du Tchad, perished there; in many ways he was the most likeable and attractive of Leclerc's subordinates, open, kind and generous.[68] Our Team Photo parted company with the 2e. D.B. when the latter left Alsace at the end of February 1945 for rest and rehabilitation in the mid-Loire valley. The division had been so badly bruised since the November breakthrough at Saverne that the breathing space was most welcome.[69] But it was also used as a Gaullist political armed force in one of the centres of Communism in France, Châteauroux, a munitions factory town. And it was wasted on a useless target, the German pocket at Royan, the head of the Gironde estuary. Increasingly bitter, the Division saw itself as wrongly deprived of the fruits of its most daring victories: the invasion of Germany east of the Rhine.[70]

66. See my *Chefs autonomistes alsaciens 1919-47* in *Saisons d'Alsace*, No. 71 (Oct. 1980) (Strasbourg, 1980), p. 73.
67. The national and international consequences of Eisenhower's initial order on 22 December 1944 to abandon all of Alsace and return to a defence line west of the Vosges are best examined in Lacouture, *De Gaulle*, II, pp. 69-76. He concludes that Eisenhower, while typically American in his slowness to grasp the political repercussion stemming from his order, did not act from "pusillanimity," giving new orders to the American and French forces to hold in Alsace at the first signs of the slowing of Hitler's Ardennes offensive. The revenge of the returning Nazis to Alsatian territory already liberated by the Allies (Haguenau north to the Pfalz border at Wissembourg) was typical of the war on the Eastern front: massacres, deportations, scorched earth.
68. See his completely disarming portrait in Repiton-Préneuf et al., *La 2e. D.B. en France*, p. 149.
69. The most moving account of the suffering, hardships and, above all, psychological damage is Captain Jacques Branet, *L'Escadron. Carnets d'un cavalier* (Paris, 1968).
70. Jean Julien Fonde, *J'ai vu une meute de loups. Avec la 2e. D.B. du Maroc à Berchtesgaden* (Paris, 1969), pp. 191-203. Compagnon sees the withdrawal from the

At the last moment Leclerc's impatience won out and he "disobeyed" again, sending his armor and troops straight across France to become one of the units under the command of General Patch, slicing through Bavaria and the Tyrol. The 2e. D.B.'s prize, a photographer's dream come true, was the taking and sacking by his *Meute des Loups* of the Berghof and above all the Adlershorst, Hitler's cherished personal hideaways above Berchtesgaden.[71] It was General Jean de Lattre de Tassigny who was sent to the formal surrender ceremonies in shattered Berlin on 8 May 1945. But it was Leclerc's division which got the spoils of war. One of the 2e. D.B.'s favourite characters, a *titi de Paris* who hung around headquarters, emerged from the burning Berghof, covered with soot but dragging behind him a gold and silver suit of armor of Shogun Japan, given to Hitler by his ally, Hirohito.[72] (The *titi* quickly disappeared into the shadowy world of fenced art in Paris and was never heard from again.) In a quite odd way, this triumph of booty redeemed the 2e. D.B.'s prowess. It became our totem for the climactic reversal: from Defeat in 1940 to Victory in 1944-1945.[73]

---

front as a "pénitence" for Leclerc's refusal to follow de Gaulle's orders to "amalgamate" untrained F.F.I. forces into the 2e. D.B., as de Lattre was doing with his largely North African and colonial First French Army. Compagnon, *Leclerc*, p. 604.

71. Repiton-Préneuf et al., *La 2e. D.B. en France*, pp. 152-155. Leclerc did not waste time by getting permission from a hostile de Gaulle for his lightning dash, but went straight to General Walter Bedell Smith, Eisenhower's Chief of Staff. Compagnon, *Leclerc*, p. 604.

72. The Berghof plunder included Hitler's entire private library the contents of which were grossly inferior to their splendid gold and silver bindings. Two volumes were given each officer by Leclerc himself. Cdt. (General) André Gribius, *J'ai connu cette armée* (Paris, 1967), p. 8.

73. After breaking with de Gaulle over the future of Indochina, Leclerc was brought home from the Far East in early 1947 to become Inspector-General of French Forces in North Africa. He was killed in an airplane crash near Colomb-Béchar on 28 November the same year. Rumors of sabotage are without foundation, although the Communists regarded Leclerc as another Cavaignac in taking Paris from their grasp in 1944, and the ultra-Gaullists viewed him – to use their leader's choice description – as having the "caractère d'un cochon." In 1952, he was made a Marshal of France.

XIII

THE TRAUMA OF 1940

A Disaster and its Traces

Stanley Hoffmann

Is it really necessary, fifty or more years later, to remind people what a great disaster it was? In just seven weeks one of the great powers in a still Eurocentric international system collapsed and had to accept, in conditions that flagrantly insulted its pride and honor, the victor's occupation of more than two-thirds of its territory. An army considered the world's strongest was defeated in a matter of days by a swift, bold adversary. An almost unanimously accepted strategic doctrine proved itself out-of-date and calamitous: two million soldiers were taken prisoner. Once again a political regime failed to survive a military debacle, but the death of what had been France's longest experience of liberal democracy resulted from a suicide with elements of shadowy intrigue and abject repentance; and that was followed by an almost complete abdication on behalf of a venerated but disquieting old man. For the first time many of the new *messieurs* as well as some of the older ones then confessing their sins not only urged the French, like Renan after the defeat of 1871, to study and emulate the victor's triumph, but also to repudiate a major part of the nation's history and traditions in order to throw themselves into the victor's political and ideological wake, in its irresistible advance toward the future. Knocked out by the breadth of the catastrophe, and even more by an exodus that uprooted some of the world's greatest home-bodies and threw men and women in love with security and crippled with habits onto jammed-up, even bomb-stormed roads, France demonstrated what an insightful author recently called a quasi-biological need to recover and withdraw.[1]

Everything, then, was affected and thrown into question: the army and the political regime, the policies leading up to the war, also the very identity of the nation, what Montesquieu would have called the "general spirit" of the French political community, the nature of its elites, the behavior of its social groups and the validity of an economic system that seemed too timid and cramped compared with the victor's dynamism. In 1814-15 the disaster could be blamed on a man who had insisted on reigning alone; in 1871 on a regime born of a coup d'état, whose leader had declined with age. But this time everyone felt implicated, even if the search for scapegoats once again unveiled the universal tendency of penitents to try and turn themselves into judges.

So there is reason to believe that an unprecedented traumatism in French history would have left not just marks but deep, telling scars, even visible wounds in subsequent history and memory. But that is not really the case. The marks, scars and wounds are there, but they immediately raise two hard questions. First, how can one distinguish, in their source, the disaster of May-June 1940 from the disaster of the preceding years – the long decline, complex and discontinuous, of the period between the wars – and especially from the black years following the armistice? The debacle is just one episode – certainly the most violent and extensive – in a whole series of traumatisms: the years from 1934 to 1936, then Munich, then the great division between the supporters of Vichy, the collaborators, the temporizers and the Resistants, and finally the quasi- civil war of 1943-44. Obviously, various people's memories of the 1940 catastrophe are colored, even shaped, by memories from before and after. Like the French Revolution, the convulsive years of 1934-46 are a whole: divisible for historians, of course, and for those who were then engaged in action, yet still a whole

---

1. Jean-Louis Crémieux-Brilhac, *Les Français de l'an 40*, vol. II (Paris, 1990), p. 714.

because of the chain and mesh of circumstances that seemed inexorably to drag individuals and groups from one ordeal to another, also because of the contrast between the relatively stable, calm world before and the altogether different world afterwards. There is not, there cannot be (except, of course, in the personal memories of various people about specific cases and moments) any memory of the disaster which is entirely distinct and distinguishable from what preceded and what followed.

I have said that this whole was divisible for historians and engaged participants. But here appears another obstacle, which gives us an important, yet oblique lesson about national memory and history. There is a stunning contrast between the proportions of the May-June 1940 catastrophe and the role it plays in the country's intellectual production (what the English and the Americans call *the record*). Let's look at what might be called historical analyses. There are studies done by military men and examinations of military strategy and tactics, sometimes highly technical, but probably the best synthesis in the domain was written by a professor in Switzerland.[2] There are lots of descriptive works – from Benoist-Mechin to Paillat and Amouroux – giving us tons of anecdotes and details rather than analyses. As far as comprehensive views that try to look at things from on high and plunge into their very depths, I see only three, all written soon after the defeat or the Liberation: Marc Bloch's *L' Etrange défaite*, Leon Blum's *A L' Echelle humaine*, and the beginning of General de Gaulle's *Mémoires de guerre*. Jean-Louis Crémieux-Brilhac's summa, which deduces from a massive amount of data and often unpublished documents interpretations and conclusions that refine, without unsettling, the insights and judgments of the "three greats" just mentioned, did not appear until 1990. Compared to the vast number of books and articles on Vichy or the 1930s or even the more spotty writings on the Resistance and the Liberation, there is not much at all.

There is even less in art and literature. For the disaster of May-June 1940, *Le Silence de la mer* has no literary equivalent. A few novels have in a way captured the soldiers' confusion and humiliation, probably the best known being the last published volume of Sartre's

---

2. Ladislas Myzyrowicz, Autopsie d'une défaite (Lausanne, 1973).

Les Chemins de la liberté. No one will take offense if we say that there is no best-seller nor any book that can be compared to Stendhal's accounts of Waterloo or Tolstoi's renderings of the war in Russia. There are only two films worth mentioning: Pagnol's *La Fille du puisatier*, made while Marc Bloch was doing his citizen's self-examination in the summer of 1940, and *Les Jeux interdits*, Réné Clément's 1952 film. Yet in both cases the debacle does not really play the starring role. In Pagnol's film it frames a quite classical story of seduction and redemption; Clément's overwhelming images about the exodus from northern France are merely the prelude to a moving story about unhappy children and some rather rough peasants.

One cannot say that the glass is empty, but it is certainly not running over. A book about the debacle-syndrome modeled on Henri Rousso's work on the Vichy-syndrome would probably be brief.

The Humiliating Catastrophe

Yet we must examine memories that just barely whisper a word or two. As is the case for all studies of memory, we must be precise about our subject. We are not concerned with what an individual remembers – on this point, the memories of various people just tell us what they did, saw and felt over those few weeks. We are talking about collective memory, certainly a debatable notion,[3] but here I am using the term to designate not some "Durkheimian" phenomenon, but rather the common denominator of a great number of individual memories. It also means the memory of official partisans or groups who try, for various purposes, to suggest or even impose a given interpretation of events. Although so-called collective memory certainly has its functions, it is not really instrumental and manipulative, a form of ideology aimed at action (Robert Frank[4] also considers public memory, but I am inclined to see it only as the memory of the group – perhaps very broad and representative – that is in power at a given time – perhaps very long).

3. See the remarks of Marie Claire Lavabre in Denis Peschanski, Michael Pollack and Henry Rousso, eds., Histoire politique et sciences sociales (Paris, 1991), pp. 272-278.
4. "Bilan d'une enquête" in *La Mémoire des Français* (Paris, 1986), pp. 371-373.

Two characteristics, and only two, emerge from a study of collective memory as defined above. The first is quite obviously a very strong sense of catastrophe, the feeling that something quite out-of-this-world just blasted into daily life with almost cosmic speed (cf. Bloch's chosen title), a feeling all the stronger since everyone, from the public authorities on down, had apparently tried to keep up a normal life during the "phony war." In the collective memory of World War I, long, fierce pain is the dominant factor. In May-June 1940 it is the feeling of brutal, unexpected blows to the heart and the head, which produced a double displacement: physical or geographical (the exodus, prison-camps, exile or London for certain individuals) and mental, History with a capital H, which, after having threatened and growled in the wings for a long time, violently burst on stage and suddenly swept, quite against their will, those who were knocked out from the private into the collective sphere. Sartre will be my sole example here. In his *Carnets de la drôle de guerre* and his *Lettres au castor* he remained detached from barracks-life while pursuing his own work and the psychological dissection of those around him. Yet, after being whisked off to a German camp, he finally discovered the first-person plural, a group-sense and political community.

The other characteristic is humiliation, even shame. Since this feeling is so obvious and understandable, there is no need to insist. But two of its corollaries require exegesis. The first is the quite ordinary psychological tendency to look for salves and excuses. Many works (including Crémieux-Brilhac's fine volumes) emphasize triumphal moments and heroic examples in order to remind us and to show that not everything was a mess, that if certain requisites had been fulfilled, as in 1914, the nation could have kept its self-respect: the Saumur cadets, Colonel de Gaulle's counter-attacks, Raoul Dautry's reforms of industrial mobilization, etc ... As for the excuses, the most striking – which show so well how memory slips into myth (this is, by the way, a phenomenon just as common in triumphal memories as in humiliated ones) – are those about a "knife in the back" (as in Germany after 1918), meaning the famous fifth column, a self-justifying myth par excellence,[5] and

---

5. Crémieux-Brilhac, pp. 557-560.

those citing the numerical superiority of German forces and weaponry, a claim now settled by historians. After having proclaimed and believed that their side would (ultimately) win because of their strength, they had to console themselves by saying that they had lost because, without sufficient help from the Allies (which is not entirely wrong), they had confronted a stronger enemy (false, as far as numbers are concerned).

The other corollary, which results both from the humiliating shock and the flagrant insufficiency of the consoling myths, is the phenomenon that accounts for the relative vacuum I wanted to underscore from the very start: a certain refusal of, or at least reticence about, self-examination, about looking oneself right in the face, to use J.-P. Rioux's expression,[6] a refusal or reticence that is reflected in the absence of commemoration, except for June 18th. As Robert Frank has said, "the mournfully memorable is not easily commemorated"[7]; there are celebrations for the Liberation, rather than for the May '45 victory. Is that because the debacle was the prelude (and the consequence) of too many searing divisions? Frank has underlined the fact that the French actually commemorate quite a few events that wildly divided the nation. Yet one has to bring in a factor that explains why these particular harrowing events only fed the feelings of humiliation and therefore fostered the psychological impossibility of any commemoration. This factor also explains why there was so little self-examination after 1945. It is the tide of self-flagellation, of "maceration" (Léon Blum's word for it)[8] in the disaster's aftermath. These masochistic displays were of an altogether special sort. Unlike Blum's and Bloch's self-critical X-ray exams (is it just a coincidence that they were both Jewish?), the statements I am alluding to – beginning with Marshall Pétain's speech on 20 June 1940, which André Gide found "quite simply admirable,"[9] although he was promptly disappointed (as early as the 24th): "ever since the victory, a festive spirit has triumphed over the spirit of sacrifice," etc ... – these words were the opening salvos of the new Franco-French war. These were not signs of a

6. *La France de la 4ème République* I (Paris, 1980), p. 264.
7. Frank, p. 377.
8. *La Prison, le procès, la déportation* (Paris, 1955), p. 412.
9. *Journal 1939-42* (Gallimard, 1946), p. 44.

serene, stoic determination to undertake self-analysis, but instead manifestations of a grim tendency to blame one's sins on someone else, to plunge down into shame all the better to drag out, for one's own relief, the guilty parties. The slide from self-examination to denunciation, starting in June '40, then the oft-repeated hunt for scapegoats throughout the black years and after the Liberation (for example, the first interpretations of the Vichy regime and the collaboration) can help explain a certain vacuum or a relative silence surrounding the disaster.

That slide also reveals another characteristic, less unusual, of the memory of disaster. Such memory is divided against itself, a confrontation of constructions where truth and myth mix together for very precise purposes. First off, there was the instantaneous memory of Vichy, which died with the regime, except among Pétain's last faithful followers, but that is no reason to forget its range and strength in 1940-41. Thus, the diary of man named Chobaut, quoted by Crémieux-Brilhac,[10] is a perfect example of the ultra-fast slide from calling into question the "average citizen" (egotistical, sterile, petty), an uneasy critique insofar as Chobaut was himself part of that group, to adopting the Pétainist vulgate: not just work, family and country – these were, in essence, "unanimist" themes – but also the hunt for the guilty ones: political parties, big bankers, etc .... meaning the transition to a memory of exclusion, which makes the instigators carry the burden of the disaster and releases the author from any responsibility. The study of this apparently instantaneous "fabrication" of Vichy's official memory has been done so well and so often that there is no need to dwell further upon it, except to emphasize that there was in fact nothing instantaneous about it. It was the popular version of an analysis that Maurras had long been making, that had spread throughout the right-wing[11] and grown stronger because of the Popular Front and opposition to it. For a certain amount of time it was used both as an explanation of a colossal, outrageous phenomenon – the debacle – and as an excuse for preserving only a partial and partisan image of that event. Thus, a bewildered,

---

10. Crémieux-Brilhac, I, pp. 610-614.
11. Cf. Robert Soucy, *Le Fascisme français 1924-33* (Paris, 1989).

The Trauma of 1940

knocked-out nation tried to raise its spirits by returning to archaism and rejecting a major part of itself.

There are two other kinds of memory, rivals in antidefeatism. Despite their desire to be agents of unification, even unanimism, they too had their scapegoats, although certainly fewer than the official memory of 1940-44: Communist memory and Gaullist memory. Communist memory looks like a second coat of paint, spread over a first whose colors are a bit unpleasant. As we know, the picture of the defeat and the explanation that Jacques Duclos and Maurice Thorez tried to propagate during the summer and fall of 1940[12] started with the notion that the war was just the imperialists' way of getting even with each other, that it was imposed on the French by the bourgeoisie's fierce hatred for the Soviet Union and the workers. Once Hitler attacked Stalin, the earlier calls for immediate peace, then for struggle against "the bourgeoisie and its 'socialists'," "the veritable scourge of the masses," turned into an appeal for patriotic resistance against the invader and his lackies. Yet the Communist Party's manufactured memory kept hammering on the bourgeoisie's responsibility for the debacle, while presenting the French Communist Party and the workers as the only ones who did not lay down or disgrace themselves before May 1940. With this memory they meant at one and the same time to make their new or refound allies feel guilty and to lay the foundations for the Party's demands for purges and social, economic and political changes in France. Later, after the Liberation, especially after the failure of the tripartite system, the classical Communist analysis of the debacle became inseparable from the celebration of the heroic, exemplary role that the "Martyr's Party" played in the Resistance and the renewed denunciation of unreliable, deceitful allies.

In Gaullist memory – which has scarcely varied over the years – the traitors took the part that the trusts and cartels enacted in Communist memory, and the Resistance, inside and outside France, replaced the Communists. As in Communist memory, one finds here the myth that nearly the whole nation was upright in resistance. Yet Gaullist memory dwells much more on the black years, projecting them, as Raoul Girardet has said,[13] in an "evan-

---

12. Cf. Stéphane Courtois, *Le PCF dans la guerre* (Paris, 1980), pp. 500-528.
13. Raoul Girardet and Pierre Assouline, *Singulièrement libre* (Paris, 1990), p. 34.

gelico-epic" light, rather than on the trauma of 1940 (of which Communist memory cannot avoid speaking precisely because it has to erase the awkward image of a party temporarily but energetically defeatist). Is this because the heroic tale of the General began on June 18th, J-Day, Year I of the great legend? Or because it was truly difficult to put on France bewildered by the debacle a cloak of righteousness and glory, even partly imaginary? Or because it was all to the advantage of the great man's pedagogy of regeneration, which to some extent required a clear conscience and pride, even sham, to fit within the simple, striking and archetypal frame of the Fall, followed by the Call and the long collective ascent toward Unity and Salvation? Yet there remains a contrast between what can be called the official Gaullist version of history, which skims over the defeat, and de Gaulle's analysis in the first volume of his *Mémoires de guerre*, which attacks with well-documented eloquence the military's conformism and the feeble, divided stagnant "esprit du régime" (a narrower and more purely political explanation than the ones given by Bloch and Blum).

There remain two difficult questions (which may never be answered, especially the first. First, how many French people have really believed these mythical versions of the past? The instantaneous Pétainist memory, as a thousand sources tell us, "took" very quickly for a great part of the population; yet subsequent events really jolted these believers, some of them changing bit by bit their vision of the world and others settling down into out-and-out skepticism. We have fewer signs indicating how representative Communist and Gaullist memories were.

Second, insofar as these two memories (like Vichy memory) were in some way inculcated from top to bottom and anything but spontaneous, what will remain of them, now that the Communist Party is withering and dying and that the General's Gaullism is ebbing back or becoming an object of research and study rather than an article of faith and a program for action? If they are growing dim, won't the relative vacuum which I mentioned at the beginning get even bigger? Since this traumatism (unlike the Revolution or even the Commune) has not engendered any ideology (Vichy's ideology preceded the regime), won't we have in the future only the scholars' "memory" of the disaster, meaning the patient (and not necessarily harmonious) memory of the historians – who naturally tend to privilege either the causes (in the 30s or the phony war) or the effects? That is what has been done, for example, by J.-B. Duroselle[14] whose analysis of the decadence of the 30s is very close to de Gaulle's and P. Laborie, who underscores the link between various people's attitudes toward the debacle and their attitudes toward Vichy.[15] All things considered, the scholars' memory – still a bit thin – joins up with individual recollections: the image emerging from them both, and which is different from the mythified versions of groups, judges nearly everybody most severely (Laborie in fact discusses these two striking phenomena, a certain pulling back into the French hexagon at the very moment when the outside world was upsetting everything and an enduring, festering collective fear in the years before the disaster). Finally, with a few touch-ups, we come back to Marc Bloch – participant, witness and historian – rather than to Blum, who was also a sharp, sensitive critic of society and his own party, but – understandably – too indulgent toward a regime that he declared more unhappy than guilty, in order to defend it against its Vichy or pro-Nazi detractors.[16]

The Uses of Defeat

One can see that it is not easy to close in upon the memory of the disaster. It is not much easier to understand where this great shock stands in French history. I've already underscored the multiple dimensions of the defeat. It was certainly the most serious event in the nation's modern history – except in one significant way: from a biological view-point, the Napoleonic wars and the WWI victory cost France many more human lives than May-June 1940 (yet the initial widespread resignation to defeat can be explained by the horrible blood-letting of 1914-18).

What we can attempt to describe here is two series of effects, two ways in which the traumatism of 1940 has weighed upon the history

---

14. *La Décadence* (Paris, 1979).
15. *L'Opinion française sous Vichy* (Paris, 1990).
16. *A l'échelle humaine* (Paris, 1945).

of contemporary France. There are good reasons for distinguishing between what I shall call action-effects and question-effects. By action-effects I mean the policies that were carried out in order to repair damage, get the country back on its feet and undo in a way the defeat. The first finding (banal but important) is that the French have been deeply divided about the lessons to be learned from the event. At first, there were those resigned to it (sometimes triumphantly, because for them the enemy was inside France) and those revolted by it ("ah, how incredibly dumb," said the General, "with boundless fury");[17] there were apostles teaching the proper use of humiliation, preachers holding forth on expiation and regeneration through suffering against the champions of resurrection through combat and reconquered honor. In the first camp were the celebrants of National Revolution and temporization, as well as the propagandists who supported the "New Europe" and adjustment to the ostensibly victorious Fascists; in the other camp, those who thought it essential to re-establish a state worthy of the name and those who saw salvation coming above all from social regeneration. It would have been doubly amazing if all the French had drawn the same lessons from the debacle. That had never occurred in their history (which probably explains why the great myths of fusion, around a King or Leader, or of the general will, hold such fascination), and because the unity ostensibly reconstituted between May '39 and May '40 was too fragile to survive the shock.

Let's skim over the lessons and acts of Vichy and the collaborationists. During Vichy and after the Liberation, various measures and policies were implemented to prevent France from falling back into the errors and weaknesses that had caused the debacle. Two Vichy provisions can be mentioned here: the higher birth-rate policy (initiated, in fact, under Daladier) designed to correct a disastrous demographic curve in comparison with prolific Germany, and the managed-economy policy – which Vichy carried out for several reasons, going from simple necessity in times of scarcity to faint desires for modernization (which, by the way, were occasionally tainted with collaborationist schemes). Various Resistance groups also had many reasons to call for such measures, going from

17. *Mémoires de guerre: L'Appel* (Paris, 1989), p. 39.

the Communists' revolutionary will to the Gaullists' nationalist Colbertism. Whatever the reason, one can read between the lines and see the haunting memory of what was to be henceforth avoided: the cramped, contorted, brainless, inefficient economic system of the 30s, which led to an industrial mobilization considered a huge failure.

Among the various lessons and imperatives animating postwar policy, the most important were the following. First came the will to become a great power once again. This ambition inspired the entire new politico-administrative class coming out of the war and the Resistance, even if the means conceived toward this end were hardly up to the task, even if the analysis of the upheavals affecting the international system was often quite poor and blind. Since humiliation had to be erased, since its most painful sign was the loss of precious rank, the high level before the fall had to be reconquered. For de Gaulle and many others, nuclear arms were part of this new *Revauche*; for certain individuals (including de Gaulle in 1945), the restoration of the Empire was another means; many of these people were the ones whom decolonization hit the hardest, because they did not see it (as did most of the English) as an adjustment to irresistible "winds of change," but as yet another shameful surrender, another debacle. Take for instance Georges Bidault, the Resistance leader, who championed a second Resistance, or the historian Raoul Girardet, traumatized all over again by Dien Bien Phu.[18] The reason why Yalta created a scandal and why the French elites rallied to a mythic interpretation of the conference was the exclusion of France, despite its victory. This was taken as an unjust humiliation imposed by the Allies on a country disgraced by the common enemy, a country which could speak for an abused Europe. A great part of French history since the Liberation is composed of repeated efforts, worthy of Sisyphus, to erase the unjust Fall in a merciless world where only an organized Europe could henceforth claim the hotly desired rank.

Another lesson and imperative, which still counts today, even for those who now realize that France is no longer a very great power: the will to independence – which was certainly nourished

18. Girardet, p. 133.

not only by the shameful defeat and armistice, but also by the memories of the "English governess" of the 30s and the nightmares of occupation and collaboration. The crucial example is the Gaullist choice of a policy of independence rather than one of influence (independence was, of course, meant to lead to influence, but that is not always the case in this world, and sometimes influence is only achieved, as the Federal Republic of Germany understood so well, through diminished independence). The Fourth Republic's bitter divisions caused by the clash between wishes for autonomy and objective weakness are also related to the traumatic heritage of the black years. And on one specific point, the deep desire to regain rank and the will to independence influenced not only the leaders' policies but also the citizens' behavior. France in the 30s had been nibbled away by pacifism, or rather by pacifisms showing up in every quarter, in nearly all the political parties and interest groups, engendering strange alliances between "antiwar fighters" of the Left and the Right. Compared with all the other West-European countries, France after '44 was the least well disposed toward pacifism or unilateral disarmament.

The debacle weighed on foreign policy in yet a third way. Although London had been General de Gaulle's point of departure and operational base, the unpleasant memories of May-July '40 (Dunkerque, Mers-el-Kébir) and France's occupation by Germany gave French diplomacy its postwar direction: France distanced itself from London, and even in order to "contain" Germany, it has been almost magnetized by that same country, at first by way of French repressive policies, then in European cooperation.

There were other lessons turned into imperatives, too well-known to be analyzed at length here: the desire to regenerate the elites and to reintegrate the working class. Here too, the experience of the '30s and of Vichy play an important role, but the individual analyses and group-memories concerning French behavior in May-June '40 had denounced the errors and inadequacies, if not the treachery, of the political, economic and military leaders and underscored the painful consequences of the workers' poor integration into the national community.

I have already underlined the convergence between the lessons drawn from the disaster and those that the new leaders and the

The Trauma of 1940

French nation as a whole, after the Liberation, deduced from the dramas of 1940-44. Thus, the extraordinary voluntarism of the two post-war Republics is like a massive repudiation of the temporization and passivity that had characterized the phony war and Vichy's Golden Age (1940-42). There was, however, no convergence on one essential issue. The imperative that nearly everybody deduced from the regime's decomposition in June-July '40 had been the need to strengthen the Executive branch – even Léon Blum had recognized that the Republic was not synonymous with the parliamentary system. Yet the experience of Vichy's arbitrariness, the rehabilitation of the parliamentary Republic because of its enemies' excesses, the Resistance's suspicions about the General and the Communists' maneuvers resulted in 1946 in the quasi-restoration of the Third Republic (despite its repudiation by the people in 1945). One had to wait until a fresh humiliation, caused by the two Algerian revolts (1954 and May '58), killed yet another Republic and called back de Gaulle. Then he could finally put into action *his* memory of the catastrophe, including the famous Article 16 of the new Constitution, whose purpose was to provide strength, even to a new Albert Lebrun, during a national emergency.

It may be, now that we are nearing the century's end, that the question-effects are even more interesting. By this I mean the profound uncertainties, the cracks that the trauma of May-June '40 brought forth in the French conscience or the nation's political culture, the questions that were not really answered by the above-mentioned measures. I shall consider three, as hypotheses.

Has the French intelligentsia really recovered from the shock of 1940? Of course, for yet another twenty years at least, intellectuals of the style born in the eighteenth century and fortified during the Romantic period still reigned by their rhetoric and aspired to their traditional role as the nation's conscience, as a spiritual power talking on an equal footing (at least!) with the secular powers. Yet typical French intellectuals had thought systematically (if not always intelligently) about the nation's essential problems, convinced that they were offering solutions to the whole world's problems: the vocation of universality, which characterized the Jacobin model of national integration, was the proud mark of this kind of French intellectuals who had actually produced this model. During the Occupation, then after the Liberation, certain intellectuals, often full of genius, kept on wanting to think of all humanity. Yet on closer examination, one realizes in the first place that they had been shaped in France before the disaster: they continued on their same old trajectory; second, that their writings turned more and more away from the analysis of social problems toward either moralism or metaphysics; that the solutions they recommended for these problems (when they took interest in them) derived more and more from foreign models. They could still claim to be universal thinkers insofar as they did moral philosophy, pure philosophy or psychology but not political philosophy (or else, like Raymond Aron, a powerful but partial exception to my rule, hid it behind sociological rigor), or brought foreign remedies into France. Although the old model was still running, its wheels were not really touching the native soil any longer. And after the intellectual generation of the '30s – after Sartre, Camus, Malraux, Bernanos, S. Weil – there came very different kinds of intellectuals: they produced theories about epistemology, not the State, or they were humble (or not so humble) specialists of the social sciences. Is this development related to the defeat of '40? Some assert that this mutation is a result of the change in modern society and knowledge, that the model of the intellectual denounced by Tocqueville had anyhow already served its time.[19] I am not so sure. Or at least things aren't so simple. The *de facto* devaluation of France has something to do with the curious mix of depoliticization and imported political delirium that the post-war intelligentsia displayed.

The prewar intelligentsia, even when spewing curses – and except for the disgusted ones, like Drieu and Rebatet, who relished the decadence that they voraciously denounced – had no real doubt about France's ability to solve its problems all by itself, and therefore for others. The postwar ones, it seems to me, doubted it – and so reflected a widely-felt, nagging uncertainty about that ability, in spite of all the efforts for renewal. J.P. Azéma has talked about the failure (at least in part) of the "new beginnings" and the

---

19. This is Michel Crozier's thesis in "La révolution culturelle," *Preuves* (January 1966), pp. 3-13, (February 1966), pp. 11-18.

renovators' feelings of failure.[20] An economic and social modernization undertaken with a mix (ultimately contradictory) of State-controlled capitalism (*dirigisme*) within France and openness to other countries, late but rapid urbanization, a real revolution in agriculture (to the detriment of the peasantry's traditional structure), two political regimes seeking synthesis between democracy and efficiency: all this, which deliberately and systematically turned its back on the various ailments of the French debacle, was still not enough to prevent a certain shortness of breath, the return of old viruses (xenophobia and racism) that many had hoped dead and gone, a vague feeling of maladjustment (for example, in the cases of the educational system, industry and the Jacobin model). The self-satisfaction felt before the '30s, which in the following years was shaken from top to bottom by what I have called the tyranny of the exterior,[21] then by the defeat, never really took root again, despite the Gaullists' efforts (and did not de Gaulle himself think that he had written "the last pages of our greatness"?) This is the second aspect of the post-trauma questioning.

There is yet a third aspect: the questions about the national State. Those who wanted to erase the humiliation did not put the State in doubt; hence, the desire to regain rank and independence that I have already mentioned. The declining Third Republic was blamed for its growing short-sightedness and isolationism, its devotion to a policy of defense behind an illusory fortified barrier, the contradiction between this stance and the alliances into which it had entered; Vichy was blamed for its willful blindness, its retreat into the myth of the native soil, its inability to form a worldperspective. Yet, paradoxically, a certain myopia would still prevail: the Resistance had scarce interest in the outside world, Gaullism emphasized, in a pedagogical reaction to France's humiliation, the self-made salvation of France alone; and those who understood that France's future was Europe hardly knew how to get the point across and often gave the impression that Europe was either a way of evacuating the nation's problems or a defensive, constrained adjustment to the "German problem." The mental spasms about the national

20. *De Munich à la Liberation* (Paris, 1979), p. 358.
21. *Essais sur la France* (Paris, 1974).

State, which result of course from France's entire past history (many pasts, but all concurring on this point) lead up to this odd result fifty years later: Germany, once crushed (even much more than France in 1940), now reunified, and conceiving of itself as a "post-national" State, whose sovereignty is partially transferred to the Länder and partially to the European Union, seems in a better position to dominate that Union than France, whose policies are European while its vision of itself is national. Can France still secure its future in a national framework? This question has been asked by Raoul Girardet, a nationalist bowled over by the defeat, then by decolonization. All of France's leaders (even Pétain) have answered – yes, of course!; but French policy has often shown that there was a great gap between proud words and hard facts, between the rooster's cock-a-doodle-doo and the chickencoop; the question remains indeed open since the great collapse and its sinister aftermath.

Thus, we find ourselves back at our beginning: the hard time France has examining itself, perhaps out of fear of the resulting conclusions, not to mention the divisions such examination could bring forth. Of course, we are in the domain of speculation rather than of scientific rigor. But even when such rigor is possible, doesn't it inevitably lead us to speculation?

This essay originally appeared in François Bédarida and Jean-Pierre Azéma (eds.), *La France des années noires* (Paris, 1993). It appears here with the permission of the Editions du Seuil, and was translated by Gretchen van Slyke.

Contributors

Martin S. Alexander is Professor of International Politics at the University of Wales, Aberystwyth.

Philip Farwell Bankwitz† was Professor of History at Trinity College.

Omer Bartov is John P. Birkelund Distinguished Professor of History at Brown University.

Joel Blatt is Associate Professor of History at the University of Connecticut, Stamford.

John C. Cairns is Emeritus Professor of History at the University of Toronto.

Michael Jabara Carley is Professor of History at the University of Akron.

Vicki Caron is the Diann G. and Thomas A. Mann Professor of Modern Jewish Studies at Cornell University.

Carole Fink is Professor of History at Ohio State University.

Stanley Hoffmann is the Paul and Catherine Buttenwieser University Professor at Harvard University.

William D. Irvine is Professor of History at Glendon College, York University.

Contributors

Nicole Jordan is Associate Professor of History at the University of Illinois in Chicago.

William Keylor is Professor of History and International Relations and Director of the International History Institute, Boston University.

Elisabeth du Réau is Professor of History at La Sorbonne (Université de Paris, III).

Robert J. Young is Professor of History at the University of Winnipeg.

www.ingramcontent.com/pod-product-compliance
Lightning Source LLC
Chambersburg PA
CBHW071146070526
44584CB00019B/2680